Temple Beth Am

This book has been donated by

In honor of

THE PASSIONS
OF THE
MATRIARCHS

THE PASSIONS
OF THE
MATRIARCHS

ഇരുഇരു

Shera Aranoff Tuchman

and

Sandra E. Rapoport

KTAV Publishing House, Inc.

Library of Congress Cataloging-in-Publication Data

Tuchman, Shera Aranoff.
  The passions of the matriarchs / Shera Aranoff Tuchman & Sandra E. Rapoport.
    p. cm.
  Includes indexes.
  ISBN 0-88125-847-4
  1. Matriarchs (Bible). 2. Women in the Bible. 3. Bible. O.T. Genesis--Commentaries.
I. Rapoport, Sandra E. II. Title.
  BS575.T82 2004
  222'.110922'082--dc22
                                        2004009435

Published by
KTAV Publishing House, Inc.
930 Newark Avenue
Jersey City, NJ 07306
Email: orders@ktav.com
www.ktav.com
(201) 963-9524
Fax (201) 963-0102

In loving memory of my grandmother

Safta

and my daughter

Danelle Rebecca

z'l

୫ S.A.T. ଔ

୫ଔ୫ଔ

In loving memory of my parents

Rebecca Menaged Sharon and Gabriel Sharon

z'l

୫ S.E.R. ଔ

TABLE of CONTENTS

ഇൗരുഇൗരു

ACKNOWLEDGMENTS xi

INTRODUCTION xiii

BEFORE YOU BEGIN.. xix

GENEALOGY OF THE MATRIARCHS... xx

PART I: **SARAH**

1 Introduction to Sarai, Abram's Wife 3

2 Sarai's Abduction By Pharaoh 6

3 Infertile Sarai Chooses A Surrogate...13

4 God Promises Sarai a Child and Changes Her Name.............22

5 Sarah's Rejuvenation 28

6 Sarah's Abduction by Avimelech..37

7 Sarah's Pregnancy and the Birth of Isaac 50

8 The Children of Sarah and the Handmaiden 58

9 Abraham Heeds Sarah's Plea..61

10 Sarah is Separated From Isaac: The *Akeida* 67

11 The Death of Sarah 71

12 Sarah is Eulogized, and Buried in *Ma'arat Ha-machpela*........78

13 Epilogue to Sarah 81

PART II: **REBECCA**

14 The Birth of Rebecca 85

15 The Quest for Rebecca...86

16 Abraham Delegates Eliezer to Find a Wife for Isaac................89

17 The Manservant Imposes His Own Tests 90

18 Rebecca at the Well 92

19 Rebecca Passes The Manservant's Tests................................96

20 Rebecca Reveals Her Identity...100

21 The Manservant Meets and Negotiates with Rebecca's
     Family...102

22 A Proposal of Marriage 105

23 Rebecca Meets Abraham's Conditions and Accepts
     the Marriage Proposal...109

24 Rebecca's Perilous Journey to Isaac.....................................113

25 The Unexpected Encounter of Rebecca and Isaac................115

26 Isaac Takes Rebecca as His Wife, Loves Her, and is
     Comforted 120

27 Abraham's Remarriage and Death 128

28 Rebecca's Infertility 132

29 Rebecca's Difficult Pregnancy 137

30 The Prophecy 141

31 Rebecca Gives Birth to Rival Twin Sons................................143

32 Jacob Convinces Esav to Relinquish His Birthright..............145

33 Isaac and Rebecca in Avimelech's Palace............................147

34 The Deception 155

35 Jacob is Sent Away 165

36 The Death of Rebecca's Nursemaid 170

37 The Unrecorded Burial of Rebecca 175

38 Epilogue to Rebecca 176

PART III: **RACHEL AND LEAH**

39 Rebecca and Isaac Command Jacob to Take a
     Proper Wife 181

40 Rachel Appears at the Well 188

41 The Kiss and the Cry 193

42 Jacob Meets Rachel's Father 197

43 Leah and Rachel: Lavan's Daughters 201

44 Jacob Loves Rachel and Offers a Proposal 204

45 Jacob Demands His Bride 208

46 The Wedding Night 211

47 Zilpah the "Handmaiden" 214

48 The Morning After 215

49 Bilhah the "Handmaiden" 220

50 Jacob Weds Rachel 221

51 Unwanted Leah is Redeemed 224

52 Leah Bears Jacob's First Four Sons 228

53 Rachel's Anguish and Jacob's Ire 234

54 Rachel Offers Bilhah as a Surrogate 243

55 Bilhah Bears Jacob Two Sons 247

56 Leah Offers Zilpah as a Surrogate 250

57 Zilpah Bears Jacob Two Sons 252

58 Rachel Barters for *Dudaim*; Leah Barters for Jacob 255

59 Leah Achieves Her Desire 259

TABLE OF CONTENTS

60 Leah Bears Jacob Two More Sons and a Daughter..............263

61 Rachel Finally Bears a Son, and Names Him Joseph 268

62 Jacob Begs Leave of Lavan 275

63 Lavan Detains Jacob 278

64 Jacob Confers with Rachel and Leah 281

65 Jacob and His Family Flee Lavan's House..........................285

66 Rachel Steals the *Teraphim*...287

67 Lavan Pursues Jacob 290

68 Jacob Utters a Fateful Curse 293

69 Lavan's Futile Hunt for the *Teraphim* 298

70 The Aftermath of the Search 306

71 A Nocturnal Encounter and Jacob's Name Is Changed
     to Israel..309

72 Esav and Jacob: A Dreaded Reunion..................................311

73 Jacob's Tragedies Begin 312

74 Rachel Suffers a Perilous Labor..314

75 A Dying Rachel Names Her Newborn Son 319

76 Rachel's Death..321

77 The Bilhah Affair...325

78 Finally, Jacob Returns Home 331

79 On His Deathbed, Jacob Reflects Upon Rachel....................334

80 But Jacob is Buried with Leah 340

81 Epilogue to Rachel and Leah 344

GLOSSARY 349

INDEX OF SOURCES 361

GENERAL INDEX..365

ACKNOWLEDGMENTS

We have been blessed with extraordinary husbands, Alan Tuchman and Sam Rapoport, respectively, who not only understood our passion for learning, but encouraged and respected it.

My mother, Freda Appleman Aranoff, often watched us work and offered us intelligent suggestions, which we invariably implemented. My husband, Alan, provided us with valuable historical perspectives on the biblical events we were studying.

Our children, Ari, Micole, and Andy Tuchman and Benjamin, Ezra, and Sarah Rapoport, were part of this project as well. They cheerfully exchanged *quantity* mothering time for intense *quality* time.

Ari's wife, my daughter-in-law, Beth Samuels, read the manuscript at every stage and gave us valuable critical insights. Micole and my niece, Maya Bernstein, encouraged us with their enthusiastic reception of the manuscript's early chapters, and Micole created our genealogy table. Andy performed the not-insignificant task of shelving and re-shelving hundreds of books over the course of the past two years. Benjamin offered us interesting relevant material, and he, Ezra and Sarah provided us, often at a moment's notice, with crucial and creative technical computer support.

We are grateful to our sisters, Gaya Aranoff Bernstein and Diane M. Sharon, for their challenging and important suggestions about our manuscript.

Chava Aranoff painstakingly reviewed every word—Hebrew and English—for spelling and grammar, and Joanna Mazur conscientiously researched the glossary. Steve Siebert, typesetter extraordinaire, skillfully formatted our text so that the English and the Hebrew present a seamless whole.

We are grateful to Dr. Ellen Frankel and Rabbi Chaim Potok, *z'l*, for their words of encouragement when this manuscript was in its early stages. Blu Greenberg not only encouraged us from the beginning, but has been a true friend to us, ultimately introducing us to our publisher. We extend our heartfelt thanks to Bernie Scharfstein, our beloved publisher at KTAV, for understanding and sharing our vision for this book.

Sandra wishes to thank her teachers, Devora Steinmetz and Rabbi David Silber, for igniting and sustaining her rigorous intellectual love of Torah.

Our thanks to Rabbi Haskel Lookstein for providing a welcoming environment for women's learning at our synagogue, Congregation Kehilath Jeshurun, the home of our morning *shiur*.

Finally, the women in Shera's Thursday morning *shiur* are thoughtful, intelligent, stimulating, and articulate, and their encouragement over the past ten years has been a driving force in the creation of this book.

INTRODUCTION

ᏚᏙᏟᏗᏚᏙᏟᏗ

M y earliest childhood memories of women learning originate with my grandmother, *Safta*, Bina Appleman, sitting at her dining room table, studying the Bible or listening to a Talmud lecture over radio station WEVD. It was as natural for me to see her learning, as it was to see her cooking, sewing or keeping house for her husband and four children. Learning Torah was an integral part of *Safta's* life. Also, my mother, with a degree in Hebrew Literature from the Jewish Theological Seminary, continues even today to study biblical texts. Watching women learning Torah was intrinsic to my life, generating within me a love for Torah learning. My father, Harry Aranoff, *z'l*, a self-taught man, intermingled daily conversation with Scriptural teachings.

This book reflects my studies of the past fifteen years. It is not only the product my own learning, but is also the result of relationships with people from whom I learned and whom I taught.

I was fortunate to spend several years in a weekly study session with Rabbi Jack Bieler, then scholar-in-residence at Congregation Kehilath Jeshurun in Manhattan. He introduced me to a wide selection of biblical exegeses. Rabbi Bieler taught me how to take a seemingly simple phrase of text and follow it through centuries-old paths of commentary on a fascinating, scholarly treasure hunt. I also studied with Rabbi Israel Rosenberg, of blessed memory. He infused in me an appreciation of Jewish spirituality as reflected in The Tanya, the philosophical treatise by Rabbi Shneur Zalman, one of the founders of the Lubavich movement. Rabbis Bieler and Rosenberg, together, gave me the skills to pursue my love of learning, nourishing my brain and soul, stimulating within me the desire to search for deeper meaning in my life, within the framework of Torah and traditional commentaries.

Thereafter, I began to study by myself, drawn naturally, I suppose, to study those chapters which involved women. I read the texts about the biblical matriarchs, searching to understand these women, wanting to identify with them. But my solitary studies at first left me dissatisfied; they raised unanswered questions. Why were these biblical women viewed as paradigms of "Woman?" Why do we bless our daughters to be like Sarah, Rebecca, Rachel and Leah, when, at least on the surface, their lives were difficult and flawed? The written biblical text, which records at length and in minute detail the religious and national history of the Jewish people, only affords us a mere glimpse of the private and intimate lives of these women. Their thoughts, feelings, words and actions, when recorded in the text, appear almost as an outline, begging to be fleshed out.

I learned that feminist biblical scholars, over the past twenty-five years, have sought to fill this need, placing issues of gender at the core of their studies. Often, they interpreted the biblical stories as marginalizing women, and they attributed patriarchal bias to the Bible. These scholars injected their own creative solutions into the biblical lacunae. While their opinions hold appeal for many readers, I, myself, was driven to delve into more ancient sources, to study the traditional commentaries, or *mephorshim*. Reading these time-worn pages of exegesis, I entered the intriguing world of the Jewish scholars who lived centuries ago. These commentaries are known, to name only a few, as *Midrash Rabbah*, Rashi, the Maharal, Ibn Ezra, Sforno, Ramban, Rashbam, the *Netziv*, the *Gr'ah*, *Alshich*, *Chatam Sofer*, and *Meshech Chachmah*, joined by relevant talmudic scholars. Standing on their shoulders are more modern traditional *mephorshim* such as *Torah Temima*, *Sha'arei Aharon*, and Nehama Leibowitz. These treasure chests of biblical commentary reveal missing elements of the personae of the biblical women.

Torah scholars have been recording and interpreting these commentaries for almost three thousand years, but their scholarship has been hidden from interested students for two major reasons. First, most of these sources had not—and until today still have not—been translated into English, so these works were available only to those fluent in Hebrew and Aramaic. Secondly, these ancient texts primarily were studied in the Rabbinical School, or *Kollel*, post-graduate learning centers for men only. It is solely a recent phenomenon that advanced learning centers for women have been thriving. The Kollel rabbis' time and efforts primarily were involved in interpreting the 613 biblical commandments, the *Taryag Mitzvot*, and their countless legal derivatives. The women, of necessity, had been immersed in their all-consuming roles of wives and mothers. They rarely had the time or education to delve into what may have interested them as well; namely, the personal lives of the biblical protagonists.

If the ancient sources had been readily available, modern students of the text could now be cognizant of the breadth and sensitivity of some of these commentators, and specifically of their insight into the passions that ruled the biblical woman's mind, body and soul. Certainly, these commentators are not unanimous in their praise of biblical women; often they are critical. But in studying these sources *as a whole*, one cannot but marvel at their understanding and sensitivity. Studying the trove of commentaries allows one to piece together an understanding of the matriarchs while still remaining grounded in traditional Orthodox sources.

As I read these commentaries, I began to discover our fore-mothers, who are portrayed so sparingly in the Torah itself. The matriarchs emerged, not as one-dimensional figures, but as complex, formidable women possessing an array of universal passions. Their thoughts are uncovered, their voices given sound, their actions more fully explained. In gaining some knowledge of them, we begin to better understand ourselves, for their thoughts are often our thoughts, their drives our drives, their words our words, their bodies our own. I could begin to identify with them, learn from them, know them, and begin to better know myself.

Eleven years ago, when a few close friends asked if I would teach them what I had been learning, my study group was born. We began meeting at my home, studying at my diningroom table. As the group outgrew the size of my table, Rabbi Haskel Lookstein, the rabbi of Congregation Kehilath Jeshurun, graciously allowed us the use of the synagogue's library. How wonderful it was to be sitting around that large conference table surrounded by shelves filled to overflowing with rows of ancient texts.

It was, at first, not uncommon for men in the synagogue to stop in to ask us if we were a congregational Sisterhood planning committee. After several years, however, the men began to accept as perfectly natural the thirty to forty women who met at eight in the morning in the same synagogue library where the men had just unwound their *tefillin*. We women pored over abstruse texts for the next hour-and-a-half, reading, dissecting, and arguing over a biblical phrase, all with the guidance of the *mephorshim*. Reluctantly, at the end of the class, we exited the hallowed room and re-entered our individual secular worlds as homemakers, lawyers, physicians, psychologists, social workers, teachers, office managers, real estate agents, administrators, and college students. Our backgrounds also were varied, from those who did not understand even a word of Hebrew, to those who, like myself, had a yeshivah education with a knowledge of Hebrew and Aramaic.

The study group participants forced my private, spare-time hobby of studying ancient texts, into the open classroom. With their encouragement and enthusiasm, they propelled me into what became a second full-time job. Each week I spent many hours unearthing even more commentaries so I could present them at our meetings. This class has been ongoing for over ten years.

From this group of women, there emerged someone with whom I formed a special bond. Sandra Rapoport, also a yeshivah graduate with knowledge of Hebrew and Aramaic, often articulated a word for which I was at a loss, completing my sentences, and as often, my thoughts. Her boundless drive and energy, coupled with her articulate command of language skills, made Sandra my invaluable collaborator in writing this book. When she agreed to write with me, to help me capture in the written word the vitality that was present in the study group, the idea of this book became a reality.

Our project entailed studying and selecting from hundreds upon hundreds of pages of commentaries that I had amassed over the years. This material served as an outline for this book. Sandra and I have labored together over the past two years as *chevruta,* as study partners, reading, analyzing, discussing and winnowing the biblical commentaries. We have endeavored always to remain loyal to the Torah text and scholars, faithfully quoting all selected commentaries by author, chapter and verse.

This arduous biblical journey has brought me a deeper understanding and appreciation of the Torah text, though the more I study, the more evident it becomes that I have only just begun to scratch the surface of the wisdom within its venerable pages. I have been immeasurably enriched by finding not only answers to my own questions, but also answers to questions I had even not thought to ask, as well as an awareness of those questions that are unanswerable. These answers, and questions, are now before you.

— Shera Aranoff Tuchman

BEFORE YOU BEGIN

හ◌ඡහ◌ඡ

B efore you begin reading this book, there are three points to bear in mind.

First, *The Passions of the Matriarchs* has been written to correlate by chapter and verse with the Hebrew Bible, also known as the Torah. Although this is intended to be read and understood on its own, the reader's appreciation is enhanced if one follows along with the biblical text. One then can glance backward, or look forward, to a sentence that has just been explained, or that will soon be explicated. This is important, for many pages in this book often are devoted to a few significant biblical words.

Second, long passages in italics are the authors' own paraphrased translations of the biblical narrative, and are not intended as literal substitutions for the biblical text.

Third, while our book is written in English, numerous passages are footnoted in the original Hebrew or Aramaic. Please bear in mind that this book was written to be read and understood *without* the necessity of comprehending these foreign language quotes. We have included them because the richness and poetic beauty of the Hebrew or Aramaic words often are diminished in translation, and those who understand the original Hebrew will appreciate the beauty of the ancient texts. To those of you who do not read Hebrew, these passages can safely be ignored without compromising the flow of our book. Those readers who do understand the Hebrew quotes will reap additional satisfaction in this dimension as well.

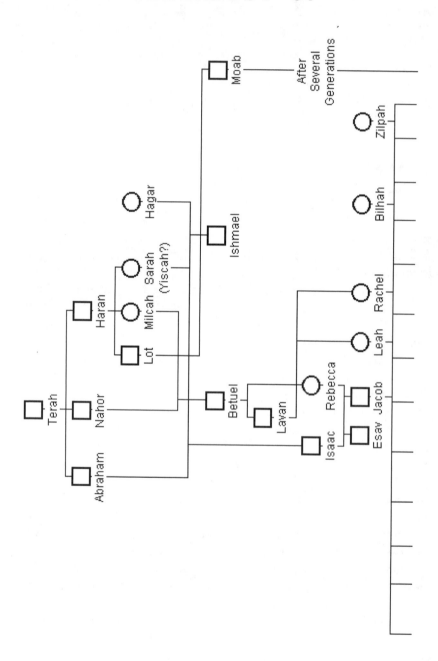

THE MATRIARCHS

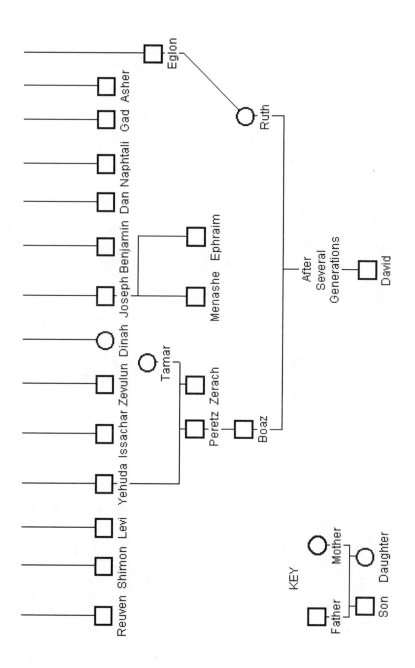

Reuven Shimon Levi Yehuda Issachar Zevulun Dinah Joseph Benjamin Dan Naphtali Gad Asher

Eglon

Ruth

Tamar

Peretz Zerach

Boaz

Menashe Ephraim

After Several Generations

David

KEY

Father Mother

Son Daughter

PART I

SARAH

౭౮Cశ౭౮Cశ

ONE

৵০৪৵০৪

Introduction to Sarai, Abram's Wife

GENESIS 11:29

T he matriarch Sarah is first introduced in the Bible in an inauspicious manner at the end of a long line of begats, tucked into the midst of this verse of Genesis, the first book of the Hebrew Bible.

> And Abram and Nahor took themselves wives; the name of Abram's wife was **Sarai**, and the name of Nahor's wife was Milcah, the daughter[s] of Haran, [who is] the father of Milcah and the father of **Yiscah**.

This woman who is so minimally described in the text, but who is destined to be the founding matriarch of a nation, silently cries out to be more fully portrayed. The text introduces her simply as "Abram's wife, Sarai."[1] It is the commentator, Rashi, who further identifies Sarai as Yiscah,[2] the daughter of Abram's deceased brother, Haran. Since Haran had died leaving two orphaned daughters, Milcah and Yiscah (Sarai), Abram and his remaining brother, Nahor, each married one of his maiden nieces in order to perpetuate Haran's memory. Nahor married Milcah, and Abram married Yiscah. Rashi

---

[1] שֵׁם אֵשֶׁת אַבְרָם שָׂרָי.

[2] יִסְכָּה

3

explains that Abram's wife, Sarai, possessed the additional name of
Yiscah.[3] The Hebrew root of that name, *SaCHo*,[4] has several
meanings: "to foresee, to view, or to possess royal bearing." Rashi
highlights the first, imbuing her with prophetic ability. Sarai was called
Yiscah because she *saw into the future* with Divine inspiration:[5] The
Talmud itself (*Megilla* 14a) confirms this quality, by naming Sarai one
of the seven biblical prophetesses.[†] Rashi continues explicating Sarai's
alternate name, using the same Hebrew root-word, meaning *to view*,
declaring that all people *viewed* her beauty.[6] Finally, using the third
definition of her name, Rashi announces Sarai's *royal bearing*.[7]

Based solely on the *p'shat*, or strict textual reading of this one
verse, the reader is afforded no identification of Abram's wife, nor
any glimpse of her qualities. "Sarai" is only a name. It is the
commentaries who supply Sarai with a provenance, who enrich our
introduction to her by painting a more complete portrait of her, from
the merest textual mention of her name. We now expect Abram's
wife, the unknown Sarai, daughter of Haran, to be prophetic, lovely
to look at, and regal.

GENESIS 11:30

The text itself, which until now has supplied the reader only with
Sarai's name, now dramatically adds a single portentous fact: the
tragic flaw that will inform her entire life. *Sarai was [also] barren, and
she had no children.*[8] The reader is unprepared for this revelation. We
have just been introduced to Sarai, whom we know is destined to be
the first matriarch. We are certainly not expecting that she will be
unable to be a mother. And yet the text belabors the fact of her
barrenness, stating in the same verse *both* that she was barren *and*

[†]The other six biblical prophetesses mentioned in the Talmud are Miriam,
Deborah, Chana, Avigayil, Chulda, and Esther.

---

3 **יסכה**

4 **סכה**

5 יסכה. זו שרה, על **שסכתה** ברוח הקדש.

6 ושהכל **סוכין** ביופיה

7 לשון **נסיכות.**

8 ותהי שרי עקרה אין לה ולד.

that she had no children. The commentary *Midrash Rabbah* (38.14) resolves this apparent redundancy by stating that whenever the text uses the words, *and she had none*,[9] it foreshadows a change of status.[10] The reader should therefore expect that the barren Sarai will eventually conceive and bear a child.

GENESIS 12:5

The barren Sarai is Abram's counterpart in his mission to introduce his God to the Canaanite world. She has accompanied Abram in his wanderings out of Haran, encountering proselytes as they travel. The text states that Abram takes his wife, Sarai, and Lot, his brother's son, and all their possessions, *and also the souls **they made** in Haran*.[11] The Bible uses the plural form *aSu*,[12] indicating "the souls *they made* in Haran." *Midrash Rabbah* (39.14) tells us that Abram converted the males, and Sarai the females.[13] Thus, the text credits them equally in the creation of uncountable converts to monotheism. *Siftei Chachamim*, a supercommentary on Rashi, states that because a convert is likened to a newborn, it is as if Sarai, Abram's barren wife, gave birth to a multitude of new souls.[14] Thus, according to the commentaries, the physically barren Sarai, herself unable to bear a child, "gives birth" to a multitude of new souls, mitigating the sting of her infertility and elevating her to the level of an equal partner with her husband in this mission.

---

9 אין לה

10 אמר רב לוי, בכל מקום שנאמר **אין לה** הוה לה.

11 ואת הנפש אשר **עשׂוּ** בחרן.

12 עשׂוּ

13 ואת הנפש אשר עשו, אלא, אלו הגרים שגיירו . . . למה אמר עשו? אלא ללמדך שכל מי שהוא מקרב את העובד כוכבים ומגיירו, כאלו בראו.

14 כי גר שנתגייר כקטן שנולד.

TWO

ॐ○३ॐ○३

Sarai's Abduction
By Pharaoh

GENESIS 12:10–13

A bram and his wife, Sarai, were living in the land of Canaan, the place where God had directed him, when a severe famine struck the land. Therefore, Abram and Sarai journeyed down to Egypt, where food was plentiful. It is only as they neared the gates of Egypt that the text, through Abram's eyes, acknowledges Sarai's exquisite beauty. **Now** *I know that truly you are a woman of beauty.*[1] It is the commentaries who wonder how, as Sarai's long-time husband, Abram could have remained unaware of Sarai's beauty until this moment. Rashi suggests that until now Abram had in truth not ever viewed his wife's beauty because of the couple's modesty. The commentary relates that it was only due to "a singular happenstance" which revealed Sarai's beauty to Abram on their way to Egypt that day.[2]

The commentaries, or *mephorshim*, describe the precise moment that Abram became aware of Sarai's loveliness. The *Midrash Tanchuma* envisions the two of them in the heat of a desert afternoon, preparing to cross the Nile River at the border of Egypt.

---

[1] **הנה-נה** ידעתי כי אשה יפת-מראה את.

[2] עד עכשיו לא הכיר בה מתוך צניעות שבשניהם. ועכשיו על ידי מעשה הכיר בה.

6

Abram happened to look up from his task of guiding his weary caravan. He saw, at that moment, his wife's reflection in the still waters of the river, and he became physically desirous of her. Before this instant, out of *extreme conjugal modesty,* Abram had never beheld Sarai directly. This chance daylight viewing *of Sarai in reflection* allowed Abram at long last "to see" her beauty in the clear light of day.[3] The Maharal and *Siftei Chachamim,* explaining Rashi, describe the moment differently. The Maharal states that on their journey to Egypt, while fording the river, Sarai inadvertently bared her thighs. It was *at that moment* that Abram became aware of Sarai's sensuality.[4] *Siftei Chachamim* adds that Sarai had lifted her skirts out of the path of the rushing water, inadvertently affording her husband a view of her lovely form.[5] The Talmud (*Bava Batra* 16a) confirms Abram's instant of awareness: "Until then, I did not know."[6] *Now* he knew. The text, which until now only hinted at Sarai's beauty in its use of her alternate name, Yiscah, in verse 11:29, now explicitly appreciates her loveliness, through Abram's explicit and overdue reaction.

Abram is at a literal and figurative crossroads at the border of Canaan and Egypt. Abram, not a wealthy man, is an itinerant nomad searching for food for his household. Having just been struck with the reality of Sarai's loveliness, Abram is becoming aware that his wife's beauty might well pose a threat to his life.

The commentaries wonder why the Bible mentions only that *Abram* arrived at the portals of Egypt. Where was Sarai his wife? Should not the text have said, "And it came to pass, when Abram *and Sarai were* coming into Egypt?" *Midrash Rabbah* (40.5) answers that Abram had hidden Sarai in a locked chest to shield her beauty from the prying eyes of the Egyptian border guards. Abram's objective was to smuggle his beautiful wife into Egypt undetected. When the guards demanded that Abram open the sealed box so they could assess its contents for tax purposes, Abram demurred. The guards said, "well

---

3 באותה שעה הלכו שניהם. כיון שהגיעו לפילי של מצרים ועמדו על היאור, ראה אברהם אבינו בבואה של שרה באותו נהר כחמה זורחת.

4 לא נכנס יצר היופי בלבו, אבל על ידי מעשה שגילתה שרה שוקה, ראה היופי שלה.

5 שהיו עוברין בנהר וצריכה היתה להגביה בגדיה, וראה שהיתה יפת מראה.

6 מכלל דמעיקרא לא הוה ידע לה.

then, we will have to tax you for importing garments." When Abram readily agreed, they greedily escalated their assessment to that of *silken* garments. Abram still agreed to pay. The suspicious guards further escalated their demand to the exorbitant duty for precious stones. Even so, Abram agreed to pay. The guards, by now expecting Abram's chest to contain an inestimable treasure, forced Abram to unlock it. When he did so, Sarai stood up, dazzling the guards, and all the land of Egypt, with her beauty.[7]

Abram, witnessing the effect that Sarai is having on the armed guards, and laboring under his own kindled awareness of his wife's desirability, becomes desperate. He therefore whispers in supplication to Sarai: "*Please* forgive me, but I have only just become aware of your beauty," and "*Please* tell the Pharaoh that you are my sister."[8] He tells Sarai that he is terrified that when the Egyptians consider her beauty, they will kill him in order to possess her. Abram therefore entreats Sarai to identify herself as his sister rather than his wife, *in order that things will go well for me on your behalf.*[9]

This intrigue troubles the commentators. *Levush Haorah*, a supercommentary on Rashi, asks, "How could Abram insinuate to Sarai that she betray her marriage vows?"[10] As it states in the Talmud (*Sanhedrin* 74a), "illicit sexual relations" is one of the three commandments—the others are idolatry and murder—for which a person must give up his life rather than transgress.[11] It was thus incumbent upon Abram to risk his own life rather than to put Sarai's honor at stake by having her pose as his sister.

Ramban agrees. In his commentary on this verse he explains that "Abraham our father" was so mortally frightened that he erroneously committed a great sin by placing his righteous wife in harm's way. Ramban suggests that Abram should have had the faith to rely on God's intervention to save them both rather than suggest

---

7 ויהי כבא אברם מצרימה ויראו המצרים. ושרה היכן היתה? נתנה בתיבה ונעל בפניה . . .
אמרו ליה מטכסין את טעין. אמר דמטכסי אנא יהיב. מרגלין את טעון. אמר אנא יהיב דמרגלין.
אמרין ליה לא אפשר. אלא דפתחת וחמית לן מה בנוה. כיון שפתחה הבהיקה כל ארץ מצרים
מזיוה.

8 אמרי-**נא** אחתי את . . . הנה-**נא** ידעתי. . . . .

9 למען ייטב לי בעבורך.

10 יש מקשין איך הותר לשרה לומר אחי הוא, והלא גלוי עריות, יהרג ואל יעבר.

11 כל עבירות שבתורה אם אומרין לאדם עבור ואל תהרג, יעבור ואל יהרג, חוץ מעבודה זרה,
וגלוי עריות, ושפיכות דמים.

the wife-sister ruse.[12] The Zohar (*Tazriya* 52a), also incredulous that Abram placed Sarai in a life-threatening situation to save himself, asks: "Can we believe that a God-fearing man like Abram should speak thus to his wife in order that he may be well treated?!" The Zohar resolves this issue by explaining that at the gates of Egypt Abram saw a guardian angel accompanying Sarai. The Zohar elevates Sarai to such a high plane that *her own merit* summons a guardian angel to watch over her in Egypt. Faced with the text's grim fact that Abram has placed his wife's life in jeopardy, the commentaries justify his behavior by explaining Abram's expectation that Sarai's guardian angel would save her from harm.

The Zohar thus concludes: "The truth is, that Abram relied on his wife's merit, and not on his own merit" to warrant Divine intervention forestalling Pharaoh's evil intention. Abram expected God to intervene on *her* behalf, acknowledging that Sarai's merit was greater than his own.[13] In truth, we will see in the following verses that it is God, and not Abram, who attends to Sarai's honor.

GENESIS 12:14–16

Abram's concerns were not fanciful. His apprehensions were realized when the Egyptians, taking one glimpse of Sarai, appreciated her exquisite beauty.[14] The reader will note that, in a work that is widely noted for its brevity, Sarai's beauty is stressed: *for she is **very** lovely.*[15] *Midrash Rabbah* (40.5) teaches us that the Hebrew word *iSHa*,[16] *woman*, in verse 14, reminds us of Eve's beauty, since the Hebrew word *iSHa*,[17] *woman*, was first used to describe Eve, the first woman in the Bible. The text's use of the word *Me'oD*,[18] meaning

---

12 ודע כי אברהם אבינו חטא חטא גדול בשגגה, שהביא אשתו הצדקת במכשול עון מפני פחדו פן
יהרגוהו; והיה לו לבטוח בשם שיציל אותו ואת אשתו. . . .

13 האי קרא קשיא. אלא אברהם . . . לא סמיך על זכותא דיליה . . . אלא על זכותא דאתתיה
. . . ולא עוד, אלא דחמא חד מלאכא אזיל קמה, ואמר ליה לאברהם, לא תדחל מנה, קב"ה
שדר לי . . . לנטרא לה מכלא. וכדין לא דחיל אברהם מאתתיה, אלא מניה, דלא חמא עמיה
מלאכא, אלא עמה. אמר הא היא מתנטרא, ואנא לא נטירנא.

14 ויהי כבוא אברם מצרימה, ויראו המצרים את האשה כי יפה היא מאד.

15 כי יפה היא **מאד**.

16 אשה

17 אשה

18 מאד

much or *very*, teaches us that Sarai was *much more* beautiful than Eve.

Sarai, a woman of such exceptional beauty that she captured the interest of a Pharaoh, was then forcibly taken[†] to Pharaoh's palace.[19] Simultaneously, as Sarai is being led away by Pharaoh's guards, the Bible describes the wealth that is being heaped upon Abram:

> And he had sheep, **and** oxen, **and** he-asses, **and** men-servants, **and** maid servants, **and** she-asses **and** camels.[20]

We draw the reader's attention to the spate of nouns used by the Bible, connected only by the *vav* or the word *and*. This breathless narrative reinforces Sarai's presumed worth to Pharaoh. It also fortifies the use of the word *much*[21] in verse 14. Abram received *much* in the exchange.

GENESIS 12:17

Alone with Sarai in his private chambers, Pharaoh is stricken by God with an undefined great plague *because of **the matter** of Sarai, the wife of Abram*.[22] Rashi identifies the plague as a skin disease that rendered sexual intimacy difficult.[23] The commentaries wonder why Pharaoh was so stricken. Was this plague a miraculous measure that *prevented* Pharaoh from sexually approaching Sarai? Or was the plague a *punishment* for his abduction of her? The commentaries go to great lengths to explain *this matter*.[24] *Kli Yakar* states that *the*

[†]The Hebrew root-word, קח, meaning *to take*, which is used here, generally connotes *marriage*, but it also appears in two other famed biblical abductions: that of Dinah, when she *was taken* by Shechem (Genesis 34:2: וירא אותה שכם בן חמר החוי נשיא הארץ, ו**יקח** אותה), and that of Esther, when she *was taken* to the palace of Achashverosh in the city of Shushan (Esther 2:8: ו**תלקח** אסתר אל בית המלך).

---

[19] ו**תקח** האשה בית פרעה.
[20] ולאברם היטיב בעבורה; ויהי-לו צאן ובקר וחמרים ועבדים ושפחות ואתנת וגמלים.
[21] מאד
[22] וינגע ד' את פרעה נגעים גדלים . . . על-דבר שרי אשת אברם.
[23] שהתשמיש קשה לו.
[24] על דבר

matter of Pharaoh's ailment was directly attributed to the simple fact that Sarai was really Abram's wife, and not his sister, and was thus forbidden to the king under any circumstances.[25] Therefore, Pharaoh duly deserved the plague he suffered, both as a preventive measure, and as a punishment.

The unvoweled root-word *DaVaR* [26] can mean both *the matter of* [27] and *speech*.[28] *The matter of* [29] Sarai's abduction and its consequences, described above, is the *p'shat*, or the plain textual reading of this phrase. Rashi and *Midrash Rabbah* favor the second meaning of the root-word, meaning *speech*. Rashi attributes Pharaoh's affliction to Sarai's spoken word.[30] A careful reading of the text, however, does not record Sarai speaking in this episode. It is the commentaries who, for the first time, allow us to "hear" Sarai's unrecorded *speech*.

Midrash Rabbah (41.2) sets the scene. The commentary describes that throughout that night Sarai lay prostrate in Pharaoh's chambers. She cried out to The Creator, saying, "Help me! My faith in You is greater even than that of my husband, Abram. For Abram left his homeland only after he received the word directly from You, while I went forth based on faith alone. I heard Your promise only from the mouth of my husband, for You did not speak directly to me."[31] In her *midrashic* cry to God Sarai is desperately hoping that she will be rewarded because of her profound faith. Her husband, Abram, left his homeland only after God's express assurance of a blessing; while Sarai left on faith alone, for God had not yet spoken directly to her.

Amazingly, the commentary explains, now God answers Sarai's plea with a direct promise to her, alone. God answers her, "Whatever I do, I do for your sake."[32]

Thus, when Rashi attributes Pharaoh's plague directly to un-recorded words[33] that Sarai uttered, he was relying on the *midrashic*

---

[25] לפי שהיתה אשת איש על כן באו עליו נגעים אלו.

[26] דבר

[27] דבר

[28] דבּוּר

[29] דבר

[30] על דברי שרה: על פי דבורה.

[31] כל אותו הלילה היתה שרה שטוחה על פניה ואומרת: רבון העולמים! אברם יצא בהבטחה, ואני יצאתי באמונה.

[32] אמר לה הקב"ה: כל מה שאני עושה, בשבילך אני עושה.

[33] דבּוּר

conversation between Sarai and God where she cried out for aid and was answered. Pharaoh's plague, then, was God's means of protecting her.

After describing Sarai's unrecorded conversation with God, the *Midrash* continues, and describes another unrecorded, private confrontation, this one with Pharaoh. Sarai repeatedly told the king that she was forbidden to him because she was the wife of another man, but the king did not heed her pleas.[34] The *Midrash* then infuses Sarai with the power to summon Divine assistance. God positioned a guardian angel in Pharaoh's chambers, visible only to Sarai. When Pharaoh approached her with immoral intentions, coming close enough to touch her slipper, Sarai ordered the angel to strike the king with his whip. When she ordered, "Strike!" he struck, and when she ordered, "Desist!" he desisted.[35] The commentaries thus invest Sarai herself with the power to summon Divine aid during her dark hours of captivity.

GENESIS 12:19

Although through the words of the commentaries Sarai is safely protected, the biblical text itself is ambiguous regarding Sarai's fate. Pharaoh says, *And I took her to me, [intending] to make her my wife.*[36] One naturally wonders, did Pharaoh rape Sarah? The commentaries unequivocally answer this question in the negative. They unanimously maintain Sarai's marital integrity. Ramban affirms that Pharaoh's intended objective was to *marry* Sarai, and install her as the queen. He never intended merely to use her as a concubine.[37] Having suffered a humiliating plague and an inability to consummate his liaison with Sarai, a frustrated Pharaoh summarily returns Sarai to her husband, and has them both escorted—along with their newfound wealth—out of Egypt. Abram and Sarai then return to Canaan.

---

34 שהיתה אומרת לו: אשת איש אני. ולא היה פורש.

35 כל אותו הלילה היה מלאך עומד ומגלב בידו. הוה אמר לה: אין אמרת מחי, מחינא. אין אמרת נשבק, שביקנא.

36 ואקח אותה לי לאשה.

37 שהיה רצונו שתהיה זאת אשתו המולכת. לא תהיה פלגש לו.

THREE

൸൙൸൙

Infertile Sarai
Chooses A Surrogate

GENESIS 16:1–2

E ven as ten years pass, Sarai remains barren. Nearly despairing of ever being able to bear Abram the son God has promised him, Sarai speaks for the very first time in the Bible itself. The text, so sparing with the words of women, finally allows Sarai to speak here. It is impossible for her not to do so. She is driven to express her imperative desire for a child. How deep and powerful must this desire for a child flow in Sarai. It is so deep that although she is unable to conceive a child herself, she accedes to the desperate alternative of sending a surrogate to her husband's bed. It is so strong, that the text for the first time allows us to hear Sarai's desperation, as she concedes at long last the virtual certainty that she will never bear a child, and that this must be God's will:

> *And Sarai said to Abram: Behold now, God has withheld children from me; come, please, and take my handmaiden as a concubine; perhaps my family will be built up through her.*[1]

Rashi identifies Sarai's Egyptian handmaiden, Hagar, as a princess, the Pharaoh's daughter. She has been a personal maid to

---

[1] ותאמר שרי אל-אברם: הנה-נא עצרני ד' מלדת. בא-נא אל-שפחתי; אולי אבנה ממנה.

13

Sarai ever since Abram and Sarai left Egypt. Even in his frustrated and angered state, Pharaoh had realized that Sarai's salvation was due solely to a Divine intervention that far outweighed his own powers. He thought to himself: It is preferable that my daughter be a handmaiden in Sarai's home, than a mistress in her own home in Egypt.[2] Pharaoh was reluctantly impressed with Sarai's holiness, and thought his daughter would thrive in her household.

Believing, as she did, that it might have been her own infertility that left Abram childless, Sarai strategically offers her husband a surrogate. The *mephorshim* are not insensitive to Sarai's wrenching ambivalence. Even while she delivers to Abram an alternative to barrenness, she harbors the secret hope that she will yet be blessed with her own child. Sforno suggests that Sarai's act is a calculated decision on her part to use her jealousy constructively.[3] Her intention is to stimulate her own reproductive hormones through the powerful surge of her emotions. She has not yet despaired completely of becoming biological mother to Abram's promised heir.

Rashi says that Sarai's words, *perhaps my family will be built up through her,*[4] teach us that without children of her own, Sarai would effectively be annihilated.[5] Therefore, concerned that her own powers are insufficient to induce her own fertility, Sarai once again calls upon her personal relationship with God to save her; in this instance, from dying barren. Rashi adds that Sarai hopes that God will recognize her merit in bringing Hagar to Abram, and will reward her with a child from her own womb.[6] Although she offers a surrogate, Sarai still acknowledges God as the ultimate source of all blessings. According to *Midrash Rabbah* (45.2), Sarai resisted the urgings of the local women who pressed potions and talismans upon her to cure her of her barrenness. Sarai's belief remains strong, and she reaffirms that any hope of childbearing rests with God alone, not with magical

---

[2] בת פרעה היתה. כשראה נסים שנעשו לשרה, אמר:מוטב שתהי בתי שפחה בבית זה, ולא גבירה בבית אחר.

[3] אולי הקנאה תעורר הכח לפעולותיו.

[4] אולי אבנה ממנה.

[5] מי שאין לו בנים, שאינו בנוי אלא הרוס.

[6] בזכות שאכניס צרתי לתוך ביתי.

charms.[7] She has hopes that God will reward her for bringing a surrogate into Abram's tent.

Abram agrees with surprising alacrity to Sarai's request. She barely has had time to articulate her amazing suggestion when the text tells us that Abram, without even offering token resistance, hearkens to her voice and takes another woman to his bed. The *mephorshim* obviously are troubled by this. Ramban suggests that Abram was so desirous of having children that the moment Sarai suggested surrogacy, he acceded.[8] Rashi vests Sarai with Divine intuition in this episode. The text appears redundant when it states, *And Abram hearkened **to the voice of** Sarai*.[9] Why are the words *the voice of* even necessary? Is it not sufficient to state, *And Abram hearkened to Sarai*? The extra Hebrew word *LeKoL*[10] (meaning *to the voice of*) thus invites Rashi's interpretation that Sarai was following a Divine intuition, a special inner voice.[11] Perhaps this is the reason Abram, recognizing his wife's prescience, hastily acquiesces, and accepts Hagar.

GENESIS 16:3

And Sarai, the wife of Abram, took Hagar the Egyptian, her handmaiden . . . and gave her to her husband Abram as his wife.[12]

Notwithstanding the implementation of her own suggestion that Abram take a surrogate, the text clearly states that Sarai remains Abram's wife. Ramban states that she relinquished neither her marital rights nor her faith that she would one day bear Abram's heir.[13] Therefore, Sarai is still referred to in this verse as *Abram's wife*,[14] as he is still referred to as *her husband*,[15] even though Hagar is given to

---

[7] אמרה: ידעתי אנא מהיכן היא סיבתי. לא כשם שאומרים לי: קמיע היא צריכה . . . אלא הנה-נא עצרני ד' מלדת.

[8] אף על פי שאברם מתאוה מאד לבנים, לא עשה כן בלא רשות שרי.

[9] וישמע אברם **לקול** שרי.

[10] לקול

[11] לרוח הקדש שבה.

[12] ותקח שרי **אשת** אברם את הגר המצרית שפחתה . . . ותתן אותה לאברם **אשה** לו **לאשה.**

[13] כי שרי לא נתיאשה מאברם, ולא הרחיקה עצמה מאצלו.

[14] אשת אברם

[15] אישה

Abram *to be his wife.*[16] Perhaps the double use of the root-word
iSHa,[17] *wife,* and still another use of the sound-alike *iSHaH,*[18] a
homophone meaning *her husband,* is a presaging to students of the
text that there are too many wives in this one household. The
following verses bear this out.

GENESIS 16:4

Hagar immediately becomes pregnant by Abram. The speed of
her conception, contrasted with Sarai's inability to conceive, enables
Hagar to devalue Sarai. *And when Hagar saw that she had
conceived, her mistress was lowered in her esteem.*[19] Rashi is explicit.
He equates—in Hagar's mind—a woman's righteousness with her
ability to become pregnant. While Hagar herself is silent in this verse
of the Bible, Rashi gives her a voice in order to explain the text's
statement that she treated Sarai with contempt: "My mistress, Sarai,
cannot be as perfect as she appears. If she were truly righteous, her
God would certainly have given her children by now. Yet He has not
done so, and it is I who became pregnant even after my very first
intimacy with Abram."[20] The *mephorshim* grapple with this profound
philosophical difficulty. *Midrash Rabbah* (45.4) asks, Why were the
matriarchs barren? Could the reason have been that God desired
their prayers? Or that The Almighty sought a more mutual
communication with them? Could God have had their welfare in
mind, and sought to extend their pleasurable time alone with their
husbands? And to prolong their youthful appearance by deferring
pregnancy?[21] *Midrash Rabbah* has offered these several hypotheses
perhaps because no single answer was sufficient. Whatever the Divine
reason for Sarah's barrenness, the stark fact remains that as Hagar's
belly swelled with child, Sarah's womb remained empty.

---

[16] לוֹ לְאִשָּׁה

[17] אִשָּׁה

[18] אִישָׁהּ

[19] וַתֵּרֶא כִּי הָרָתָה, וַתֵּקַל גְּבִרְתָּהּ בְּעֵינֶיהָ.

[20] אמרה: שָׂרִי זוֹ אֵין סִתְרָהּ כְּגָלוּיָהּ; מַרְאָה עַצְמָהּ כְּאִלּוּ הִיא צַדֶּקֶת, וְאֵינָה צַדֶּקֶת, שֶׁלֹּא זָכְתָה
לְהֵרָיוֹן כָּל הַשָּׁנִים הַלָּלוּ, וַאֲנִי נִתְעַבַּרְתִּי מִבִּיאָה רִאשׁוֹנָה.

[21] שֶׁהקב"ה מִתְאַוֶּה לְתִפְלָּתָן וּמִתְאַוֶּה לְשִׂיחָתָן . . . כְּדֵי שֶׁיִּהְיוּ מִתְרַפְּקוֹת עַל בַּעֲלֵיהֶן בְּנוּיָּין . . .
כְּדֵי שֶׁיֵּצְאוּ רוֹב הַשָּׁנִים בְּלֹא שִׁעְבּוּד . . . כָּל זְמַן שֶׁהָאִשָּׁה מְקַבֶּלֶת עֻבָּרִין הִיא מִתְכַּעֶרֶת.

GENESIS 16:5

Sarai is shocked and angered both by Hagar's haughtiness and by Abram's passive acceptance of Hagar's officiousness. *Sarai said to Abram: My anger is directed toward you.*[22] The *mephorshim* offer different reasons for this anger. Rashi voices Sarai's complaint against her husband: "*You* must bear the brunt of the responsibility for the discord in this house. First, when you entreated God to bless you with sons to carry on your name, you prayed only for yourself, and not for us both. You said, 'What use to me are my riches when *I* remain childless, with no son of *my* flesh to inherit me?'" (Genesis 15:2–3).[23] "You failed to pray that God would fulfill His covenant of fertility through both of us, through *our* union."[24]

"Second, you witnessed Hagar's contempt of me, and you stood by silently."[25] Thus, not only is Sarai dismayed that Abram prayed to God for an heir for *himself,* but she also could not bear Abram's apparent disregard for her constant pain as Hagar grew more boldly insolent. Alshich suggests that Sarai suspected that Hagar's stinging and haughty words reflected Abram's private assurances to Hagar that the child *she* was carrying would be the covenantal heir.[26]

Sarai obviously is feeling betrayed. Her intention in introducing Hagar's surrogacy was that she would retain her position as matriarch, while Hagar would function solely in a reproductive capacity. Instead, Sarai feels she has lost her status as mistress of Abram's house, and her hope to nurture Hagar and Abram's child as her own. Sarai tells him, "Hagar no longer respects or heeds me."[27] Perhaps Sarai harbored a hope that Abram would speak up to reassure her, or even that he would castigate Hagar. He does neither of these things. By his silence, Abram further demeans Sarai in Hagar's eyes. A depleted and emotionally exhausted Sarai cries out

---

[22] ותאמר שרי אל אברם: חמסי עליך.

[23] ויאמר אברם: אדני ד', מה תתן לי ואנכי הולך ערירי? . . . הן לי לא נתת זרע . . .

[24] עליך אני מטילה העונש. כשהתפללת להקב"ה . . . לא התפללת אלא עליך, והיה לך להתפלל על **שנינו**, והייתי אני נפקדת עמך.

[25] ועוד; . . . שאתה שומע בזיוני ושותק.

[26] חששה שרי פן מה שהוקלה בעיניה היה כי אברהם אמר לה כי **בולדה** יקרא לו זרע.

[27] ואקל בעיניה

to Abram in the biblical text: "Let God be the judge of our relation-ship!"[28]

Abram and Sarai's marriage is buckling under the strain of years of frustrated hopes. The Talmud (*Bava Batra* 58a) relates the story that in the next world Abram is seen sleeping in Sarai's arms while she strokes his head. The observer is assured by an awakened Abram not to be embarrassed; Abram tells him that he has not interrupted an intimate physical episode, because, in Abram's words, "There is no passion here."[29] Was this absence of marital passion, so cryptically described in the Talmud by Abram, a continuation of their earthly relationship?

GENESIS 16:6

Sarai's admonition gives Abram pause. Sforno notes that Abram immediately relegates Hagar back to her handmaid status.[30] Abram then tells Sarai to do with Hagar as she will.[31] The Bible states that *Sarai dealt harshly* with Hagar.[32] Sarai is suffering from her own protracted infertility. Her insecurity is exacerbated by Hagar's easy fertility and her contemptuous behavior. This is the only time that the text reveals a lapse in Sarai's self-control. The text is ambiguous about the nature of Sarai's lapse. What exactly did Sarai do to Hagar? The *mephorshim* offer several theories. *Midrash Rabbah* (45.6) interprets Sarai's act of returning the recently emancipated Hagar to handmaid status as the "harsh" behavior noted in the verse. After serving as a handmaiden to Sarai for ten years and then briefly tasting pampered freedom as Abram's pregnant concubine, the return to servant status was torture for Hagar.[33]

Midrash Rabbah continues that once Hagar fulfilled her function as surrogate by becoming pregnant, Sarai removed her from the master's bedroom.[34] For Hagar this, too, was torment. She began as

---

[28] ישפט ד' ביני וביניך.

[29] דיצר בהאי עלמא ליכה.

[30] שאינה משוחררת ממך.

[31] הנה שפחתך בידך; עשי-לה הטוב בעיניך.

[32] ותענה שרי.

[33] מאחר שעשינו אותה גבירה, אנו עושין אותה שפחה.

[34] מנעתה מתשמיש המטה.

handmaiden to the mistress Sarai; was elevated to concubine to the master Abram, then was summarily demoted to handmaid status to Sarai once again. Of course this must have been "torment" to Hagar.

According to Sforno, Sarai's behavior toward Hagar—whatever form it took—was necessary and justified, in order to restore their servant/mistress relationship. It was crucial for Hagar to recognize that *she* was the servant, and to cease her denigration of her mistress.[35] Rashi's interpretation of the "torment" is that Sarai caused Hagar to work with much effort.[36] *Midrash Rabbah* characterizes the "harsh" treatment as delegating to Hagar tasks that were unsuited to her in her new status. Fetching water and towels to the bath was no longer appropriate work for the master's concubine. Ramban, however, faults *both* Sarai and Abram for their behavior in this episode.[37] According to Ramban, Sarai and Abram both sinned in their treatment of Hagar. Perhaps if their relationship had been less strained, Abram and Sarai could better have weathered the turbulence of surrogacy.

The modern Bible scholar, Nehama Leibowitz, in her work, *Studies in Bereshit (Genesis)*,[†] strives to understand Ramban's harsh criticism of Sarai, considering that according to Nehama, "Sarah's reactions are surely understandable. After selflessly offering Hagar to her husband she sees herself triumphed over by her handmaid. Who would condemn Sarah for her behavior?" While Nehama herself feels there were extenuating psychological circumstances at work that mitigate an outright condemnation of Sarai, she explains that Ramban makes no allowances for Sarai's treatment of her handmaid. Nehama presents her understanding of Ramban's criticism:

> "Perhaps the Torah wished to teach us that before man undertakes a mission that will tax all his moral and spiritual powers he should ask himself first whether he can maintain those same high standards to the bitter end. Otherwise, man is liable to descend from the pinnacle of altruism and selflessness into much deeper depths than would ordinarily have been the case. Had

[†]Leibowitz, N. (1973). *Studies in Bereshit (Genesis)*, Fourth Revised Edition (Jerusalem: Hemed Press), p. 155.

---

[35] כדי שתכיר שהיא משועבדת, ולא תבזה עוד את גברתה.

[36] היתה משעבדת בה.

[37] חטאה אמנו בעני הזה, וגם אברהם. . . .

Sarah not wished to suppress her instincts and overcome *every*
vestige of jealousy for her rival, had she not dared to scale these
unusual heights of selflessness, she would not have fallen victim
to the [Ramban's] sin of 'Sarah dealt harshly with her.'"[38]

Sarai's initial impulse of proffering a surrogate to her husband
was such a laudable act that it was almost inevitable that over time it
would become injected with ordinary human weakness, and would
end in tragedy.

Hagar flees from *Sarai's* presence.[39] *Midrash Rabbah*, noting
that the biblical text only states that Hagar flees from *her* presence
and not from *Abram's*, suggests that Hagar was fleeing only from
Sarai; her relationship with *Abram* was far from over.

GENESIS 16:7–16

Hagar's flight leads her to an oasis by the road. There, an angel
of God addresses her as Sarai's *handmaid* [40] and questions Hagar.
Hagar describes to the angel that she has fled from *her mistress*
Sarai.[41] The angel then exhorts Hagar to return to *her mistress*.[42] By
the triple use of the words indicating Hagar's menial status, the text
supports Sarai's reestablishment of the servant/mistress relationship.
Thereafter, the angel predicts that Hagar will give birth to a son whom
she must name Ishmael, which translates from the Hebrew words
YiSHMa-el,[43] meaning "God will hear your plea."

Heeding the angel's voice, Hagar returns to her mistress and
bears Abram a son, whom *he* names Ishmael.[44] The reader will note
that it is Abram who names Hagar's son, and not Hagar herself, as

---

[38] אולי רצתה התורה ללמדנו, כי המתמתח מעל לקומת אנוש ומקבל על עצמו משימות שמעל
לכוחו—ייטיב לשאול עצמו תחילה, אם יוכל לעמוד בהן עד הסוף. שאם לא כן, מוטב לו לאדם
שיחיה לפי כוחותיו ולפי הנדרש ממנו, כי אם רגע יעלה מעלה ביכולת היותר ובהבאת קרבן
ובכבישת כל יצר אנושי . . . הן אם לא יוכל גם לשהות על אותם רוכסי ההרים שאליהן
טיפס והגיע לרגע, סכנת שיפול מטה בהרבה ממה שהיה בזמן היותו במישור.

[39] ותברך מפניה

[40] **שפחת** שרי

[41] מפני שרי **גברתי** אנכי ברחת

[42] שובי אל-**גברתך**

[43] ישמע אל

[44] ותלד הגר לאברם בן, ויקרא **אברם** שם-בנו אשר-ילדה הגר ישמעאל.

the angel instructed. One could infer from the *p'shat* that Abram and Hagar resumed, at the very least, an intimate exchange of words; for how else would Abram have known to comply precisely with the angel's directive if Hagar had not confided in him? Rashi's solution attributes Abram's knowledge of the child's name to Divine revelation.[45]

Because the text and the commentaries are silent as to Sarai's reaction to the birth of a son to Abram, we can assume that Sarai realizes she has no choice but to silently accept Hagar's elevated status. Sarai desperately wants Abram's child, even if it is fated to be through a surrogate.

---

[45] ויקרא אברם שם וגו'. אע"פ שלא שמע אברהם דברי המלאך שאמר " וקראת שמו ישמעאל,"
שרתה רוח הקודש עליו וקראו ישמעאל.

FOUR

಼಼಼಼

God Promises Sarai
a Child and
Changes Her Name

GENESIS 17:1–14

Thirteen years pass. Sarai, now eighty-nine years old, remains sterile. All this time, she has watched another woman, her own handmaid, raise Abram's son. Abram, on the other hand, is a vital ninety-nine years old when God next appears to him. In this encounter God reaffirms His promise to Abram that he will be *the father of a multitude of nations*,[1] and seals His word by changing Abram's name to Abraham.[2] God also promises him the land of Canaan as his everlasting possession throughout generations. As evidence of Abraham's acceptance of God's sovereignty, he is commanded to circumcise all newborn males in his household when they reach eight days of age. This *mitzvah*—or commandment—of circumcision, a sign of God's Covenant, must be performed through-out each subsequent generation.

---

[1] אב המון גוים

[2] והיה שמך אברהם כי אב-המון גוים נתתיך.

At the same time that God changes Abram's name to Abraham, God acknowledges Sarai's partnership in the Covenant by also changing her name, from Sarai to Sarah.[3] The Talmud (*Brachot* 13a) explains the significance of these name changes, and states that the additional Hebrew letter *hay* added to Abram's name makes him ruler over not just the land of Aram, but over *all* nations.[4] Similarly, regarding Sarai, the Talmud elevates her to princess over not merely her own nation, but over the entire world, incidentally fulfilling the third definition of Yiscah, meaning regal (see Chapter 1).[5]

Midrash Rabbah explains the name change as follows: God took the letter *yud* from Sara**i**[6] (the numerical value of the Hebrew letter *yud* equals 10), and divided it equally between her new name, Sara**h**, and Abram's new name, Abra**h**am, giving to each of them an additional Hebrew letter *hay* (the numerical value of each letter *hay* equals 5).[7]

Thus, say these *mephorshim*, God crowned Abraham through the merit of his wife Sarah.[8] Abraham's honor and greatness therefore originate with Sarah.[9] Students of the text will recall that Abraham himself understood Sarah's worthiness at the portals of Egypt. At that time, he said to Sarai, *in order that things will go well for me on your behalf*.[10] *Matnot Kehuna*, a commentary on *Midrash Rabbah*, suggests that Abraham's statement in Egypt presages the crowning glory that God grants to him and Sarah in this verse, twenty-three years later; that Abraham's honor and greatness are derived from Sarah's merit, and not her greatness from his.[11]

---

3   שרי אשתך לא-תקרא את שמה שרי, כי שרה שמה.

4   בתחלה נעשה אב לארם, ולבסוף נעשה אב לכל עולם כולו.

5   בתחלה נעשית שרי לאומתה, ולבסוף נעשית שרה לכל העולם כולו.

6   שרי

7   יו"ד שנטל הקב"ה. משרי נחלק חציו לשרה וחציו לאברהם.

8   בעלה נתעטר בה.

9   נתעטר ממנה בכבוד וגדולה.

10   למען ייטב לי בעבורך.

11   והיא לא נתעטרה בבעלה.

According to Rav Soloveitchik,[†] because "there was an existential interdependence between both, . . . Abraham could not be a 'father' of multitudes if Sarah were not [also] crowned as a 'mother' queen of this multitude."

GENESIS 17:16

In a parallel manner to His recent promise to Abraham, God follows His pronouncement of Sarah's name change with an astounding promise on her behalf. He now promises to bless Sarah with a child of her very own, saying that this child will be the fruit of Sarah's relations with her husband, Abraham. God states that *Sarah* is destined to be the mother of the nations and kings that God had promised Abraham (in Genesis 17:6) would issue from his loins.[12] God's words concerning Sarah's blessing are remarkably similar to His blessing to Abraham.[13] The parallel blessings promise that a multitude of nations will be born from Abraham and Sarah.

This is a momentous declaration, for at this moment the reader grasps that Sarah herself will conceive her own biological child from Abraham. The text states, *I will bless her,* and then adds, **and moreover** *I will give you a son from her.*[14] *Siftei Chachamim* asks, Would it not have been sufficient for the text to say, "I will bless her with your son?" What do the words *and moreover* add to our understanding of God's blessing? The commentary's solution is that the biblical verse is comprised of two parts because God blesses Sarah with two distinct blessings. The first phrase blesses Sarah with a return to youthful fecundity. This primary blessing must naturally precede the second phrase, the blessing that Sarah herself will conceive Abraham's son.[15]

[†]Soloveitchik, J. B. (1989). *Man of Faith in the Modern World: Reflections of the Rav, Volume Two* (Hoboken, NJ: KTAV Publishing House, Inc.), p. 86.

---

[12] ונתתיך לגוים ומלכים ממך יצאו.

[13] והיתה לגוים מלכי עמים ממנה יהיו.

[14] וברכתי אותה **וגם** נתתי ממנה לך בן.

[15] מאי וברכתי אותה, ואחר כך וגם נתתי ממנה לך בן? אלא ודאי קאי על הברכה שקודם לכן, והוא הנערות.

GENESIS 17:17

An astonished Abraham falls on his face upon hearing God's prediction of Sarah's fertility, and he laughs out loud.[16] The commentators offer varying interpretations of the simple word VaYiTZCHaK,[17] *and he laughed.* Rashi cites Onkelos on the word VaYiTZCHaK,[18] *and he laughed,* and translates it to mean "and he rejoiced,"[19] in Aramaic. Alshich questions this definition. It is unlikely that the word VaYiTZCHaK[20] (*and he laughed*) connotes pure joy; for if this were so, why then does Abraham harbor doubt in his heart in the second half of this verse?

> *And Abraham said in his heart: Can this happen to someone like me, who is a hundred years old, and to my wife Sarah, who is ninety years old, that she will give birth?*[21]

Ibn Ezra explains that Abraham's doubt is based not on theological grounds, but on the laws of nature. "How can my aged seed yield fruit? Even more unbelievable, how can a woman who has ceased her menses conceive?"[22] Rabbi Samson Raphael Hirsch, explaining Abraham's laughter at the news that Sarah will give birth, states that in this verse the word "*TZeCHoK*[23] is used without exception for ironic laughter . . . laughter that has in it a certain denying . . . of the matter which excited the laughter."

GENESIS 17:17–21

Instead of responding with unequivocal joyous laughter to God's promise that he will conceive a child *with Sarah,* Abraham responds fearfully to God's promise. Abraham is worried that his thirteen-year-old son, Ishmael, will have no place in God's revealed plan: *If only*

---

[16] ויפל אברהם על-פניו ויצחק.

[17] ויצחק

[18] ויצחק

[19] וחדי

[20] ויצחק

[21] ויאמר בלבו הלבן מאה-שנה יולד, ואם שרה הבת תשעים שנה תלד?

[22] תמה בעבור היות זרע הזקן קר, על כן לא יוליד. והתימה הגדול, איך תלד אשה שנפסק דמה?

[23] צחק

You will let Ishmael live! [24] Alshich points out that Abraham's objection fails to take into account Sarah's longtime dream; Ishmael is son of *his* seed, but what of Sarah? Should not Abraham's reaction *also* have been to rejoice that God has seen fit to grant Sarah's lifelong prayer?[25] Perhaps that is a reason for God's remonstrance of Abraham in the next verses. In these verses God addresses both of Abraham's concerns. First, that Sarah is too old to conceive; and second, that his son, Ishmael, will be disinherited. God responds sequentially: To Abraham's doubt of Sarah's ability to conceive (verse 17), God reassures Abraham in verse 19 saying, *Not so! Sarah your wife* **shall bear** *you the true covenantal son, whom you shall name Isaac. . . .*[26] Not only has God promised Abraham that he will, indeed, sire a son with Sarah, but God has named him as well. Isaac is destined to be the true covenantal son, and the second patriarch. As to Abraham's fears for Ishmael, God's response appears in verses 20 and 21: *And as for Ishmael, I have heard your concerns, and I will also bless* **him** *with multitudes. . . .*[27] God reiterates, *But I will establish My covenant* **with Sarah's son**, *Isaac. . . .*[28] The reader will note that the phrase, *and I will establish My covenant . . .* appears twice in God's response to Abraham: once in verse 19,[29] and again in verse 21.[30] This repetition reinforces the centrality of "the Covenant" and the covenantal heir in God's plan for continuity of the chosen people. God wanted Abraham to realize that Ishmael was not this covenantal heir.

Rav Soloveitchik, in his chapter on this biblical portion, describes God's conversation with Abraham at this precise moment. According to the Rav, God tells Abraham that His covenant cannot be realized without Isaac. The Rav teaches that Ishmael is not worthy of being the covenantal heir because he is the son of Hagar. The covenantal heir must be the son of both *Sarah* and Abraham. Therefore, the Rav concludes, Isaac will represent *both* Abraham and Sarah. There is no

---

[24] לו ישמעאל יחיה לפניך!

[25] והלא אם הוא יתרצה בזה לבדו, שרה לא תתרצה, כי מה לה בטובת ישמעאל?

[26] ויאמר אלהים אבל שרה אשתך **ילדת** לך בן וקראת את שמו יצחק . . . והקמתי את בריתי אתו לברית עולם. . . .

[27] ולישמעאל שמעתיך הנה ברכתי אתו והפרתי אתו והרבתי **אתו** במאד מאד. . . .

[28] ואת בריתי אקים את יצחק, אשר תלד לך שרה. . . .

[29] והקמתי את בריתי

[30] ואת בריתי אקים

covenant without Sarah. The Rav teaches that the covenant was entrusted to the two: man and woman.[†]

Tucked into verse 19 is God's personal command that Abraham name Sarah's promised son Isaac.[31] The root-word *TZeCHoK*,[32] meaning *laughter*, forms the basis of Isaac's name. Rashi says the reason for the name was "because of the laughter."[33] The reader is aware that the only "laughter" that has taken place in the text as of yet has been Abraham's laughter in verse 17, when he laughed in response to the unlikely news that he would have a child with Sarah. God is emphasizing here that only *their* child, who will be named Isaac after the "laughter," will be the recipient of God's covenant.[34]

GENESIS 17:23–28

Obeying God's command in 17:10, as a sign of the Covenant, Abraham immediately circumcises himself, his thirteen-year-old son, Ishmael, and his entire male household.[35] The stage is now set for news of a covenantal heir, and the upcoming verses bear this out.

[†]Soloveitchik, J. B. (1989). *Man of Faith in the Modern World: Reflections of the Rav, Volume Two* (Hoboken, NJ: KTAV Publishing House, Inc.), p. 86.

---

[31] וקראת את שמו יצחק.

[32] צחק

[33] על שם הצחק.

[34] את יצחק, אשר תלד לך שרה למועד הזה, בשנה האחרת.

[35] בעצם היום הזה נמול אברהם וישמעאל בנו, וכל אנשי ביתו.

FIVE

෯෮ඏ෮ඏ

Sarah's Rejuvenation

GENESIS 18:8

It is *in the heat of the day*,[1] and Abraham is sitting at an opening of his tent at the crossroads, recuperating from his circumcision. Suddenly in the distance he sees three strangers facing him. Abraham runs to greet them, and offers them his hospitality, which they accept. As the strangers wash their dusty feet and rest under a tree, Abraham hastens into the tent, and excitedly urges Sarah to bake cakes for their guests, while he hurries off to prepare a tender calf for their meal. The food is prepared, served and eaten outside the tent.

Rashi notes that the text in verse eight mentions that Abraham himself brings their guests the calf, the milk and the butter; all the food originating with the livestock. Conspicuously absent from the text is mention of the cakes that Abraham had expressly asked Sarah to bake.[2] Rashi questions, What of Sarah's baked goods? Apparently, on the very day of the strangers' arrival at her tent, Sarah's menses miraculously resumed, signaling her renewal but rendering her ritually impure. Thus, the dough that she kneaded was prohibited to her

---

¹ כחם היום

² ויקח חמאה וחלב ובן-בקר אשר עשה. . . .

28

guests.[3] Unbeknownst to Abraham and Sarah, their three guests are in truth messenger-angels sent by God. According to Rashi (in verse 18:2), one of the angels' missions was to heal Abraham following his circumcision; the second's role was to deal with the destruction of the city of Sodom; and the third angel's duty was to herald Sarah's rejuvenation.[4]

GENESIS 18:9

The angel asked Abraham, Where is Sarah, your wife? And he answered, She is here, inside the tent.[5] Rashi wonders: Would not the angels have known of Sarah's precise whereabouts? Why was it necessary for them to ask? He answers his own rhetorical question, saying that the angels sought thus to endear Sarah to her husband by emphasizing her modesty.[†] She modestly remained inside the tent, out of the strangers' sight.[6]

GENESIS 18:10

Sarah's angel promises that when he returns in a year's time, Sarah already will have borne her son. Sarah, still inside the tent, hears the angel's prediction, as the tent flap is directly behind the

---

[†]This extreme modesty is a virtue extolled in the Talmud. In *Yevamot* 77a, the sages are discussing the reason that Ruth—the ancestor of both King David and the Messiah—a Moabitess, was permitted to enter the congregation of Israel, despite the strict prohibition against Moabite *men* (Devarim 23:4). They reasoned that although the Moabites were punished for failing to greet the newly-freed Hebrews on their way out of Egypt, the Moabite *women* were forgiven, because it was their modesty which properly kept them at home. כל כבודה בת מלך פנימה.

---

[3] לחם לא הביא? לפי שפירסה שרה נדה . . . אותו היום, ונטמאת העיסה.

[4] אחד לבשר את שרה, ואחד להפוך את סדום, ואחד לרפאות את אברהם. שאין מלאך אחד עושה שתי שליחות.

[5] ויאמר אליו, איה שרה אשתך? ויאמר, הנה באהל.

[6] יודעים היו מלאכי השרת שרה אמנו היכן היתה, אלא להודיע שצנועה היתה כדי לחבבה על בעלה.

seated guests.[7] Rashi points out that the verse ends with the words *VeHu aCHoRaV*,[8] *and it—the tent flap—is behind him*. Thus, we can assume that Sarah heard the angel's message because in the heat of the day the tent flap was open.

GENESIS 18:11

In light of this astonishing news, that Sarah will bear a son in one year's time, the Bible reminds its readers that both Abraham and Sarah are extremely old, and that Sarah ostensibly had ceased having regular menses.[9] *Siftei Chachamim* explains that Sarah attributed her bleeding that day to overexertion during her hasty preparation for her guests. When it occurred, she had no inkling that God was restoring her youth to her.[10]

GENESIS 18:12–15

And so Sarah laughed silently to herself, wondering: At this withered stage of my life will I [now] be rejuvenated? And my husband is [also] old.[11]

As they did with Abraham, the commentaries discuss the nature of Sarah's laughter. The strict textual reading of the words[12] is: *She laughed internally*. Ibn Ezra explains that Sarah's laughter was undetectable; it was within her soul.[13] Rashi explains that the words mean that Sarah's focus is on her internal body. She laughs, thinking, "Is it possible that this aged uterus will sustain an embryo? That these shriveled breasts will nourish a child with milk?"[14] *Siftei Chachamim* offers the additional explanation that Sarah begins to question the

---

7   ויאמר שוב אשוב אליך כעת חיה, והנה בן לשרה אשתך, ושרה שמעת פתח האהל והוא אחריו.

8   והוא אחריו

9   ואברהם ושרה זקנים באים בימים, חדל להיות לשרה ארח כנשים.

10   היתה סבורה שמקרה הוא, ולא חזרת וסת . . . מכח מהירת הלישה, שאמר אברהם, "מהרי" וכו'.

11   ותצחק שרה בקרבה לאמר: אחרי בלתי היתה לי עדנה? ואדני זקן.

12   ותצחק בקרבה

13   וטעם בקרבה "בנפשה."

14   מסתכלת במיעה ואמרה: אפשר הקרבים הללו טעונים ולד? השדים הללו שצמקו מושכין חלב?

origin of her bleeding of that day. After she sees her blood she wonders, "Have I injured myself, or can this be my menses?"[15]

The *Netziv*, on the other hand, attributes to Sarah a high degree of faith in God's ability to work miracles on her behalf. When Abraham revealed to her God's promise (in 17:21) that *she* would bear his covenantal son, Sarah steadfastly believed this could happen. She expected, however, that given her advanced age, God would supersede the laws of nature to enable her to give birth, and not have her conceive in the natural manner. But so great was her faith, according to the *Netziv*, that she would not have been surprised had God enabled even a stone to become pregnant.[16]

Sarah's laughter reflected her delight that God's promise to her that she would give birth to a child of her own apparently was about to be fulfilled in a natural manner. As the day progressed, Sarah noticed that her body had begun to show signs of rejuvenation. The Talmud (*Bava Metzia* 87a) describes that her breasts began to firm, her wrinkles to soften. Her youthful beauty was restored.[17] At that point Sarah shed her last doubt that her morning's bleeding was indeed a restoration of her youth. She understands that God would work His miracle for her within the laws of nature. She appreciates that her body was readying itself for pregnancy.[18] For the *Netziv*, then, Sarah's inner laughter reflects her last doubt. It concerns her aged husband, Abraham. For *he* has exhibited no signs of rejuvenation.[19]

The text states that God confronts Abraham, questioning Sarah's laughter. God asks,

> *Why did Sarah laugh about this, saying, "Is it really true that I will give birth, and I am so old?" Is anything too miraculous for God to accomplish?* [20]

---

[15] אמרה כן שמסופקת, כלאמר; "הדם שראיתי כבר מסופקת אני בזה, אם הוא וסת שלי או לא."

[16] מתחלה כשהגיד לה אברהם דבר ד', לא צחקה ולא התפלאה מזה, וידעה שלא יפלא מד' לתת הריון גם לאבן.

[17] נתעדן הבשר ונתפשטו הקמטין, וחזר היופי למקומו.

[18] אבל בראותה שהיא נעשית ילדה, והיתה לה עדנה, הרי רצונו יתברך שהלידה תהיה בדרך הטבע.

[19] התפלאה . . . שלא ראתה באברהם שום שנוי.

[20] ויאמר ד' אל אברהם, למה זה צחקה שרה לאמר: האף אמנם אלד ואני זקנתי? היפלא מד' דבר?

According to Rashbam, it is not God who is thus questioning Sarah's laughter. Rather, it is one of the angel-messengers who is visiting them.[21]

Sforno interprets Sarah's laughter as incredulity at the angel-messenger's blessing of fertility. Sforno says that Sarah likened the possibility that she would give birth at the age of ninety to God's ability to resurrect the dead. This is a miraculous feat which only God—and not even His angel-messenger—could accomplish. It is precisely because the prediction came from the *angel*, and not from God, that Sarah allowed herself to laugh.[22]

The reader will recall that Abraham also laughed in the face of God's promise that Sarah would bear him a son in her old age (Genesis 17:17). In contrast, Abraham's laughter went unchallenged. *Ohr Hachayim*'s commentary reflects the difficulty with the text's disparate treatment of Abraham's and Sarah's laughters. Why does God question only Sarah's laughter, and not her husband's?[23] The commentator answers his own question by explaining that Abraham's joyous laughter was an *immediate* response to God's promise of their fertility; while Sarah's joyous laughter found expression only after she felt the physical changes of rejuvenation.[24] Perhaps God expected that Sarah's joyous laughter would have occurred earlier, *immediately* after hearing the angel's prediction through the open tent flap. Instead, she only allowed herself to believe in the angel's prediction after seeing the physical evidence of God's miraculous power.

Notwithstanding the *mephorshim*'s differentiations between Abraham's and Sarah's laughter, the fact remains that the same word *TZeCHoK*[25] (meaning *laughter*) elicits different responses in the text. Abraham's laughter goes unchallenged, while Sarah's laughter is questioned. This is not merely a semantic problem, but a serious philosophical issue as well. This issue is so serious that it is one of the fourteen biblical phrases that Jewish scholars in the third century

---

21 "ויאמר ד':" המלאך הגדול שבהם.

22 שחשבה שהיה דבר **המלאך** ברכת נביא בלבד . . . לא נבואה ושליחות האל ית' . . . כי אמנם להשיב הבחרות אחר הזקנה הרי הוא תחית המתים.

23 כי אברהם גם כן צחק כשאמר לו ד' בשורות הזרע . . . ולא ראינו שהקפיד ד' על שצחק אברהם . . . מה נשתנה צחיקת שרה מצחיקת אברהם?

24 כי אברהם בעת הבשורה צחק משא"כ שרה; לא צחקה בעת שנתבשרה, אלא בעת שראתה עדנה.

25 צחק

B.C.E. actually *altered* when they were forced to translate the Hebrew
Bible into Greek for the Egyptian king, Ptolemai II.

The Talmud (*Megilla* 9a) relates the story that King Ptolemai,
desiring an accurate Greek translation of the Jewish Bible,
sequestered seventy-two Jewish scholars knowledgeable in both
Hebrew and Greek. Without revealing to them his ultimate purpose,
Ptolemai isolated the scholars in seventy-two separate houses with the
identical instruction: "Transcribe for me the Torah of your teacher,
Moses."[26] Miraculously, the Talmud tells us, all seventy-two scholars
translated the Torah in precisely the same manner. When they
reached our verse in Genesis (18:12), *Sarah laughed internally,*[27] all
seventy-two scholars, aware that Sarah's laughter is met with Divine
censure while Abraham's is not, altered the Hebrew wording from
BeKiRBaH,[28] meaning *internally,* to *BiKRoVeHa,*[29] *in the presence of
others.* This audacious alteration transformed Sarah's silent—and
ostensibly permissible—laughter, into a public—and therefore
objectionable—display of laughter. Such an unprecedented
replacement of Torah text (that is, substituting the words "*private*
laughter" with their virtual antonym "*public* laughter") demonstrates
how truly difficult it is, even for scholars, to comprehend God's
disparate reaction to Abraham's and Sarah's laughters.

Ohr Hachayim, then, without ever referring to the Talmud's
vignette, explains in essence that it is the *timing* of Sarah's laughter
(whether it was silent or public) that triggers God's reaction in these
verses.

Ever Sarah's protector, God, in relaying to Abraham Sarah's
reaction to the news of her impending fertility, strategically omits her
phrase about Abraham's advanced age at the end of verse 12: *But
my master is old!* [30] Rashi briefly explains God's strategy. God did not
wish to instill discord between husband and wife by reminding
Abraham that Sarah was acutely aware of *his* advanced age.[31] The
Talmud agrees. *Bava Metzia* 87a states that peace between a

---

[26] מעשה בתלמי המלך שכינס שבעים ושנים זקנים, והכניסן בשבעים ושנים בתים, ולא גילה
להם על מה כינסן. ונכנס אצל כל אחד ואמר להם: כתבו לי תורת משה רבכם.

[27] ותצחק שרה בקרבה.

[28] בקרבה

[29] בקרוביה

[30] ואדוני זקן

[31] שנה הכתוב מפני השלום, שהרי היא אמרה "ואדוני זקן."

husband and wife is so desirable an end that God Himself altered Sarah's words.[32]

Although God now reiterates the angel's promise to Abraham, saying that at this time next year Sarah will deliver a son, still God withholds from Abraham Sarah's doubts about her husband's virility. Nevertheless, God questions Abraham, asking,

> *Why did Sarah laugh?* (18:13) *And she denied this, saying, "I did not laugh," because she was fearful. And it was said to her: No, you did laugh.*[33]

This verse presents several problems. First, what is Sarah's reaction to God's challenge? Second, why does she react in this fashion? And third, who is it who responds to Sarah's behavior? On the first point, understanding Sarah's reaction to God's challenge, the *p'shat* meaning of the words,[34] *and Sarah denied,* is that she actually denied that she laughed upon hearing the angel's news that she would give birth. But the Hebrew word for "she denied"[35] can also mean "and she cowered." This cowering reaction is understandable in light of the next words in the verse,[36] *because she was fearful.* Quite probably Sarah was frightened at being confronted by both God and Abraham right after the onset of her physical rejuvenation. In contrast, Alshich proposes that Sarah *does not deny* that she laughed; she denies only that the reason for her laughter was the improbability that *she* could bear a child. Sarah already believed (18:12) that God was readying *her* for pregnancy. Alshich's explanation is that Sarah laughs because of the improbability that her centenarian husband, Abraham, could father her child.[37]

---

[32] גדול שלום, שאפילו הקדוש ברוך הוא שנה בו.

[33] ויאמר ד' אל אברהם, למה זה צחקה שרה? . . . ותכחש שרה לאמר: לא צחקתי, כי יראה;
ויאמר: לא, כי צחקת.

[34] ותכחש שרה

[35] ותכחש

[36] כי יראה

[37] היא צחקה באומרה "ואדוני זקן." והוא אמר לה שצחקה לאמר: "ואני זקנתי." והנה הצחוק היה
אמת; אך לא מטעם זה.

Whether Sarah's fear caused her to issue a denial or to cower, the reader should infer from the *p'shat* that Sarah was terrified when God challenged her. Alshich, however, explains that Sarah feared that God had revealed to Abraham her statement, *and my husband is [also] old,*[38] implicating Abraham as the cause of their infertility. Sarah was unaware that to promote marital harmony God only revealed to Abraham her statement that *she* was old. Sarah feared that Abraham's ire would be kindled by her reference to *his* advanced age, and that he would provoke a confrontation with her in the presence of their guests.[39]

Ohr Hachayim gives us an additional insight into Abraham's state of mind. He suggests that Abraham was frightened that Sarah's laughter would cause God to renege on the angel's promise that Sarah would bear his son. His long-lived hope for a child with Sarah, now so palpably close, was threatened.[40] His son by the handmaid, Hagar, up until this moment his only hope for an heir, all at once seemed not enough. Abraham wanted the promised child with Sarah.

The final question presented by our verse is, Who responds to Sarah's words? Is it God, or is it Abraham? Who says to Sarah, *"No, you did laugh."* The reader should envision the scene of this conversation. Sarah is at the open tent flap; Abraham is standing by after his three guests have been served their noonday meal, when God questions Abraham about Sarah's laughter. Sarah, Abraham, and the messenger-angels are privy to God's query in verse 13 asking *"Why did Sarah laugh?"* After the text informs the reader that *"Sarah was frightened,"* it goes on to say, *"No, you did laugh."* The commentaries are divided as to whom this phrase is attributable. The reader can understand the difficulty, as either of the parties to the conversation could have interjected it.

Sforno proposes that *Abraham* is chiding his wife with this phrase. Abraham knew that if God said that Sarah laughed, then she most certainly did so, because God would not lie. It follows that Abraham believed Sarah was not speaking truthfully, and he would not allow any mitigating excuse for her denial.[41]

---

[38] ואדני זקן

[39] היא יראה פן יתקוטט עמה. . . .

[40] לבל יחשוב אברהם כי לצד הקפדת ד' על שרה ישוב ד' מדברו הטוב אשר דבר אליו.

[41] ויאמר [אברהם], לא. שידע כי לא איש אל ויכזב, ולא האמין לה כלל.

On the other hand, *Torah Temima*, quoting the Talmud (*Yerushalmi* 87), is emphatic that it is not Abraham, but *God* who is addressing Sarah here. The commentator points out that Sarah is the only woman to whom God speaks. He uses the words, *"No, you did laugh"* from this verse as a proof-text.[42] However, the super-commentary on *Torah Temima* reminds us that the Talmud refers to six other prophetesses in addition to Sarah; surely God spoke directly with them, as well? Moreover, does it not state in the Torah that "[God] said to the woman [Eve]" (Gen. 3:16), and also that "God said to Rebecca " (Gen. 25:23) ? How can *Torah Temima* state that God spoke only with Sarah?

The supercommentary distinguishes the matters about which the six other biblical women are prophesying. God's discourse *with them* is limited to matters of state, while God's discourse with Sarah is of a personal nature. As regards Eve and Rebecca, the Yerushalmi Talmud states that they received God's words via an intermediary, and not from God directly.[43] Furthermore, *Torah Temima* recounts that there exist varying levels of prophecy, and that Sarah reached an intimate level of prophecy that was unattained by the other prophetesses.[44]

---

[42] לא מצינו שדבר הקב"ה עם אשה, **אלא עם שרה בלבד,** שנאמר, **ויאמר, לא, כי צחקת!**

[43] דרשא זו בכלל צריכה באור, דהא מצינו כמה נשים שנביאות היו. כמו שנאמרו במגילה י"ד א', שרה, מרים, דבורה, חנה, אבגיל, חולדה, אסתר. וא"כ איך אמר לא מצינו שדבר הקב"ה עם אשה, הלא מכיון דנביאות היו; הלא דבר עמהן. וצ"ל דהדבור עם הנביאות היה בעניינים כוללים, הנוגעים לכלל האומה. משא"כ על עסקי עצמן לא דבר, כי אם עם שרה. והא דכתיב בחוה אל האשה אמר, וברבקה ויאמר ד' לה. מפרש בירושלמי דהיו האמירות על ידי מתורגמן.

[44] . . . בשרה הגיעה מדרגת הנבואה עד קצה המדרגות, והיינו מדרגת נבואה שלמה.

SIX

ഓരുഓരു

Sarah's Abduction
by Avimelech

GENESIS 20:1–2

S hortly thereafter, God destroys the inhabitants of Sodom for their intransigent evil. Abraham and his household have journeyed south, to the city of Gerar, fleeing the destruction, where a familiar scenario begins to unfold. There, Abraham tells the inhabitants of Gerar that his beautiful wife, Sarah, is his sister.[1] The precise translation of this phrase is: *And Abraham said to his wife, Sarah, "she is my sister."* Obviously, the direct translation is confusing. How could Abraham speak *to* Sarah, using the pronoun *she*, in the third person? Rashi and Ibn Ezra both state unequivocally that the Hebrew word *el,*[2] *meaning to*, often is understood as *al,*[3] meaning *pertaining to*. Therefore, the phrase can be understood as *And Abraham said, pertaining to his wife, Sarah, "she is my sister."*[4] From this phrase we deduce that while Sarah is the important subject of her husband's pronouncement, there is clearly no dialogue between them. Sarah may be

---

1 ‏ויאמר אברהם אל שרה אשתו אחותי היא.‏

2 ‏אל‏

3 ‏על‏

4 **‏אל שרה אשתו:‏** ‏על שרה אשתו;‏ **‏אל שרה אשתו:‏** ‏כמו‏ **‏על.‏**

37

standing right beside Abraham at the gates of Gerar, but Abraham speaks of her as if she is not present.

Not unexpectedly, Avimelech, the king of Gerar, sends his servants to Abraham's dwelling place, and abducts Sarah.[5] The reader will recall that years before, in a similar fashion, using similar language, Pharaoh "took" Sarah to his palace in Egypt.

Therefore, on the surface, this abduction appears to mimic Pharaoh's taking of Sarah from Abraham decades earlier. There are several differences, however. In the earlier incident, it is a famine that impels Abraham's migration to Egypt. Here, Rashi says that Abraham, whose mission is to convert souls to monotheism, is seeking more populous territory in which to pitch his tent. He also is fleeing the base immorality of Sodom, which had trapped his nephew, Lot.[6]

Also, in the earlier episode, Abraham beseeches Sarah to identify herself as his sister. Yet, in these verses, Abraham makes the now-familiar misrepresentation *without* any consultation with his wife. Rashi condemns Abraham's action by saying that not only did Abraham not request Sarah's permission, but he proceeded against her will and specifically to her detriment.[7] The Maharal explains that Abraham knew that had he requested her complicity, Sarah would have refused, the excruciating memories of the prior betrayal and near-rape still clear in her mind.[8] Alshich agrees:[9] Abraham acts peremptorily because he strongly suspects that Sarah would not give her consent to the wife/sister ruse. Sarah is bitterly aware of the grave consequences to herself of agreeing to declare that she is Abraham's sister. Abraham knows this, but still he presents her as his sister.

Students of the text must wonder what is motivating Abraham to repeat this scenario some twenty-three years after he first did so? The *mephorshim* also are understandably troubled by this episode. Alshich asks: Why, knowing what occurred in Egypt, does Abraham still proceed with this subterfuge?[10] Ramban explains that Gerar was a more civilized place than Egypt was, and Avimelech more honorable

---

5 וישלח אבימלך מלך גרר ויקח את שרה.

6 כשראה שחרבו הכרכים ופסקו העוברים והשבים, נסע לו משם. ד"א: להתרחק מלוט. . . .

7 כאן לא נטל רשות, אלא על כרחה, שלא בטובתה, לפי שכבר לקחה לבית פרעה על ידי כן.

8 בודאי לא תעשה מעצמה ברצונה, אחר שראתה שנלקחה לבית פרעה.

9 כי מר לה מאד על מה שקרה לה עם פרעה.

10 ישוב לאמר,אחותי היא, כמו זר נחשב ולא חש פן יקרנו כאשר קרה לו עם פרעה.

than Pharaoh. Therefore, Abraham did not expect an abduction here. But he was still somewhat wary of Avimelech's power and position. After all, Abraham is still only an itinerant tent-dweller, albeit now he is a wealthy one. For this reason, says Ramban, a cautious Abraham resorted to the "sister" subterfuge.[11]

Alshich persists, asking why Abraham presented the lovely Sarah as his sister in a city of strangers; he must have suspected the outcome would endanger her. Why did Abraham *again* place Sarah in a situation where only a miracle could extricate her?[12] Was he perhaps relying on Sarah's special relationship with God to protect her again? It seems that Abraham did, indeed, expect a miracle to save Sarah. The *Netziv* agrees with this supposition. Whenever Abraham journeyed to a place that God had not specifically directed him to visit—such as here in Gerar and formerly in Egypt—Abraham feared that God's protection would not follow *him*.[13] In these situations, Abraham relied on God's continual protection of Sarah.

Whatever Abraham's reasons for not securing Sarah's assent and for repeating the "sister" subterfuge, the reader should note that Sarah does not speak in the text throughout this episode. Sarah is once again taken by force from her husband's tent to the palace of a king. We can but imagine the broad gamut of emotions that Sarah is experiencing and not expressing.

GENESIS 20:3–5

Avimelech is in a deep sleep that night when God appears to him in a dream. God tells Avimelech that he is in peril of death because he has abducted Sarah; and moreover, that she already is the proper wife of another man. During his dream, Avimelech distances himself from Sarah and justifies his behavior to God, saying: "Lord, would you kill even a righteous nation? Did not Abraham himself tell me this woman was his sister? And she herself said 'he is

---

[11] אבל המלך הזה תם וישר, גם אנשיו טובים; רק אברהם חשד אותם, והיה אומר לכל: אחותי היא.

[12] ולמה סמך על הנס?

[13] בכל מקום שהלך ולא היה על פי ד' ורוח הקדש, היה ירא שלא יהיה שם ההבטחה.

my brother.' With an innocent heart and with clean hands I took her."[14]

A comparison of Avimelech's protestation of innocence here, to verse two, where Abraham said, "she is my sister,"[15] will show that Avimelech is not being truthful. Nowhere does the text quote Sarah as explicitly agreeing with Abraham, saying "he is my brother."

God concedes to Avimelech that even if Sarah's "taking" had been initiated with the proper intentions—such as to take a beautiful woman as a wife—nevertheless God's intervention was necessary to stop Avimelech from going too far and thus sinning against God, Sarah's protector. God instructs Avimelech to return Abraham's wife to him, and further assures Avimelech that as Abraham is a prophet, he will *know* that in truth Avimelech's intentions were honorable, and therefore would not avenge himself against the people of Gerar. Abraham will then intercede on Avimelech's behalf to avert the Divine death sentence threatening him and his subjects.

Somewhat reassured, Avimelech drifts in and out of sleep. This entire dream sequence begs elucidation. There is an apparent redundancy in verse three, where God tells Avimelech: *Behold you will die because the **woman** you have abducted already is the **wife** of another man.* While the Hebrew word *iSHa*,[16] used twice in the text, can mean both "woman" and "wife," the commentaries explain the reason the Torah uses the word *iSHa* [17] twice here. *Torah Temima* states that both uses are necessary because the death penalty is due to Avimelech not so much for the "taking" of Sarah the *woman* (the commentary implies that an *un*married woman lawfully *could* be taken against her will), but also because he abducted a *wife* whose marriage already had been consummated. She was not lawfully available to any man other than her rightful husband.[18] Abarbanel, on the other hand, is emphatic that the reason the text twice refers to Sarah's status as a woman *and* as a wife is to signify that Avimelech is doubly in jeopardy of losing his life at God's hand. First, for taking Sarah by force and *against her will*, even assuming Avimelech

---

14 ואבימלך לא קרב אליה; ויאמר, אדני, הגוי גם צדיק תהרג? הלא הוא אמר לי אחתי הוא, והיא
גם הוא אמרה אחי הוא; בתם לבבי ובנקיון כפי עשיתי זאת.

15 ויאמר אברהם . . . אחתי הוא

16 אשה

17 אשה

18 מדלא דכתיב והיא אשת איש . . . דעיקר העונש מיתה הוא משום בעולתו של בעל.

thought he was abducting an available virgin; and second, for abducting a woman who was in fact *married* to another man.[19]

After God enunciates the threat to Avimelech, the king attempts to exonerate himself before God. The burning question again is, exactly what transpired between the king and Sarah? Rashi replies that Avimelech never touched Sarah; rather, Sarah's guardian angel stood between her and Avimelech and permitted no contact.[20]

GENESIS 20:5–6

Abarbanel explains that in his plea, Avimelech points out that both Abraham and Sarah had told him that she was his sister. Thus, the king claims that even had he lain with her he would not have been required to return her to Abraham, who gave his implicit permission to the king to take Sarah.[21] *Ohr Hachayim* has Avimelech relying upon his *droit de seigneur*, his right as a monarch, to take any desired virgin to his bed. The *Midrash Tanchuma* adds that Avimelech told God that when Abraham announced that Sarah was his sister, Avimelech sought corroboration. Avimelech recounts that he turned to Sarah, and when she agreed, Avimelech—still searching for the truth—inquired of the caravan's camel drovers, donkey drivers and servants. They all told him "She is his sister."[22] Avimelech continues, telling God that therefore, having done all in his power to assure her availability, "With my innocent heart and with my clean hands have I taken Sarah."[23]

According to the *Netziv*, the phrase "with my innocent heart" means that Avimelech took Sarah not in a blind passion, but with the deliberate, honorable purpose of taking Abraham's sister as his lawful wife.[24] As far as the "clean hands" argument is concerned, the *Netziv*

---

19 שהיה חייב מיתה משני צדדים. האי מפני בחזקה ומבלי רצונה,ובין שתהיה פנויה ובין שתהיה אשת איש, לא היה לו ללקחה שלא כרצרנה. ועל זה אמר "על האשה אשר לקחת." והצד השני להיות אשת איש והוא אמרו "והיא בעולת בעל."

20 לא קרב אליה; המלאך מנעו.

21 אף שהיה שוכב עמה, לא היה ראוי לעונש כיון שהוא אמר אחותי היא והיא ,גם היא אמרה אחי הוא . . . אף שאשכב עמה, איני מחייב לחזירה לו.

22 הוא אמר לו אחותי היא, ולא האמנתי עד ששאלתי אותה. וגם היא אמרה אחי הוא; ולא האמנתי עד ששאלתי לחמרים ולגמלים שלה, ואמרו אחותי היא.

23 בתם לבבי ובנקיון כפי עשיתי זאת.

24 בתם לבבי: לא דרך תאוה, כי אם בלב תמים חפצתי לקחת אחות אברהם לאשה.

interprets it to mean that Avimelech separated from Sarah immediately after she insisted that she was truly Abraham's wife.[25] God accepts only the first part of Avimelech's plea, acceding only that his heart may well have been pure. This is clear because in the text (in verse six) God expressly acknowledges Avimelech's first defense, while completely ignoring the second. The *mephorshim* wonder why God did not accede to the second half of the plea as well. Did God disbelieve Avimelech's second argument that he had "clean hands?"

Rashi answers that while Avimelech may not have begun with the intention of committing a sin, he still is not wholly innocent, as he did abduct Sarah.[26] *Siftei Chachamim* elaborates that implicit in God's deliberate omission is His disbelief of Avimelech's argument that his hands were clean in the entire "taking" episode.[27] Several *mephorshim* define "clean hands" not only in its spiritual sense, but also in its physical sense. Rashi, quoting the *Midrash Rabbah*, suggests that Avimelech's hands are actually "unclean" because he did lay his hands upon Sarah.[28] This is the reason that God only accepted Avimelech's statement that his *intentions* were pure, because his *hands* most assuredly were not.[29]

The rejuvenated Sarah, blessed a second time with her beautiful face and form, is forced now also to relive the nightmare of being held against her will on account of her extreme desirability. Once again, she finds herself alone with a king in his chambers. Still again, her protests of her unavailability fall upon ears deafened by desire. *Midrash Rabbah* (52.13) points out that, as before, Sarah is Divinely protected. Her guardian angel literally pushes Avimelech's hand away from her.[30] It is thus clear from the text (verse six) and the commentaries that it was God—and not Avimelech's strength of character—who prevented Avimelech from "taking" Abraham's wife.[31]

The phrase in the text, *therefore I prevented you from touching her*, prompts both Rashi and the *Netziv* to state unequivocally that

---

25 ובנקיון כפי: אחר כך, כשאמרה שהיא אשת אברהם, פירשתי ממנה.

26 אמת שלא דמית מתחלה לחטוא, אבל נקיון כפים אין כאן.

27 היה לו לאמר כי בתום לבבך ובנקיון כפיך עשית זאת, כמו שכתוב אבימלך בעצמו.

28 הדא אמרה משמוש ידים יש כאן.

29 אמר הקב"ה: באחת זכית, ושקרת באחת.

30 מלאך דחפו מעליה.

31 על כן לא נתתיך לנגע אליה.

whatever transpired in the king's chambers that night did not culminate in physical intimacy. Rashi says that God's statement to Avimelech underlines that he was not as free from culpability in this incident as he protested he was. Rather, that it was God who prevented Avimelech from sinning against Sarah. God did this by weakening Avimelech's virility.[32]

The *Netziv* elaborates on Rashi, saying that God specifically prevented Avimelech from even touching Sarah, in order that his passions not be aroused. For if he had but touched her, he would have set into motion a tragic, inexorable chain of events. Recognizing that Avimelech was not strong enough to control himself, it was God who rescued Sarah from Avimelech's baser desires.[33] God's plan was that Sarah's revived youthfulness would kindle *Abraham's* awareness of her, and that her long-awaited pregnancy would yield the covenantal son God had promised the couple in chapter 17. This child's provenance must be uncontestable. There was nothing less at stake here than the continuity of Abraham and Sarah's Divine mission, and Avimelech's lust had no place in this plan.

GENESIS 20:7

What of Abraham? While Sarah and Avimelech were aware of God's intervention behind Avimelech's closed chamber doors, how was Abraham to know that his wife remained *his alone*? According to Rashi, that is the reason the text states, *Return this man's wife, for he is a prophet.*[34] Logically, the verse could have been complete without this phrase. The verse would then have read, "And now, return this man's wife to him." Following up with the phrase "because [Abraham] is a prophet" would seem irrelevant to Avimelech and to the reader. Rashi explains that it was absolutely necessary that God characterize Abraham as a prophet here. He thus would possess the knowledge that the relationship between Avimelech and Sarah was unconsummated. Rashi states that without this awareness, Abraham

---

32 לא ממך היה שלא נגעת בה . . . שלא נתתי לך כח.

33 מנעתיך מנגוע בה ממש, כדי שלא תבוא לתוקף יצר הרע, שאז היית מחליט לבוא עליה. ושוב לא היה סיוע מן השמים.

34 השב אשת האיש, כי נביא הוא.

may very well have despised and rejected his wife, Sarah, after she had been with another man, albeit against her will.[35]

GENESIS 20:8–10

Following God's dire warning to Avimelech, the king awakens, summons his court and privately relates to them God's ultimatum: he must return the beautiful Sarah to Abraham the Hebrew, or else face death at God's hand. Avimelech's confidants are understandably terrified at what their simple abduction has wrought. Avimelech calls Abraham to the palace and aggressively challenges him, saying: "What have you done to us? What sin have I sinned against you that you have caused me and my kingdom hitherto-unheard-of torments? What motivated you to promulgate this ruse, presenting your wife as your sister?"

Rashi asks, to what "torments" is Avimelech referring? God's warning was wholly verbal. Yet the text in verse nine does allude to *Ma'aSiM*,[36] meaning "actions," deeds or torments. Rashi answers that Avimelech's outrage is a direct response to the terrible plague that Abraham's deception has wrought. This "torment" was a complete occlusion of all bodily orifices of Avimelech and his courtiers, namely: the closing off of all semen ducts, urinary and excretory paths, and auditory and olfactory tracts.[37]

The elaborate description of this plague in the text is necessary in order to put to rest any present or future suspicion that Sarah's eventual child is not Abraham's.

GENESIS 20–11

Abraham responds to the king, justifying his behavior with two explanations. First, he tells Avimelech that upon approaching the city of Gerar and after assessing the morality of its people, he thought that

---

[35] ואל תהא סבור שמא תתגנה בעיניו ולא יקבלנה.

[36] מעשים

[37] מכה, אשר לא הורגלה לבא על בריה, באה לנו על ידיך: עצירת כל נקבים של זרע, ושל קטנים, ורעי ואזנים וחוטם.

the inhabitants were not God-fearing; that they would slay this old man in order to possess his beautiful and desirable wife.

The Talmud (*Bava Kama* 92a) supports Abraham's assessment of Gerar's inhabitants. The measure of a townspeople's worthiness is taken when they greet the stranger or the wayfarer. Upon greeting such a traveler, the townspeople should offer him food, drink and refreshment, just as Abraham did when he greeted the three angels in chapter 18. By way of contrast, the inhabitants of Gerar accosted Abraham's dusty caravan at the gates of the city, and—spying the old man in the company of an exquisite younger woman—examined him as to the nature of his relationship with her. "Who is this woman? Is she your wife, is she your sister?" The sages support Abraham's genuine fear of Gerar's godlessness. The townspeople's inappropriate inquiry into Sarah's virginal status in their initial contact with Abraham was the tipoff as to their dishonorable character.[38]

GENESIS 20:12,13

Abraham justifies his use of the word "sister" with the now-familiar argument identifying Sarah as his sister as well as his wife. He tells Avimelech, *she is in fact my sister, the daughter of my father, but not the daughter of my mother; and so she became my wife.*[39] He further explains that as a kindness to him, Sarah allowed him to present her as his sister throughout their wanderings.

The obvious issue here is that Sarah is, in fact, Abraham's niece—the daughter of his deceased brother, Haran—and not his sister. Rashi justifies Abraham's use of the word "sister" by pointing out that Abraham, Terah's son, and Sarah, Terah's granddaughter, are considered progeny of the same father for purposes of their filial relationship. Thus, one's grandchildren are considered as one's children.[40]

Rashbam further explains that the Bible uses Abraham's argument to justify the conjugal relationship between a brother and a half-brother and -sister. While siblings issuing from the same mother

---

[38] אכסנאי שבא לעיר, על עסקי אכילה ושתיה שואלין אותו, או על עסקי אשתו שואלין אותו? אשתך היא? אחותך היא?

[39] וגם אמנם אחתי בת אבי היא, אך לא בת אמי; ותהי לי לאשה.

[40] בני בנים הרי הן כבנים; והרי היא בתו של תרח.

were forbidden to marry each other, Abraham and Sarah each had different mothers. Thus, their marriage was considered legitimate, and any resulting children would be worthy recipients of God's promise to Abraham and Sarah in chapter 17, verse 16:

And I will bless her, and moreover I will give you a son through her; and I will bless her, and she shall be a mother of nations; kings of nations will issue from her.[41]

GENESIS 20:14–16

Partially appeased by Abraham's "sister" explanation, Avimelech takes sheep and oxen, men-servants and maid-servants, and heaps them upon Abraham. He also returns Sarah to him. Avimelech then makes a generous pronouncement, inviting Abraham to settle anywhere in his country that appeals to him. Alshich points out that Avimelech is offering Abraham his sovereign protection to counteract Abraham's express fear that the townspeople would harm him in order to possess his wife.[42]

The transaction is not yet complete. After gifting Abraham with livestock, cattle, and servants, and offering his sovereign protection, Avimelech now turns and speaks directly to Sarah. The king says to her, "On your behalf I gave your brother Abraham one thousand pieces of silver. This sum will veil you and protect your reputation in the land."[43] Rashi points out that the king goes beyond what would have been expected in returning Sarah to her brother/husband. Rashi says that Avimelech's announced gift, worth one thousand pieces of silver, is made specifically to appease and to honor Sarah; such an immense gift will testify that Avimelech relinquished her against his will, and only because God miraculously appeared to him and instructed him to do so.[44]

While Rashi views the king's gift as having two components, part in livestock to appease Abraham, and part in silver coin to appease

---

[41] וברכתי אתה וגם נתתי ממנה לך בן; וברכתיה והיתה לגוים; מלכי עמים ממנה יהיו.

[42] אל תירא שיהרגוך על דבר אשתך, כי תהיה בטוח כי אהיה שומר לראשך.

[43] ולשרה אמר, הנה נתתי אלף כסף לאחיך. הנה הוא לך כסות עינים לכל אשר אתך, ואת כל ונכחת.

[44] לכבודה כדי לפייסה; הנה עשיתי לך כבוד זה . . . הנה הממון והכבוד הזה לך כסות ענים . . . יודעים יהיו שעל כרחי השיבותיך, ועל ידי נס.

Sarah, Ramban differs in his perception of Avimelech's gift. Ramban views Avimelech's offering as *livestock only*, whose entire *value* is one thousand pieces of silver. Thus, according to Ramban, nothing of monetary value was given to Sarah by the king. Avimelech's attempt to mollify Sarah is done not with coin but with words. The king is aware that the woman of beauty and honor whom he covets has value far beyond the price of sheep and oxen.[45]

We must remember that the king and his court are still suffering from the physical effects of God's plague. All their bodily functions remain at a standstill. Avimelech knows that this can be commuted only through Abraham's prayers. He successfully mollified Abraham with the gift of livestock; but he knows that appeasing Sarah's sensibilities is more complex. He has seen that she is a woman who must be appealed to verbally. Rashi is of the opinion that Sarah *allows* the king to appease her with his gifts. Ramban, on the other hand, is emphatic that Sarah *does not* accept Avimelech's apology for her abduction. He states that Sarah also rejects Avimelech's monetary overtures.[46]

The commentaries each base their opposing conclusions on the same three Hebrew words in the text:[47] *And before **all** [men] you will be able **to stand** and defend yourself.* The Hebrew word *NoCHaCHaT*[48] can mean either literally "to stand," or figuratively "to stand fast." Sforno says that Avimelech's tangible gift gave Sarah the ability to stand firm and to offer tangible proof of her worth against all slanderers of her reputation. Thus can he appease her.[49] Ramban defines the *p'shat* differently. Ramban states that Sarah was *not* appeased. He defines the words *V'et Kol*,[50] *and all this*, to mean *despite all* the valued gifts that Avimelech showered upon her and Abraham, Sarah *stood fast*,[51] and refused Avimelech's attempt to win her forgiveness for abducting her.[52]

---

[45] היו הצאן והבקר והעבדים שנתן לו שוים אלף כסף . . . והגיד הכתוב שפייס את אברהם בממון ואת שרה בדברים.

[46] שרה **לא** נתפייסה לו.

[47] ואת **הכל** ונכחת

[48] נכחת

[49] ובעיני **כל** שומע, ובעיני **כל** נוכחת, שתבקש אולי לגנותך.

[50] ואת **כל**

[51] ונכחת

[52] אבל עם **כל** זה היתה מתוכחת עמו בטענות לאמור: שלא תמחל לו.

If this episode were to end according to Rashi and Sforno, both Abraham and Sarah would be appeased, Avimelech's guilt would be assuaged, and there would be a congenial closure to an incident that began in deception and terror. Ramban rejects this pat solution, still achieving closure but on a higher plane for Sarah. Ramban's solution has Abraham accepting Avimelech's guilt offering and praying to God on behalf of the king and his subjects. He posits that Sarah, however, rejects any attempt to mollify her, and that she stands alone, unforgiving of Avimelech's abduction of her. Building on Ramban's reasoning, we can understand that Sarah does *not* say, "I will not forgive your abduction of me!" but rather asks rhetorically, "*How can I* forgive you after all you have put me through?" We must not lose sight of the fact that this is the second time that Sarah has survived a traumatic abduction. Sarah twice allowed herself to be imperiled in order to save Abraham. Ramban is clear that Sarah's unforgiving stance is to her credit. To Ramban, Sarah's refusal to forgive Avimelech is eloquent testament to her steadfast character.[53]

GENESIS 20:17,18

Abraham prayed for the health of the repentant Avimelech, and the king, his wife and her handmaids were healed from the plague that God had wrought, totally sealing off all of their bodily channels. The pregnant women of Gerar were allowed to give birth, undoing the punishment they bore because of the abduction of Sarah, Abraham's wife. Alshich implies that the reason the text enumerates specifically that Avimelech was healed, is so that the reader clearly understands that when Sarah was alone in his presence, he was emphatically "un-healed," and it was therefore physically impossible for him to have impregnated her.[54] *Ohr Hachayim* states further that the reason the text uses the double emphatic form of the verb "closed" [up all the orifices],[55] is to make it absolutely clear to any

---

53 שלא תמחל לו, ובשבחה דבר הכתוב, ואברהם נתפייס ויתפלל עליו.

54 היות לו עונש זה . . . כי היתה עתידה ללדת מאברהם . . . על כן עצר ד' כל רחם, ויסתום כל נקביהם.

55 עצר עצר

doubters that Sarah's future pregnancy was not to be credited to Avimelech, but to her husband, Abraham.[56]

Ramban once again draws on the text to point out God's defense of Sarah's propriety and honor. He observes that verses 17 and 18 deliberately omit any reference to the graphic details of Avimelech's ailment or of his cure. Yet, these same verses specifically describe the punishment and cure of the women of Gerar. Why the omission concerning Avimelech? Ramban answers that the status of Avimelech's bodily functions has no proper place in the text now that Sarah has been safely returned to her husband, Abraham.[57]

The final words of this chapter, *because of the matter of Sarah, Abraham's wife*,[58] should ring a bell in readers' memories. This precise phrase appeared in the first abduction episode with Pharaoh at Genesis 12:17 (*and Pharaoh was stricken by God with a great plague **because of the matter of Sarai, the wife of Avram***).[59] There, as we discussed at length in the first pages of our section on Sarah, the Hebrew root-word[60] could mean either "the matter of" or "speech." Here, Rashi again clings to the *midrashic* meaning of the words,[61] "because of Sarah's *words*." Surprisingly, he does not elaborate for the reader what Sarah's missing words are. He allows the reader the necessary space within which to empathize with Sarah. The unelaborated silence at the conclusion of this emotionally wrenching episode is fairly bursting with Sarah's inchoate speech.

---

[56] שלא יאמרו: מאבימלך נתעברה שרה.

[57] ולא פרש הכתוב חולי אבימלך, והזכירו ברמז; דרך מוסר וכבוד לשרה.

[58] על-**דבר** שרה אשת אברהם

[59] על-**דבר** שרי אשת אברם.

[60] דבר

[61] על-דבר שרה

SEVEN

୫୦୧ଞ୫୦୧ଞ

Sarah's Pregnancy
and the Birth of Isaac

GENESIS 21:1–5

God "listens" to Sarah's silent anguish, and remembers His promise to her that she will bear Abraham's son. Her rejuvenation
complete, Sarah now conceives and bears Abraham's son in his old
age, at the time of year prescribed by God via His messenger at the
flap of Abraham's tent that fateful noon. Abraham named his son that
Sarah bore him "Isaac," and he circumcised his son, Isaac, when he
was eight days old, thus fulfilling God's command. Abraham was one
hundred years old at the birth of his son, Isaac.

GENESIS 21:1

And God remembered Sarah. . . .[1] Verse one opens with the
Hebrew word *PaKoD*,[2] an unusual term for "He remembered."
Midrash Rabbah (53.5–6) and its commentaries relate what,
specifically, it was that God remembered concerning Sarah. The
reader will recall that when we are introduced to Sarah and Abraham,

---

[1] וד' פקד את שרה.

[2] פקד

50

the Bible refers to "the souls they made in Charan," crediting Sarai as an equal partner with her husband in creating souls for monotheism. Here, God repays Sarah in kind. He "remembers" her unabated zeal in gathering converts, and now rewards her with her very own biological child.[3]

Why does God choose to reward Sarah at this precise moment in time? The answer is, because Sarah has shown herself, again and again, unwilling to yield to anyone but her husband, even though her overwhelming desire for a child of her own has crescendoed over decades. *Yefei To'ar*, a supercommentary on *Midrash Rabbah*, quotes a biblical law (*Bamidbar* 5:28), saying even if a married woman were voluntarily to sequester herself with another man, thereby engendering jealousy in her husband, if she is innocent of adultery, God will reward her afterwards with a pregnancy by her husband.[4] How much more so the matriarch Sarah, who was forced twice into seclusion with kings, against her will, specifically in order to save Abraham's life! Sarah should, as proof of her steadfastness, be rewarded *at this time* with a child *by Abraham*.[5]

Another supercommentary on *Midrash Rabbah*, *Mishna d'Rabi Eliezer*, actually pinpoints Sarah's time of conception to the day of her reunion with Abraham, the day after she was released from Avimelech's palace.[6] The *mephorshim* are not content just yet to move on to the birth of Isaac—surely the momentous crux of this story—without a discussion of the nature of passion and its role in the conception of Isaac. Their discussion is based on the very first word of this chapter, *And God* [remembered Sarah]. They seek to teach us that God's direct providence is central to Isaac's birth. *Midrash Rabbah* understands this from the Torah's specific use of God's name in the opening sentence. It is clear to the rabbis that overseeing the process of Sarah's pregnancy and delivery was not delegated to a messenger-angel, but was reserved for God alone. The reader will recall (Genesis18:2) that in the Torah, messenger-angels are typically

---

[3] ‏. . . שרה הפקידה אצלי מצות ומעשים טובים. החזיר לה הקב"ה מצות ומעשים טובים‏
‏אברהם ושרה הפקידו נפשות אצלי כמו שכתוב, "ואת הנפש אשר עשו בחרן ", ואני מחזיר‏
‏להם נפשות.‏

[4] ‏ואם לא נטמאה האשה וטהרה היא, ונקתה, ונזרעה זרע.‏

[5] ‏כיון שאשה הגורמת לבעלה לקנאה כי הסתירה עצמה עם איש אחר, נפקדת אם טהורה היא;‏
‏כל שכן שרה, שלוּקחה בעל כרחה, פשיטא שראויה היא להפקד.‏

[6] ‏אברהם בא עליה יום אחד אחר שיצאה מבית אבימלך.‏

used for particular tasks. There is not only a messenger-angel for directing pregnancy, but also one for awakening passion. *Midrash Rabbah* is explicit that the messenger-angel for passion was *not* called upon to infuse desire in Sarah, for Sarah had no need of it; God was watching over her.[7]

Yefei To'ar explains that when God created human beings—desires and all—God gave them the ability to carry out the Divine commandments via thoughts, words, and deeds. These thoughts, words, and deeds are in fact the human manifestations of God's spiritual messengers.[8] According to the commentator, a person's own desires are themselves God's messenger-angels. The entire process of having a child, for instance, is accompanied by a melange of strong desires. Here, in the case of Sarah, *one* desire assumed primacy over all others. Sarah's desire for a child was so strong that it eclipsed the other desires buried within her. To borrow the rabbis' imagery, God's messenger-angel *of passion* was standing by; Sarah did not call upon him. She had no need of the messenger, because *God remembered her*, and was directing the outcome.[9]

The *mephorshim* understood that Sarah's driving passion was to bear Abraham's child. She wanted *their* child to be the heir to God's covenant. All her other passions became of no account.

GENESIS 21:2

And Sarah conceived, and she bore Abraham a son in his old age, at the appointed time that God had promised him.[10] Sarah finally achieves her goal of bearing Abraham's child. Notably, this verse twice refers to Isaac's parentage. The verse states both that *Sarah* conceived and bore him, and that he was *Abraham's* son of his old age. Rashi says that the reason for this emphasis is to allow no room for any slanderous speculation, given that Sarah had been sequestered in Avimelech's household for the duration of that one

---

7 אף על גב דאמר רבי הונא מלאך הוא שהוא ממונה על התאוה, אבל שרה לא נצרכה לדברים הללו, אלא הוא בכבודו.

8 כל כח מן הכחות הגופניות יקרא מלאך. שענין מלאך: שליח, עושה רצונו יתברך.

9 פקידת שרה היתה בנס גמור, מבלי מבוא ענין טבעי. ונפקדה שלא מדרך הפקידה הטבעית.

10 ותהר ותלד שרה לאברהם בן לזקניו, למועד אשר דבר אתו אלקים.

day.[11] Moreover, the use of the Hebrew term, "son of his old age,"[12] seems to be a contraction of two other Hebrew words: *Ziv iKuNiN,*[13] meaning "the precise image of Abraham." This is an indication to us that the face of the infant Isaac was the image of Abraham, further confirming his parentage.

GENESIS 21:3

The next verse, dealing with the naming of Isaac, continues to belabor the emphasis on his parentage. Here, the verse would have been complete if it simply had stated: And Abraham named his son Isaac. Instead, the text embellishes the now-familiar refrain that the son whom Abraham named is the son born to him by Sarah.[14] On the subject of Isaac's naming, the *Meshech Chachma* reminds us that "Isaac" was the name that God Himself chose for the covenantal son in Genesis17:19. Here, Abraham is carrying out God's command by naming him "Isaac."[15]

GENESIS 21:4

This verse, the third consecutive sentence describing Isaac's birth, naming, and now his circumcision, again identifies Isaac—somewhat redundantly—as "Abraham's son." Verses two through five in this episode refer *eight* times either to the fact that Isaac is Abraham's son, or to the fact that Isaac is the son that Sarah bore to Abraham. Clearly the purpose of the repetition is to establish without a shadow of a doubt exactly whose child Isaac is. The text puts to rest with this verse any disquiet, past or future, associated with Isaac's provenance.

---

[11] שלא יאמרו מביתו של אבימלך הוא.

[12] בן לזקוניו

[13] "זיו איקונין"

[14] ויקרא אברהם את שם בנו הנולד לו אשר ילדה לו שרה: יצחק.

[15] כאשר צוה אותו אלקים: מוסב גם על "ויקרא שמו יצחק," (פסוק ג), כאשר צוה וכו', "וקראת שמו יצחק" (בפרק יז פסוק יט).

GENESIS 21:5

This verse emphasizes Abraham's age as one hundred years old at the birth of his son, Isaac. Yet verse one of this chapter, which identifies Sarah as Isaac's mother, does not mention Sarah's chronological age. The *Netziv* explains that although Sarah's chronological age was ninety years, because she had experienced her rejuvenation, it was not noteworthy that the "young" and lovely Sarah was Isaac's mother; it was expected.[16]

GENESIS 21:6

And Sarah said: God has made laughter for me; whoever hears will laugh with me.[17]

The matriarch Sarah, who suffered two abductions without speaking in the text, does not remain silent when the issue of her child is at stake. In fact, Sarah's voice is heard in the biblical text only when her desire for a child becomes paramount. See above, at Genesis 16:2, 16:5, 18:12 and 18:15, which are the verses where Sarah feels compelled to speak because of her passion for a child. Now that Sarah finally has given birth to a child, the reader can expect that Sarah's voice will be heard.

Onkelos defines *TZeCHoK*,[18] the root-word of Isaac's name, to mean "joy."[19] Joy is the undiluted emotion that Sarah is experiencing after Isaac's birth. Sforno delves deeper into Sarah's emotions. He characterized her joy as so deep that it overshadows her perception of newborn Isaac's pain at his circumcision.[20] Rashi explains that Sarah's joy extends beyond her own ambit, to encompass the surrounding multitudes: On the day of Isaac's circumcision, many other persons' hopeful prayers were answered along with Sarah's, and much happiness emanated from her.[21]

---

[16] ואברהם בן מאה שנה, אבל לא כתיב עוד "ושרה בת תשעים שנה," שהרי כבר נהפכה לילדה.

[17] ותאמר שרה: צחק עשה לי אלקים;כל השמע יצחק לי.

[18] צחק

[19] ואמרת שרה: חדוא עבד לי ד'.

[20] אף על פי שיש צער צער מילה לתינוק, הקל יתברך נתן שמחה בלבי. לפיכך כל השומע יצחק לי וישמח בעדי, ולא ידאג בשביל צער המילה.

[21] בו ביום הרבה תפלות נענו עמה, ורב שחוק היה בעולם.

Alshich explains that even though her son's name was God-given, and Abraham bestowed it upon the child, Sarah was careful to preemptively erase any negative connotation in Isaac's name that might be reminiscent of her original laughter (in Genesis18:13), commemorating her present joy.[22] The *Meshech Chachma* puts Sarah's concern to rest, saying that God had chosen Isaac's name even *before* Sarah laughed. He reasons that it is difficult to believe that God would select a name for the covenantal heir if that name were reminiscent of an event that displeased him.[23] In fact, the commentator is explicit (echoing Rashi in Genesis17:19) that their son's name was to be "Isaac," after *Abraham's* laughter. Sarah's statement in this verse (21:6) that "God has made laughter for me" is her manner of investing her son's name with relevance *for her*. The *Meshech Chachma* finds this endearing, saying that Sarah's interpretation of her son's name is a meaningful way for her to participate in his naming ceremony. He understands that her desire to so participate is a quality that mothers universally possess.[24]

GENESIS 21:7,8

Holding her son to her breast following his circumcision, Sarah is overwhelmed with sublime happiness. Rashi characterized Sarah's words in this verse as those of extreme praise and fealty to God.[25] She spontaneously praises God, saying: "[How great is God!] No one ever would have thought to say to Abraham 'Sarah will nurse sons!' Yet [God is so great that] I have given Abraham a son for his old age."[26]

Abarbanel expounds on this verse's Hebrew word for an expression of high praise, *MiLLeL*.[27] Because it is an unusual usage,

---

[22] חששה פן יהיה שם יצחק מזכרת עון מה שצחקה היא . . . רק כי צחוק עשה לה אלקים כי שמחה ד'. ומי יוכיח כי הפירוש הוא זה ולא אחר.

[23] **ולפני** שצחקה שרה בפרק יח פסוק יב! כי קשה לומר שיקרא את שמו על שם מאורע שלא מצא חן בעיני הקב"ה.

[24] בכל זאת קראו יצחק על שם שאברהם שמח. ולכן אמרה שרה "כל השומע יצחק לי," להשתתף בקריאת שמו, כדרך האמהות.

[25] לשון שבח וחשיבות

[26] ותאמר: מי מלל לאברהם "היניקה בנים שרה," כי ילדתי בן לזקוניו.

[27] מלל

the commentator infuses it with special meaning. Sarah is keenly aware that God has bestowed a great blessing upon her by allowing her to bear Abraham's son at this stage of her life. The use of the word MiLLeL,[28] meaning "to extol," indicates that Sarah rightly senses God's even greater munificence: He did not stop at opening her womb; He allowed Sarah to experience the added satisfaction of nursing her own son until the time for his weaning arrived.[29] It is as if God is rewarding Sarah, measure for measure. She was steadfast for ninety years, and now she will reap the full blessing of motherhood. Abraham also understands this, and while he did not make a community celebration at Isaac's birth, or even at his circumcision, he is moved to celebrate at his weaning two years later. Rashi specifies that Sarah continued to nurse Isaac for twenty-four months.[30] It is as if Sarah aptly exclaims here: "How great is God that I not only gave birth, but that I am also nursing my son!" God's blessings are truly appreciated by Sarah and Abraham.

Students of the text should ask, Why does the verse say "Sarah will nurse *sons*," when we all know that she only bears one son? Rabbi Samson Raphael Hirsch expresses the *p'shat* response that Isaac and all subsequent generations emanating from Isaac had their origins at Sarah's breast. It was Sarah, after all, who nourished the first covenantal child. The text credits Sarah with this, and is hinting to us that Isaac is the first of countless future "sons of the covenant" who will issue from her. *Midrash Tanchuma* advances a different reason for the use of the plural word "sons." He says that Sarah *truly* nursed many sons. How is this so? The *midrash* explains that the women of the day, skeptical that ninety-year-old Sarah could have given birth, suspected that the new baby was really Hagar's, and that Sarah was presenting it as her own. To test their theory, these women visited Sarah in her tent and thrust their hungry infants toward Sarah, demanding that she nurse their sons. Once they saw that mother's milk flowed freely from Sarah's breasts, their wagging tongues were

---

[28] מלל

[29] כאשר ראתה שרה שמלבד הלידה, עוד הגדיל השם עמה חסד במה שנתן לה חלב בשדיה להניק את בנה . . . שלא היו לה שדים צומקים, אבל שדים נכונו להניקו . . .

ובעבור אותו נס העצום עשה אברהם משתה גדול ביום הגמל את יצחק . . . ולכן לא עשה משתה על הלידה, ולא על המילה . . . אלא על הגגמל וההולדה וההנקה.

[30] לסוף כ"ד חדש

silenced.[31] Still, Sarah was exceedingly modest. She was content to nurse her son in solitude, hugging to her breast the private fulfillment that came from knowing that God answered her prayers completely. *Ohel Yaakov* describes that Abraham was not satisfied with this purely private bliss. Consistent with his mission to spread God's glory among the peoples of the world, he told his wife that the miraculous event of Isaac's weaning was not a time for modesty. He instructed Sarah to bare her breasts to the women at Isaac's weaning celebration, thereby demonstrating to them God's ability to perform miracles for those who believe in Him. Sarah acquiesced, and nursed her son in their presence.[32]

GENESIS 21:8

The Talmud (*Bava Metzia* 87a) also asks the same question, How may sons did Sarah nurse?[33] The Talmud sets the scene at Isaac's weaning ceremony: Ever since Isaac's birth, gossip-mongers had been spreading the tale that Isaac was not the natural son of Abraham and Sarah, but a foundling they picked up in the market-place, and passed off as their own. To squelch the rumors once and for all, Abraham and Sarah invited the important townspeople to the weaning ceremony—husbands, wives, and children—and instructed them to leave their wet-nurses at home. The matriarch Sarah, whose milk had dwindled as she weaned Isaac, was now miraculously able to nurse the multitude of thirsty babies that day. Her breast milk flowed as if from a gurgling fountain.[34]

---

[31] כיון שילדה שרה היו נשי אומות העולם תמהים לומר: אפשר שילדה? והיו אומרין אלו לאלו: והלא זקנה שרה! ושמא שפחתה היא. מה היו עושות? היו נוטלות בניהן והולכות אצל שרה, ואומרות לה: היניקי את הילד הזה, והיתה מניקה את בניהם, שנאמר: היניקה **בנים** שרה.

[32] אמנו שרה הייתה צנועה יותר מדי. אמר לה אבינו אברהם: אין זו שעת הצניעות, אלא גלי דדיך כדי שידעו הכל שהתחיל הקב"ה לעשות לנו נסים. מיד גלתה את דדיה.

[33] קמה בנים הניקה שרה?

[34] אותו היום שגמל אברהם את יצחק בנו, עשה סעודה גדולה. היו כל אומות העולם מרננים ואומרים: ראיתם זקן וזקנה שהביאו אסופי מן השוק ואומרים: בנינו הוא . . . מה עשה אברהם אבינו? הלך וזימן כל גדולי הדור, ושרה זימנה את נשותיהם, וכל אחת ואחת הביאה בנה עמה ומניקתה לא הביאה. ונעשה נס בשרה אמנו ונפתחו דדיה כשני מעיינות; והניקה את כולן.

EIGHT

ଋଓଋଓଋଓ

The Children of Sarah
and the Handmaiden

GENESIS 21:9

At Isaac's weaning party, Ishmael—Abraham's son by Hagar, the Egyptian handmaiden—is a mature, strapping youth of more than fourteen years of age. He already is an accomplished marksman with bow and arrow. Ishmael has grown to young manhood under his mother's Egyptian influence, and as such he is familiar with both idolatry and immorality. As time passes, and Isaac grows in height and in understanding, he is at the impressionable age of pre-adolescence. Because Isaac is growing up in the same household as Ishmael, Sarah is more wary than ever of Ishmael's influence on her son. *And Sarah saw Hagar the Egyptian maid's son whom she had borne to Abraham, making sport.*[1] The commentaries are aware that Sarah has turned the proverbial deaf ear to Ishmael's questionable behaviors from the time of Isaac's birth up until this point.

What were these behaviors? The key Hebrew word in this verse that gives the commentaries pause is the final word *MeTZaCHeK*,[2] whose root-word means "laughter." In our previous discussions of this root-word concerning Abraham's and Sarah's "laughters," the *TZeCHoK*[3] (laughter) was either vocalized or silent, but it never

---

[1] ותרא שרה את בן הגר המצרית אשר ילדה לאברהם מצחק.

[2] מצחק

[3] צחוק

58

devolved into behavior. Here, however, the text informs us that "Sarah *saw*" Ishmael's laughter. Since the more proper verb would have been "Sarah *heard*" his laughter, the commentaries uniformly concur that Ishmael's "laughter" was associated with his actions. What behaviors did Sarah witness? Ishmael's behaviors are implied by the word *MeTZaCHeK*.[4] Sforno says that beginning with Isaac's birth, Ishmael engaged in imitative teasing behavior that he learned from the gossip-mongers, saying that Isaac was not Abraham's true son, but Avimelech's illegitimate son. Sarah, preoccupied with pregnancy, labor, childbirth, and new motherhood, paid no heed to the teenager's taunts.[5]

Midrash Rabbah (53.11) further describes Ishmael's taunting. Upon the birth of Isaac, when Abraham's household was rejoicing, Ishmael derided the well-wishers, saying their joy was misplaced; that *he* was the first-born son of the wealthy Abraham, and that *he*—and not the newborn—would inherit the prescribed double portion at his father's death.[6] *Chatam Sofer* does not take Ishmael's slander lightly. He identifies it unequivocally as *LaSHoN HaRa*,[7] the basest tale-bearing, which can lead to venal sins.[8] Abarbanel differs from Sforno's assertion that Sarah was preoccupied, saying that, on the contrary, she was fully aware of Ishmael's slanderous taunts even as early as Isaac's birth. She bided her time, however, and refrained from complaining to Abraham, knowing that her husband's allegiance was to his healthy, strapping son, Ishmael, over the precarious newborn Isaac. Sarah was wise enough to wait until Isaac had matured physically, because only then, to paraphrase Abarbanel, could Abraham appreciate the ripened fruit that was Isaac.[9]

---

[4] מצחק

[5] מלעיג על המשתה שנעשה בבית אברהם באמרו שנתעברה מאבימלך . . . שמע בזאת אחר כך מליצני הדור, ואם באולי בעת הלידה היה מצחק לא הרגישה בו שרה שהיתה אז טרודה.

[6] אין לשון הזה של צחוק, אלא לשון ירושה. שבשעה שנולד אבינו יצחק היו הכל שמחים. אמר להם ישמעאל: שוטים אתם! אני בכור, ואני נוטל פי שנים.

[7] לשון הרע

[8] בן הגר המצרית מצחק . . . לשון הרע שקול נגד ג' עבירות: עבודה זרה, גלוי עריות, שפיכת דמים . . . כי אמר "מאבימלך נתעברה שרה."

[9] לא בקשה שרה שיגרש את האמה ואת בנה רק לפי שאין ספק שיקשה אברהם לעזוב את בנו הודאי ישמעאל ,איש גדול ושלם בקומתו, בעבור הספק שהוא ביצחק . . . אחרי שגדל יצחק בשניו וקומתו והיה כשאר כל אדם, היה ראוי שיחזיק בו אברהם כבן יורש, ויעזוב את הקליפה וידבק בפרי.

Ordinary sibling rivalry between an older son accustomed to being the favored only child, and a younger interloper, is how Ibn Ezra characterizes Ishmael's behavior. This rivalry was irksome to Sarah, but did not threaten Isaac's well-being, so initially she took no action.[10] It was only when the teasing and taunting evolved into behavior that actually threatened Isaac's moral, spiritual and physical existence that Sarah intervened. Rashi stretches the limits of the word *MeTZaCHeK*.[11] He very specifically attributes to Ishmael the three sins of idolatry, illicit sexual relations and even murder. He derives these sins from the Bible's use of the word *MeTZaCHeK* [12] in this verse, and in three other textual references where the same Hebrew root-word is used to mean each of the specified sins.[13]

Torah Temima, relying on the merit of Abraham's righteousness, disagrees with Rashi's severe interpretation that states that in Abraham's house Ishmael engaged in the three venal sins. Rather, the commentator suggests that the word *MeTZaCHeK* [14] refers to Ishmael's constant boasting about his firstborn's double-portion inheritance due to him after Abraham's death.[15]

The *Midrash Rabbah*, elaborating on the word *MeTZaCHeK*,[16] adds a description of what Sarah saw transpire between Ishmael and her son. One day, under the pretext of showing Isaac their future inheritance, Ishmael lured the boy from his mother's tent, and led him into the fields. Once there, he set Isaac up as a target, and began shooting arrows at him saying, "I am only making sport!"[17] *Yalkut Shimoni* is straightforward in his characterization of Ishmael's "sport." He views it as lethal. According to the commentary, this was an attempt actually to murder Isaac.[18]

---

[10] מצחק: כי כן מנהג כל נער; ותקנא בו בעבור היותו גדול מבנה.

[11] מצחק

[12] מצחק

[13] מצחק: לשון עבודה זרה . . . ד"א, לשון גלוי עריות, ד"א: לשון רציחה.

[14] מצחק

[15] ואני אומר,חס ושלום שיהיה בביתו של אותו הצדיק מי שעושה כן, אלא אין צחוק זה אלא ירושה, שהיה ישמעאל מצחק ואומר אני בכור ונוטל שני חלקים.

[16] מצחק

[17] אמר ליה ישמעאל ליצחק: נלך ונראה חלקנו בשדה. והיה ישמעאל נוטל קשת וחצים ומורה כלפי יצחק, ועושה עצמו כאלו **מצחק** . . . כן איש רמה את רעהו ואומר: הלא **מצחק** אני.

[18] נטל קשת וחצים . . . וראה יצחק יושב לבדו וירה עליו חץ להרגו.

NINE

৪০০৪৪০০৪

Abraham Heeds
Sarah's Plea

GENESIS 21:10

H ow much longer can Sarah merely observe Ishmael's actions and remain silent? Her protective instincts for Isaac must soon impel her to intercede with Abraham. Sarah has avoided such a confrontation for as long as possible but now, afraid for Isaac's very survival, Sarah speaks up to her husband. The biblical text is normally sparing when quoting speakers. It is even more selective recording the speech of women. As we have discussed above, the text records Sarah's words only when they relate to her life's passion: to bear and nurture a child. Here, then, the Bible records Sarah's words for the last time:

> *[Therefore,] she said to Abraham: Send away this maidservant and her son, because this maidservant's son will not inherit along with my son, with Isaac.*[1]

Although banishing Hagar and Ishmael may appear unduly harsh, Alshich justifies it, saying that when Sarah realized that Ishmael's behavior truly went beyond acceptable limits, she trembled

---

[1] ותאמר לאברהם: גרש את האמה הזאת ואת בנה, כי לא יירש בן האמה הזאת עם בני, עם יצחק.

61

with fear lest Isaac learn to imitate Ishmael. The *midrash* elaborates upon Sarah's final statement, giving her further voice. Alshich allows us to hear Sarah's cry: "If Isaac were to adopt even one of Ishmael's perverted values, how could I go on living?" Fearing this terrible possibility, Alshich says that Sarah was driven by terror and hopelessness to exhort Abraham to send away the maidservant and her son.[2]

Rabbi Abraham, the son of the Rambam, says that God looked into Sarah's heart and saw no hatred for Ishmael there. Rather, God saw that Sarah was motivated solely by her passion to nurture Isaac to his full potential.[3]

The *Netziv* points out that Sarah has a lingering fear that Isaac is still perceived by some as Avimelech's son, and not Abraham's. By sending Ishmael away, Abraham proves to the world that Isaac *is his* child. For Abraham would not likely send away Ishmael if he were his only biological son—no matter how much he sought to please his wife, Sarah—unless Isaac were also the son of his loins.[4]

Moreover, Alshich reminds us that Sarah has never forgotten God's promise that her son—and her son alone—will be the one to inherit God's legacy. Sarah reminds her husband in this verse that it is her son—Isaac—who is the one who was chosen by God to be the covenantal heir, and not the handmaid's son.[5] Sarah knows she must preserve Isaac's moral and physical well-being so that he will grow to inherit the promised Covenant.

The Ralbag says it was necessary for Sarah, *acting under Divine inspiration*, to take such a drastic step—asking Abraham to send Ishmael away—in order to separate Isaac from Ishmael's evil influence.[6] Thus, the reader has seen that the commentators justify

---

[2] כאשר [ראתה] שרה הדבר הרע הזה ותתאבל באמת באמור: אם לוקח יצחק אחד ממדות ישמעאל כאלה, למה לי חיים! על כן חרדה לאמר: גרש . . . בל ילמוד יצחק ממנו.

[3] לפי שהוא יתעלה ראה את מחשבתה בסתר בזה; כי טובה הוא להצלחת יצחק בשלימותו; לא שנאה לישמעאל.

[4] ובזה ידעו הכל כי יצחק בנך הוא; שהרי לא יעשה אדם גדול כאברהם שיגרש בנו יחידו בשביל אהבת אשתו.

[5] ולבל יאמר לה . . . אגרשני מעל פני, על כן הקדימה ותאמר לו גרש האמה הזאת ואת בנה . . . ויצא זה לשרה **ממאמר יתברך** באומר: אבל שרה אשתך יולדת לך בן . . . והקימותי את בריתי אתו לברית עולם . . . ואת בריתי אקים את יצחק אשר תלד לך שרה.

[6] שהיתה הסבה **מהש"י** לגרש את ישמעאל כדי להפרידו מעל יצחק בעבור שלא ילמד יצחק ממעשיו הרעים.

Sarah's action of protecting Isaac from Ishmael's threatening behaviors. Abraham, however, views the matter very differently.

GENESIS 21:11

And this **matter** seemed very wrong in Abraham's eyes, because of his son.[7] The commentaries ask, to what matter, DaVaR,[8] is the text referring? What, specifically, is troubling Abraham? Abraham is troubled, according to Rashi, not only because he is facing the awful necessity of sending Ishmael away, but also because he fears that all that he has heard about Ishmael's evil doings is true.[9] Levush Haorah synthesizes Rashi's two interpretations. He says that Abraham was aware of Ishmael's behavior even before Sarah's exhortation. To the contrary, Abraham had admonished Ishmael repeatedly over the years, but to no avail. Abraham looked upon sending Ishmael away as a last resort, desiring to keep him close at hand for as long as possible, while attempting to influence him to the good. But it now appeared that Abraham had no choice but to send Ishmael away, as he posed an actual physical danger to Isaac.[10]

GENESIS 21:12

God seeks to allay Abraham's anxiety about Ishmael's fate. Moreover, God also addresses Abraham's subconscious concerns regarding Hagar, for in verse 11 Abraham's fear concerns solely Ishmael. God, however, knowing Abraham's innermost thoughts, reassures him here about the handmaid as well. And God said to Abraham: Let it not be repugnant in your eyes on account of the young man and your handmaiden.[11] One would assume that these

---

[7] וירע **הדבר** מאד בעיני אברהם, על אודות בנו.

[8] **דבר**

[9] ששמע שיצא לתרבות רעה . . . ופשוטו: על שאמרה לו לשלחו.

[10] וירע הדבר מאד בעיני אברהם: שוודאי שהיה רע ומר בעיניו, זה ימים רבים על התרבות רעה על ישמעאל **קודם שתאמר לו שרה** . . . וידע רוע מעלליו והוכיחו על זה, ולא קבל תוכחה. והיה מצטער על זה מאד, אבל לא רצה לשלחו, כי היה מצפה אולי יחזור לתשובה, על ידי שיוכיחו תמיד. ולכך עכשיו שאמרה לו שרה "גרש וכו' . . . " וירע בעיניו.

[11] ויאמר אלקים אל אברהם: אל ירע בעיניך על הנער ועל אמתך.

assurances from God concerning Ishmael and Hagar would have satisfied Abraham. What follows, therefore, is the most extraordinary statement in the Bible concerning the matriarch Sarah. *Whatever Sarah says to you, heed her voice, for it is Isaac who will be known as your issue.*[12]

Amazingly, God issues a directive to the patriarch Abraham to heed his wife Sarah's words in all matters. Rashi's interpretation of God's words have become the benchmark for any commentary on this verse. He states that God tells Abraham that Sarah's voice is the voice of prophecy. Furthermore, that her prophetic ability exceeds Abraham's.[13] Mizrachi, a supercommentary on Rashi, uses this verse as the proof-text for the statement that Sarah was a prophetess. He then refers to the very first Rashi cited in Chapter 1 above, and points to Sarah's alternate name, Yiscah, which readers of the text will recall translates to mean "seer," because she was destined by God "to see" with Divine inspiration, or "to prophesy."

Torah Temima agrees with Rashi concerning Sarah's ability to prophesy.[14] The commentary on *Torah Temima* expands on Sarah's prophetic ability, instructing us that God would never have exhorted Abraham to obey Sarah's directives without question if she were not greater than he in prophecy.[15] The *Netziv* questions the text's use of the phrase *SHeMa BeKoLaH*,[16] translated as "listen *within* her voice," rather than the more common *SHeMa LeKoLaH*,[17] meaning simply "listen *to* her voice." The commentary interprets "listen *within* her voice" to indicate that God wanted Abraham to heed not only the simple intention of Sarah's words, but also her deeper objectives. God wished Abraham to listen carefully and to learn from Sarah's wisdom.[18]

Ohr Hachayim states that God's amazing statement to Abraham to heed Sarah's voice validates her directive to Abraham to send away Ishmael and Hagar.[19] According to the commentator, God's

---

[12] כל אשר תאמר אליך שרה שמע בקלה, כי ביצחק יקרא לך זרע.

[13] שמע בקולה: בקול רוח הקדש שבה; למדנו שהיה אברהם טפל לשרה בנביאות.

[14] מלמד ששרה אמנו נביאה היתה.

[15] משום דאם לא, לא היה הקב"ה מרשה לאברהם לשמוע בקלה בלא גבול וקצבה. . . .

[16] שמע **ב**קלה

[17] שמע **ל**קלה

[18] ולא אמר שמע **ל**קלה . . . אבל **ב**קלה. משמעו שידקדק ויתבונן בדבריה.

[19] בא הקב"ה והצדיק דברי שרה, ואמר לו כל אשר . . . שמע בקלה.

instruction to Abraham to obey Sarah is His explicit acceptance of Ishmael's and Hagar's banishment.

GENESIS 21:13–21

From this point on in the story of Ishmael's banishment, the text resolutely refers to Ishmael either indirectly or in the third person. The story identifies him only as "the boy," *HaYeLeD*,[20] "the lad," *HaNa'aR*,[21] or "the handmaid's son," *BeN Ha'aMaH*.[22] In these verses he is never again described as Abraham's son, as he was before God commanded Abraham to heed Sarah's voice. For instance, in 21:9 the text had referred to Hagar's son "whom she bore to Abraham."[23] Also, in 21:11 the text had referred to Ishmael specifically as Abraham's "son."[24] *Ohr Hachayim* makes it very clear that this substitution signifies a shift in Abraham's focus. Abraham now understands Sarah's objective in banishing Ishmael. *Ohr Hachayim* points out that Abraham finally admits in his heart that Isaac is his true covenantal son. The commentator cites verse 14, where reference to Ishmael is now relegated to "the boy," instead of "his son."[25]

In this vein, the narrative continues. God reassures Abraham that "the handmaid's son" will also become a nation despite his banishment. Obeying God's words, Abraham sends away Hagar and "the boy." Abraham provides her with bread and a jug of water, and Hagar wanders in the desert of Beersheva. When her water jug is empty, Hagar, unwilling to hear "the boy's" cries, leaves him under a tree, and weeping, she watches him from afar. God hears "the lad's" cries and sends His angel to reassure Hagar—as He did to Abraham—that "the lad" will become a great nation. He directs Hagar to a well of water, from which she slakes "the lad's" thirst. And God watched over "the lad," and he settled in the Paran desert and

---

[20] הילד

[21] הנער

[22] בן האמה

[23] את בן הגר המצרית **אשר ילדה לאברהם**

[24] על אודות **בנו.**

[25] ותמצא שחזר אברהם והודה לדבריה. דכתיב, וישכם אברהם וגו' ואת הילד וגו', **ולא אמר את בנו.**

became a huntsman. "His mother" later brought him a bride from her native Egypt.

Finally, for the first time, a contented Sarah dwells alone with Abraham and Isaac. With the divisive concubine and her troublesome son gone, Sarah is free to experience the fullness of her life. Presumably she and her husband raise Isaac in the ways of their God. Unfortunately, the text omits any details of these halcyon years, but we can readily imagine Sarah's delight in them.

TEN

ଷୠଔଷୠଔ

Sarah is Separated
From Isaac: The *Akeida*

GENESIS 22:1–3

Years later, Abraham faces the supreme test of his religious obedience: the *Akeida,* the "binding of Isaac." God calls upon him to take his son, Isaac, and offer him as a sacrifice. Abraham, the quintessential man of faith, unhesitatingly proceeds to carry out God's command.[1] Ever since God had commanded Abraham to heed Sarah's voice following her directive to send away Hagar and Ishmael (in 21:12), there is no further textual reference to her. In fact, not only does Sarah never speak again, but the biblical text does not even refer to her until it records her death. Therefore, we cannot be sure whether Sarah even knew about the impending sacrifice of her son, Isaac. And if she were aware of it, did she acquiesce, or did she argue and try to restrain Abraham? Did she cry out to God or was she silent? Sarah's entire life has been bound up with her passion to mother the covenantal child. Ironically, now—at this moment of the fruition of her dreams—Isaac's very existence hangs in the balance. This is why Sarah's silence in the text is thunderous.

---

[1] ויהי אחר הדברים האלה והאלקים נסה את אברהם . . . ויאמר קח-נא את בנך . . . את יצחק . . . והעלהו שם לעלה. . . . .

67

The commentators attempt to answer these questions. *Sefer Tosfot Hashalem* proposes that Sarah knew nothing of Abraham's plans. Abraham feared that had he disclosed to Sarah the true nature of his mission that day, she would have refused to let him go; had he absconded with Isaac without telling Sarah his whereabouts, she would likely have feared the worst, gone mad and killed herself. Therefore, Abraham told Sarah only that he was taking Isaac away in order to educate him.[2]

God's directive to Abraham (in 22:2) to "take your son," *KaCH-Na*,[3] translates as "*please* take;" not as a command, but as a supplication. *Ohr Hachayim* interprets these words as a Divine hint to Abraham, suggesting that he mollify Sarah, convince her with soft words to allow him to take Isaac away.[4] And so, that entire night, Abraham entreats Sarah to allow Isaac to accompany him in order to learn Torah.[5] Even as dawn is breaking, Abraham cannot bring himself to disclose to Sarah the true reason he seeks to take Isaac from her.

The reader will recall that when Abraham stood at the gates of Egypt so many years before, he used the same word of supplication to Sarah, saying *iMRi-Na*.[6] "*Please* tell the Pharaoh that you are my sister." Both in that verse (Genesis 12:13) and here, according to *Ohr Hachayim*, Abraham uses the same beseeching term, because he anticipates that his wife's initial response will be to resist, or to deny his request.

Sefer Tosfot Hashalem elaborates on the scenario of that fateful evening preceding the *Akeida*. The commentator allows us to glimpse into Sarah and Abraham's tent, and overhear them in conversation. Abraham approaches Sarah and proposes a feast. He tells Sarah, "Prepare food and drink so that we might celebrate tonight." Amidst her preparations, Sarah asks, "Tell me, what is the special occasion that requires such a feast?" Abraham responds, "God has commanded me to bring Isaac up to Mount Moriah, to educate him

---

2 אמר אברהם: אם אודיע, נשים דעתן קלות ולא תשמע לי; ואם לא אודיע לה, תחנק עצמה שלא תראה את יצחק. אמר לה: יש מקום שאני רוצה לחנך את הנער.

3 קח-**נא**

4 רמז לו שיקח את שרה בדברים להתרצות אליו להליכו עמו.

5 אמרו ז"ל: כי כל אותו הלילה היה אברהם מפייס לשרה להסכים עמו שיוליכנו ללמדו תורה עד אור הבוקר.

6 אמרי-**נא**

there in the ways of God's commandments. He has told me to bring Isaac to *that* mountain, and to no other." Sarah yields to this, saying: "Take him there in peace."[7]

Verse three describes the haste of Abraham's actions early the next morning. He arose at dawn while the household slept, silently saddled his mule, roused his two manservants and Isaac, split the firewood for the altar, and set out for Mount Moriah.[8] Alshich explains the text's use of the Hebrew word *VaYASHKeM*,[9] "and he rose up early in the morning." Abraham arose from his bed, careful not to wake Sarah, because he feared her questions about his furtive preparations. Perhaps she would ask: "Where are you headed so early this morning?" Or she might note his hasty bundling of the firewood onto the donkey, and question, "I see you've taken the fire and the kindling, but you've forgotten the lamb to be sacrificed." To avoid Sarah's inevitable flood of questions, Alshich suggests that Abraham took his son and crept silently away into the morning mist.[10]

How grateful Torah students must be to these venerable commentators, who allow us to continue to hear the echo of Sarah's voice even though the actual flow of her words in the text has ceased.

GENESIS 22:4–24

After a three-day journey, Abraham and Isaac ascend Mount Moriah alone. There, in faithful obeisance to God's command, Abraham binds Isaac to the altar. Ibn Ezra, commenting on verse 22:4, mentions that there are three *midrashic* opinions as to Isaac's age at the time of the *Akeida*. Some say Isaac was thirty-seven years of age; others that he was age five; but Ibn Ezra himself favors the

---

[7] ביום שניסהו הקב"ה אמר אברהם לשרה: תקני מאכל ומשתה ונשמח היום. מיד תיקנה. אמרה לו: מה טיבה של שמחה זו ומשתה גדול? אמר לה: הקב"ה צוה לי לעלותו להר המוריה ולחנכו שם במצוות, ולא במקום אחר. אמרה, קחהו לשלום.

[8] וישכם אברהם בבקר ויחבוש את חמורו, ויקח את שני נעריו אתו ואת יצחק בנו, ויבקע עצי עלה ויקם, וילך. . . .

[9] וישכם

[10] וישכם אברהם וכו': לשלא ירגישו בדבר ויגיע לאזני שרה. ולבלתי הניח לה מקום לשאול אנה פניכם מועדות? והנה האש והעצים, ואיה השה לעולה? על כן מיהר בהשכמה, ויחבוש בעצמו את חמרו טרם ירגישו אפילו נעריו . . . לא יבצר מלשאול להם שרה מה זה ועל מה זה.

opinion that Isaac was close to thirteen years of age when his father took him to Mount Moriah.[11]

While he is holding the sacrificial blade to Isaac's throat, an angel of God interrupts the sacrifice, prohibiting Abraham from carrying out the deed. The angel accepts the aborted sacrifice *as if* Abraham had in fact sacrificed his son. In Isaac's place, Abraham slaughters a ram and offers it to God. As a reward for Abraham's fidelity to God, the angel reassures him that this selfsame son, Isaac, whom Abraham did not withhold even from God's altar, is destined to carry on God's covenant with Abraham. Although the repercussions of the trauma of the *Akeida* will inform Isaac's life, the reader will note that the biblical text is silent concerning its immediate effect on Abraham and Isaac.

Afterwards, Abraham returned to his waiting manservants and settled in Beersheva. There he learns that, in contrast to his and Sarah's lifelong quest for children, his brother Nahor and his wife Milcah—Sarah's sister—have had eight sons. The text lists them by name. While students of the text are accustomed to reading series of begats, this listing is noteworthy because none of Nahor's grandchildren is mentioned, save one child, a daughter born to Betuel, named Rebecca. The significance of this listing, according to Rashi, is to introduce us to Rebecca, who is destined to partner Isaac in the emerging dynasty of the Hebrew people.[12]

Ba'al Haturim gently links the birth of Rebecca, Isaac's future wife, with the forthcoming narration of his mother's death. The commentator points out that the Bible does not leave the reader without hope. As Sarah's "sun" is setting, the text hints to us that a matriarchal successor's light is just beginning to dawn.[13] Even though Sarah's life is ending, we are comforted by the knowledge that Rebecca is waiting in the wings. Sforno elaborates, saying that we should derive solace from the fact that only after Rebecca—a worthy replacement for the righteous Sarah—is born, could the text relate Sarah's death.[14]

---

[11] ורז"ל אמרו שהיה יצחק כעשר בן שלשים ושבע שנים . . . ואחרים אמרו שהיה בן חמש שנים . . . והקרוב אל הדעת שהיה קרוב לי"ג שנים. . . . .

[12] ובתואל ילד את רבקה: כל היחוסין הללו לא נכתבו אלא בשביל פסוק זה.

[13] עד שלא שקעה שמשה של שרה, זרחה שמשה של רבקה.

[14] אחר שנולדה רבקה הראויה למלאת מקום שרה . . . כאמרם ז"ל: שאין צדיק נפטר מן העולם אלא אם כן נולד צדיק כמותו.

ELEVEN

৪৩৪৩

The Death of Sarah

GENESIS 23:1–2

And these were the years of the life of Sarah: one-hundred years, and twenty years, and seven years; the years of the life of Sarah. And Sarah died in Kiryat Arba, which is Hebron, in the land of Canaan. And Abraham returned to eulogize Sarah and to weep over her.[1]

The reader must be reeling from these two momentous events, following one on the heels of the other, and separated only by the announcement of Rebecca's birth. First, we learned of the near-death of Isaac, and now we read of the actual death of Sarah. Because there still has been no mention of Sarah *in the text*, since God instructed Abraham to "heed Sarah's words," our questions continue to intensify. On the night preceding Isaac's departure, our questions centered on whether Sarah had foreknowledge of Abraham's intention. Now, with the recording of her death, not only do we feel profoundly bereft, but we also are driven to know all the details of Sarah's final days. Did she ever learn the true nature of Abraham's plan? If so, did she know that it was ultimately Divinely averted? And finally, did she ever see Isaac again?

---

[1] ויהיו חיי שרה מאה שנה ועשרים שנה ושבע שנים; שני חיי שרה. ותמת שרה בקרית ארבע
הוא חברון בארץ כנען; ויבא אברהם לספד לשרה ולבכתה.

At the outset, however, the commentators make much of every last word in the text that describes Sarah's death, as if they are loath to leave her. Rashi explains the somewhat stilted structure of the first verse in this chapter. He says the reason the years of Sarah's life are delineated separately (i.e., "one-hundred years, *and* twenty years, *and* seven years") is that we must derive meaning from each segment. Despite Sarah's travails, at one-hundred years of age she was as morally pure as she was at twenty, the year she left her father's house to marry Abraham. And at twenty years of age she had the innocent physical beauty of a seven-year-old.[2]

The *Netziv* questions the double use of the words "the years of the life of Sarah," *VaYeHi CHaYei SaRaH*[3] and *SHNei CHaYei SaRaH*,[4] which are stated twice in Hebrew in verse one. Would not only one mention have sufficed? The commentator offers a beautiful interpretation, saying that the words "the life of Sarah" are mentioned twice to highlight that a human life is comprised of two ontological elements. One is the mere passage of time from birth until death; the *quantity* of one's years. The second is the *quality* of our lives; the times that are marked by exultation and not melancholy.[5]

The commentator continues, pointing out that not only are there two aspects of living in the human condition, but also that Sarah actually led two lives. He derives this from the final three words of verse one, **SHNei** *CHaYei SaRaH*,[6] which can be translated both as "the *years* of the life of Sarah," and as "the *two* lives of Sarah." What were these two lives? According to the *Netziv*, Sarah's first life consisted of the ninety years preceding Isaac's birth; her second life began with her miraculous rejuvenation, and lasted thirty-seven years, until her death.[7]

---

[2] לכך נכתב שנה בכל כלל וכלל, לומר לך שכל אחד נדרש לעצמו: בת ק' כבת כ' לחטא . . . שהרי אינה בת עונשין אף בת ק' בלא חטא, ובת כ' כבת ז' ליופי.

[3] ויהי חיי שרה

[4] שני חיי שרה

[5] שני חיי שרה מיותר; והנה כבר פרשנו פרוש חיים בלשון הקדש משתי משמעות: אחת חיים ולא מות; ב' שמח ועלז ולא עצבון.

[6] **שני** חיי שרה

[7] ונראה עוד לפרש על פי הפשט: משמעות "שני" מספר שני. ובאשר שרה נעשית ילדה אחרי זקנתה וחזרה לספר חליפות השנים. . . . בראשונה היתה תשעים שנה ובשניה ל"ז שנה. בסך הכל שני חיי שרה היו מאה ועשרים ושבע שנה.

Finally, in the nature of a eulogy, at this moment of Sarah's death, the *Netziv* is moved to explain his version of why God told Abraham to heed Sarah's voice (at 21:12). Students of the text will recall that Rashi reasoned that God's statement implied that Sarah's prophetic ability exceeded Abraham's. The *Netziv* here reminds us that the definition of a prophet is one to whom God speaks directly. Since God spoke directly with Abraham on a continuing basis, and spoke with Sarah but once (at 18:15), how could Rashi have meant that Abraham's actual prophesying ability, *NeVuaH*,[8] was second to Sarah's? Rather, the *Netziv* takes pains to distill Rashi's intent by redefining "prophecy" as it applies specifically to Sarah. He explains that Sarah exceeded Abraham in the quality of Divine inspiration, *RuaCH HaKoDeSH*,[9] which visits a person of solitude and descends upon her once she possesses the ability to receive it. God need not speak to her in order for her to possess this rare gift. Thus, extols the *Netziv*, Sarah transcended Abraham in the quality of Divine inspiration. This required her to *infer* God's desired direction, plan the proper route to achieve God's aims, and execute God's wishes. Such intuitive perception was the nature of Sarah's greatness.[10]

Given her intuitive level of prophecy, the juxtaposition in the text of the *Akeida* and Sarah's death inexorably leads the *mephorshim* to conclude that Sarah *must have divined* the contingency of Isaac's existence, and that somehow this *knowledge* precipitated her death. This inference is necessary because the text does not mention Sarah's knowledge of the *Akeida*. The commentaries differ on the nature of what Sarah "knew," and how this apprehension killed her.

Rashi explains that by the text's placement of the event of Sarah's death in the chapter immediately following that of the *Akeida*, we learn that there exists a cause-and-effect relationship between the two events.[11] It is certainly plausible that when Sarah heard of the

---

[8] נבואה

[9] רוח הקדש

[10] ואחר כל זה יש להתבונן במה שאמרו שאברהם היה טפל לשרה בנביאות. ואין זה אלא תימא: האדם הגדול אשר דבר עמו ד' כל פעם היה טפל לשרה שלא דבר עמה ד' כי אם דבור אחד . . . אלא הכונה הוא שהיה טפל ברוח הקדש . . . רוה"ק הוא מה שאדם מתבודד ומשרה עליו רוה"ק ויודע מה שרואה. אמנם לא דבר עמו ד' . . . אבל ברוח הקדש היתה שרה מצוינת יותר מאברהם אבינו.

[11] ונסמכה מיתת שרה לעקידת יצחק לפי שעל ידי בשורת העקידה . . . מתה.

terrifying happening of the *Akeida,* she immediately expired from grief.

Pirkei d'Rabi Eliezer sets the scene: After the *Akeida*, a disgruntled Satan, who had sought Isaac's death—perceiving that Isaac is alive and well—turns his evil intentions to Sarah. Appearing before her in the guise of a human, he whispers to her: "Eh! Old woman! Haven't you heard the latest news?" She tells him, "No." He continues, "Your old man took your son, Isaac, and sacrificed him on an altar to his God. And the boy was crying out and wailing, and there was no one to save him." At these words, Sarah herself cried out three times, her soul departed, and she died. The commentator states that the three blasts of the *shofar* on Rosh Hashana immortalize Sarah's anguished cries.[12]

According to *Siftei Chachamim*, the messenger of doom need not even have been a supernatural Satan, whose mission was to destroy Sarah. It could have been an ordinary man, a wayfarer from Mount Moriah relating to her the true story of the *Akeida*. Before he could relate the happy ending—that Isaac was saved from death—and in the instant he paused in his telling to catch his breath, Sarah became overwhelmed by his news, and her soul departed and she died.[13]

Rashi differs from these commentaries in an important detail. According to Rashi, Sarah died even as she learned the truth, that Isaac in fact *survived* the *Akeida,* narrowly *escaping* death. Rashi teaches us that Sarah died of extreme anguish—of existential angst—upon hearing of Isaac's *near*-death. In that instant Sarah realized that although Isaac survived, her entire life *could have been* annihilated by the razor's edge of Abraham's sword. The ninety years she spent pining for a child, her thirty-seven years of ecstatic motherhood, her entire existence had approached the brink of extinction. Sarah's experiencing the tenuousness of Isaac's life was

---

[12] וכשבא אברהם מהר המוריה, חרה אפו של סמאל . . . הלך ואמר לשרה: אי שרה! לא שמעת מה שנעשה בעולם? אמרה לו, לאו. אמר לה: לקח אישך הזקן לנער יצחק והקריבו לעולה. והנער בוכה ומילל שלא יכל להנצל. מיד התחילה בוכה ומיללת. בכתה שלש בכיות כנגד תקיעות, ופרחה נשמתה ומתה.

[13] ואיחר המגיד לסיים דבריו ולומר לה שניצל ולא נשחט . . . שעה מועטת קודם לכן נבהלה כל כך מדבריו ופרחה רוחה ונשמתה.

more than she could bear. According to Rashi, *this knowledge* is what killed Sarah.[14]

The ultimate question still looms: Given Sarah's deep-seated faith, how can we reconcile her death of "profound grief?" Should not Sarah's faith in God's justice have shielded her from the ill effects of the news of the *Akeida*? The reader will associate the fact that Sarah died following the *Akeida* with an assumption that she died of overwhelming *grief*. This inference does not necessarily follow according to *Sefer Tosfot Hashalem*, who posits a counter-intuitive argument. He proposes that Sarah's death at this precise time was from the emotion of overwhelming *happiness*, not grief. He draws this conclusion by asking rhetorically, How could Sarah, a woman of such enormous faith in God, have *grieved* over God's choice of her son as a sacrifice? The commentator answers that on the contrary, Sarah's faith was so great that she was able to extract undiluted *joy* from the fact that God selected her son for reasons known only to God.[15] It was this powerful flood of emotion that killed her. Thus, according to this commentator, Sarah died not of grief, but from the tidal wave of joy.[†]

The reader might well wonder why God did not intervene this final time to save Sarah's life, as it had been saved at every crisis juncture until now. The *mephorshim* grapple with this as well. *Yefei To'ar* explicitly states that in fact Sarah's life was *not* cut short. Rather, Sarah was destined to die at this time, and therefore God allowed the angel of death to take her.[16] *Sha'arei Aharon* confirms that the one-hundred-and-twenty-seven years that Sarah lived were the Divinely-

---

[†]The Talmud (*Ketubot* 62b) supports the hypothesis that intense *psychological* emotions—whether joy or grief—can certainly have a *physiological* effect. It relates the tale of a scholar who returns to his home after an absence of twelve years. Upon recognizing her beloved husband walking towards her, the scholar's wife's heart stopped beating, and her soul fled her body. אזל יתיב תרי סרי שני בבי רב. הוה יתיבא דביתהו קא נהלה קמאה. דל עינה, חזיתיה, **סוי לבה, פרח רוחה.**

---

[14] שנזדמן בנה לשחיטה **וכמעט שלא נשחט**, פרחה נשמתה ממנה ומתה.

[15] וא"ת וכי היתה שרה מצטערת במה שבחר השם בבנה להיות לעולה! לכן יש לפרוש פרכה רוחה **מרוב שמחה.**

[16] ומתה שרה מאותו צער: . . . משמע שמתה בלא זמנה. זה אין קושיה . . . יש לומר שמלאך המות סבב למצא מקום ליטול נשמתה ואי לא דבא קצה, לא הוה יכל לה.

allotted years of her life, undiminished by the *Akeida*. The *Akeida* served as the vehicle to bring about her preordained death.[17] The Zohar also appreciates the intrinsic connection between Sarah's life and that of her beloved Isaac. It states that the last thirty-seven years of Sarah's life—those years beginning with Isaac's birth until the time of the *Akeida*—were *the real* "life of Sarah." The commentary derives this interpretation from the first Hebrew word of chapter 23: *VaYiHiYu*,[18] *And **these were** [the years of the life of Sarah].* The sum of the numerical value of each Hebrew letter comprising this word totals thirty-seven (each *vav* equals six, each *yud* equals ten, and the *hay* equals five). It is an instructive allusion that the Bible could not accurately narrate Sarah's death without subtly linking it with Isaac's life. Thus, the first word in the chapter of the Bible named for Sarah's death has the numerical value of the years of Isaac's life until that time.[19] The common point of departure for all these *mephorshim* is that the *Akeida* must have impacted on Sarah's death because the latter event follows the former so closely in the text. In contrast, *Sha'arei Aharon* gives pause to these interpretations by reminding us of the five verses (at Genesis 22:20–24) separating the two momentous events. These verses, whose sole purpose ostensibly is to introduce the reader to the birth of Rebecca, Sarah's successor and Isaac's future wife, serve another important role. According to the commentator, Rebecca's birth is narrated *before* Sarah's death in order to inform us that Sarah in fact *knew* of the birth of her grand-niece. He points to the beautiful symmetry of both Sarah and her sister, Milcah, giving birth miles and years apart, to children who are destined to wed and perpetuate God's covenant. This knowledge allowed Sarah to die in peace.[20]

---

[17] אלו היו שנים שנקצבו לה מראש אלא שהסטן השתמש אמתלא זו כדי ליטול ממנה נשמתה.

[18] ויהיו

[19] אמר רבי חייא . . . דהא כד אתעקד יצחק, בר תלתין ושבע שנים הוא, וכיון דאתעקד יצחק, מיתת שרה . . . ואינן תלתין ושבע שנין, מיומא דאתייליד יצחק, עד שעתא דאתעקד, אינון **הוו חיי שרה ודאי**, כחושבן ויהיו, בגימטרי"א תלתין ושבע שנין הוו.

[20] נסמכה מיתת שרה ללידת מלכה, להורות שנתבשרה שרה שפקד השם את מלכה אחותה גם היא, ונתן לה בנים, ובתוכם רבקה הצדקת הראויה לבנה, וכל זה להורות שבאתה אל אבותיה בשלום.

Along these lines, Ibn Ezra quotes the *Gr'ah*, who states that Sarah lived an additional eleven years after the *Akeida*.[21] Thus, according to the *Gr'ah*, Sarah's final moments were not anguished. Rather, she was granted the time to live out her days satisfied that God's promise to her and to Abraham would be fulfilled through Isaac.

---

[21] אמנם הגר"א כתב בפירושו לסדר עולם, . . . וצריך לומר לפי דעתי ששרה מתה י"א שנים אחרי העקידה.

TWELVE

ဆဝဆဝဆ

Sarah is Eulogized, and Buried in *Ma'arat Ha-machpela*

GENESIS 23:2

The *Netziv* asks, why does the text say, *And Abraham returned to eulogize Sarah, and to weep over her,*[1] with the eulogy mentioned before the weeping? Under ordinary circumstances, one would expect that the weeping would precede the eulogy. The commentator explains that the text's positioning of words is deliberate and accurate. When Abraham returned to Hebron after Sarah's death, he was greeted by throngs of people surrounding Sarah's house. As their communal leader, his first task was to eulogize Sarah. Abraham's private weeping and mourning for her came second. The commentator goes so far as to suggest that Abraham's grief was mitigated by the fact that Sarah had already fulfilled her life's goal of raising Isaac. It was Abraham's public eulogy of her—not his private tears—that was most needed by Sarah's followers. Abraham saw this and met that need.[2]

---

[1] ויבא אברהם לספד לשרה, ולבכתה.

[2] אברהם בא ממקום רחוק לשם . . . נתקבצו המון העם סביב הבית . . . מיתת שרה לא גרם לאברהם שינוי בהליכות עולמו עוד שהרי כבר נתגדל יצחק בנה שהוא התכלית, והספדה רבה על פי חשיבותה. משהוא הקדים לספוד לה ואחר כך לבכותה.

78

Alshich's interpretation of the text's phrasing is that when a righteous person dies, one is obligated first to eulogize her, so that the community will recognize her righteousness, and thereafter to mourn her passing. Abraham behaved accordingly. The eulogy he spoke and the tears he shed properly mourned the passing of the generation's most righteous woman.[3]

On the subject of the eulogy itself, the text is silent and the *mephorshim* add very little commentary. *Ma'ayna Shel Torah* explains that Abraham paid homage to Sarah's essence: he praised her preeminence as a mother. How exceptional was Sarah, that she was able to achieve the pinnacle of motherhood by molding a son such as Isaac, who was prepared to joyfully give up even his own life to serve God.[4] Abraham pointed out to the congregants that Sarah's accomplishment was her ability to successfully imbue her son with her vision of the one true God, much as she had done with the numerous converts whom she taught to believe in monotheism.

The *Midrash Tanchuma* (*Chaye Sarah*, note 3) relates the exquisite *midrash* that although these verses of the biblical text omit the actual words of Abraham's eulogy of Sarah at her funeral, his eulogy of her exists in another portion of the Holy Scripture. The commentary explains at length that chapter 31 of the Book of Proverbs, known as "Eshet Chayil" ("Woman of Valor"), is a thirty-one-verse paean to the matriarch Sarah. The *midrash* states, "Sarah *is* the 'Woman of Valor.'"[5]

GENESIS 23:3–19

Abraham rose from the presence of his deceased wife,[6] in order to deal with the pressing task of finding Sarah a worthy burial place. He approached the sons of *Cheyt*, landowners in Hebron, and negotiated the public purchase from them of the Cave of Machpela

---

3 שלא על בחינת אשתו עשה, רק למה שהיא שרה מפאת עצמה, שחייב אדם להספיד ולהוריד דמעות על אדם כשר.

4 כאשר הספיד אברהם את שרה וביקש לספר את מעלותיה, ציין את מעשה העקידה . . . אם היא חינכה בן כזה, המוכן למסור נפשו מתוך שמחה, אפשר להבין מזה עד היכן הגיעה מעלותה.

5 זה שאמר הכתוב אשת חיל מי ימצא, הדברים על מי נאמרו, לפי שכתיב למעלה ויבא אברהם לספוד לשרה ולבכותה, התחיל בוכה ומספיד, ואמר . . . "אשת חיל זו שרה. . . ."

6 ויקם אברהם מעל פני מתו.

and the field surrounding it. Finally, Sarah was laid to rest in the Cave in the field of Machpela—*Ma'arat Ha-Machpela*—in Hebron, in the land of Canaan. The commentator *Sha'arei Aharon* relates a *midrash* that Sarah died with a "Divine kiss," because only the righteous who died in this manner could merit being buried in the Cave of Machpela.[7]

---

[7] במערת המחפלה לא היו נקברין רק המתים בנשיקה . . . כיון שראה אברהם שפניה מאורות, ומוכיח דמתה בנשיקה.

THIRTEEN

ಬಂದ∞ಲ

Epilogue to Sarah

*God should establish you as He did **Sarah**, Rebecca, Rachel, and Leah.*[1]

In traditional homes every Friday evening, we confer this blessing on our Jewish daughters after the Sabbath candles are lit. Considering the fraught saga of the life of Sarah the matriarch, we are naturally led to wonder: Do we really seek to bestow such a life upon our own daughters? Sarah's life as it appears in the *p'shat* is *not* one that we would hope our daughters would relive. We would hardly wish our daughters to experience dislocation, famine, abduction, infertility, the trauma of surrogacy, a sometime-indifferent husband, vexatious stepchildren, or the near-death of a long-awaited child. To most properly answer this question, we have delved beyond the *p'shat* and relied on the *mephorshim* to enlighten us. The commentaries elevate our understanding of Sarah's character, allowing us to comprehend the manifold qualities that enabled Sarah to live a fulfilled life.

The driving force underlying Sarah's actions was her passionate desire to bear a child. This passion informed all of Sarah's thoughts, words and actions. Blessed with a long-awaited son, she nurtured him on the vision of the one true God, empowering him to become

---

[1] ישמך אלקים כ**שרה**, רבקה, רחל ולאה.

81

Abraham's covenantal heir, the second generation in the progression of the incipient Jewish nation.

We extract from this Sabbath benediction the prayer that our daughters will walk in Sarah's footsteps, possessing, as she did, the clarity of vision and endurance of will to fulfill themselves as Jewish women.

PART II

REBECCA

ഔ ഇ ഔ ഇ

FOURTEEN

ഇൗരുൽരുൽ

The Birth of Rebecca

GENESIS 22:20–24

The birth of Rebecca, the second matriarch, is recorded in the Torah even before we are told of Sarah's death. *And Betuel begat Rebecca; [Betuel was the eighth] of the eight sons whom Milcah bore for Nahor, Abraham's brother.* Rebecca's name stands out in these verses as the only enumerated grandchild, of all the grandchildren born to Milcah and Nahor. According to Rashi, the only reason the Torah even inventories their eight children is in order to focus the reader's attention on Rebecca's provenance.[1] After reading these verses, we are reminded that Rebecca is the granddaughter of Milcah, Sarah's sister, and of Nahor, Abraham's brother, and thus is a worthy successor to Sarah.

---

[1] כל היחוסין הללו לא נכתבו אלא בשביל פסוק זה.

FIFTEEN

&0&3&0&3

The Quest for Rebecca

GENESIS 24:1–9

Following Sarah's death and burial, the Torah recounts for us that Abraham—by now very advanced in age—is blessed by God with *all* material things.[1] Abraham, however, sees that his son Isaac remains unmarried, and that his own death is approaching. He recognizes that without a proper marriage for his son, God's promise to him and Sarah may never be fulfilled. The *mephorshim* are struck by the irony of Abraham's "having it all" in verse one, and yet the text's devoting the next nine verses to his plan for acquiring what he is missing. According to the Ramban, without generational continuity, Abraham's wealth, possessions, honor, longevity and progeny still do not fulfill his most fervent desire: to insure that Isaac will father worthy children.[2] Abraham therefore vests his oldest, most trusted manservant with the task of traveling to Aram-Naharayim to acquire a suitable bride for Isaac from among Abraham's family. The *Netziv* and other commentaries identify this venerable servant as Eliezer.

---

[1] ואברהם זקן, בא בימים, וד' ברך את אברהם **בכל.**

[2] ברך את אברהם בכל: בעושר, ונכסים,וכבוד, אורך ימים ובנים. וזאת כל חמדת האדם. והזכיר הכתוב לאמר: כי היה שלם בכל, לא חסר דבר זולתי שיראה בנים לבנו.

86

The reason Abraham chooses Eliezer is obvious according to the simple reading of the text. He was, after all, Abraham's most trusted servant, in command of all *his* possessions.[3] The *Netziv* first restates that the emphasized pronoun "his" (*Lo*[4]) in verse two relates to *Abraham's* possessions.[5] Eliezer was vested with the care of all that was "his," interpreted as "all that belonged *to Abraham*." The commentator then offers a more subtle interpretation of this verse. He suggests that the words should not be read that Eliezer was in command of all that was *his master's*; that is, all that belonged to Abraham. Rather, that Eliezer was in command of all that was *his own*. That is to say, that Eliezer was strong enough to rule over his own desires, notably his sexual passions.[6]

That Eliezer is able to suppress his natural inclinations is vital in order to insure that the prospective bride will be delivered to Isaac in her untouched, virginal state. Alshich states that Abraham and Isaac know this about Eliezer, and so they can send him on this mission with confidence.[7]

The *Netziv* also offers an explanation as to why it is that Abraham delegates *this* most important mission, while in the past he, himself, hurried to the tasks. The reader will recall, for example, that a recuperating Abraham himself hurried to ready the meal for the three angel-messengers on that fateful noon; and that he rose at dawn before his household to saddle his own mule on the way to the *Akeida*. The commentator suggests that it was only Abraham's extremely advanced age which prevented him from making this crucial match-making journey himself, to carry out this vital mission.[8]

Rabbi Abraham, son of the Rambam, suggests, alternatively, that it was actually Sarah's death that awakened this immediate need for Abraham to see Isaac wed. For had Sarah still been alive, neither Isaac's bachelorhood nor Abraham's advanced age would have impelled him to act at this time, because Abraham would have relied

---

3 עבדו זקן ביתו, המושל בכל אשר **לו.**

4 לו

5 מושל בכל אשר לו היינו בכל אשר **לאברהם.**

6 משמעו שולט ביצרו שהיה נוגע אך לנפשו בעניני תאוה וכדומה.

7 למה לא חשש לזה אברהם? . . . לזה אומר המושל בכל,שהוא יצר הרע, ויוכל לכובשו ולעמוד נגדו.

8 שאברהם היה זקן בא בימים מבואר שהוא נוגע לענין כי לולא זה לא היה מצוה לעבדו אלא הוא בעצמו היה מזדרז למצוה רבה זו ליתן אשה זו ליצחק. **שבזה תלוי כל התכלית.**

on Sarah to attend to the fulfillment of God's Covenant, and to find a proper bride for Isaac even after his death. His wife's unexpected death left Abraham with the stark realization that now he alone was responsible for Isaac's future.[9]

---

[9]   ולא נתעורר להשיאו אלא אחר מיתת שרה כאשר לא היה שם אחריה מי שיסדר את מצב יצחק.

SIXTEEN

꧁꧂꧁꧂

Abraham Delegates Eliezer
to Find a Wife for Isaac

A braham entrusts Eliezer to act in his stead to find the wife for Isaac, imposing three inviolate conditions upon him. So vital is it that Eliezer carry out Abraham's specific requirements that Abraham extracts an oath from Eliezer to this effect. Abraham's first condition is that the chosen woman must not be a daughter of the local Canaanites. His second requirement is that the chosen woman should hail from Abraham's country and kindred. Third and finally, Abraham insists that the chosen woman be willing to leave her country and family, and journey to Isaac in Hebron. In the event that Eliezer finds the proper woman to be Isaac's bride, who meets only the first two conditions but is not willing to leave her family and homeland to follow a stranger to a strange land, Abraham absolves his servant of his oath.

SEVENTEEN

༺ఌ༻ఌ

The Manservant
Imposes His Own Tests

GENESIS 24:10–14

Eliezer sets out on his journey to Aram-Naharayim at the head of a caravan of ten camels heavily laden with dower gifts. Arriving at his destination, he approaches the well at the outskirts of the town at eventide, intending to water his travel-worn and thirsty animals. Coincidentally, this was the precise time of day that the town's maidens gathered at the well to draw water for their households. Perhaps overwhelmed by the sheer number of young women he sees coming down the path to the well, Eliezer begs the God of his master Abraham to direct him to the right one. Eliezer cleverly devises a test so that he can immediately distinguish the girl who possesses the quality he seeks, thus adding his own fourth condition: she must embody the characteristic of *chesed*, an active compassion for the welfare of others. He proposes to ask each girl, "Please lower your water jug so that a stranger might quench his thirst." If she answers, "Certainly, please drink. And I will draw water for your thirsty camels as well," this would then be a sign that the God of Abraham has chosen that maiden for Isaac.

Rashi notes that Eliezer's added condition that the girl must embody *chesed* is not one of the three requirements that he swore to

90

Abraham. However, if she possesses and exhibits this additional quality it will show that the girl is worthy to enter Abraham's household.[1] Clearly, Eliezer is using this quality to narrow the field among the maidens who may be Abraham's kindred. The *Netziv* says that Eliezer's prayer is that God will come to his assistance, and cause *only a girl who meets Abraham's three conditions* to fulfill this fourth requirement.[2]

Ma'ayna Shel Torah adds that Eliezer's extra test was intended to demonstrate not only the maiden's *chesed*, but also her sensitivity and intelligence. Eliezer planned to ask the girl to allow a stranger to drink directly from the lip of the vessel. He was curious to see whether she would be foolish enough to bring the possibly-contaminated water home to her family; or insensitive enough to spill the unused remainder on the ground at his feet; or intuitively keen enough to devise an alternate response. By offering to water the stranger's camels directly after he drinks from the jug, the chosen girl would artfully dispose of the used water without humiliating the stranger. Thus, the maiden will also exhibit the desirable qualities of good judgment and perspicacity.[3]

---

1. ראויה היא לו שתהא גומלת חסדים וכדאי ליכנס בביתו של אברהם.

2. יהי רצון שתהיה **אותה** אשר הוכחת, וממילא אם אין כאן האשה אשר הוכחת, לא תמצא בתולה שתענה ותאמר כך.

3. ביקש אליעזר. . . . לבחון אותה בכל, . . . לכן ביקש ממנה להשקותו מים מתוך הכד גופו, כי אז יראה מה תעשה במים שישארו בתוך הכד אחרי שתייתו; אם תקח אותם הביתה . . . שמא חולה הוא והדביק את המים במחלתו; ואם תשפוך אותם ארצה . . . יהא בזה משום עלבון כלפיו . . . לא תישאר בפניה עצה אחרת, כי אם לומר: "גם לגמליך אשקה" כדי לשפוך את שארית המים לפני הגמלים, ואז תצא ידי הכל. ובכן, אם היא תעשה כך, יהא זה סימן מובהק, שלא זו בלבד שהיא מחוננת במידות טובות, אלא שהיא גם נבונה ופיקחת למצוא עצה טובה בשעת הצורך.

EIGHTEEN

ဆံုးဆံုး

Rebecca at the Well

GENESIS 24:15

Eliezer has barely finished formulating these new conditions, when God answers his prayer. Rebecca—daughter of Betuel, granddaughter of Milcah, Sarah's sister, and Nahor, Abraham's brother— goes out and approaches the well, shouldering her water jug. The Malbim is quick to state that this is the very first time that Rebecca has joined the other maidens to draw water at dusk. The commentator describes that God assigned to Rebecca a guardian angel who urged her *to go out* that evening.[1] The Zohar (132a) focuses on the text's use of the term "goes out" (*YoTZeiT* [2]) when it describes Rebecca's approach to the well. The text should perhaps have said "Rebecca comes to" the well, unless we are meant to infer from the term "goes out" that Rebecca was exiting a particular site. In fact, the Zohar states that the precise use of the word "goes out" is meant to teach us that God Himself *took Rebecca out* of her family's influence and brought her to the well that evening.[3]

---

[1] הטעם שיצאה רבקה עתה אף על פי שלא יצאה מעולם . . . עורר אותה מלאך ד'
שתצא. . . .

[2] יצאת

[3] "והנה רבקה יוצאת" באה מבעי ליה, שהקב"ה **אפיק לה** מכל אינון בני מתא. דכלהו חייבין,

The *mephorshim* deal cursorily with the issue of Rebecca's age at this time. Rashi alludes (at Genesis 25:20) to her age as an improbable tender age of three years.[4] Tosfot, in the Talmud (*Yevamot* 61b), cite her age as a marriageable fourteen.[5] Considering that the Bible in the following verse refers to Rebecca as a "young woman," *Na'aRa[H]*,[6] and not as a "young girl," the reader can therefore assume that she was of a comfortably marriageable age when she arrived at the well on that fateful day.

GENESIS 24:16

And the young woman is exceedingly beautiful to behold, a virgin, unknown to any man; she goes down to the watering-hole, fills her water-jug and comes back up.[7]

The reader will recall that the Hebrew term *Me'oD*,[8] meaning "very" or "exceedingly," also was used by the Torah to describe Sarah's exquisite beauty (Genesis 12:14), comparing it favorably with that of Eve, the first woman. Here, *Sha'arei Aharon* similarly uses the Torah's term *Me'oD*,[9] "exceedingly," also to equate Rebecca's beauty with the legendary fairness of Eve.[10]

The commentaries next deal with an apparent redundancy in this verse. The verse states both that Rebecca was a virgin *and* that no man knew her. Would not only one of those expressions have sufficed? As the readers might expect, the commentaries assign each of these phrases discrete and important meanings. The *Netziv* takes the *p'shat* approach. He states that first, Eliezer noticed Rebecca's *virginal* modesty. She hung back while the other young women boldly approached the shepherds gathered at the well. Second, that truly *no man knew her*, meaning that as Eliezer watched, he saw that the

---

והיא יוצאת מכללא דלהון.

[4] המתין לה עד . . . ג' שנים ונשאה.

[5] דרבקה נערה היתה . . . והרב רבינו שמואל חסיד משפיר"א הוכיח שהיתה בת ארבע עשרה.

[6] נער[ה]

[7] והנער טובת מראה מאד בתולה ואיש לא ידעה, ותרד העינה ותמלא כדה ותעל.

[8] מאד

[9] מאד

[10] טובת מראה מאד, בזיו איקונין של חוה.

shepherds mingled with the other maidens, but that none approached Rebecca, because she was unknown to them.[11]

Rashi interprets the apparent redundancy by explaining that not only was Rebecca's *virginity* intact, but also that *no man knew her* in *any* physical sense.[12] Rashi explains the phrase "no man knew her" to mean that it was acceptable among the heathens at that time for unmarried females to engage in all manner of physical intimacy with a man short of natural consummation, still remaining technical virgins. The parallel phrases in this verse underline, therefore, that Rebecca was both virginal *and* untouched in any way.[13]

The commentary on *Torah Temima* demonstrates how truly miraculous it was that "no man knew" Rebecca. At that time, incest was customary: fathers slept with their own virgin daughters before their weddings. The commentator interprets the phrase "and no *man* (*iSH* [14]) knew her," identifying "the man" as Rebecca's father, Betuel. The text is informing the readers that contrary to the communal norm, Rebecca remained untouched.[15] By their explanations of this verse, the commentaries have allowed us to glimpse the moral depravity of the Arameans. That Rebecca is able to remain utterly apart from these influences is attributed to her credit.

Shouldering her water-jug, Rebecca descends the steps to the well, fills her jug, and ascends the path toward home. The *Netziv* points out that the text's use of the words "descends" and "ascends" (*VaTeReD . . . VaTa'aL* [16]), hints at Rebecca's modesty. For unlike the other maidens who bent over immodestly to draw their water, Rebecca politely descended the shallow steps at the base of the public well, drew her water from an upright position, and then began her homeward journey.[17] *Midrash Rabbah* (60.5) interprets the word "ascends" (*VaTa'aL* [18]) to add a miraculous touch to Rebecca's task.

---

[11] [אליעזר] התבונן בה שאין לה דבר עם אנשים כמו שראה שאר בתולות, שהכל מכירין אותן, באשר היו רגילין בכל יום להיות עם הרועים אצל הבאר, וגם לא היו צנועות. אבל **אותה** . . . . לא ידעה אדם.

[12] בתולה: ממקום בתולים. ואיש לא ידעה: שלא כדרכה.

[13] לפי שבנות הגוים היו משמרות מקום בתוליהן ומפקירות עצמן ממקום אחר. העיד על **זו שנקיה מכל.**

[14] איש

[15] אין **איש** אלא אביה, שכך היה מנהגם של ארמיים לשכב עם בנותיהם בתולות. . . .

[16] ותרד . . . ותעל

[17] ראה שהיא לא שחה עצמה לשאוב ככל השואבות, שזה אינו דרך צניעות.

[18] ותעל

While she descended the steps expecting to draw the water with some difficulty, the water wondrously *rose up* to the mouth of the well, allowing her effortlessly to complete her job.[19] The *midrash* wants the reader to appreciate that this girl Rebecca is someone very special in the text, as miraculous events accompany her appearance.

---

[19] כל הנשים יורדות וממלאות מן העין, וזו, כיון שראו אותה המים, מיד **עלו.**

NINETEEN

࿓ఠ࿓ఠ

Rebecca Passes
The Manservant's Tests

GENESIS 24:17–18

E liezer, the manservant, runs towards Rebecca, importuning her: "Would you be so kind as to pour me a few drops of water from your jug?" Rebecca, who until now has been described in the text, speculated about and—unbeknownst to her—critically observed from afar, speaks for the first time: "Drink, my lord." And she at once lowers her water jug from her shoulder, handing it to the stranger so that he might drink.

One could assume that Eliezer singled out Rebecca as the object of his pursuit simply because of the qualities already mentioned: her virginal loveliness and her exceptional modesty. But Rashi adds that the manservant—already drawn to observe her because of these qualities—witnessed the supernatural occurrence of the water rising to greet her.[1] It was at that moment that Eliezer realized that she might well be the girl he was seeking, and he ran toward her in order to test his theory. Rebecca's every action speaks of her fine character. The Rokach reasons that Rebecca went to the trouble of lowering the jug to her hands rather than more easily tipping it from her shoulder, in order to keep the dusty stranger at a respectable distance. Otherwise,

---

[1] וירץ העבד לקראתה: לפי שראה שעלו המים לקראתה.

he would have come intimately close to Rebecca to drink his fill from her shouldered pitcher.[2] Not only does Rebecca show actual *chesed* to the stranger by giving him the water; she also inadvertently demonstrates her propriety in the modest manner of her offer.

GENESIS 24:19–21

Rebecca gives the stranger more than the bit of water that he requests; she allows him to drink his fill. Observing that his ten camels were standing by, she then tells him: "I will also draw water for your thirsty camels." She readily emptied the remaining water from her jug into the watering-trough, running back and forth from the well to the trough until all the camels were watered.

Ohr Hachayim notes that Rebecca deals with Eliezer's camels only after he has drunk his fill. In fact, she does not even mention the beasts in the same breath that she offers him his drink. She initially only says, "Drink, my lord" (Verse 18). This demonstrates her consideration of the thirsty stranger, revealing her intention to allow him to drink unhurriedly. Had she said to him right away, "Drink my lord, *and then* I will water your thirsty beasts," Eliezer might have rushed through his drinking in order to ease her task.[3] Also, *Sha'arei Aharon* adds that because Rebecca did not mention the stranger and his beasts in the same breath—she says "Drink, my lord" in verse 18, and "I will water your camels also" in verse 19—we are meant to observe her awareness of the stranger's sensibilities. The man's needs certainly precede those of his camels. Had she offered to water them both at the same time it might have been perceived as discourteous to his honor.[4]

All these subtleties are not lost on Eliezer. Rashbam states that it was Rebecca's latest words, "and I will also give your camels to drink," that stunned him to the realization that the God of his master Abraham may have answered his prayer.[5] He recalled his own test from verse 14: "And the girl who answers my request for water

---

2   שאם היה שותה על שכמה, היה מסתכל בה.

3   וטעם לא אמרה תכף ומיד "גם לגמליך . . ." . . . נתכוונה הצדקת . . . שאם היתה . . . יש מקום לו למהר להקל טורחה . . . יחשוב כי הוא זה כל הטורח וישתה כחפצו, לאט לאט.

4   שתה אדני . . . גם לגמליך אשאב: היה במשמע שאליעזר וגמליו הכל אחד, כלומר שנזהרה בכבודו.

5   הבין שזימן לו הקב"ה מה שביקש.

saying, 'drink and I will water your camels also,' *she* will be the chosen one for Isaac." By exhibiting the quality of *chesed*, this modest beauty had fulfilled Eliezer's condition, and even appeared to exceed his hopes.

Eliezer watches in stunned silence as Rebecca hurries about her task. He waits with bated breath to see if, at long last, his mission is about to succeed. Sforno is struck by the text's use of the Hebrew word *MiSHTa'eH*,[6] meaning Eliezer *stood gazing* at Rebecca *in awed silence*. The commentator reasons that this strong word conveys the servant's wonderment at the alacrity and swiftness of the girl's actions. Readers should take note of the eight action words in verses 18 through 20 describing Rebecca's behavior:[7]

> And she **quickly** went down; and she **lowered** her water jug from her shoulder; and she **gave him** water to drink; and she **completed** the task; and she **hurried** and **emptied** her pitcher; and she **ran** yet again to the well; and she **drew** water for his camels.

Alshich notes that Eliezer's wonderment is not at whether Rebecca is the chosen girl; her demonstrated qualities have already convinced him of that. Rather, that upon watching her cheerfully— and with dispatch—going about this arduous, charitable task of watering every last camel, he is wondering at his great good fortune that Abraham's God has answered his prayers so swiftly and completely.[8]

GENESIS 24:22–23

And when the camels finished drinking, Eliezer took a golden ring and arm bracelets of substantial worth, and, readying them for a gift, he asked the girl, "Tell me, if you please, whose daughter are you? Is there place in your father's house for me and my entourage to lodge?" The Abarbanel is not troubled by the fact that the text states that Eliezer *took* the dower gifts *before* he positively identified the girl as Abraham's kin. Rather, the text's meaning flows smoothly: He *took*

---

6 משתאה

7 ותמהר, ותרד, ותשקהו, ותכל, ותמהר, ותער, ותרץ, ותשאב.

8 היה מקום לחשוב אולי היה מפקפק בנסיון . . . לזה אומר לא כן הוא, כי אם אדרבה. והאיש משתאה, משתוקק אליה . . . כי אמר בלבו הנה מהנסיון ידעתי כי היא האשה . . . אך עדין אפשר יגמור הדבר ולא על ידי בדרכי זה . . . ולכן בראותי אשר כלו הגמלים לשתות לגמרי, אז נחה דעתו.

the bracelets, he asked her identity, *and then* he presented them to her.[9]

The text specifies that the two golden bracelets that Eliezer is holding are *aL YaDeHa*,[10] meaning either "on her hands," or "for her hands." *Ohr Hachayim* implicitly answers the question of how the text can say the bracelets are *on* her hands, when Eliezer has not yet offered them to Rebecca. The commentator suggests that the Torah uses the words "on her hands" to hint to us that Eliezer's bracelets miraculously fitted the girl Rebecca as if they were made to fit her arms' measurements.[11] *Sha'arei Aharon*, quoting *Tiferet Tzion*, adds that the perfect fit of Eliezer's bracelets was the final miraculous sign to the manservant that he had achieved his quest for his absent master. The commentator states that Abraham gave these bracelets to his trusted servant as a sign: When he found the girl who met all the other tests, the final signal to the manservant would be whether the two bracelets fit her arm perfectly. If they did—as the text here suggests—then Eliezer could be assured that she was the perfect match for his master's son, Isaac.[12]

Eliezer inquired of the girl, "Tell me please, who are you, and do you have a place for us to lodge?"[13] The *Netziv* seizes upon this phrase, laden with implicit questions: Eliezer is not simply asking the girl who her father is. He is really asking Rebecca to *tell* him *the story* [†] of her provenance.[14]

[†]Readers may recognize the letters of the word הגד, *HaGaD*, which forms the basis of the word *Haggadah*, the book read on Passover that *tells the story* of the redemption from Egypt.

---

[9] היותר נכון, ראשונה שאל בת מי את? ואחר כך נתנה לה. ולכן לא אמר הכתוב "ויתן לה," אלא "ויקח."

[10] על ידיה

[11] על ידיה: פירושו כאלו נעשו כשיעור זה

[12] דאברהם מסר הסימן לאליעזר מהצמידים דהאשה. שיהיו הצמידים כפי מדת ידיה. זהו לעד שהיא ראויה ליצחק.

[13] הגידי-נא

[14] הגידי-נא לי: משמעות הגדה. לפרש כל הפרטים שבענין. ומזה הבינה שאין השאלה רק לדעת שם אביה לבד, אלא כל היחוס.

TWENTY

ଧ୦ଓଧ୦ଓ

Rebecca Reveals
Her Identity

GENESIS 24:24–27

Understanding the servant's unexpressed query, Rebecca replies expansively: *I am the daughter of Betuel, who is the son of Milcah and Nahor.*[1] The dignified nature of Rebecca's reply is highlighted if the reader focuses on the Hebrew word for "I" that is used in this verse, *aNoCHi.*[2] The text uses the regal word for the personal pronoun to give weight to Rebecca's response, and stature to her character. Rebecca then replies to the servant's second inquiry: *We have plentiful straw and animal feed, as well as sufficient room for lodging.* Hearing the girl's responses, Eliezer gratefully bows low before God, saying, "Blessed is the God of my master, Abraham, who has not withheld *chesed* from me; and who has led me to the house of my master's kin." Eliezer now knows that it is *this girl* whom God has chosen for Isaac.

Rebecca's words allow the commentaries and the reader to view a more detailed image of the girl who will wed Isaac. The *Netziv* explains that Rebecca's first response to Eliezer establishes her

---

[1] ותאמר אליו, בת בתואל **אנכי,** בן מלכה אשר ילדה לנחור.

[2] אנכי

100

prominent lineage from both her parents.[3] Rabbi Abraham, son of the Rambam, mentions that the order of Rebecca's reply—she answers the stranger's two questions in the order they were asked—discloses her qualities of courtesy, intelligence and understanding.[4]

GENESIS 24:28–33

The girl ran to her mother's house to tell her all that had just transpired. We can envision the girl Rebecca, newly bedecked in golden nose-ring and bracelets, racing breathlessly into her mother's tent. She surprises her mother and the others present, excitedly relating her recent adventure. Her brother Lavan, seeing his sister's treasures and overhearing Rebecca's story, runs out of the women's compound all the way to the well to greet the stranger, who is still waiting there by his camels. Lavan invites Eliezer to come into his house, saying he has made room for both the stranger and his camels. Lavan then busies himself unharnessing and feeding Eliezer's beasts, providing his road-weary guests with water to wash the dust from their feet. He also sets a place for Eliezer, but the manservant demurs, saying he will not eat until he has told his tale. At this pronouncement, Lavan invites Eliezer to "Speak on!"

Rashi states that Rebecca ran directly to her mother's tent, and not to her father to relate the afternoon's events, because the women of that time had separate tents from the men where they attended to household and personal matters. Also, a daughter is more likely to confide in her mother than in her father.[5]

On the other hand, according to the Sforno, her brother Lavan ran in the other direction toward Eliezer, for one purpose only. Lavan's motivation was not primarily altruistic, extending hospitality to a complete stranger. Rather, his eye was on the stranger's heavy purse.[6]

---

[3] בן מלכה: והיא יחוס גדול יותר משארי בני נחור.

[4] ותאמר אליו בת בתואל: תשובה זו מורה לא רק אל האדיבות בלבד, אלא גם אל הפיקחות והתבונה.

[5] לבית אמה: דרך הנשים היתה להיות להן בית לישב בו למלאכתן, ואין הבת מגדת אלא לאמה.

[6] וירץ לבן אל האיש: לראות אורח עשיר שבא לעיר, לא להכניסו לביתו.

TWENTY-ONE

৪০ଓଃ৪০ଓଃ

The Manservant Meets
and Negotiates
with Rebecca's Family

In inviting Eliezer home, Lavan says to him, "Don't tarry out here by the well, as I have cleared the house for you." *Midrash Rabbah* (60.7) states that Lavan could not have had the time to ready the house for the guests, because as the text states, he ran to the well as soon as he saw the bedecked Rebecca and heard her tale. Yet the text emphasizes Lavan's assurance to Eliezer that he has *cleared the house* for him and his beasts. The commentary's solution is that Lavan, having learned from his sister that Eliezer is Abraham's messenger, quickly cleared the house of any trace of idolatry.[1] Lavan was clever enough to discern that any emissary from the house of Abraham—the man widely reputed even then as the father of monotheism—would be uncomfortable in the presence of idols. It was Lavan's intention to put Abraham's manservant at ease, not out of any consideration for Eliezer, but so that he would be caught off-guard, and thus pose an easy target for robbery. According to *Sha'arei Aharon*, Lavan has his eye on Eliezer's weighty saddlebags.[2]

In fact, the *Chatam Sofer*, quoted in *Sha'arei Aharon*, tells us that Lavan's lust for riches was insidious. The commentator relates that during the welcoming meal Lavan slipped a poison into Eliezer's

---

[1] ואנוכי פיניתי הבית: מטנופת של עבודת כוכבים.

[2] וירץ לבן אל האיש. מתחילה רץ כאיש נבהל להון, כששמע אדם עשיר בא, ורצה לגזול ממנו.

food, but that God's angel switched the platters, sparing Eliezer from certain death, and killing Betuel instead.[3] This angel may be the one mentioned in Genesis 24:40. There, Eliezer refers to the guardian angel whom his master, Abraham, prayed would shield Eliezer from all harm while on his mission.[4]

Yalkut Shimoni explains that it was specifically on account of Abraham's merit that the poisoned platter was switched. Eliezer was saved because he had yet to fulfill his mission. But why was Betuel singled out for death? The commentator recounts that Rebecca's father, Betuel, was the ruler of Aram-Naharayim, and as monarch he exercised his *droit de signeur* and customarily deflowered the virgin brides on their wedding nights. The elders of the town had recently approached Betuel, warning him that when his own daughter became a bride they expected that he would treat her no differently than he had treated their daughters; that he would commit the same abhorrent act upon Rebecca as well. They threatened to murder both him and his daughter if she went to her marriage bed an untouched virgin.[5]

By causing Betuel's untimely death, God averted this potential double-edged disaster, thereby preserving Rebecca for Isaac alone. This notion that Betuel has died early in Eliezer's negotiation is an opinion held by some of the commentaries. Radak, however, holds that Betuel was old and senescent.[6] While he was physically present throughout the marriage discussion, his place as head of the household has been supplanted by his son Lavan.

GENESIS 24:34–48

Rebecca's father, Betuel, her brother, Lavan, and Eliezer are gathered with the family's menfolk for the evening meal. With the

---

3 וייַשׂם לפניו לאֵכול: שֶׁנָתנו לו לאליעזר סם המת במאכלו, ובא המלאך והחליף את שלו בשל בתואל.

4 ויאמר [אברהם] אֵלָי: ד' אשר התהלכתי לפניו ישלח מלאכו אתך והצליח דרכך. . . .

5 ובזכות אברהם נתחלפה הקערה, ואכל בתואל ממנה ומת . . . ומפני מה מת בתואל? שהוא היה המלך בארם נהרים וכל בתולה שתנשא בועל אותה לילה ראשונה . . . נתקבצו כל השרים ואמרו: אם הוא עושה לבתו כשם שעשה לבנותינו, מוטב. ואם לאו, אנו הורגים אותו ואת בתו. לפיכך מת, כדי שינצל אליעזר ורבקה.

6 כי בתואל זקן היה.

untouched repast spread out before him, Eliezer recounts for the girl's family the deserving background of Isaac, his master's son. Radak points out that Eliezer is detailing Isaac's fortune in order to reinforce for them that Isaac's future bride will enjoy—along with Isaac—the benefits of Abraham's wealthy legacy. This is important lest Betuel fear that Ishmael, the son of Abraham's concubine, Hagar, will inherit the traditional, first-born's double portion.[7]

Eliezer then eloquently reiterates the conditions imposed upon him by his master for choosing a bride for his beloved son, Isaac. With his audience now in thrall, Eliezer skillfully proceeds to narrate for them how the God of Abraham guided him to their very well; how their selfsame daughter met his spontaneous test for *chesed*; how she labored cheerfully to water his caravan of camels, and how her revealed lineage led him inevitably to their tent.

---

7   אַף עַל פִּי שֶׁיֵּשׁ לוֹ בֵּן מֵאִשָּׁה אַחֶרֶת . . . נָתַן לוֹ [לְיִצְחָק] אֶת כָּל אֲשֶׁר לוֹ.

TWENTY–TWO

80 C3 80 C3

A Proposal of Marriage

GENESIS 24:49

E liezer, finally arriving at the purpose of his mission, appeals to Rebecca's family to deal *kindly* and *truthfully* with him and with his master Abraham.[1] He presses them for an answer: Will they allow him to take their daughter, Rebecca, from the bosom of her family to a distant land to wed Abraham's son? The words "kindness and truth"[2] may seem incongruous in the context of negotiating an arranged marriage. What is the nature of the "kindness and truth" that Eliezer seeks here? The Sforno interprets sending one's daughter in marriage to a distant place, relinquishing a betrothal to a local youth and the attendant closeness to one's future grandchildren, as the kindness, or *chesed*, that Betuel and Lavan can grant to Abraham.[3] And Ibn Ezra interprets "truthfulness," or *eMeT*,[4] to mean that Betuel will not renege on this *chesed* once he has given Eliezer his word.[5]

---

[1] ועתה, עם ישכם עשים חסד ואמת את אדני, הגידו לי. ואם לא, הגידו לי, ואפנה על ימין או על שמאל.

[2] חסד ואמת

[3] חסד: כדי להפיק רצון אדוני, תבטלו רצונכם ותסכימו לשלוח את בתכם בארץ מרחק, ולא תחושו לקנות בה קרובים בארצכם.

[4] אמת

[5] ואמת: לקיים דבר החסד.

It is here that Eliezer lives up to Abraham's expectations of him as a consummate negotiator. He already has exposed his intention to obtain Rebecca as a bride for his master's son. But sensing the gold-lust in Betuel and Lavan, he cannot resist backing off a bit, saying to them in the second half of this verse, "Tell me now, sirs, if you agree to my proposal. But if you do not agree, do not hesitate to tell me that also, so that I can pursue my options one way or the other."[6] The text's Hebrew expression for "one way or the other" is *that I may turn to the right or to the left.*[7] According to Rashi, Eliezer was presenting a veiled ultimatum to Betuel and Lavan:

> Do not think that you are the only kin of my wealthy master whom I can visit. On the one hand I can consider the daughters of Isaac's brother, Ishmael, or I can journey to the land to the left, and consider the daughters of Abraham's nephew, Lot.[8]

The *Netziv* posits that Eliezer had not the slightest intention of abandoning Rebecca now that he had been Divinely directed to her. Rather, that Eliezer knew full well that Rebecca was the chosen bride, and that if he could not obtain her from Betuel and Lavan via the straightforward approach (as in verses 34–48), then he would go about acquiring her in some undisclosed roundabout manner.[9]

---

6 . . . הגידו לי, ואם לא, הגידו לי, ואפנה על ימין או על שמאל.

7 על ימין או על שמאל

8 על ימין: מבנות ישמעאל. על שמאל: מבנות לוט, שהיה יושב לשמאלו של אברהם.

9 על ימין או על שמאל: אחפש עצות לדבר; וימין ושמאל הוא קניני לאופנים שונים בדרך הישר,
או בדרך עקלתון.

GENESIS 24:50–51

Following Eliezer's ploy, Lavan and Betuel are quick to respond that as God's hand truly seems to be directing this matter,[10] Eliezer should take Rebecca to be Isaac's wife and promptly return with her to his master. Even idolaters such as Lavan and Betuel recognize from Eliezer's narrative that Divine providence was at work orchestrating this match. The Talmud in *Moed Katan* (18b) credits verse 50 with being the Bible's proof-text for the notion of God's intimate involvement with matchmaking.[11] The Talmud quotes Lavan's and Betuel's response to Eliezer that "this matter originated with God."

GENESIS 24:52–56

Elated that Rebecca's family has agreed to the match, Eliezer bows gratefully to God and then reaches into his saddlebags and brings forth jewelry wrought of silver and of gold, and fine clothing fit for a bride, and presents them all to Rebecca as a gift from his master. Rebecca's brother and mother, however, receive only token gifts. From this point forward, the text makes no further mention of Betuel. *Midrash Rabbah* (60.12), concurring with *Chatam Sofer* and *Yalkut Shimoni*, holds that Betuel was killed because he sought to prevent the match.[12] In contrast, Radak states that Betuel is still alive, but that Lavan has assumed the role of family spokesman in Betuel's dotage, and that Betuel is not mentioned in the text because he is no longer of any consequence.[13]

Freed of the burden of his mission, Eliezer, along with his entourage and Rebecca's family, eat and drink a festive meal well into the night celebrating the betrothal. Early the next morning, Eliezer and his men awaken and beg their leave to return to their master Abraham. Because the text reports in verse 55 that only Rebecca's brother and mother try to delay Eliezer's leave-taking—again making no mention of her father, Betuel—*Sha'arei Aharon* reiterates that Betuel himself ate from the poisoned food Lavan had intended for

---

[10] מד' יצא הדבר.

[11] מד' אשה לאיש. מן התורה דכתיב "ויען לבן ובתואל ויאמרו מד' יצא הדבר."

[12] ובתואל היכן הוא? ביקש לעקב, וניגף בלילה.

[13] לאחיה ולאמה: כי הם היו עקר הבית כי בתואל זקן היה.

Eliezer, and that as a result, Betuel died during the night (see Chapter 21).[14]

 Yalkut Shimoni credits Eliezer with the ability to perceive Rebecca's guardian angel. The angel has kept Rebecca from harm as she came of age in her father's house. Now he is tarrying outside Lavan's tent, a silent sentinel eager to accompany Rebecca safely on her journey to Isaac.[15] Eliezer, viewing the impatient angel, redoubles his efforts to take the girl Rebecca right away, despite Lavan's and his mother's attempts to deter his immediate departure. Eliezer persists, reminding them that he is but God's messenger in this mission, and that they should not stand in his way.

---

[14] בתואל היה אוכל מההוא תבשיל ומצאוהו בשחרית שהוא מת.

[15] והשכים העבד בבקר וראה את המלאך עומד וממתין לו בחוץ.

TWENTY-THREE

୫୦୯ଽ୫୦୯ଽ

Rebecca Meets Abraham's Conditions and Accepts the Marriage Proposal

GENESIS 24:57–58

Finally, Lavan and his mother appear to accede, saying to Eliezer, "We will summon the damsel and hear from her own lips" whether she will agree to accompany you now.[1] Responding to her summons, and at their specific inquiry, Rebecca states unhesitatingly, "I will go." Rashi derives from this episode the principle that a maiden cannot be wed, according to Jewish law, except with her consent.[2] The Radak fine-tunes this notion, pointing to verse 51 as the place where Rebecca's *first* consent to the match was obtained. There, Lavan and Betuel blessed the match, and presented the consenting Rebecca to Eliezer to signify that the negotiations were at an end, saying, "Behold Rebecca is standing here before you, take her and go."[3] The commentaries infer that Rebecca had to have consented there, for to this day a single girl is never betrothed without her permission.

---

[1] ויאמרו נקרא לנער[ה], ונשאלה את פיה.

[2] מכאן שאין משיאין את האשה אלא מדעתה.

[3] ונשאלה את פיה. נשאליה מה תאמר אם תרצה ללכת מעתה, כי **מן הנראה** שעל הנשואים שאלוה כשאמרו: "הנה רבקה לפניך" (פסוק נ"א), כי אין משיאין את האשה שלא מדעתה.

Rebecca's laconic response, *eLeCH* [4] (*I will go*), is resounding in its speed and forthrightness. The girl whom God has selected to be the second matriarch is not a passive pawn. At the well, when Eliezer asked her for a sip of water, she suggested of her own volition that she water the stranger's camels as well; a daunting task. Here, this same girl, faced with the opportunity to leave her home and birthplace, her parents and brother, stands straight and sure in their presence and answers "I will go!" to their query. She was intelligent enough to discern that her family wished to keep her in their possession for a twelvemonth—ostensibly to prepare her bridal goods—while in reality they sought to extract from Abraham's servant more in the way of a substantial bride-price. *Sha'arei Aharon* says as much.[5]

Rashi suggests that Rebecca's famed reply was uttered assertively, not simply compliantly. She was telling her family that with *or without* their consent, she was determined to go with Eliezer and to wed Isaac.[6] Otherwise, suggests *Siftei Chachamim*, in response to her family's question (*Will you go with this man?*), Rebecca could have uttered a simple "Yes."[7] *Ma'ayna Shel Torah* explains that Rebecca's assertive answer reflected her faith that her betrothal to Abraham's son was Divinely orchestrated.[8] How else could she have found the strength to stand alone against her brother's and mother's wishes that she remain?

GENESIS 24:59–61

Having failed in their design to delay Rebecca's departure and enrich themselves, Rebecca's family has no choice but to send her on her way, accompanied by her beloved nurse, Deborah, and her handmaids. (The commentator Chizkuni points out that Rebecca's long-time nurse, Deborah, is the unnamed "governess" alluded to in

---

4 אלך

5 כשנגמר השדוך שאמר "הנה רבקה לפניך, קך ולך,". . . וייציא [אליעזר] כלי כסף וזהב ונתן לרבקה, וללבן נתן מגדנות, ולא כסף וזהב . . . על כן צדד צדדים לעכב הדבר . . . ורבקה שהיתה חכמה גדולה והבינה . . . על כן אמרה "אלך."

6 ותאמר "אלך." מעצמי, ואף אם אינכם רוצים.

7 למה כתיב "אלך" ולא כתיב "הן" או "כן"?

8 ותאמר אלך. אפילו אם לא תרצו, שכן **מן השמים** יכריחו אתכם להסכים.

the text at verse 59. We know this because much later in Rebecca's saga, the Torah takes care to record the death of "Deborah, the governess of Rebecca" at Genesis 35:8.[9] We will discuss its significance when we reach that verse.)

Ramban points out that once her family gave her their final permission to go, Rebecca sprang into action. She immediately summoned her handmaids to ride out on the very camels she had watered the day before.[10] The commentator *Akeidat Yitzchak* stresses that notwithstanding Rebecca's youth and provincial inexperience, she wrested control of her leave-taking from Eliezer and gathered her maidens herself, mustering them and all their belongings and swiftly readying them for the journey.[11]

As the caravan is poised to leave her family's compound, Lavan blesses his sister. The reader will note that there has been no mention in the text of a dowry gift to Rebecca from her family. All the wedding gifts enumerated here have been flowing only from Abraham. *Midrash Rabbah* (60.12) interprets this to mean that the only "dowry" Rebecca receives are Lavan's words of blessing.[12] *Matnot Kehuna*, a supercommentary on *Midrash Rabbah*, presents an even less flattering portrait of Lavan, adding that not only did he gift her solely with words and no material wealth, but even those few words of blessing were hollow, uttered only with his lips, and not from his heart.[13]

Lavan calls out to Rebecca: "Our sister! May you be the forebear of tens of thousands; may your children be worthy to inherit the gates of their enemies."[14] Rashi's interpretation opposes that of *Midrash Rabbah* that Lavan's parting words were hollow. Rather, Rashi relates Lavan's words to the blessing given to Abraham and Isaac after the *Akeida* in Genesis 22:17. The Hebrew words are nearly identical. There, as here, the blessing is that God will "greatly multiply"

---

[9] ואת מנקתה. בנעוריה, והזכירה עכשיו שלא תתמה לכשתגיע לפרשת מיתתה, בראשית ל"ה:ח.

[10] אחר שנתנו רשות שתלך רבקה ומיניקתה ועבד אברהם ואנשיו, קמה רבקה וקראה נערותיה ותרכבנה על הגמלים.

[11] ותקם היא ונערותיה. אמר שעם היותה קטנה נתאמצה וקמה בעצמה ונערותיה עמה ותלכנה וכו'.

[12] לא היו מפרינין אלא בפה.

[13] לא היו נותנין לה נדוניא אך דבר שפתים . . . בפה ולא בלב.

[14] את היי לאלפי רבבה, **ויירש זרעך את שער שונאיו.**

Abraham's "seed," and his children will "inherit the gates of their enemies."[15]

According to Rashi, Lavan is aware of God's blessing to Abraham and Isaac atop Mount Moriah, and in his parting words to Rebecca he seeks to invoke God's same promise of fertility upon his sister.[16]

Moreover, says Rashi, Lavan's wishes are specifically directed to the secret hope of the bride-to-be: That even though she lived in a time of polygamous mores, she would yet be privileged to be the beloved one-and-only wife of her husband, and sole mother of his children.[17] Sforno interprets Lavan's blessing similarly, adding that he prays that Isaac will cherish Rebecca and appreciate her goodness and that only through her—and not through another wife—will God's promise of fertility be fulfilled.[18]

---

[15] והרבה ארבה את זרעך . . . **וירש זרעך את שער אויביו.**

[16] את וזרעך תקבלו אותה ברכה שנאמר לאברהם בהר המוריה.

[17] יהי רצון, שיהא אותו הזרע ממך ולא מאשה אחרת.

[18] היי נוחה לבעלך בדרכי טובך באופן שאת בלבד, ולא אשה אחרת.

TWENTY-FOUR

৵৩৵৩

Rebecca's Perilous Journey to Isaac

O n their way at last, the caravan was comprised first, of Eliezer, Abraham's manservant, walking briskly before the lead camel, holding fast to the reins of Rebecca's beast. Ramban explains that Eliezer is mindful of the seriousness of the last leg of his mission. It is for this reason that the text in verse 61 states that *they followed after the man, and the servant took Rebecca and traveled on his way.* The *p'shat* explanation, according to the commentator, is that Eliezer knows the way, and therefore he is in the lead. Also, that his sworn duty is to watch over Rebecca, and to deliver her safely to Isaac.[1] Rebecca's governess, along with her numerous handmaids, followed in line on Abraham's camels.

Alshich points out that we learn from this verse how—for the sake of propriety—neither Eliezer nor his men reach out to assist Rebecca as she climbs onto her camel. As the text states, *Rebecca and her damsels rode upon the camels,* to stress that the women assisted one another to mount the camels. The men kept to themselves.[2]

---

[1] אחרי האיש, כי הוא מורה הדרך לפניהם. וטעם ויקח העבד את רבקה וילך: לספר בזריזותו כי אחרי צאתו מן העיר ותלכנה כל הנשים אחריו. לקח העבד רבקה עמו: לא תפרד ממנו ולשמרה בדרך מכל מכשול.

[2] ותקם וכו'. אמר כי אפילו להרכיבה על הגמל לא היה על ידי האיש, כי אם היא ונערותיה ותרכבנה.

Torah Temima and its supercommentary point out that the text understands how simple proximity in such a situation could perhaps lead first to impure thoughts, and then—potentially disastrously—to improper deeds. If Rebecca had been riding the camel directly in front of Eliezer, so that she was constantly in his line of sight for the duration of the journey, he may have begun to frame fantasies about the beauty he was escorting.[3] Thus, the text places Eliezer at the head of the caravan, with Rebecca behind him. The only sights in his line of vision are stretches of uninhabited road and rocky hillsides.

Yalkut Shimoni explains that Rebecca and her damsels were prepared to endure the rigors of the seventeen-day journey from Aram-Naharayim to Hebron. They are stunned, therefore, to be nearing Abraham's home a mere three hours from the moment of their leave-taking from Lavan. The commentator emphasizes the miraculous foreshortening of their journey, attributing it to Rebecca's guardian angel whose Divine task it was to see Rebecca safely from her family's tent to Isaac's. The angel was unwilling to risk leaving Rebecca in Eliezer's charge overnight, specifically to avoid tempting the stalwart servant, so the angel miraculously caused the caravan to arrive at its destination before dark.[4]

---

[3] אחרי האיש. ולא לפני האיש. מלמד שלא יהלך אדם אחורי אשה, משום הרהור.

[4] מקרית ארבע עד חרן, מהלך יז' ימים . . . בשביל שלא יתיחד העבד עם הנערה בלילה, נקפצה הארץ לפניו, ובשלש שעות בא לחברון לעת תפילת הערב.

TWENTY–FIVE

ഇരുജ്ഞ

The Unexpected Encounter
of Rebecca and Isaac

GENESIS 24:62–65

A s evening approaches, the caravan comes upon a lone man in an open field. This lone figure is Isaac, who has returned to his home from the north, and is meditating in the field before nightfall. At this moment his eyes behold the caravan of camels approaching. Rashi wonders: Why is Isaac out in the field at this time? He answers that Isaac had just returned from his own mission to fetch Hagar for his father, in order to soothe Abraham's loneliness in his very old age.[1] Radak is of the opinion that Abraham's sizable livestock holdings necessitated that Isaac travel frequently between the northern provinces and his home in Hebron. It was on such a homeward trek that Isaac met Eliezer's caravan.[2]

The reader may wonder why the text portrays its two main protagonists encountering one another for the first time in this field, in the middle of nowhere? Why does Rebecca not meet Isaac in the comfort and security of Abraham's tent?

The *Netziv* is singular in his understanding of this famed encounter on a purely psychological plane, and the commentator has

---

[1] שהלך להביא הגר לאברהם אביו שישאנה.

[2] היה לו ליצחק מקנה או שום עסק באותו המקום הנקרא באר לחי ראי, והיה הולך ושב שם.

115

no quarrel at all with an uninhabited field as the backdrop. Rebecca is overwhelmed by her first vision of a man who is deep in contemplation, his arms raised in prayer, the setting sun at his back. She sees a tall figure, clad in the flowing robes of a nomad, perhaps even wrapped in a voluminous prayer shawl. With his arms outstretched, his ethereal silhouette limned in gold, Rebecca may have wondered: Who is this? Is it an angel of the Lord? Is it a man? She is awestruck and perhaps a bit frightened by this unexpected sight.[3] Isaac—raising his downcast eyes at the conclusion of his prayer—is startled by the sudden arrival of the caravan. He then sees Rebecca, who at that moment also is staring at him, a seeming specter.

Several commentators understand the moment of encounter between Rebecca and Isaac to be one of immediate connection and instant attraction. Z'ror Hamor states unequivocally that when their eyes met across the expanse of the field, they knew that each was the other's intended mate.[4] Mishna d'Rabi Eliezer, a commentary on Midrash Rabbah, characterizes Isaac as exceedingly handsome. The commentator uses the Hebrew phrase YeFeH To'aR,[5] an expression used very sparingly in the Bible, and only to describe the physical beauty of heroes and heroines such as Joseph, Rachel and Esther.[6] Breishit Rabbati adds that Rebecca's vision of Isaac instantly fulfilled her romantic fantasy of a husband.[7]

According to the Netziv, just as the God of Abraham directed Eliezer to encounter Rebecca at the well, so, too, God is orchestrating the apparent chance meeting between Isaac and Rebecca in this open field. The commentator is certain that it is God's design that Rebecca's initial encounter with Isaac will set the tone for their future relationship. God does not want their marriage to be filled with the daily verbal jousting between a wife and her husband. God's intent is that from Rebecca's very first glimpse of Isaac she will be at once

---

3 ספר הכתוב כי . . . ית' סיבב שיפגע יצחק ברבקה בדרך ותהא נבעתת ממנו בתחלת הכרתה
אותו . . . בעודו עומד ומתפלל והיה אז כמלאך אלקים נורא מאד . . . ראתה ידיו שתוחות
בתפילה. על כן נבעתה מאד.

4 ותשא רבקה את עיניה ותרא את יצחק. להורות שהיא בת זוגו, כלומר, כמו שהוא נשא עיניו,
כן היא נשתה עיניה. . . .

5 יפה תאר

6 לפי שהיה [יצחק] יפה תאר כמו יוסף . . .

7 צפתה שידו שתוחה, הרהרה תאוה שכיבת בעל.

smitten and reverent, even viewing him as slightly otherworldly. This first meeting is to set the pattern, and over the course of their life together Rebecca will lack the heart to confront Isaac, even if the truth is on her side. She will thus be driven to find other means to achieve her righteous ends.[8]

The reader is led to question, at this juncture, why the *Netziv* is definitive in his characterization of Rebecca's relationship with Isaac as one where she must hold her peace and take only furtive action, even if her righteous end will ultimately justify the furtive means. Or even why, coming on the heels of our description of the matriarch Sarah—a woman who certainly confronted her husband Abraham in order to achieve *her* righteous ends—we are affirmatively told that the second matriarch will achieve *her* goals by *avoiding* confrontation with Isaac. The reason cannot be that Rebecca is timid, as we already have witnessed her forthrightness and bravery in the face of strong familial pressure. The commentator implies that it is God's wish that Isaac be shielded by his wife and spared any contention. Rebecca's task is to soothe her husband's body and soul, as she takes the matriarchy one generation further along toward fulfillment of God's promise. Perhaps Isaac's trauma and triumph at the *Akeida* was wrenching enough for one lifetime.

Mesmerized by Isaac's stare, Rebecca falls from atop the camel. The commentators differ on the nature of Rebecca's "fall." Did she actually ever hit the ground? Did she injure herself? Rashi's interpretation is that Rebecca merely inclined her body deferentially upon seeing Isaac's splendid appearance.[9]

Siftei Chachamim explains why Rashi felt it necessary to depart from the *p'shat*, which would seem to clearly indicate that Rebecca actually fell to the ground. This supercommentator on Rashi states that had Rebecca actually fallen from her seat on the camel onto the ground, the text would have said "she fell off the camel, onto the ground," instead of "she fell from atop the camel."[10] These commentators interpret the text to mean that Rebecca's act was

---

8 ויצחק בא, וגו'. אם היה העבד בא עמה תחלה לבית אברהם . . . לא היתה נבעתת מפחד
יצחק, והיתה מתנהגת עמו כמו כל אשה עם בעלה. והזמין ד' לפניו באותה שעה אשתו . . .
וכל זה הקדמה להסיפור . . . ומכל מקום לא מצאה רבקה לב להעמיד את יצחק על דעתה
דברים נוכחים, כי היא יודעת האמת. . . .

9 ראתה אותו הדור . . . הטתה עצמה לארץ, ולא הגיעה עד הקרקע.

10 ותפל מעל הגמל. ולא כתיב מהגמל או ותפל לארץ.

volitional. Sforno agrees, saying that Rebecca merely inclined her head out of obeisance to Isaac.[11]

Rashbam also has Rebecca remaining on the camel's back, but has her shifting her position from astride the camel—her stance throughout the journey—to side-saddle, which is the more modest saddle position, but is difficult to maintain safely during a long ride.[12]

In contrast to those who feel that Rebecca's fall from the camel was volitional, *Yalkut Shimoni* is certain that Rebecca's "fall" from the camel was an actual plunge. Rebecca foresaw in a flash of Divine inspiration the strife that would result from Esav, one of their future children, and so shaken was she that she lost her balance and fell to the ground.[13] Rebecca's fall was in fact a serious one, so much so that her accidental drop from such a height resulted in internal injury. The commentator goes so far as to state that this fall caused her to rupture the physical signs of her virginity.[14] Alternatively, Rebecca may have ruptured her virginal membranes while she was *still astride* the camel on her ride to Hebron. This might be the reason for Rashbam's focus on her mounted position during the journey. After all, this was likely her first trip by camel any distance from her home. Her father and brother were loath to let this untouched beauty out of their sight except to fetch water at the public well on that fateful day. Therefore, any injury to her maidenhood had to have occurred after she mounted Abraham's camel. This delicate issue is dealt with by the commentaries later on in Rebecca's story, the morning after Isaac has taken her to his heart and to his bed.

Having composed herself following her "fall" from the camel, Rebecca inquires of the servant Eliezer, "Who is this man in yonder field who is coming toward us?" The servant replies, "He is my master [Isaac]." Immediately after learning the man's identity, Rebecca draws her veil across her face. *Sha'arei Aharon* interprets this as Rebecca modestly veiling all but her eyes from Isaac's perusal.[15] Sforno teaches us that Rebecca's veil covered her entire face, even her eyes. She sought to protect herself from Isaac's reflected glory, much as

11 הכניעה ראשה בהיותה על הגמל, לכבוד יצחק.

12 לצניעות. לפי שהיתה רוכבת כמו איש משום ביעתות.

13 לפי שראתה ברוח הקודש שעתיד לצאת ממנו עשו הרשע, נזדעזעה.

14 ותפל מעל הגמל. ונעשת מוכת עץ, ויצא ממנה דם בתולים.

15 נתנה הצעיף על פניה שלא היה נראה ממנה כי אם עיניה.

Moses required a veil to cover his face after his confrontation with God at Sinai.[16]

GENESIS 24:66

After Rebecca veils herself, Eliezer greets Isaac, overflowing with the news of the success of his mission. He recounts for Isaac all that he did, and all that transpired since he left Abraham's tents bent on his quest. Rashi states that Eliezer divulged to Isaac in detail the miracles which God had wrought, leading him to select Rebecca as the chosen bride. For instance, how God answered his prayers and summoned the girl Rebecca to the well, and also how God foreshortened the journey in order to bring this matter to a rapid conclusion.[17] Rashbam elaborates, saying that Eliezer enumerated the miracles which pervaded his visit in Aram-Naharayim in order to make it absolutely clear to Isaac that God's presence at every step of his quest is the evidence that it was God who chose this girl Rebecca to fulfill Isaac's destiny.[18]

Rav Bachya helps us to understand Rashi and Rashbam, both of whose interpretations of this verse invoke God's miracles, when in fact the text itself makes no mention of God here. The commentator reasons that when the Bible states "all that *he* did," the word "he" can refer both to all that *Eliezer* did to fulfill his obligation to Abraham, as well as all that *He*—God—did, miraculously, to lead Eliezer to Rebecca.[19] Isaac is now assured that it was God's providence that led Eliezer to select Rebecca as his mate.

---

[16] ותתכס. כי יראה מהביט, על דרך ויסתר משה פניו.

[17] גלה לו נסים שנעשו לו, שקפצה לו הארץ, ושנזדמנה לו רבקה בתפלתו.

[18] להודיעו נסים שנעשו לו, לדעת כי בת מזלו היא.

[19] "אשר עשה." מתייחס גם לאליעזר וגם להקב"ה.

TWENTY–SIX

Isaac Takes Rebecca as His Wife, Loves Her, and is Comforted after His Mother's Death

GENESIS 24:67

And so Isaac brought her into the tent of his mother Sarah, and he took Rebecca unto him and she became his wife, and he loved her; and Isaac was then comforted after [the loss of] his mother.[1]

Some commentaries suggest that Isaac returned home from the *Akeida* to find his mother still alive (see Chapter 11). Even if Isaac were fortunate enough to have spent time with Sarah before she died, it must still have been wrenching for him to bring his bride into his mother's empty bedroom even some years later. According to the *p'shat*, however, one can infer that Sarah had died without ever seeing her son Isaac again. According to Radak, three years have passed since Sarah's death.[2] Ever since her death, Sarah's private tent has been maintained in pristine condition. One can but imagine Isaac's anguish if upon his return after the *Akeida*, he found that his mother had not survived the shock of his near-death. He surely could not bring himself to enter the tent where he last left his mother sleeping in the predawn as he and his father slipped out on their way to Mount Moriah. How much more difficult must it be, therefore, for

---

1 ויבא יצחק האהלה שרה אמו, ויקח את רבקה ותהי לו לאשה ויאהבה, וינחם יצחק אחרי אמו.

2 היו לה שלש שנים שמתה כשלקחה יצחק רבקה.

120

Isaac *now* even to contemplate supplanting his mother's mythic presence with a new bride? Similarly, how strong must the shoulders of his new bride be to be able to bear the weight of Sarah's fabled stature! It is in their interpretations of this verse that the commentaries demonstrate their exquisite sensitivity to the fraught psychological drama that the protagonists are silently enacting.

Ramban sets the scene. He describes how Sarah's private tent, so long a focal point for her converted followers, had been kept by these women exactly as it had been on the day that Sarah died. Sarah's faithful—who kept the tent of their honored mistress—were wary that Abraham would bring another woman into the matriarch's tent. They were certain that its only fitting and proper occupant would be Isaac's future wife. With the passing of years, all were hopeful that once Isaac married they could naturally end their vigil. When Isaac escorted Rebecca into his father's enclave that evening, led her to the entrance to his mother's house, and then ultimately into its sanctum to make her his wife, the wait was over for all concerned.[3]

While Sarah's faithful kept her tent *structurally* intact for three years after her death, *Midrash Rabbah* describes the four *spiritual* elements that graced Sarah's home and that vanished with her death. First, during Sarah's lifetime, a Divine cloud hovered over the door to her tent. At her death, the cloud evaporated, only to return upon Rebecca's setting foot at the tent's entrance.[4] *Yefei To'ar* identifies Sarah's "cloud" as the Divine presence and Holy inspiration. For not only did Sarah and Rebecca oversee the physical necessities of their household; they also embodied its spiritual requirements.[5] Their supremely intelligent and understanding souls merited that the cloud signifying the Divine presence should bless their tent.

Rebecca becomes heir to the second of Sarah's hallmark qualities upon her entering the venerated tent. During Sarah's lifetime, her tent's doors were open to all, particularly encouraging women to approach her home and partake of its bounties. While she generously dispensed food to road-weary wayfarers and to curious

---

[3] כי מעת שמתה שרה לא נטו אהלה. כי אמרו לא תבא אשה אחרת אל אהל הגבירה הנכבדת. וכאשר ראה רבקה, הביאה אל האהל ההוא לכבודה, ושם לקחה.

[4] כל ימים שהיתה שרה קיימת היה ענן קשור על פתח אהלה. כיון שמתה פסק אותו ענן וכיון שבאת רבקה חזר אותו ענן.

[5] אשר פירש ענן השכינה והנבואה. וזה כי שרה ורבקה הסתכלו לא לבד בעניני הגופניים, אך גם בעניני הרוחניים, ונתעלו בשכלם עד שזכו לענן השכינה.

others, Sarah also treated them to their first taste of ethical monotheism. This physical and spiritual largesse ceased abruptly when Sarah died. In reality, then, her death left a physical and spiritual void, and the mere presence of the tent these three years—absent the woman—was a daily reminder that Sarah's successor was awaited. *Midrash Rabbah* (60.16) teaches us that when Rebecca became mistress of Sarah's tent, this same bountiful generosity returned.[6]

Third, even when Sarah had kneaded her dough to bake bread, *challah*, for her guests, the visitors watched her recite a prayer and tear off a symbolic corner of her dough, thereby drawing God's presence into her dwelling. Sarah did not merely preach the Godly life; she *lived* it, and anyone entering her tent witnessed this. This, too, was implicit in Rebecca's legacy from Sarah, and the *mephorshim* confirm that with Rebecca's presence in the tent, she brought *mitzvot*—the observance of God's commandments—back into Sarah's home.[7]

Finally, Rebecca's weekly kindling of the Sabbath candles restored the physical and spiritual light that Sarah had ignited during her lifetime. Sarah's tent, dark and lifeless for three years, was returned to its splendor under Rebecca's ministry.[8]

Of these four enumerated recurrences that are described in *Midrash Rabbah*, Rashi quotes only three of them: Sarah's challah, her Sabbath candles, and the Divine cloud. *Siftei Chachamim* explains that Rashi quotes these three because they relate particularly to a woman's obligation to fulfill these *mitzvot* as she presides over her home. The fourth *mitzvah*—of hospitality to guests—which Rashi does not mention, is just as incumbent upon men as it is upon women. After all, both Sarah and Abraham welcomed wayfarers and pilgrims into their tents all the years of their lives. Just as Sarah had brought God's benediction into her home as she baked her bread, so did Rebecca do so. As Sarah blessed the lights ushering in the Sabbath, so did Rebecca. The Divine cloud that covered Sarah's tent

---

6 כל הימים שהיתה שרה קיימת היו דלתות פתוחות לרווחה. וכיון שמתה שרה, פסקה אותה
הרווחה. וכיון שבאת רבקה, חזרה אותה הרווחה.

7 וכל ימים שהיתה שרה קיימת היה ברכה משולחת בעיסה. וכיון שמתה שרה, פסקה אותה
הברכה. כיון שבאת רבקה, חזרה.

8 כל ימים שהיתה שרה קיימת נר דולק מלילי שבת ועד לילי שבת. וכיון שמתה, פסק
אותו הנר. וכיון שבאת רבקה, חזר.

during her lifetime symbolized the holiness of the marital bond. And it is because Sarah adhered to the *mitzvah* of *nidah*—permitted and prohibited sexual relations between a wife and her husband—that the Divine cloud hovered over her tent and preserved its inhabitants.[9]

Sha'arei Aharon states that Sarah's observance of the latter *mitzvah* of *nidah* transformed her simple tent into a spiritually holy sanctuary, allowing God's spirit to permeate her home. So holy was Sarah's tent that the commentary therefore likens Sarah's death to the destruction of the holy Temple.[10] The same Divine, protective cloud that dissipated with Sarah's death reappeared when Rebecca took over.

The Talmud (*Shabbat* 31b), confirms the importance of these three *mitzvot: nidah, challah*, and kindling the Sabbath candles, in a woman's life. In fact, the *failure* to keep these commandments generates a state of unholiness, rendering a woman vulnerable during the hours of childbirth, when she is most susceptible to danger.[11] The Talmud then wonders: if *women* are held accountable during childbirth, at what time in their lives are *men* held accountable before God? Reish Lakish answers: Men are vulnerable whenever they cross "the narrow bridge" between safety and danger.[12] That is to say, as Rabbi Steinsaltz explains in his commentary,[†] men traverse "the narrow bridge" throughout their entire lives, and thus are *always* accountable for their actions. A woman also faces accountability at all times, but she is most vulnerable when she crosses "the narrowest bridge," which occurs when she is at the point of childbirth.[13]

Abraham recognized the pivotal role Isaac's future wife would play in continuing his and Sarah's legacy, and therefore he expended great resources to find a proper wife for him. The *Chatam Sofer*

[†]Steinsaltz, A. (1989). *Babylonian Talmud* (Israel: The Israel Institute for Talmudic Publications), Vol. 2, *Shabbat* 31b.

---

[9] כנגד ג' מצות שהנשים מצוות בהן. כנגד חלה, "ברכה מצוייה." כנגד הדלקה, "נר דלוק." וענן קשור הוא ענן השכינה, וזהו לכבוד קדושת טהרה. שהיתה [שרה] זהירה בנדתה לטהר עצמה, כי הטהרה מביאה לידי רוח הקודש.

[10] לולא שׂשרה היתה מתנהגת בטהרה, לא היה מקום להשראת השכינה . . . ומשמתה שרה, נסתלקה השכינה, כלומר נחרב המשכן.

[11] על שלש עבירות נשים מתות בשעת לידתן: על שאינן זהירות בנדה, בחלה, ובהדלקת הנר.

[12] וגברי, היכא מיבדקי? אמר ריש לקיש: בשעה שעוברים על הגשר.

[13] שבשעת הסכנה נפרעים מאדם על כל חטאיו.

beautifully characterizes the Jewish woman's role.[14] It is *she* who will build the proper Jewish home by seeing to both the religious and the concrete needs of her household. All this is borne on her shoulders, sustained by her will.[15] Rebecca embodied *Chatam Sofer*'s ideal: by her observance of *mitzvot*, she restored the splendor of Sarah's tent.

Thus, for both women and men, a Jewish life is contingent on the observance of *mitzvot*. The *mitzvot* that Rebecca inherited from Sarah and incorporated into her life, continued the nascent Jewish religion and propelled it into the next generation.

The Zohar (133b) confirms the exclusivity of Sarah's tent in everyone's consciousness. Even the master Abraham respected its sanctity. Not only did he restrain his concubine from venturing inside it, but even he could not bring himself to enter her tent after Sarah's death.[16] In fact, Radak recounts that in keeping with the custom of those times, a husband and wife each retained separate tents within which to conduct their daily routines. When it was time for conjugal relations, the husband generally came to his wife's tent.[17]

In Sarah's absence, then, Abraham had no need to enter her tent, and he did not do so. Sarah's tent stood empty and unoccupied from the time of her death until Isaac brought Rebecca home. All the commentators agree that Rebecca arrived in Isaac's bed untouched by any man; neither her father, Betuel—the monarch of Aram-Naharayim—nor her brother Lavan, nor any admiring shepherd or camel drover, nor the servant Eliezer had ever laid a hand upon her in an improper way. Of course this issue, delicate though it may be, is of paramount concern in assuring the integrity of Abraham's dynasty. For if Rebecca had been taken by another man before she arrived in Isaac's tent, she could theoretically be carrying another man's child. This would have been insupportable.

Although the *mephorshim* agree unequivocally that Rebecca was a virgin, they disagree over whether or not she possessed *physical signs* as proof of her virginity. *Yalkut Shimoni* presents both

---

[14] לבנות בית בישראל

[15] עיקר עבודת ד' ית' וגם לרבות כל עניני עולם הזה. **באשר היא תלויה**, כי ידוע לכל משכיל, יודע ומבין.

[16] ואברהם אע"ג דאינסיב, לא עאל בההוא ביתא, ולא אעיל לה להאי אתתא תמן . . . ובאהל דשרה, לא אתחזי אתתא אחרא, אלא רבקה.

[17] כי כן היה מנהג בימים ההם להיות אהל לאיש בפני עצמו ולאשה בפני עצמה, וכשהיו שוכבים יחד היה האיש בא אל אהל האשה.

scenarios. First, that Rebecca did possess the physical signs of virginity; and secondly, that while Rebecca was in fact a virgin, she had traumatically lost the physical proof of her purity. The commentator first suggests that although Eliezer was Abraham's most trusted servant, the reality that Eliezer had Isaac's future bride in his keeping for any length of time greatly troubled Abraham. (Perhaps Abraham remembered how his own passionate desire for his wife Sarah was kindled on their way to Egypt so many years ago. See Chapter 2.) He suspected the servant might have wronged the beautiful Rebecca on the journey to Hebron, and was distraught at the prospect. Therefore, to ensure Rebecca's suitability, Abraham cautions Isaac to look for objective signs of her virginity when he takes her to his bed. Once Isaac is assured that Rebecca is as perfect as Sarah had been, her place as Isaac's wife is secured.[18] Notwithstanding Abraham's initial suspicions concerning Eliezer, as a reward for Eliezer's faithful and blameless service to him, Abraham grants him his freedom.[19]

Yalkut Shimoni then turns to the second possibility, that Rebecca could have traumatically ruptured her virginal membranes yet still arrive at her marital bed in a pure state. But how could Isaac have believed her to be virginal even though the bodily signs were absent? By way of response, the commentator presents a fascinating tale of Rebecca's fall from the camel. He posits that she fell from the camel onto a roadside bramble hedge, thereby rupturing her membranes and bleeding onto the ground. The Almighty immediately instructed Gabriel, her guardian angel, to descend to earth to watch over Rebecca's blood, in order that it not dry up, disappear or become disturbed by any creatures or roadside travelers. God was preserving proof of Rebecca's purity against future doubters.

Later that night, in their marital bed, Isaac is shocked to find no evidence of virginal blood. He suspects Eliezer of having taken advantage of Rebecca on the journey from her father's house. Rebecca swears to her husband that Eliezer never touched her, and she relates to him the episode of her injury on the bramble hedge. They go out together to inspect the site of her fall, and miraculously, the blood-

---

[18] אמר אברהם ליצחק: העבד הזה חשוד על כל עבירות שבתורה ומרמה בידו . . . הבא הנערה האהלה והוציא בתוליה באצבע. אם טהורה היא בבתוליה הרי היא ראויה לך. וכך עשה . . . ואחר כך לקחה לאשה.

[19] ובשביל שגמל אליעזר חסד ליצחק, הוציאו לחירות.

stained branch is exactly where Rebecca said it would be, perfectly preserved. Isaac then recalls that Rebecca's fall from the camel occurred immediately after she first saw him standing in the field. Isaac understands from all this that Rebecca is innocent. The Almighty, eager to reward the servant Eliezer for being unjustly accused, allows him to enjoy the pleasures of paradise.[20]

And he loved her; and Isaac was then comforted after [the loss of] his mother. The peace that had eluded Isaac in the years following Sarah's death becomes embodied in this young woman Rebecca. Isaac's love for her yields the comfort he has so sorely needed following Sarah's death. Otherwise, the Ramban asks rhetorically, why would the text juxtapose Isaac's marriage with an allusion to his period of mourning for his mother? [21] Satisfied that he has wed his soul-mate, Isaac finally is comforted for the death of his mother. Rashi explains that because it is customary for a husband to find comfort in his wife, especially after his mother's death, this verse clearly makes sense.[22] *Pirkei d'Rabi Eliezer* reminds us that for three full years after her death, Isaac wholeheartedly mourned his mother Sarah. Isaac's marriage to Rebecca enabled him to forget *the sadness* of his mourning for Sarah, while allowing him to retain *the joy* of his memories of their years together.[23]

The *Netziv* explains the Bible's use of the words "and she became his wife" *and* "he loved her." *Both* phrases are necessary for our understanding of Isaac's marriage to Rebecca. The commentator points out that the first statement in this verse—that Isaac took Rebecca to be his wife—neither proves nor disproves that he loves her, because Isaac was *obligated* to wed the girl that was chosen for him. The fact that the Bible immediately adds the second phrase—that Isaac loves her—proves to us that even though she was

---

20 נעשית מוכת עץ ויצא ממנה דם בתולים. מיד אמר הקב"ה לגבריאל, רד ושמור את הדם, שלא
יסריח ולא יהיה בו מום. בא יצחק עליה ולא מצא בה בתולים. חשדה מאליעזר. אמר לה:
בתוליך היכן הן? אמרה לו: כשנפלתי מהגמל נעשיתי מוכת עץ . . . נשבעה לו שלא נגע בה.
הלכו ומצאו העץ צבוע דם. מיד ידע יצחק שהיא טהורה. אמר הקב"ה . . . מה אעשה לעבד
הזה? . . . הכניסוהו חי לגן עדן.

21 וזה טעם ויאהבה וינחם. ירמוז היה מצטער מאד על אמו, ורחק ממנו מנחם עד שנחם באשתו
באהבתו אותה. כי מה טעם שיזכיר הכתוב אהבת האיש באשתו?

22 אחרי אמו. דרך ארץ, כל זמן שאמו של אדם קיימת, כרוך הוא אצלה. ומשמתה, הוא מנחם
באשתו.

23 לאחר שלש שנים לקח את רבקה ושכח **אבל** שרה אמו.

chosen for him, he *also* fell in love with her.[24] The reader will recall that there was no mention of the word "love" in the text when Abraham took Sarah to be his wife, yet they both were able—together—to establish the foundation for the Jewish people. Was the "love" a necessary, explicit element? Later on in this book, we will follow through on this theme of the love of the patriarchs for their wives, as the saga of the final two matriarchs, Rachel and Leah, unfolds.

The Zohar (133b) ascribes one of the four hidden aspects of love to each of the four phrases in this verse, and credits Rebecca with embodying *all* of them in Isaac's imagination. The first phrase, "and he took Rebecca," represents one facet of love; "and she was a wife to him" is a second facet; "and he loved her" is third, and "Isaac was comforted" describes the fourth face of love.[25] We can infer from the Zohar's commentary that "and he took Rebecca" represents their *sexual* union; "and she was a wife to him" represents *motherhood*; "and he loved her" indicates that she was his *soul-mate*; and "Isaac was comforted" represents Rebecca's ability to bring *God's holiness* into their marriage. Thus, we learn that Rebecca encompasses the ideal woman to Isaac. She embodies all of her husband's fantasies of what a woman should be.

---

[24] ויאהב. דמזה דכתיב ותהי לו לאשה? אין הוכחה שאהבה . . . הוצרח הכתוב לפרש שמצא ממנה קורת רוח מאהבה.

[25] יצחק ברזה דארבע דסטירו דרבקה, דכתיב ויקח את רבקה חד, ותהי לו לאשה תרי, ויאהבה תלת, וינחם יצחק אחרי אמו הא ארבע.

TWENTY–SEVEN

ꙮꙮꙮ

Abraham's Remarriage
and Death

GENESIS 25:1–18

And Abraham took yet another wife, and her name was Keturah.

The Bible here makes an eighteen-verse digression annotating Abraham's "second family" immediately following the account of his son, Isaac's, love-match with Rebecca. The overarching purpose of this segment is to emphasize that the additional children who issued from Abraham's later unions were irrelevant from the standpoint of Abraham's covenant with God; only Isaac—his son with Sarah—merited the distinction of "covenantal son," heir to his parents' teachings and bearer of God's message and *mitzvot* to the next generation. Thus, the text's mere recitation of the names of Abraham's additional issue in verses one to four is followed in verse five by the statement, *And Abraham gave **all** that he had to Isaac.* Abraham gave Isaac "all" that was important and timeless: the weighty mantle of covenantal son. In contrast, verse six states that the children of Abraham's concubines were just given gifts during his lifetime, thereafter sent away from proximity to Isaac his son. Only then, in verse seven, does the Bible enumerate the one-hundred-and-seventy-five years of Abraham's life, the prelude to mention of his death in verse eight. It is Isaac, Sarah's son, and Ishmael, Hagar's son, who together bury their father in the Cave of Machpela. This is the same burial place that Abraham took such pains to purchase for Sarah, and Abraham is laid to rest by her side. Verse 11 specifies that after Abraham's death *God blessed Isaac, his son*. The Bible is careful to delineate Ishmael's progeny in verses 12 to 16, noting that among them numbered twelve princes. Predictably, these verses presage Ishmael's death in the text, at one hundred and thirty-seven years. Textually, the Bible has been sweeping up loose ends in these eighteen verses, leaving the reader with a clear field genealogically and spiritually. The only heir to Abraham left on the biblical proscenium is Isaac, his only son from Sarah, who is poised at the threshold of his life with Rebecca. The figurative mantles have passed from Abraham to Isaac, from Sarah to Rebecca.

The reader may be struck by the contrast between the Bible's description of Isaac's marriage to and love for Rebecca, juxtaposed with the verse describing that Abraham, now at the very end of his life, takes another wife—perhaps even several others. The commentaries are as perplexed as the reader. Abarbanel terms Abraham's behavior as "decidedly strange." He suggests that Abraham should have contented himself, in his very old age, with the role of "patriarch emeritus," and not fathered excessive progeny.[1]

Rashi states that the woman Keturah, whom Abraham marries in verse one of this chapter, is in fact the exiled Hagar.[2] Abarbanel surmises that Rashi is driven to identify Keturah as Hagar in order to minimize the strangeness of Abraham's behavior in marrying yet a third woman; therefore, using Rashi's interpretation, Abraham took only two wives, Sarah and Hagar.[3] Yet the question persists. In verse six the Bible uses the Hebrew plural for concubines when it enumerates Abraham's other children from these women.[4] If Keturah were in fact truly Hagar, then the text would more correctly have stated "the children of the *concubine*," leaving the word in its singular form. In truth, then, according to Abarbanel, Abraham must have taken at least one other concubine in addition to Hagar.

---

[1] ראיתי לחקור על הפרשה הזאת **דברים זרים** שראיתי בה . . . בהיות אברהם ישיש בשבע ימים לקח אשה והוליד ממנה . . . זה באמת יהיה לאברהם, קדוש ד', פועל מגונה ובלתי מסכים אל שלמותו. ובדין נאמר עליו "ויוסף אברהם" **כי היה זה תוספת ומותר.**

[2] קטורה, זו הגר.

[3] ואחשוב שהביאם לזה להמעיט בזרות הגועל הזה **שלא לקח אשה מחדש**, אבל חזר לקחת את הגר.

[4] ולבני **הפלגשים** אשר לאברהם

Midrash Tanchuma confirms that though some commentaries agree with Rashi that Abraham merely took back his exiled wife Hagar, there are also *mephorshim* who refer to the use of the plural word "concubines" to support the notion that Abraham married yet a third woman.[5]

However many women Abraham married after Sarah's death, and however many children he sired, the fact remains that regardless, he bequeathed all that he possessed to his son Isaac, including God's covenantal blessings. Also, he was buried beside Sarah, the mother of Isaac, his only covenantal son.

GENESIS 25:19–20

With Abraham's death, Isaac's story rises to prominence. The Bible recaps, in these two short verses, Isaac's birth and his marriage to Rebecca.

> *And this is the history of Isaac, Abraham's son; Abraham begat Isaac; at age forty, Isaac took Rebecca—daughter of Betuel the Aramean from Padan-Aram, sister of Lavan the Aramean—to be his wife.*

The Bible mentions Isaac's age at his marriage, but omits any reference to Rebecca's age. The *mephorshim* differ on this point. Rashi says here that Rebecca was three years old when Isaac acquired her in marriage.[6] Rashi may have been troubled by the prospect of Rebecca's tender age, as he is careful to mention, as we noted earlier, that a girl must be able to grant her knowing, wholehearted consent to her betrothal. We learn this principle, according to the commentator, from Rebecca's consent to her betrothal to Isaac in 24:57. The implication, then, is that Rebecca was older than three years. Chizkuni, using a different measure, calculates Rebecca's age as fourteen at her marriage.[7] Mizrachi, too, calculates Rebecca's age as fourteen-and-a-half-years.[8] *Torah Shlema*, on the other hand, places

---

5 הגר היא קטורה . . . ורבותינו אומרים **אשה אחרת נטל.**

6 הרי ליצחק ל"ז שנים, ובו בפרק נולדה רבקה; המתין לה עד שתהא ראויה לביאה, ג' שנים, ונשאה.

7 . . . לכן נראה שהיתה בת ארבע עשרה שנה כשנשאת.

8 נמצא שהיתה בת י"ד וחצי כשנשאה.

Rebecca's age at twenty years old when she wed Isaac.[9] *Sha'arei Aharon* acknowledges the lack of consensus regarding Rebecca's age at her marriage.[10]

However Rebecca's age is computed, all are in agreement that at the very least she was twenty-three years old when she conceived.

---

[9] ובכת"י נר השכלים אמרו שיצחק נשא את רבקה כשהיתה בת כ' שנה.

[10] ובקחתו את רבקה . . . ולפעמים המדרשים חלוקים.

TWENTY-EIGHT

ॐ∞ॐ∞

Rebecca's Infertility

GENESIS 25:21

Isaac and Rebecca are married for twenty years, and to their great sadness they remain childless. *Pirkei d'Rabi Eliezer* describes how a heartsick Isaac is inspired to bring his barren wife to his most sacred place, to the site of the *Akeida*, where his relationship with God was most tangible and personal. We can envision their trip together to Mount Moriah. Isaac leads Rebecca along the path he trod with his father Abraham that early morning over twenty years before. Alone with Rebecca atop the mountain, Isaac prays that the God who delivered him from death would now grant that his beloved wife would give birth to his child.[1] The Zohar (136b) states that Isaac's fervent prayer atop Mount Moriah rose straight to heaven, and directly to the "ears" of God Himself. Isaac's burnt-offering, sacrificed to God at the conclusion of his prayer for Rebecca, sealed his supplication, and God's answer to Isaac's entreaty was almost instantaneous.[2]

---

[1] לאחר עשרים שנה לקחה יצחק והלך עמה להר המוריה, למקום שנעקד שם, והתפלל על ההריון, ונעתר לו.

[2] ויעתר יצחק לד' לנכח אשתו. מהו ויעתר? דקריב ליה קרבנא, וצלי עלה. ומה קרבנא קריב? עולה קריב.

And Isaac entreated God on his wife's behalf, because she was childless. . . .[3] According to the *p'shat*, Isaac prayed on behalf of his childless wife, while the text makes no mention at all of any prayer or action on Rebecca's part to remedy her barren state. It is the commentaries who here infuse Rebecca with life. They provide the absent details that allow the reader to perceive Rebecca as an equal participant in their quest for a child. This verse thrusts the reader into what surely was an emotionally-charged scene. Rashi describes it, placing Isaac in one corner of their tent atop the mountain, and Rebecca in the opposite corner, each of them silently praying to God.[4] *Siftei Chachamim* states that Isaac and Rebecca were properly standing in prayer at a distance from one another—he on the one side, she on the other—to allow the space for God's presence to hover between them.[5]

Rashbam interprets this verse to mean that Isaac is praying *for* his wife, not that he is standing *opposite* her.[6] The Hebrew word *L'NoCHaCH* [7] can mean either "for" or "opposite." While Isaac and Rebecca may have physically *stood* in opposition to one another as Rashi suggests, emotionally they were unified; Isaac prays *for* Rebecca. Both husband and wife, while praying separately, are considered to be of one mind: urgently pleading with God to grant them a child.

Meshech Chachma elaborates. He explains why the text states that Isaac prays only *for his wife*. Since they were *both* childless, should Isaac *also* have prayed on *his own* behalf that God would grant them both progeny? Isaac here is praying on Rebecca's behalf, and not for himself. He does this because he remembers God's blessing to Abraham (Genesis 17:19) that he, Isaac, was destined to sire a covenantal child.[8] Therefore, because he is in no doubt that *he will* sire an heir eventually, Isaac's selfless prayer is that God should allow his beloved Rebecca—and no other—to bear him the promised child.[9]

---

[3]   . . . ויעתר יצחק לד' לנכח אשתו כי עקרה היא.

[4]   לנכח אשתו. זה עומד בזוית זו ומתפלל, וזו עומדת בזוית זו ומתפללת.

[5]   לפי שאין דרך המתפללים להתפלל זה לעומת זה

[6]   לנכח: **בשביל** [אשתו]

[7]   לנכח

[8]   וקראת את שמו יצחק; והקימותי את בריתי **אתו** לברית עולם, **לזרעו** אחריו.

[9]   כי הוא היה בטוח שיהיה לו זרע . . . רק יתכן שיוליד מאשה אחרת, לכן התפלל. . . .

Midrash Rabbah (63.3) gives actual voice to *both* Isaac and Rebecca. The reader already knows from the text that Isaac prays; the *midrash* supplies his very words. The text does not mention, however, that Rebecca prays at all; astonishingly, the *midrash* is certain that she prayed, *and* it supplies her words where the text provides none. The commentary teaches us that their prayers were parallel. Standing in his corner of the tent, Isaac supplicates God, "Creator of the world, let all the children that You are destined to give me, issue from this righteous woman." Simultaneously, Rebecca is standing in her corner of the tent, also pleading: "All children that You are destined to give me, please let them issue from this righteous man."[10]

In contrast to the extreme tension that the state of prolonged childlessness provoked between Sarah and Abraham, the commentaries stress the unity of purpose and passion between Isaac and Rebecca. The Zohar states (137b), "Now observe that Abraham did not supplicate God for children, notwithstanding that Sarah was barren."[11]

Abarbanel posits that Isaac and Rebecca were each praying on the other's behalf, for the straightforward reason that *both* Isaac and Rebecca were barren.[12] Abarbanel's source for Isaac's infertility is not the biblical text itself, but the Talmud (*Yevamot* 64a). There, it clearly states that Isaac our forefather was sterile.[13] Abarbanel stresses that Rebecca is mindful that Isaac's parents also endured a protracted period of childlessness. Perhaps that is also part of Rebecca's prayer for her husband; that he will not suffer as they did.[14] It was on the strength of *both* their supplications that God responded to them. Miraculously, Isaac became able to father a child, and Rebecca to carry it. *Ohel Yaakov* presents a beautiful interpretation of this verse. He cites the Talmud (*Bava Kama* 92a) for the notion that he who prays *for another*—though he himself is in need of the same remedy—his prayer will be answered first.[15] Here, God granted Isaac

---

[10] לנכח אשתו. מלמד שהיה יצחק שטוח כאן, והיא שטוחה כאן. ואומר: רבש"ע, כל בנים שאתה נותן לי יהיו מן הצדקת הזו. אף היא אמרה כן. כל בנים שאת עתיד ליתן לי יהיו מן הצדיק הזה.

[11] אברהם לא צלי קמי קב"ה, פיתן ליה בנין, אע"ג דשרה עקרה הות.

[12] כי היו **שניהם** עקרים . . . כי מכח התפלה נפקדו שניהם. הוא להוליד, והיא להריון.

[13] אמר רבי יצחק, יצחק אבינו עקור היה.

[14] היו שניהם עקרים. אם ליצחק שהיה לו העקרות בטבע, מסבות אביו ואמו, שהיו כן.

[15] כל המבקש רחמים על חבירו, והוא צריך לאותו הדבר, **הוא** נענה תחילה.

the fertility he sought *for Rebecca*. Another commentary, *Torat Hachida*, adds that Isaac prays *for her*, but because they are *as one soul*, when God answers Isaac, in effect *both* their prayers are answered.[16]

And God was entreated by **him**. . . .[17]

The text is clear that God is responding only to *Isaac's* prayer, not to Rebecca's. This is not problematic, because readers should recall that in the first part of this verse the text states that it is only Isaac who prays. As we have just explained, the commentaries—and not the text—supply the fact that Rebecca prays, and they supply the substance of her prayer also. Therefore, it is the commentaries who must bear the burden of explaining why—if both Isaac and Rebecca prayed—God answered only Isaac's prayer. Rashi's explanation is that Isaac's prayer took precedence over Rebecca's because Isaac was himself a righteous person, and also the son of a righteous person; while Rebecca, though herself a righteous person, was not born of righteous parentage.[18] *Torat Hachida* softens Rashi's interpretation. He stresses that Rebecca's extreme virtue is unquestioned. She merited that God would answer her prayer in her own right, notwithstanding the immoral character of her unbelieving father, Betuel.[19]

Considering that the *mephorshim* recognize that *both* Rebecca and Isaac prayed for a child, it is the commentaries who must explain why the text states that God answered Isaac's prayer and not Rebecca's. *Torat Hachida* advances two basic reasons for this. First, whenever a prayer is offered for oneself or one's family, a person's righteous lineage is taken into account. Therefore, here, it was *Isaac's* prayer that was answered. The commentaries continue, explaining that the *opposite* would be the case if one's prayer were on behalf of the community. Then, a person's unworthy parentage would actually yield *greater* advantage. In such a situation, a person who comes from unbelievers yet who has become righteous himself, could have

---

[16] שהתפלות על עצמם, **דאשתו כגופו, ובעל כאשתו.**

[17] ויעתר **לו** ד'. . . .

[18] ויעתר לו. ולא לה, שאין דומה תפלת צדיק בן צדיק לתפלת צדיק בן רשע.

[19] אבל ודאי זכותה גם כן גרם . . . אמנם מה שמיעט רבקה אינה מצד עצמותה, דצדקת היא . . . דאין החסרון מצדה כי אשת חיל היא, אלא הפגם מצד אבותיה.

even *more* influence in the realm of prayer.[20] Therefore, since Isaac's selfless prayer would benefit *both* Rebecca and himself, it was *his* prayer that bore more weight at this time. According to *Torat Hachida*, Isaac's worthy parentage reinforced his prayer. On the other hand, had Isaac and Rebecca been praying for the welfare of the *community*, the commentators state that *her* prayer, as the righteous daughter of a nonbeliever, would have prevailed.

The second reason advanced by the commentaries as to why the text specifically states "God answered *him* [Isaac]," is to underline that God was only answering *Isaac's* prayer, and no other's. Students of the text will recall Rebecca's brother, Lavan, whose parting blessing to his sister (in 24:60) was that she be "the forebear of tens of thousands." *Torat Hachida* declares that our verse negates any potential suggestion that Rebecca's long-awaited fertility is due to her unworthy brother's parting benediction.[21] The text wants us to be clear on this point: "God answers *Isaac*," and not Lavan.

And God was entreated by him, **and Rebecca his wife became pregnant**. *Ohr Hachayim* explains why this verse departs from the Bible's typical manner of announcing conception and pregnancy with words such as "and Adam *knew his wife*, . . . and she became pregnant." (Genesis 4:1) The words ". . . knew his wife," or another phrase implying conjugal intimacy, are *missing* from our verse. The commentator suggests that Isaac and Rebecca had had intimate marital relations within three days prior to this prayer scene. Isaac's prayer, then, was that their sexual intimacy would yield them the child they both fervently desired.[22] The commentator implies that Isaac's and Rebecca's marriage was a loving one. Their sexual relationship had a value all its own, independent of her ability to bear a child. In fact, it antedated his prayer for a child. As Rebecca's saga continues to unfold, we will see other indications in the biblical text that bear out this notion.

---

[20] בקשה כשמתפלל על עצמו, שזכות אבותיו מסייעתו. אבל המתפלל על צבור, **אדרבא** חשובה לפני המקום תפלת צדיק בן רשע שמניח מעשה אבותיו.

[21] כדי שלא יאמר לבן **שברכתו** עשתה פירות.

[22] טעם שלא אמר "וידע יצחק את . . . " אולי שהיתה התפלה אחר שידע[ה] תוך ג' ימים הראשונים . . . יתפלל שלא יסריח. וזו היתה תפלתו של יצחק.

TWENTY-NINE

৪০৪৪৪৩

Rebecca's
Difficult Pregnancy

GENESIS 25:22

I saac's and Rebecca's prayers were answered, and at long last Rebecca became pregnant, but her pregnancy was a turbulent one. *And the children struggled within her, and she said, if this be so, why is this happening to me?* [1] Although the *p'shat* is clear that Rebecca is experiencing excessive fetal movements since she is carrying twins, Rashi nevertheless cites a *midrash* to explain this phrase. He states that within her womb, each twin kicks in turn; one when she passes by the house of Torah study of Shem and Ever,[†] and the other when she passes a place of idolatry.[2] Rashi is alone in his interpretation of this phrase that the boys' natures were predetermined *in utero*. The commentaries widely believe that only *after* birth, and with sentience, does a person choose his path of right or wrong.

[†]Shem is Noah's righteous son, and Ever is Shem's grandson (*Siftei Chachamim*). Midrashic sources vest them with having established a place of ethical monotheistic study.

---

[1]   ויתרצצו הבנים בקרבה, ותאמר אם כן למה זה אנכי?

[2]   כשהיתה עוברת על פתחי תורה של שם ועבר, יעקב רץ ומפרכס לצאת; עוברת על פתח עבודת אללים, עשו מפרכס לצאת.

137

Torat Hachida's words exemplify this precept. He states simply that this one instance,where the unborn twins' natures appear to be formed *in utero*, is not the usual course of human nature.[3] The Talmud (*Nidah* 16b) relates that the same Divine angel that is appointed over conception and pregnancy takes a drop from the newly-created life and presents it before the Almighty, asking Him: Master of the Universe, this drop of life, what will it be? Is it fated to be strong or weak, wise or foolish, rich or poor? The Talmud continues that whether the new life will be wicked or righteous, however, is never predetermined. This is a path that is selected by each individual, according to his or her own free choice.[4] The commentaries continue to offer explanations of Rebecca's suffering. Rashbam states that Rebecca, who at first hoped she would experience a normal pregnancy, felt an excessive amount of fetal movement, and was concerned.[5] Ibn Ezra supplies a vibrant background, filling in for the reader the conversations that took place behind the scene. He explains that Rebecca inquired of her neighbors who had given birth whether they, too, had experienced such unremitting fetal movement. They fearfully replied that they had not.[6] *Midrash Rabbah* (63.6) adds that Rebecca was tireless in her quest to confirm that her pains were normal. She canvassed the tribal women, making her way from tent to tent. She received no satisfactory response.[7]

Rashi states that Rebecca's pregnancy was so complicated that she questions her own initial desire to conceive.[8] She asks herself, "I never expected this pregnancy to be easy, but these pains are so unbearable that I must question my overwhelming desire to bear a child." Ramban offers an existential interpretation to Rebecca's biblical words. His view is that her pain was so excruciating and

---

[3] אלא מוכרח משעת לידה ומה אירע להם ביעקב ועשו היה הנס.

[4] אותו מלאך הממונה על ההריון, לילה שמו. ומוטל טפה ומעמידה לפני הקב"ה, ואומר לפניו: רבש"ע, טפה זו מה תהא עליה? גבור או חלש, חכם או טיפש, עשיר או עני? ואילו רשע או צדיק לא קאמר.

[5] שהיו רצים ומתנענים בתוך גופה כדרך עוברים.

[6] והיא שאלה לנשים שילדו אם הירע להם ככה? ותאמרנה לא.

[7] היתה אמינו רבקה מחזרת על פתחיהן של נשים ואומרת להן: הגיע לכן הצער הזה?

[8] ותאמר אם כן. גדול צער העיבור. למה זה אנכי? מתאוה ומתפללת על הריון.

unbearable that she cried, "Would that I did not exist—that I should die now! Or even that I should never have been born!"[9]

Sforno elaborates on Rebecca's state of mind. He also allows us to hear her unspoken words. "If my pregnancy is so unusually difficult that I am facing imminent death in childbirth, why did my family bless me to be 'the mother of thousands?' (Genesis 24:60) And why did my husband pray that I would be the one to bear his children?"[10]

Rebecca is aware that death during childbirth is not an uncommon phenomenon. She has seen childbirth first-hand among her family, entourage, and neighbors. It is likely that—as mistress of the clan—she even assisted at numerous births. But she has been suffering exceedingly, and her primal fears have escalated with the realization that her travail is so out of the ordinary that her life—and that of her unborn child—is at risk.

Ohr Hachayim makes it clear that Rebecca is not whining about normal birth pangs. Her excruciating pregnancy has her fearing the contingency of a miscarriage. Coming after twenty barren years, Rebecca's anxiety is not trivial. Sensitive to her realistic concerns, this commentator supplies her anguished voice: "If I am to miscarry after all this time, and my womb will be left empty, with nothing to show for it, then I will have been pregnant for naught!"[11] *Ohr Hachayim* is steadfast in his defense of Rebecca. He reminds the reader that she is a righteous woman, who had withstood enormous levels of suffering in order to carry the covenantal child.

The Maharal adds that in the throes of her apprehension Rebecca decides that the ultimate explanation for her suffering must definitively lie with the Almighty. "If so," Rebecca reasons, "I must not sit by idly."[12] . . . *So she goes out to inquire of God.* . . .[13] Rashi states that Rebecca's destination was the House of Torah study of Shem.[14] *Pirkei d'Rabi Eliezer* reveals that Rebecca rouses herself though her

---

[9] והנכון בעיני, כי אמרה אם כן יהיה לי, למה אנכי **בעולם?** הלואי אינני; שאמות או שלא הייתי.

[10] אם כן . . . ואסתכן אני בלידה . . . למה זה התאווה קרובי שתהיה אני אם הזרע . . . וכן בעלי שהתפלל אלי בזה.

[11] אין הדעת מסכמת עליו שתמאס הצדקת בהריונה לצד הצער . . . היו נדחקים ביותר כשיעור . . . ולא יתקיימו במעיה . . . ולמה אנכי הרה? לרק יגעתי! ולעולם לא הקפידה על צער ההריון, כי הצדיקים יסבלו צער גדול בעולם הזה לתכלית טוב הנצחי.

[12] אם כן למה זה אנכי. יושבת בטל, ואין אני חוקרת אחר זה. אין עלי רק לדרוש אחר זה.

[13] ותלך לדרוש את ד'.

[14] לבית מדרש של שם.

agonies have brought her to the verge of death. She stuns her
entourage by announcing that she will go alone to seek God's
guidance. She travels again to Mount Moriah, the holy place that she
had visited with Isaac not nine months before. There, in the place
where God had twice answered her husband in his time of anguish,
she prays that God will disclose to her the true reason for her
suffering.[15]

---

[15] ומחבליה הגיע נפשה למות, והלכה להתפלל במקום טהור. שנאמר, ותלך לדרוש את ד'.

THIRTY

৪০০৪৪০০৪

The Prophecy

GENESIS 25:23

*And God said to her, two nations are in your womb, and two peoples
will emerge from you; and one will overpower the other, and the elder
will serve the younger.*[1]

A ccording to the *p'shat*, God speaks *directly* to Rebecca. Sforno
explains that God is responding to Rebecca's plea. God therefore
discloses to her that the reason for her excruciating pain is that she is
carrying warring twins.[2] Other commentaries say that this communication was in direct, and that God spoke to Rebecca through an
intermediary. According to Rashi, it was the prophet Shem who
delivered God's message to Rebecca.[3] *Torah Temima* (quoting
Talmud *Yerushalmi, Sotah* 87) does not go so far as to give this
intermediary a name.[4] Rashbam calls him a prophet,[5] and *Midrash
Rabbah* (63.7) calls him a messenger-angel.[6] It is interesting that some

---

[1] **ויאמר ד' לה:** שני גויים בבטנך, ושני לאמים ממעיך יפרדו. ולאם מלאם יאמץ, ורב יעבוד
צעיר.

[2] זו היא סיבת הרציצה

[3] על ידי שליח. לשם נאמר ברוח הקדש, והוא אמר לה.

[4] ויאמר ד' לה. על ידי מתורגמן

[5] על ידי נביא.

[6] על ידי מלאך.

mephorshim, ordinarily eager to vest the matriarch with holiness, appear to contradict the plain meaning of the text when they say it was God's angel who comforted Rebecca with the message that her pregnancy would yield children who would sire two nations. The reason advanced by *Sha'arei Aharon* for this apparent discrepancy is that had God spoken to Rebecca *directly*, she would have been named in the Talmud as one of the seven biblical prophetesses. The reader should recall (see Chapter 1) that Sarah is the only matriarch to appear on that list.[7] Chizkuni points out that regardless of whether it was an angel who spoke to Rebecca, or an intermediary, or even God, the true import of this verse is that *only Rebecca received the revelation* that the elder of the sons she was carrying was destined to be subservient to his younger twin. Isaac was never privy to this certitude.[8]

Rashbam attributes to this verse the reason that Rebecca will in the future favor her younger son over the elder.[9] The commentator points out that God comforted her, alleviating her two fears: first, that she would miscarry, and second, that another woman would bear the covenantal child. God assures her in this verse that she will deliver healthy twins, and moreover, divulges to her which son will be Isaac's successor. Astonishingly, God singles out Rebecca's younger son and promises to love him. Is it any wonder, then, that Rebecca also favors the younger twin over his elder brother?

---

[7] שאם היה דבר ד' עמה, למה לא מנאוה חז"ל עם שבע נביאות שמנו במסכת מגילה?

[8] ויאמר לה, **ולא לו.** לפיכך לא היה סבור שיהיה עשו רשע.

[9] ורב יעבד צעיר. ולכן אהבה את יעקב, שאהבו הקב"ה.

THIRTY–ONE

৪৩৮৩৮৩

Rebecca Gives Birth
to Rival Twin Sons

GENESIS 25:24–28

Rebecca carried her pregnancy full-term, and she gave birth to twin boys. The first emerged ruddy, covered all over with red hair, and they named him Esav. Next, his brother was born, with his hand still holding onto Esav's heel. And he named him Jacob. And Isaac was sixty years old at the time his twin sons were born. And the boys grew; Esav became a hunter, a man of the field, and Jacob was a simpler man, who chose to remain in the tents. **And Isaac loved Esav because he hunted venison for him to eat; but Rebecca loves Jacob.**[1]

The commentaries grapple with the problem of why each parent demonstrates a preference for one child over the other.

The *Netziv* explains that Isaac loved Esav because Esav catered to him, bringing him the food he loved. Not so Jacob, who was not a hunter like his brother, but a tent dweller.[2] Rebecca's love of Jacob was based on her younger son's essential nature, not upon anything he could bring her.[3]

---

[1] ויאהב יצחק את עשו כי ציד בפיו; ורבקה אהבת את יעקב.

[2] מה שאין כן יעקב; היה יושב אהל ולא שמש הרבה.

[3] ורבקה . . . אהבה את יעקב. לא הביטה אלא על המעלה והתכלית . . . משום שאהבת יצחק לא היה אלא על פי השעה. משא"כ אהבת רבקה. היתה מצד טבע הענין.

Still, Sforno teaches us that Isaac loved Jacob also, even though it is not explicitly so stated in the text. Sforno derives this from his interpretation of verse 28, which he presents as "And Isaac *also* loved Esav."[4] It was necessary for the text to point this out to us to teach us that Isaac knew that Jacob was the more worthy child.[5] Rabbi Abraham, son of the Rambam, describes the converse situation regarding Rebecca. She, too, loved Esav, though the text does not say so. But because he was a hunter and spent the bulk of his time out in the field, he was not at home to endear himself to her. By contrast, her love for Jacob grew naturally day by day, because he stayed closer to home. Thus, she developed a more comfortable, loving relationship with her younger son.[6]

The commentaries here interject several serious criticisms of Esav's character and behaviors. They state that he became an idolater, while Jacob spent his time learning (Rashi);[7] that Esav seduced women behind their husbands' backs (*Kli Yakar*);[8] that Esav feigned righteousness only to please his father (*Ohr Hachayim*),[9] while outside their home he was brutish and rash (Radak).[10]

Ohel Yaakov characterizes Isaac's favoritism of his first-born son as a natural one. He does not fault Isaac for failing to see Esav's shortcomings. Rather, the commentator credits Rebecca with knowing the truth: that Jacob is God's favorite. She possesses this foreknowledge because she sought God's counsel during her pregnancy and was answered.[11]

---

[4] ויאהב יצהק . . . **גם** את עשו.

[5] שידע בלי ספק שלא היה שלם כיעקב.

[6] ורבקה אהבה את יעקב חיבה יתרה . . . ולא שהיתה שינאה את עשו, אלא אוהבת יעקב יותר ממנו. וגברה אהבתה הטבעית ליעקב לפי שהיה יושב אהלים. ולכן היתה רגילה עמו. ועשו היה איש שדה, ולכן נתמעטה רגילותה עמו.

[7] זה פירש לבתי מדרשות, וזה פירש לעבודת אלילים.

[8] שהיה צד נשים תחת בעליהם.

[9] שהיה צד אביו בדברים.

[10] היה רק ופוחז.

[11] היה יצחק אוהב את עשו כי הוא הבכור, כמשפט שני אחים . . . אבל רבקה ידעה האמת: כי בשני בנים האלה המאוחר הוא הקדוש; כי הלכה לדרוש את ד'.

THIRTY–TWO

Jacob Convinces Esav
to Relinquish His Birthright

GENESIS 25:29–34

O ne day Jacob was at home cooking a thick soup when an exhausted Esav returned from the fields. *Torah Temima* explains that Esav's exhaustion was not merely brought on by his long day spent hunting in the fields; he had just returned from committing various acts of immorality. He publicly denied the existence of God, thus denying the essence of ethical monotheism; he scorned his birthright; denigrated his covenantal responsibility as the eldest grandson of Abraham; he raped a betrothed virgin, and even committed murder.[1]

When he saw Jacob preparing the fragrant soup, Esav exclaimed, "Please! Let me gorge myself on some of that red soup before I faint dead-away." (On account of the color of this red pottage, Esav was also known by the name "Edom," from the root-word *eDoM*,[2] meaning the color red.) And Jacob replies, "First sell me your birthright." To wit, Esav exclaims, "Here I am, about to die. What good will a birthright be to me in such a state!" But Jacob persists, saying, "Swear, now, that you give up your birthright." And

---

[1] חמש עברות עבר אותו רשע ביום ההוא: בא על נערה המאורסה, והרג את הנפש, וכפר
בתחיית המתים, וכפר בעיקר, ושט את הבכורה.

[2] אדם

145

so Esav swore, and he sold Jacob his birthright for the soup. So Jacob gave bread and lentil pottage to Esav, and Esav ate, and drank, and got up and left,[3] thus scorning his birthright.

Ohel Yaakov points to this spate of verbs as proof that Esav truly scorned his rights as first-born son of the patriarch Isaac. There is no hint of any emotion or regret in the text's summary recitation of his hasty meal and his immediate departure. The commentator states that Esav left Jacob's table and went on his merry way, sated, happy, and carefree. This is not the portrait of a man who regretted his hasty decision.[4]

ויאכל, וישת, ויקם, וילך [3]

וזהו ויאכל, וישת, ויקם, וילך, כלומר: הלך לדרכו שמח וטוב לב. מזה הוכרע "ויבז עשו את [4]
הבכורה."

THIRTY-THREE

ಬಂಡಬಂಡ

Isaac and Rebecca
in Avimelech's Palace

GENESIS 26:1–6

S ome time after Esav sold his birthright, there was a famine in the land, distinct from the first great famine that had occurred at the time of Abraham. En route to Egypt in his quest for sustenance, Isaac journeys with his wife and twin sons to Gerar, where Avimelech, the king of the Philistines, dwelt. There, God appears to Isaac, and tells him *not* to go down into Egypt, but rather to dwell in the land of Canaan, where He will protect and bless him. God further reaffirms His covenant with Isaac, saying: "To you and to your progeny will I give all of these lands, fulfilling the oath which I swore to your father Abraham." God continues to reiterate His blessing of fertility, saying that Isaac's seed will be as numerous as the stars in the heavens, and that they will inherit all these lands of Canaan. God reminds Isaac that these blessings will devolve to him and his children because Abraham hearkened to God's voice, and kept steadfastly to His commandments, laws and teachings. Isaac did as God commanded him, and journeyed no farther than Gerar.

GENESIS 26:7

The men of that place asked about his wife; and he said, "She is my sister," for he feared to say she was his wife. [Isaac feared] "Lest the men of this place will kill me for Rebecca, because she is beautiful to behold."

This is the third time that readers of the text are presented with a patriarch who declares, in the face of danger, that his wife is his sister. In years past, *Abraham* twice presented Sarah as his sister before lustful kings. Here, however, according to Ramban, Isaac echoes his father's protective pretext, just as he emulated his father's flight to Egypt to feed his family. The difference here is that Isaac relied on the Philistines' memory of their previous forcible taking of Abraham's wife, Sarah, and their subsequent covenant of peace with Abraham at Genesis 21:27. Isaac thus was hopeful that his wife would be safe.[1] In fact, *Rebecca is never abducted by Avimelech* or his henchmen. *Midrash Lekach Tov* suggests that they had learned their lesson from the episode with Abraham, when the Philistines had suffered the dire punishment of their bodily functions coming to a standstill following their abduction of Sarah.[2] Therefore, Isaac's guarded confidence in their collective memory of that event was well placed. Chizkuni adds that Rebecca was not forcibly taken because the Philistines remembered that they had been chastened once before.[3]

Readers will note that Isaac does not ask his wife's permission to use the wife/sister ruse. The *Netziv* explains that it was not overbearing behavior on Isaac's part that he did not ask his wife to be a part of this dissembling charade. When his father Abraham had resorted to this ruse concerning Sarah, she was then taken against her will and nearly raped. Isaac, knowing that Rebecca would deny him nothing, does not wish to make her an accomplice to a subterfuge that may backfire; what if the Philistines of Gerar *do not* remember

---

1 כי היה בדעתו לרדת מצרימה, והלך אל אבימלך, בעל ברית אביו . . . והנה אבימלך—מפני בריתו של אברהם—לא נגע בו ולא בביתו כלל.

2 ויאמר אחותי היא. כדרך אביו, אבל הפרש היה בין מעשה אברהם למעשה יצחק, כי אברהם בכניסתו למקום נלקחה שרה. **אבל ביצחק לא נלקחה רבקה כלל**, כי למודים היו מן אברהם.

3 לפי שהוכיחם אברהם כבר.

what their previous abduction had wrought years before? What if they were to take Rebecca from Isaac nevertheless? [4]

The *Netziv* reminds us that Rebecca's awe of Isaac was established at the moment of their first setting eyes on one another in the field that long-ago evening. Thus, she was unlikely to challenge her husband's use of the ruse.

GENESIS 26:8

Isaac and Rebecca lived thus in Gerar as brother and sister under Avimelech's protection for many months while the famine raged in Canaan.

And it came to pass, when he had been there for many days, that Avimelech, king of the Philistines, looked through the window, and saw—behold! Isaac was sporting with Rebecca, his wife! [5]

The *mephorshim* explore the meaning of the Hebrew word *MeTZaCHeK,*[6] translated here as "sporting."

What behavior were Isaac and Rebecca engaging in, and what did Avimelech witness? Rashbam teaches us that as time passed and Isaac saw that Avimelech did not molest his "sister" Rebecca as he had feared, Isaac's guard was lowered, and he acted like a husband toward her.[7] Therefore, says *Ohr Hachayim*, in the natural way of a husband in love with his wife, Isaac embraced Rebecca in the privacy of their chambers.[8] Rashi says that Avimelech actually looked into Isaac's window and beheld him in bed with Rebecca.[9]

Midrash Lekach Tov allows the reader to imagine Avimelech's growing curiosity about his guests, such that the king is reduced to peering into the window of their private quarters. The commentator

---

[4] ולא בקש ממנה שתאמר גם כן הכי כמו שעשה אברהם, משום שרבקה היתה נכנעת ביותר ליצחק . . . ולא סרה מרצונו מאומה.

[5] ויהי כי ארכו לו שם הימים, וישקף אבימלך מלך פלשתים בעד החלון; וירא והנה יצחק מצחק את רבקה אשתו.

[6] מצחק

[7] לא נזהר מעתה כל כך שלא להתנהג עם אשתו מנהג אישות, מאחר שלא נתנו לב לגוזלה ממנו.

[8] מעשה חיבה הנעשית בין איש לאשתו.

[9] ראהו משמש מטתו.

posits that the Bible's introductory Hebrew words to this verse[10] can be translated either as *After he had been there many days,* or *As daylight grew longer with the onset of summer.*[11] *Kli Yakar* agrees that Avimelech was consumed with curiosity about his guests. In fact, the king wondered why Isaac, a wealthy, eligible man, was still a bachelor.[12]

The king harbored prurient fantasies concerning the lovely Rebecca, but sought proof of her availability by watching the couple at close quarters. He thought, "If they are truly brother and sister, then why has Isaac not yet taken a wife? And if they are *not* brother and sister, then I must see proof of that first-hand." It is in this context of Avimelech's emotional maelstrom of coveting the woman but fearing the consequences, that he stares voyeuristically out of his palace window, across the courtyard into the private guest quarters, and witnesses Isaac caressing Rebecca. Abarbanel states that Avimelech understood that Isaac's playful behavior toward Rebecca, and her response to it, was inconsistent with that of a brother toward his sister.[13] Chizkuni agrees, adding that Avimelech actually saw Isaac and Rebecca in intimate preparation for marital relations.[14]

A *p'shat* reading of this verse reveals its ambiguity. *And Avimelech . . . looked through the window.* The commentaries implicitly ask: Through whose window is Avimelech peering? Is it that he looks out of his own window, specifically *into* Isaac's open bedroom window? Or does Avimelech merely look *out of* his own window onto the courtyard? As we have just explicated, Rashi, *Midrash Lekach Tov, Kli Yakar,* Abarbanel and Chizkuni interpret this verse according to the first scenario: Avimelech stared out of his own window, and into Isaac's.

Other commentaries favor the second interpretation, that Avimelech peered out of his own window in the direction of Isaac and Rebecca's, but was able to see only their closed shutters. *Siftei Chachamim* and *Levush Haorah* both explain Rashi. Neither

---

[10] כי ארכו לו שם הימים.

[11] יש אומרים אריכות הימים, ויש אומרים ימי הקיץ שהימים ארוכים.

[12] לפיכך הרהר אבימלך בליבו לאמר: אם באמת שאחותו היא, אם כך, למה אינו נושא אשה כל הזמן הארוך?

[13] רואה אותם מצחקים ומהתלים, והיה לו עמה מן הקרוב והרמיזות, מה שלא יתכן שיהיה לאדם עם אחותו.

[14] מצחק: צחוק שלפני הבעילה.

commentator is comfortable with Rashi's interpretation that Avimelech witnessed Isaac and Rebecca in the act of marital intimacy. They cannot conceive of Isaac engaging in sexual behavior in front of an open window in broad daylight. Rather, *Siftei Chachamim* states that what Avimelech viewed through his window at midday was Isaac closing the shutters to his bedroom window with Rebecca by his side. From this act, states the commentator, the king understood that Isaac and Rebecca were definitely not brother and sister.[15]

Levush Haorah agrees. He states that an obsessed Avimelech saw Isaac's bedroom window—usually opened wide to catch the daily breezes—shuttered and closed. The king understood from this subtle change of routine that Isaac desired to engage in intimate relations with Rebecca in the shadowed darkness of his rooms, away from the prying eyes of his palace neighbors.[16] Chizkuni also interprets this verse according to the latter approach. Avimelech, peering through his palace window toward Isaac and Rebecca's rooms, as was his wont, observed that their window was closed tight. Simply from this unusual fact, Avimelech discerned what was taking place behind the shutters.[17]

The *Netziv* summarizes that upon viewing Isaac and Rebecca together, Avimelech understood without any possibility of doubt that their behavior was consistent only with that of a husband with his wife.[18]

GENESIS 26:9–11

Avimelech's suspicions were thus confirmed. His longtime guests were in fact husband and wife. And so Avimelech summons Isaac before him and admonishes him, saying, "But she is your wife! Why did you say 'She is my sister?'" And Isaac replies, "Because I thought you might kill me in order to possess her." Avimelech continues to reprove Isaac, asking, "What have you done to us? One of us very

---

[15] וישקף . . . דלא תימא שראהו ממש משמש—דחלילה—לצדיק כמוהו להניח חלון פתוח! אלא שסגר החלון, ומכח זה הבין אבימלך. . . .

[16] יצחק סתם החלון, והשקפת אבימלך היה בסיבת סתימת החלון. שראה שסתמו יצחק, והבין דכדי לשמש בבית אופל סתמו, או משום כדי שלא יראוהו השכנים.

[17] בעד החלון. לא שהיה החלון פתוח אלא נעול. ומתוך שהיה נעול הבין אבימלך המעשה.

[18] את רבקה **אשתו**. עניני צחוק המיוחדים לאשה. ולא נפל ספק אולי מצחק עם אחותו.

nearly slept with your wife! You would thus have brought blame upon us!" Faced with Isaac's stoic silence, Avimelech issues a protective command to his subjects, saying: "He who so much as touches this man and his wife will surely die."

Avimelech's exclamation, "How could you have said, 'She is my sister!'"[19] suggests to Radak that *this* Avimelech was *not* the same Avimelech who had forcibly taken Sarah to his chambers years before, who had also suffered because of Abraham's reliance on the wife/sister ruse. For had he been the same man, he would surely have seen through Isaac's familiar ploy, because of what had happened with Sarah. The commentator suggests, rather, that it was customary for Philistine kings to be called "Avimelech," just as it was customary for Egyptian kings to be called "Pharaoh."[20]

Contrarily, Rav Bachya feels that Isaac's Avimelech and Abraham's Avimelech were one and the same; that Isaac was justified in returning to Gerar, because he hoped that this same king who had made an oath of peace with his father would honor it with the son.[21] And Avimelech said ". . . *one of us* nearly slept with your wife!"[22] Rashi suggests that because of Rebecca's considerable beauty, it was Avimelech himself who would have taken her from Isaac.[23] Chizkuni, however, teaches us that her beauty appealed to everyone in Gerar, be he young or old, commoner or royalty.[24]

Avimelech's actual identity is unimportant in this episode for two reasons. First, in contrast with Sarah, Rebecca was never taken from her husband's side, and spent no time alone with Avimelech. Second, also in contrast with Sarah, by the time Rebecca and Isaac had entered Avimelech's kingdom, their twin sons already had been born. The issue of Isaac's paternity—so critical because of Sarah's forcible abduction by Avimelech—is not an issue here. There is never a doubt that Isaac and Rebecca are the parents of Jacob and Esav.

---

19 ואיך אמרת אחותי הוא?

20 לא היה זה אבימלך שהיה בימי אברהם. כי אילו היה הוא, לא היה שואלו איך אמרת. כי כבר ידע בענין שרה. אבל מלכי ארץ פלשתים היו נקראים אבימלך ברוב, כמו שהיה נקרא ברוב מלך מצרים פרעה.

21 היה אותו אבימלך שהיה בימי אביו, שכרת עמו ברית והלך אליו אולי ייטב לו.

22 ויאמר אבימלך, מה זאת עשית לנו; כמעט שכב אחד העם את אשתך.

23 אחד העם: זה המלך.

24 אחד מן העם. הן גדול, הן קטן.

GENESIS 26:12–33

God blesses Isaac while he dwells in the city of Gerar, and he prospers greatly, which arouses the jealousy of the Philistines. Avimelech asks Isaac to leave his city, because his wealth and holdings have overwhelmed the inhabitants. Isaac complies, and settles in the valley of Gerar, where his men dig a well and find fresh water. Avimelech's shepherds, having dogged Isaac's footsteps, twice battle with Isaac's shepherds over his father's wells, which Isaac had re-dug at his peril, the local shepherds having seized the water for themselves. Not wishing to place his beloved wife and two young sons in greater danger, Isaac distances his family from the fray and settles in Be'er Sheva, there building an altar to God. God appears to Isaac, and reassures him that He will protect him, just as He promised his father Abraham.

Yet Avimelech, fearing Isaac's growing strength, follows him to Be'er Sheva. There, Avimelech and his army chieftains seal a peace covenant with Isaac because they see that Isaac is blessed by God. On that same day, Isaac's servants dig yet another well, finding water once again, thus assuring Isaac and his family's survival during the famine.

GENESIS 26:34–35

Many years pass, and the text records that when Esav reached the age of forty years old—the same age that his father had been when he married Rebecca—Esav married two Hittite women, Yehudit and Basmat. Sforno notes that in contrast to his father Abraham, who was preoccupied to the point of obsession over his son's marrying only a woman of his kith and kindred, the ailing Isaac did not bestir himself to seek out suitable wives for his two sons.[25] And in fact, the Bible states that Esav's Hittite wives were a source of spiritual depression *for Isaac and Rebecca*.[26]

Midrash Rabbah notices that Isaac's name is mentioned *before* Rebecca's in this verse, and the commentary offers possible

---

[25] ויהי עשו בן ארבעים שנה. ולא חשש יצחק להשיא לו ולאחיו נשים הגונות . . . כמו שעשה אביו.

[26] ותהיין מרת רוח **ליצחק ולרבקה**.

explanations. First, perhaps this is a subtle reminder to us that Isaac's sensibilities were more offended over Esav's wives' idolatrous practices than was Rebecca. For although Hagar and Ishmael had posed a threat of negative influence in Isaac's childhood, they were sent away before they could exert any lasting impression upon him. Isaac grew up in Abraham and Sarah's tents, which were devoid of any trace of idol worship, while Rebecca's childhood home contained constant evidence of these practices, where she grew accustomed—even inured—to seeing them.[27] Second, according to Rashi (in Genesis 25:22) Rebecca possessed the foreknowledge that one of her twin sons would bring her grief, so perhaps she was not as shocked at Esav's intermarriage as was Isaac. Isaac was not privy to this prophecy, and so is more taken aback by Esav's behavior.[28]

The *Netziv* teaches us that regardless of whose name is mentioned first, *both* Isaac and Rebecca are wretched at Esav's wives' behaviors.[29] Perhaps Isaac, who loved Esav, was especially vexed at his wives' inappropriate behavior, having expected better of him. Whereas Rebecca, even though she did not hold out high expectations for Esav, was nonetheless aggravated by Esav's wives' scornful behavior toward her. Both Isaac and Rebecca were embittered by Esav.[30]

---

[27] למה ליצחק תחלה? אלא על ידי שהיתה רבקה בן כומרים, לא היתה מקפדת על טנופן עבודת כוכבים.

[28] לפי שהדבר תלוי בה. שנאמר, ויאמר ד' **לה**: שני גוים בבטנך.

[29] ליצחק ולרבקה. לכל אחד באופן אחר.

[30] ולפעמים האהבה גורמת מורת רוח . . . ולפעמים השנאה גורמת מורת רוח.

THIRTY-FOUR

୫୦୯ଃ୫୦୯ଃ

The Deception

GENESIS 27:1–4

With the passage of time Isaac grew old and his eyesight weakened, so that he could not see. And he called Esav, his elder son, to appear before him, and he said to him, "My son!" And Esav answered, "I am here to do your bidding." And Isaac said, "Know, now, that I am old, and I do not know how soon I will die. Take your hunting gear, your bow and arrows. Go out into the field and hunt me some wild game. Prepare this delicacy for me the way I like it, and bring it to me to eat, so that I can bless you before I die."

According to Sforno, Isaac was offering Esav the opportunity to honor him by allowing him to perform the labor of hunting and cooking the meat that Isaac so enjoyed, thus meriting the blessing he was about to bestow.[1] This entire segment of biblical narrative is elaborated upon by the Ramban: Rebecca knows from the prophecy during her pregnancy that the elder son will serve the younger. Isaac, however, is not privy to this revelation, and as his death draws nearer, it will soon be time for him to bestow his blessings upon his heirs. Other than his substantial wealth, Isaac will be passing on the

---

[1] רצה במטעמים כדי שיתעסק בכבוד אב, ובזה תחול עליו הברכה כי גם שלא הכיר בגדול רשעו של עשו, מכל מקום לא חשב אותו לראוי שתחול עליו אותה הברכה שהיה בלבו לברכו.

155

generational or covenantal blessing that he inherited from Abraham. The drama intensifies because the reader is aware that only Rebecca knows that Esav—though he is the elder son—is not the "chosen" one for purposes of receiving the coveted generational blessing. Isaac, the bestower of the blessing, is unknowingly preparing to vest it upon an unworthy Esav.[2]

The modern commentator, Yehuda Nachshoni, emphasizes that Rebecca possessed two critical pieces of their family puzzle that Isaac was lacking. First, Isaac is not aware that the forthcoming deception is an inevitable continuation of the chain of events put into play when Esav scorned and sold his birthright to Jacob in Genesis 25:24. Once he sold it to his brother, Jacob, by rights, became the "elder," and the natural perquisites that flowed to the elder son came due him. And second, Isaac, in his innocence, fails to recognize the truly corrupt character of his son Esav, while his wife discerned all of this.[3]

The reader can envision Rebecca's coiled tension as Isaac grows older and as his eyesight dims. She cannot venture far from Isaac's tent, lest he is seized with the impulse to bless his sons. She fears that Isaac will erroneously bless Esav, the elder son, with the covenantal blessing, while Jacob, the younger twin, is the one worthy to receive it. Ramban suggests that Rebecca has modestly concealed the prophecy in her heart these many years, always expecting that her husband's own prophetic ability would give him the insight into which of his sons should receive Abraham's blessing.[4] The reader enters the scenario at this precise point.

GENESIS 27:5

Rebecca is listening when Isaac speaks to Esav his son. And Esav went out into the fields to hunt wild game.

---

[2] בעבור תברך נפשי. היה בדעתו לברך אותו שיזכה הוא בברכת אברהם . . . כי הוא הבכור, ונראה שלא הגידה לו רבקה מעולם הנבואה אשר אמר ד' לה.

[3] אין כאן אלה פעולת המשך למעשה של קנית הבכורה . . . ליצחק חסרו שני נתונים להכרת המצב. הוא לא ידע על בזוי הבכורה ומכירתו. ואף לא הכיר את אופיו המושחת של עשו. רבקה הכירה בו.

[4] לא הגידה לו, דרך מוסר וצניעות . . . או שאמרה אין אנכי צריכה להגיד נבואה לנביא.

The commentators consider how Rebecca overhears Isaac's instructions to Esav. The *Netziv* says that Rebecca's concern for Jacob impelled her to listen intently whenever her husband spoke privately with Esav.[5] *Ohr Hachayim* is confident that it is Rebecca's prophetic ability—and not a propensity for eavesdropping—that enables her to remain continuously aware of Isaac's words, even when he does not speak in her presence.[6] *Perush Yonatan* elevates Rebecca's "listening" to prophecy, as does *Ohr Hachayim*, but adds another dimension to it. The commentator states unequivocally that *only* in response to a Divine *command* to select Jacob would this exemplary woman have orchestrated the forthcoming episode.[7]

GENESIS 27:6–10

> *And Rebecca said to Jacob, her son, as follows: I have just overheard your father speaking to your brother Esav, and he said to him, "Bring me wild game, and prepare for me this delicacy, and I will eat it, and I will bless you before God in advance of my death." So now, my son, listen carefully to what I am saying, to what I am ordering you to do. Go now, if you would, to the flock, and fetch me from there two tender kid-goats. And I will prepare them as a delicacy for your father, just the way he likes it. And you shall bring it to your father to eat, in order that he will bless **you** before he dies.*

Rebecca is about to orchestrate a switch that will have profound consequences not only on a familial level, but on a generational level as well. God never condemns Rebecca, but the *p'shat* reading of this biblical drama invites the reader to decry Rebecca's behavior as manipulative at best, or deceptive at worst. In contrast, virtually all the *mephorshim* exonerate Rebecca's actions. Her plan is viewed as submission to God's design.

At the outset of this suspenseful scene, the commentator *Ohr Hachayim* states that Rebecca here is acceding to God's will as it was revealed to her in prophecy. The commentator derives this from the

---

5 ורבקה שומעת. כך דרכה. תמיד בשעה שיצחק מדבר עם עשו היא צייתנית לדעת אולי הוא נוגע ליעקב.

6 ורבקה שומעת . . . רבקה נביאה היתה, ושומעת תמיד בדברי יצחק. הגם שלא ידבר בפניה והבן.

7 שמעת ברוח קודשא. דקשיא ליה האיך יעצה לבנה דבר מרמה, אלא ברוח הקודש **נצתווה** לה.

first Hebrew letter of verse six. This conjunctional *"vav"* specifically denotes that Rebecca complied *with* God's instruction to her concerning her son Jacob.[8]

Abarbanel, agreeing with *Perush Yonatan* that Rebecca's actions are Divinely inspired,[9] understands her behavior. The commentator invites us to imagine Rebecca's initial shock at God's presumed command to present Jacob in Esav's stead. Rebecca, an intelligent and thoughtful woman, takes a critical look at her two sons and sees them as they are: On the one hand she sees her first-born son, Esav, who has been a hunter and a spiritual stranger to his mother for his entire life. He has recently married two Hittite women whose sinful and contentious ways are causing bitter strife in Rebecca's household, and are the source of his parents' misery. On the other hand, she sees Jacob, unmarried at 40-odd years old, seemingly content, as Isaac was, to manage his father's extensive flocks and to dwell in his tents. The contrast could not have been more staggering to Rebecca. The commentator tells us that she thought, "The prophecy was correct! My younger son *is* more worthy than his older brother. For how can any sons that issue from Esav and his immoral wives be fit to inherit a personal relationship with God, along with the Holy Land?"[10] In that instant of epiphany, Rebecca knew what she had to do.

GENESIS 27:8

Rebecca exhorts Jacob: *Hearken to my voice.*[11] The *Netziv* points out that whenever the Hebrew word **BeKoLi**[12] (in my voice) appears in the Bible coupled with *listen to me*, its import is that the listener is expected to pay close attention to the voice of the speaker, and to follow her instructions to the letter.[13] In this instance, according

---

[8] ‏ורבקה אמרה. תוספת וא"ו כי הסכימה היא לרוח הקודש השרויה עליה.‎

[9] ‏ברוח הקודש נצתווה לה.‎

[10] ‏גם ראתה שנשי עשו היו רעות וחטאות . . . ואיך יהיו בניהם יורשים הדבקות האלקי והארץ הקדושה? לכן השתדלה בדבר הזה.‎

[11] ‏שמע בקלי‎

[12] ‏בקלי‎

[13] ‏שמע בקלי. תיבת בקלי **מיותר** . . . אבל כבר ביארנו כל פעם דמשמעות "בקלי" הוא התבוננות ודיוק בדברי. ורמזה לו שברוח הקודש היא מדברת.‎

to the commentator, by her choice of words Rebecca was intimating to her son that her imminent plan was inspired by Divine prophecy.

Ohr Hachayim recognizes the grave import of Rebecca's plan, and vindicates her forthcoming actions. Her persuasion of Jacob to trick his father into blessing him rather than his brother is seen by the commentator as the only avenue available to her. The moment of blessing is abruptly upon them, and the commentator envisions Rebecca's ambivalence. She is, after all, aware that she is about to deceive her beloved husband, and what is more, to encourage her favored son to be an active accomplice. She *must* prevent her husband's blessing from falling to the wrong son. The commentator here elaborates upon Rebecca's words, following the Bible's use of the phrase *hearken to my voice*.[14] "Now heed my words, Jacob my son. While my advice might appear to be deceitful, and may not seem right to you, I am asking you to trust me, and to comply with the Bible's positive command to honor your mother. For I am in receipt of God's prophecy in this matter." *Ohr Hachayim* reminds the reader that the Bible teaches us to obey a prophet's instructions, in such a temporary, exigent situation as Jacob is facing, even if it appears to run counter to established law.[15]

Alshich adds to our understanding of Rebecca's strength of purpose and clarity of vision. He has her saying to Jacob:

> Heed my voice, my son.[16] But do so *not* merely to advance your own ends, in order to outsmart your brother and acquire his blessing. Heed my words solely out of respect for my wishes, without attempting to discern an underlying meaning to my strategy.[17]

Thus, the commentaries take pains to emphasize that Rebecca's action is proper, perhaps because she is in receipt of God's prophecy. She also ensures that her son Jacob truly appreciates that his

---

[14] שמע בקולי

[15] שמע בקולי. הגם שיש בדברים אלו כגניבת דעת. על כל זה יש לך לשמוע בקולי . . . מלבד חיוב מצות כיבוד אב ואם שהיא מצות עשה, גם היא נביאה. וכתוב: בדברי נביא אמת אליו תשמעון. וכבר כתבנו שיצטדק נביא באומרו לעבור על מצות ממצות התורה לפי שעה.

[16] ועתה בני, שמע בקולי.

[17] לכך אמרה ועתה בני, שמע בקולי. כלומר ואתה גם כן לא תעשה הדבר לכוונת קנות ברכות או לרמות אחיך. זולתי כדי לשמוע בקולי . . . ואל תשקף בכוונת המצוה.

acquiescence to her wishes regarding his father's blessing is the right
and proper thing to do, if only because she asks him to do it.

The reader may remember that Rebecca's words, *hearken to my
voice*[18] (in verse eight), are virtually the same words that appear in
Genesis 21:12, when God exhorts Abraham to heed the words of his
wife, Sarah, concerning the banishment of the taunting Hagar. There,
when Abraham hesitated to do as Sarah bid him, God intervened on
Sarah's behalf and said, "All that Sarah instructs you, *hearken to her
voice*."[19] *S'fat Hayeriya*, a supercommentary on *Ohel Yaakov*,
informs us that the Torah's use of identical words in both Sarah's
situation and here in Rebecca's, teaches us that God's guiding hand
directed them both.[20] The commentator continues with a brief excerpt
from the tribute to women from the Book of Proverbs (31:26),
holding Rebecca out as a paradigm for the phrase, *Her mouth is
opened in wisdom*.[21] He concludes that the phrase *hearken to my
voice* is a reference both to God's attribution of Sarah's voice of
prophecy and to Rebecca's own concomitant Divine inspiration
throughout this entire episode.[22]

GENESIS 27:11–12

And Jacob answers his mother Rebecca, saying: "But my
brother Esav is a hairy man, while I am smooth-skinned. What if my
father draws me near and feels my skin; I will appear in his eyes as a
trickster, thus bringing upon myself a curse instead of a blessing."
Ramban interprets Jacob's concern in a tender fashion. He explains
that Jacob foresees his father lovingly embracing the son who feeds
him delicacies, perhaps kissing him and placing a gnarled hand upon
his son's cheek.[23] Thus, Jacob tacitly acquiesces to his mother's plan
to substitute him for his brother, but he expresses his reservation that

---

18 שמע בקלי

19 כל אשר תאמר אליך שרה, **שמע בקולה.**

20 שמע בקולי. יען כמילת **ב**קולי מורה על דבר שנאמר "כל אשר תאמר אליך שרה, **שמע
בקולה.**"

21 פיה פתחה בחכמה.

22 ברוח הקודש שמעה את הכל.

23 אולי יקרב אותי אל עצמו לנשק לי או לשום ידו על פני כדרך חבת האב על בנו.

any blessing acquired in such a fashion might backfire and result in a curse.

GENESIS 27:13

His mother replied to him: Let your curse be on my [head], my son. Only hearken to my voice, and go, fetch [the kid-goats] to me.[24]

Rashbam explains that Rebecca cavalierly accepts Jacob's feared consequences for her scheme because she truly believes that her plan is consistent with God's prophecy that her younger son will prevail over his older brother.[25] The *Netziv* agrees, relying on the repetition here of the now-familiar phrase, *hearken to my voice*.[26] With this phrase, Rebecca is hinting to her son, Jacob, that he need not concern himself about any feared curse; that because she is privy to the prophecy that her older son will be subservient to the younger, she is confident that her plan will succeed.[27]

GENESIS 27:14–17

So Jacob went, and fetched the kid-goats, and brought them to his mother. And his mother prepared the delicacies just the way his father liked them. Then Rebecca took the choicest garments that Esav, her elder son, had left in her home, and she draped them over Jacob, her younger son. And as for the skins of the two kid-goats, Rebecca dressed them upon Jacob's hands and upon the exposed part of his neck. And she placed the savory delicacies, and the bread which she had made, into the hand of her son Jacob. *Midrash Rabbah* (65:17) paints the scene poignantly. Rebecca, acting upon her vision, can only bring her son Jacob to the threshold of his destiny. She escorts him only as far as Isaac's tent flap. There, she tells her son, "I have done all that it is within my power to do for you. Go, now, and God will do the rest."[28]

---

[24] ותאמר לו אמו, עלי קללתך בני, אך שמע בקלי ולך קח לי.

[25] עלי ועל צווארי. כלומר כי היתה בוטחת במה שאמר לה הקב"ה "ורב יעבוד צעיר."

[26] שמע בקלי

[27] שמע בקלי. הבן בדברי. כי ברוח הקודש הנני מדבר ויודעת אני שיצליח העניין.

[28] לותה אותו עד הפתח. אמרה, עד כאן הייתי חייבת לך. מכאן ואילך ברייך יקום לך.

GENESIS 27:18–29

The text then narrates the famed scene, masterminded by Rebecca, where Jacob presents himself to his father in the guise of his older brother. Isaac, perhaps suspecting that the wrong twin was before him, embraces his son and exclaims, "The voice is the voice of Jacob, but the hands are the hands of Esav!" Notwithstanding any harbored doubts, Isaac blesses Jacob with the coveted first-born's blessing. Amazingly, the crux of Isaac's blessing (at verse 29) mirrors the prophecy that Rebecca received during her difficult pregnancy. "Let the peoples of the world serve you," Isaac intones, "and nations bow down to you; *you shall be lord over your brother*, and your mother's sons will bow down to you."

GENESIS 27:30–33

No sooner does Jacob receive Isaac's blessing and depart his father's tent, when Esav returns from his hunt and presents himself to his father to be blessed. Isaac is abjectly terrified when Esav confronts him. The commentaries differ as to the cause of Isaac's terror. Was Isaac aware that the son he blessed was Jacob and not Esav? If Isaac did *not* know that he had blessed an impostor, then the "enormous terror" he feels[29] (in verse 33) when Esav appears at his tent shouldering a slain deer is readily understandable. He trembles because he realizes that he blessed the wrong son.

If, on the other hand, he *knew* that he was blessing his younger son, Jacob, then Isaac's existential terror in verse 33 is problematical. Why would Isaac "tremble" at Esav's presence if he had already seen through Jacob's ruse? A close reading of the *p'shat* would indicate that Isaac more than suspected that a deception was afoot when he questioned the son standing before him and doubted his identity. He asks, *Who are you, my son?* [30] in verse 18; *How is it that you have found [the venison] so quickly, my son?* [31] in verse 19; *Come near to me, please, so that I may feel you, my son, [to be certain] you are*

---

[29] ויחרד יצחק חרדה גדולה עד מאד.

[30] מי אתה בני?

[31] מה זה מהרת למצא בני?

truly my son Esav or not [32] in verse 21; *[But] the voice is the voice of Jacob, while the hands are the hands of Esav!* [33] in verse 22; *[Are] you my son Esav?* [34] in verse 24; and finally, *And [Isaac] smelled the smell of his clothing, and [then] he blessed him* [35] in verse 27.

Ramban states that when Esav confronts his father, Isaac trembles greatly because it is at that moment that he realizes that his beloved son Esav has forfeited his blessing forever.[36] Isaac realizes that even though it is against his own will, Esav will not be the recipient of the firstborn's blessing, because that blessing—once bestowed, even erroneously—is irrevocable.[37] Rashi agrees with Ramban that Isaac blessed Jacob unknowingly. However, Rashi adds that once Isaac realizes that he blessed the wrong son, he *consciously* affirms that the blessing should remain with Jacob: *and he shall be blessed.*[38] In this way, in the future, no one will challenge Jacob's receipt of the blessing he obtained by trickery.[39]

Isaac's suspicions are confirmed as Esav stands before him. Rashbam explains that in a flash of insight Isaac realizes that his beloved wife, Rebecca—in her wisdom—guided Jacob in the subterfuge. Isaac recognizes that Rebecca perceived what he did not: that Jacob, and not Esav, was the one worthy of the covenantal blessing. He therefore confirms aloud that Jacob's blessing should stand, and Isaac trembles no more.[40] *Ohel Yaakov* overrides the commentaries' debate on the question of whether Isaac knew—or even suspected—that he was blessing Jacob in Esav's stead. This commentator states emphatically that regardless, the Almighty approved of Rebecca's method of securing the covenantal, first-born's blessing for Jacob.[41] This is because Jacob was always intended to be its recipient.

---

[32] גשה נא ואמשך בני, האתה זה זה בני עשו אם לא.

[33] הקל קול יעקב, והידים ידי עשו.

[34] אתה זה בני עשו?

[35] וירח את ריח בגדיו ויברכהו.

[36] וזה טעם החרדה הגדולה אשר חרד. כי ידע שאבד בנו האהוב לו ברכתו לעולם.

[37] על כרחי, שאי אפשר לי להעביר הברכה ממנו.

[38] וגם ברוך יהיה.

[39] שלא תאמר: אלולי שרמה יעקב לאביו לא נטל את הברכות. **לכן הסכים וברכו מדעתו.**

[40] גם ברוך יהיה . . . ידע שבעצת רבקה עשה הכל, והיא היתה מכרת בו שראוי לברכות.

[41] אבל הקב"ה הסכים לשיטת רבקה לברך את יעקב שיהיה גביר לעשו.

GENESIS 27:34–41

When Esav learned that his younger brother had received the first-born's blessing, he cried out bitterly and asked his father to bless him nonetheless. Isaac thus was prevailed upon to confer a lesser blessing upon Esav, and as a result, Esav harbored a grudge against his brother Jacob. So Esav secretly plotted that he would bide his time until after his father's death, thinking, "whereupon I will murder my brother Jacob."

THIRTY–FIVE

Jacob is Sent Away

GENESIS 27:42–45

And Rebecca was told the words of her elder son, Esav.[1]

So she sent for Jacob, her younger son, and told him, "Behold, Esav your brother consoles himself, marking you for a dead man, as he plans to kill you himself. Now, therefore, my son, hearken to my voice, and rouse yourself and flee to Haran to the home of my brother Lavan. Stay there with him a short while until your brother's wrath has cooled, and his anger toward you has subsided, and he has forgotten what you did to him. Only then will I send for you to return home, for why should I risk losing you both in one day!"

Ramban explains that Rebecca discovered Esav's secret threat because he bragged to his close friends about his plan for revenge, and she *was told* of his bravado.[2] Rashi, however, along with other *mephorshim*, departs from a *p'shat* reading of the words "and Rebecca was told . . ." and clearly credits Rebecca's prophetic ability with enabling her to discern the hatred that lodged deep within Esav's heart. The commentator states unequivocally that the inner workings of Esav's vengeful heart were revealed to Rebecca by Divine

---

[1] ויגד לרבקה את דברי עשו בנה.

[2] שגלה סודו לאחד מאוהביו.

inspiration.[3] Radak agrees, taking Rashi one step further, actually naming Rebecca a prophetess.[4]

Rebecca, having learned of Esav's reaction, realizes now that the ruse—while successful in aiding Jacob to obtain the rightful blessing—has incensed Esav to threaten Jacob's life. Therefore, Rebecca hastily summons Jacob and uses the familiar phrase, *And now, my son, **hearken to my voice**[5]* (see 27:8 and 13), to preface her parting words to her beloved son, urging him to flee to her brother in Haran. The *Netziv* reminds the reader that the Bible repeats Rebecca's phrase word-for-word here, to reinforce for us that in this instance, also—as when she orchestrated the deception—she is speaking with rectitude, precision and depth of understanding. Jacob is exhorted to listen closely, and to apprehend the deeper meaning of his mother's words.[6]

GENESIS 27:46

From the moment Rebecca issued the momentous response—*I will go*[7] (in 24:58), consenting to journey to Abraham's land and to further his Divine mission, the course of her life was set. She met her first imperative goal and provided Isaac with heirs. Her next goal is to assure the survival of the son who is worthy of receiving Isaac's—and therefore Abraham's—blessings. Thus, Esav's angry vendetta threatens Rebecca's survival in a very real sense. For if Jacob—the worthy heir—were to be killed by Esav, then Rebecca's entire life will have been for naught.

Yet in this verse, Rebecca cries out to Isaac, "I am anguished with my life because of [Esav's] Hittite wives. If Jacob were to take a Hittite wife such as these, [and marry] of the daughters of the land, what meaning would my life have?"

This verse is a completely unexpected *non sequitur* to the dramatic outcry by Esav, and his threat to murder Jacob. The reader might rather have expected Rebecca to fly into her husband's tent,

---

3   ברוח הקדש הגד לה מה שעשו מהרהר בלבו.

4   אפשר כי בנבואה נאמר לה, **כי נביאה היתה.**

5   ועתה בני, **שמע בקלי.**

6   שמע בקלי. התבונן בדברי כי גם עתה דברה בדיוק ובעומק הדעת.

7   אלך

throw herself at his knees and cry, "Husband! Esav is planning to kill his brother Jacob! You must aid me in separating our warring sons. You must prevail upon Esav to leave Jacob be, and send Jacob away, out of Esav's reach." Instead, however, the text relates Rebecca's complaint to Isaac about Esav's Hittite wives. Because Rebecca's words and actions have so far been insightful, preemptive and even prophetic, we must uncover the reason for this verbal ploy. Rashbam cryptically states that Rebecca's cry about her misery with the Hittite women was "a wise move."[8] The *Netziv* suggests that Rebecca is following the pattern of her marriage, protecting Isaac from any unpleasantness. Rebecca brought up the subjects of the Hittite wives rather than disclose to Isaac Esav's murderous plot, in order to prevent Isaac from coming face-to-face with Esav's true intention.[9] Alshich understands that not only did Rebecca seek to protect Isaac, and to prevent her sons from slaying one another, but she also sought to obtain a wholehearted blessing for Jacob before his escape.[10]

. . . *What meaning would my life have?* [11] These three poignant Hebrew words mark Rebecca's final speech in the Bible. For this reason alone students of the text would be expected to pay close attention, to dissect and understand their meaning. However, this is not the first time that Rebecca has uttered similar desperate words at a time of personal crisis. The first time was during her troubled pregnancy, which followed her twenty childless years. There, Rebecca, terrified that she would miscarry, desperately sought some assurance that she would bear a long-awaited child. Her words in 25:22—*And she said, "If so, what meaning does my life have?"* [12]—are echoed in her cry here. In this verse, Rebecca's existential fear, repressed thus far over the course of her sons' lifetime, surfaces once again. Rebecca worries that if both her sons marry unworthy wives, then Abraham's legacy would remain unfulfilled through hers and Isaac's progeny. Devastated when she received the prophecy during her pregnancy that the elder of her unborn sons would be unworthy, she now fervently desires that at least her

---

[8] דרך חכמה אמרה רבקה ליצחק.

[9] לא רצתה רבקה להודיע ליצחק רשעת עשו.

[10] הנה רבקה . . . . התחכמה . . . . למען ישלחנו יצחק . . . שמצווהו ללכת ומברכו.

[11] למה לי חיים?

[12] ותאמר אם כן למה זה אנכי!

younger son will inherit the Divine blessing. For if not, she reasons, her life would be rendered meaningless.

The *Chatam Sofer* explains that Rebecca did not despair, even when she received the prophecy that one of her unborn sons would be unworthy, because she held onto the hope that the other son would carry on.[13] Now, however, faced with the specter of Jacob's marrying unrighteous women, Rebecca's angst overwhelms her, and she cries, "If Jacob marries a Hittite woman, a woman of this land, then why was I even born!"

GENESIS 28:1–7

Finally comprehending Rebecca's wisdom in her championship of Jacob, Isaac, of his own volition and with "open eyes," now blesses Jacob with the covenantal blessing he received from his own father. With this second blessing Isaac affirms all of Rebecca's interventions and anoints Jacob the heir apparent.

> *And Isaac calls Jacob to him and blesses him; and he commands him saying: "Do not take a wife from the daughters of Canaan. Arise and journey to Padan-Aram, to the home of Betuel, your mother's father; take for yourself a wife from there, from among the daughters of Lavan, your mother's brother, so that the Almighty God will bless you, and make [your union] fruitful, and make you fertile. And you shall [thus] become a congregation of peoples. [And God shall] give you and your progeny the blessing of Abraham: that you shall inherit the land of your journeyings, [the land] that God gave to Abraham.*

The reader can imagine Rebecca watching her husband as he knowingly blesses her younger son. Her lifelong mission is becoming actualized as Abraham's covenantal blessing is being passed to Jacob. But how bittersweet is Rebecca's moment of joy! As she watches Jacob assume his position as spiritual heir to Isaac, she also knows that for his own safety Jacob must leave her, and seek his future in Padan-Aram.

---

[13] שרבקה התפללה למה זה אנכי. פי' רמבן למה אנכי בעולם . . . ונאמר לה שני גוים. ועי"ז סבלה היסורים. עתה ח"ו אם גם יעקב ירשיע ע"י נשים כאלה . . . וזה שאמרה למה לי חיים.

So Isaac did send Jacob away, and he journeyed to Padan-Aram, to Lavan the son of Betuel the Aramean, the brother of **Rebecca, mother of Jacob and Esav**. . . . *And [thus], journeying to Padan-Aram, Jacob obeyed [both] his father and his mother.*

Nehama Leibowitz[†] rhetorically asks, "What prompted the Torah to add the apparently completely superfluous fact that Rebecca was the mother of both Jacob and Esav?" She answers that

> It is meant to teach us something new. . . . The text wished to teach us that Rebecca rescued *Jacob* from death [but] she was acting as the mother of *Esav*, too, in preventing him murdering his brother. In this hour of mortal peril she laid plans, carefully and prudently as 'Jacob's and Esav's mother,' so that she should not be 'bereaved of both of them in one day.' (See Genesis 27:45.)

Nehama understands that if Esav were to carry out his threat to kill Jacob, Rebecca would be physically bereft of her favored son, Jacob, and she would also "lose" her elder son, Esav.

> At one and the same moment the perpetrator of fratricide and the victim would be no more (one physically, the other mentally, shut out of her mind) and their mother would have lost two children as the result of the one deed of murder.[14]

For this reason, and out of Rebecca's love for both Jacob and Esav—albeit unequally—the Bible reminds the reader that as Rebecca sends Jacob away, she is fulfilling her role as mother to both her sons. Tragically, however, as she watches Jacob's form receding in the distance, Rebecca is unaware that she will never again set eyes on him.

[†]Leibowitz, N. (1973). *Studies in Bereshit*, p. 286.

---

14 מה ראתה התורה לציין עתה בסוף הפרשה את רבקה כאם יעקב ועשו . . . וכל הפרשה עסקה ביחסי רבקה אל "עשו בנה הגדול," ואל "יעקב בנה הקטן?" . . . להודיענו שלא אם יעקב בלבד היתה בהבריחה את יעקב ובהצילו אותו ממות, אלא גם אם עשו היתה בהצילה את עשו מלרצוח את אחיו . . . הנה עתה ברגע הסכנה הגדולה היא מכלכלת מעשיה בתבונה כ"אם יעקב ועשו," שלא תשכל שניהם יום אחד . . . כי שניהם בניה וביום וברגע אחד עלולה היא לשכל אותם, כי גם ההרוג וגם ההורג אינם עוד.

THIRTY–SIX

The Death of
Rebecca's Nursemaid

GENESIS 35:8

O ther than cursory mention of Rebecca's name in future chapters of the text which recount Jacob's lineage, Rebecca's story effectively ends here. Unfortunately, the text supplies no details of her life after she sends Jacob away to the house of her brother Lavan. Even Rebecca's death is not recorded in the text. The *mephorshim* themselves must feel this absence of textual detail, because they strain to deduce Rebecca's death from *this* verse, which plainly records *only* the death of Deborah, Rebecca's nursemaid.[1]

> *And Deborah, Rebecca's nursemaid, died and was buried in the foothills of Beit-El, beneath the oak that [Jacob] called "The Oak of Tears."*

Using this verse, the *mephorshim* link the *unrecorded* death of Rebecca to the *recorded* death of her nursemaid. They also offer explanations as to the reason Rebecca's death is only hinted at in the text. Rashi explains that Rebecca, in her last recorded instruction to her son Jacob, promises to send for him to return from Padan-Aram once Esav's anger is assuaged (see 27:45). The years pass and the

---

[1] ותמת דברה מינקת רבקה ותקבר מתחת לבית-אל תחת האלון; ויקרא שמו אלון בכות.

danger has subsided. Rebecca dispatches her most trusted maidservant, the one who had accompanied her so many years before on the caravan ride from her father's home in Padan-Aram to meet Isaac, her betrothed. Deborah's mission now is to bring Jacob home. According to Rashi, she dies *en route*, her mission unfulfilled.[2]

Ramban agrees that Rebecca's death is hinted at by the reference to Deborah's death and burial in this verse, but his understanding is that Deborah's death occurred not *en route to* fetch Jacob, but on her journey *back* from Padan-Aram with Jacob, his wives and his children in tow. Deborah had escorted her mistress from Padan-Aram and had remained with her when she wed Isaac many years before. According to Ramban, now, at Rebecca's urging, Deborah returned to Lavan's house where she remained in order to act as nursemaid to Rebecca's grandchildren. It was on her arduous return journey home to Canaan with Jacob and his family that the aged Deborah died suddenly.[3] This reading allows us to envision Rebecca's fulfillment in the knowledge that Jacob has married properly and has been blessed by God with many children.[4] Unfortunately, Rebecca dies before Jacob and his family return home, and although she is blessed with thirteen grandchildren from Jacob, she never sets eyes on any of them. The commentaries *infer* Rebecca's death from verse 27, where the text records Jacob's homecoming: *And Jacob **returns to his father** Isaac*.[5] Ramban emphasizes that had Rebecca still been alive at the time of his homecoming, the text would certainly have read "Jacob returned to his father *and his mother*." The commentator stresses that because it was *Rebecca's* intervention that secured for Jacob all his blessings, and it was also *her* wisdom that guided Isaac to send Jacob to Padan-Aram, the absence of any reference to Rebecca in the verse describing Jacob's homecoming implies that she died in his absence.[6]

---

2 מה ענין דבורה בבית יעקב אלא לפי שאמרה רבקה ליעקב: ושלחתי ולקחתיך משם, שלחה דבורה אצלו לפדן ארם לצאת משם, ומתה בדרך.

3 וזהו ענין הרמז. והיתה דבורה עם יעקב כי אחרי שבאת עם רבקה, שבה לארצה, ועתה תבא עם יעקב לראות גבירתה, או להתעסק בגדול בני יעקב, לכבוד רבקה ולאהבתה, והיתה בביתו.

4 רבקה . . . שלחה דבורה אצלו לפדן ארם להוציאו משם, ולחוס על ילדיו.

5 ויבא יעקב אל יצחק אביו.

6 ואלו היתה רבקה שם, היה מזכיר אל אביו **ואל אמו**, כי היא השולחת אותו שם, והגורמת לו כל הטובה, ויצחק בעצתה צוה אותו ללכת שם.

Rabbi Abraham, son of the Rambam, offers yet another possible scenario involving the death of nursemaid Deborah. Rebecca, having endured her son's absence for twenty years while Esav's wrath cooled, is now near death herself. She sends a messenger to Padan-Aram for Jacob so that she can see him one last time. Deborah, her beloved and trusted servant, waits at the crossroads for Jacob to arrive home. Seeing Jacob approach, Deborah runs out to greet him and hastens to escort him to her mistress' bedside. Unfortunately, both are too late, as Rebecca dies before seeing her beloved son this one last time.[7] In fact, Chizkuni confirms that Rebecca indeed sent for Jacob in time before her death, but that due to Jacob's procrastination, Rebecca died without seeing him.[8]

The reader may legitimately ask why an event as important as Rebecca's death is not specifically mentioned in the Bible? Why is it relegated solely to allusion and inference? In contrast to *Sarah's* burial, Rebecca's burial is devoid of panoply. According to Ramban, the Bible did not wish to reiterate Rebecca's existential solitude by explicitly mentioning her unattended death. The stark reality was that her beloved son Jacob did not arrive home in time to bury her; her other son, Esav, remained estranged from her; and her husband, Isaac, in failing health and nearly blind, was by now extremely old and incapable even of leaving his own bed. The text did not wish to state that Rebecca was buried by strangers. The Ramban softens even this latter insult, however, by suggesting that Esav ultimately did in fact bury his mother, in a singular act of respect for her.[9]

Otzar Ishei Hatanach—quoting *Pesikta Rabbati* (12.22)—explains that *Rebecca herself*, sensing her end was near, and aware that neither Isaac nor Jacob would be able to escort her coffin to its burial place, issues an order that her burial should take place at night, under cover of darkness. She does not wish her funeral to draw idle gossip concerning Esav, her sole pall bearer. For these reasons,

---

7 ואמרו בהליכת דבורה אליו כי רבקה שלחה אותה כדי שתביא אותו . . . ויתכן שכאשר יעקב
קרב אל הארץ יצאה דבורה לקראתו והיתה דבורה מעיצה עליו לבוא מהר.

8 שלחה רבקה את דבורה אחר יעקב להחזירו . . . ולא רצה לבא.

9 יתכן לומר שלא היה לה כבוד במיתתה, כי יעקב איננו שם, ועשו שונא אותה ולא יבא שמה,
ויצחק כהו עיניו ואננו יוצא מביתו. ולכן לא רצה הכתוב להזכיר שיקברוה בני חת . . . בעבור
שהיה עשו יחידי בקבורתה. . . .

Rebecca's death and burial are not highlighted in the text in the manner that Sarah's was.[10]

The biblical text records that Jacob and his children bury Deborah, Rebecca's nursemaid, under an oak tree in the foothills of Beit-El, beneath the oak that Jacob called "The Oak of Tears."[11] Ramban continues his hypothesis that Rebecca's death is coincident with her nursemaid's. He points to the fact that Jacob names the place "The Oak of Tears." Given the importance of names in the Bible, Ramban is loath to believe that Jacob is commemorating only the maid's death. Her death alone would not have warranted excessive mourning and the naming of her burial place after the tears shed at her death. Rather, reasons the commentator, the tears referred to in this verse are shed by Jacob over *his righteous mother's* death. He mourns her passing excessively, realizing how great must have been Rebecca's love for him, to have first secured for him the covenantal blessing, and then to have had no alternative but to send him away to safety. Jacob cries for his mother's one fleeting moment of triumph of purpose, which evaporated the same instant she overheard Esav's threat on his life. Jacob's tears are for his beloved mother, who died before he returned from his exile in Padan-Aram, and they are also for himself. For in saving himself, Jacob simultaneously became bereft of his mother's presence.[12]

GENESIS 35:9

And God appeared to Jacob . . . and blessed him.[13]

What blessing does God bestow upon Jacob immediately after Deborah's death? *Midrash Rabbah* (81.5) characterizes this as the

---

[10] כשמתה רבקה הוציאו אותה בלילה, **והיא צוותה כן.** אמרה: יעקב הצדיק בני אינו כאן, יצחק הצדיק בעלי יושב בבית מפני שכהו עיניו, יוצאוני ביום ויהא רשע זה [עשו] הולך לפני מיטתי והיו אומרים "אוי מן הדד שזה הניק!" לכן ציותה להוציאה בלילה, ולא נכתב מיתתה כשל שרה.

[11] ותקבר מתחת לבית-אל תחת האלון, ויקרא שמו אלון בכות.

[12] קרא שם המקום ההוא אלון בכות כי אין בכי ואנקה על המנקת הזקנה שיקרא גם המקום עליו. אבל יעקב בכה והתאבל **על אמו הצדקת** אשר אהבתיהו, ושלחה אותו שם ולא זכתה לראותו בשובו.

[13] וירא אלקים אל יעקב . . . . ויברך אתו.

blessing for mourners,[14] corroborating the *mephorshim's* hypothesis that Rebecca's death was coincident with the recorded death of her nursemaid's. The *Netziv* adds that this verse describes God's expression of solace to the grieving Jacob.[15]

---

[14] ברכת **אבלים** ברכו.

[15] ויברך אותו ברכת **תנחומים**.

THIRTY-SEVEN

೮೦ೞ೮೦ೞ

The Unrecorded Burial
of Rebecca

The text makes no mention of Rebecca's burial place. But the Talmud (*Eruvin* 53a) is definitive in placing Rebecca in the Cave of Machpela, along with Sarah and Abraham.[1] Rebecca, her life's work complete, is accorded this honor and is laid to rest in the tomb reserved by Abraham especially for burying his dead. Her beloved husband, Isaac, is eventually buried by her side.

---

[1] מאי מכפלה? שכפולה בזוגות . . . אמר רבי יצחק קרית הארבעה זוגות . . . אדם וחוה,
אברהם ושרה, יצחק ורבקה, יעקב ולאה.

THIRTY–EIGHT

ଚ୦୯ଓଚ୦୯ଓ

Epilogue to Rebecca

*God should establish you as He did Sarah, **Rebecca**, Rachel and Leah.*[1]

On one level, Rebecca's tale is a grand, near-mythic love story. A beautiful and pure young girl, the object of an extensive and perilous quest, is discovered at the village well and passes the tests that foretell her fitness to be the chosen bride of Abraham's heir. Although she is born into a house of idolatry, Rebecca's own determination, faith, and foresight propel her into Isaac's arms and elevate her to be Sarah's successor. As the story is told thus far, we can certainly understand how Rebecca's life could be one we would hope our own daughters might relive.

However, the reality of Rebecca's existence was far from idyllic. She left her family and birthplace at a young age, traveled to a distant and strange land with only her trusted nursemaid as a companion, and although she married a man who truly loved her, she suffered twenty anguished years of infertility. Her eventual but turbulent pregnancy culminated in the birth of rival twins, after which time her marital integrity was threatened by a powerful and lustful king. Years later, Rebecca engineered a monumental deception which engendered a profound hatred between her sons, culminating in a

---

[1] ישמך אלקים כשרה, **רבקה**, רחל ולאה.

176

vow of fratricide. Thereupon Rebecca sends her hunted son away, and she is fated never to see him again. Many years pass and Rebecca dies alone, unattended by those whom she loved most.

Knowing the difficult drama of Rebecca's life, why do we still bless our daughters to be like her? We hope our daughters will emulate Rebecca's overriding ability to discern what was right, and to employ all of her resources in order to realize this vision. In fact, Rebecca's proper choices actually altered the presumed course of primogeniture, which would have placed Abraham's covenantal blessing in Esav's hands, and not in Jacob's.

Early on, Rebecca exhibited physical beauty, intelligence, and the quality of *chesed*, lovingkindness, which distinguished her from the other young women at the well. She also exhibited resolute confidence sparked by the intuitive foresight which marked her. These characteristics enabled Rebecca to assume primary responsibility at every stage of her life.

Rabbi Adin Steinsaltz, in his chapter on Rebecca in his work *Biblical Images*, eloquently summarizes Rebecca's clarity of vision:

> She *knew* that she must water the camels; she *knew* that she must go with the stranger, Abraham's servant, that this was her fate. When she saw Isaac, she *knew* that this was *the* man; and when she bore his sons, she *knew* which of them should receive the birthright.[†]

Rebecca was blessed with a husband who perceived and loved in her all the facets of his ideal woman, and who empathized with her existential needs; when she was barren he was "barren," and he prayed for her to conceive. Rebecca was further blessed with the wisdom to discern when to offer lovingkindness, and when to withhold it. Although this knowledge necessitated deception, Rebecca was graced with a husband who validated even that, saying, "Indeed he *shall* be blessed," at Genesis 25:33.[2]

When we bless our daughters to be like Rebecca we pray that—like Rebecca—they will meet life's challenges by choosing the

---

[†]Steinsaltz, A. (1984). *Biblical Images* (New York: Basic Books), p. 44.

---

correct path, guided by God's teachings. Acting in this inspired manner, Rebecca propelled Abraham's covenantal vision to the third generation through the chosen son, Jacob, and his wives.

PART III

RACHEL AND LEAH

ഇൽ രൃ ഇൽ രൃ

THIRTY–NINE

ಬಿ೮ಬಿ೮

Rebecca and Isaac Command Jacob to Take a Proper Wife

GENESIS 27:46

And Rebecca said to Isaac, "I am sick to death from dealing with [Esav's wives], the daughters of Chet. If Jacob [also] takes a wife from among the daughters of Chet—who are local [Canaanite] girls—then of what value is my life!

I n Part II, "Rebecca," the reader was immersed in the rivalry between Rebecca's sons, Esav and Jacob. Jacob was forced to flee his brother's wrath after surreptitiously receiving the firstborn's blessing. In this verse, the beginning of the story of the next generation, the text highlights Rebecca's lament that she would not be able to bear it if her beloved son Jacob were to take a wife from among the local Canaanite girls, as Esav did. Did Rebecca urge Jacob to flee to Padan-Aram in order to escape his irate brother, or did she urge Jacob to run to her father's house in order to secure him a spouse from among her kindred? Was Rebecca's focus on the immediate past, or was her intent to orchestrate Jacob's future?

The commentaries credit Rebecca with both purposes. Rashbam explains that Rebecca here only speaks of her concern over a wife for Jacob because she is intuitively aware that the ailing Isaac would not be able to bear the knowledge that Esav had sworn to slay Jacob.

Chizkuni understands that while Rebecca's stated purpose is to secure a suitable bride for Jacob, her *intention* is also to separate the warring brothers. Thus, Rebecca's last spoken words in the Bible underscore her wisdom, as she both protects her husband and plans for her son's future.

GENESIS 28:1–5

So Isaac called Jacob [to his side], blessed him and commanded him as follows: "Do not take a wife from the daughters of Canaan. Rouse yourself! And go to Padan-Aram, to the home of Betuel, your mother's father. And take for yourself a wife from there, a wife from the daughters of Lavan, your mother's brother. **And may the Almighty God bless you, make you fruitful, make you into a congregation of peoples, and may God bestow Abraham's covenantal blessing upon you and your children to inherit the land that the Almighty gave to Abraham. . . ."** [1]

Nehama Leibowitz[†] explains that Isaac deliberately bestowed the covenantal blessing *upon Jacob* minutes before he fled to Padan-Aram. The commentator points out that earlier, when Isaac had thought he was blessing his elder son, Esav, the blessing he had bestowed was of "abundance, fatness, power, and dominion—material blessings. But the Abrahamic mission, the blessing of seed and the promise of the land, were not bequeathed to Esav, since such a spiritual blessing cannot be conferred by succession but only granted to the one who is deserving of it." Isaac *knowingly* bestowed his father's generational blessing upon his second-born son because his firstborn son had violated an implicit trust when he married Hittite wives, embittering his parents' spirit. "Esav by his own behavior, by his intermarriage with the idolatrous inhabitants of the land, forfeited his right to such a blessing. It cannot be argued, that had Jacob not deceived Esav, Esav would have been chosen to become the third Patriarch and ancestor of the Jewish people." Nehama thus teaches us that the *p'shat* itself proves that although

[†]Leibowitz, N. (1973). *Studies in Bereshit*, pp. 272–278.

[1] . . . וקל שדי יברך אתך ויפרך וירבך והיית לקהל עמים, ויתן לך את ברכת אברהם לך ולזרעך אתך לרשתך את ארץ מגוריך אשר נתן אלקים לאברהם.

Isaac sought to bless his elder son, Esav, first, he reserved for Jacob the *covenantal* blessing. Rebecca's famed "switch" did not alter Isaac's demonstrated intention.[2]

> *Thus Isaac sent Jacob away, and he traveled to Padan-Aram, to Lavan, the son of Betuel the Aramean, the brother of Rebecca, mother of Jacob and Esav.*

GENESIS 28:7

> *So Jacob, obeying the wishes of both his father and his mother, set out on his journey to Padan-Aram.*

Jacob understands that he has received two disparate mandates from his parents. His father has just ordered him to seek a wife from among his mother's family, and his mother has urged him to escape his brother's sworn vengeance. This is the reason the biblical text tells us that Jacob is obeying the wishes of *both* his father and mother when he journeys to Padan-Aram.

GENESIS 28:10–22

On the way to Padan-Aram, Jacob rests for the night, using stones to pillow his head. In a dream, he encounters the God of his father and grandfather, who reaffirms that *he* will be the recipient of the tripartite covenantal blessing consisting of the land, the nation, and Divine protection. Jacob builds an altar there, commemorating God's validation of his quest, and he names the place Beit-El ("The House of God"). He pledges his fealty to God and vows a speedy return to his father's house.

---

[2] שובע, שומן, כלכלה, בריאה ודשנה, שפע נכסים, שלטון וכוח—כל זה מיועד לעשו. אך היעוד האברהמי, ברכת הזרע והבטחת הארץ לא לעשו היו מיועדים מלכתחילה, כי אין ברכת אברהם עוברת בירושה לבכור כבכורתו, אלא לראוי בלבד . . . ועל ידי שהוציא עשו עצמו מכלל מורשת אברהם בהתערבבו בעם הארץ־הכנענים, גם לא זכה עוד בברכה זו "שלא תאמר: אילולא שרימה יעקב באביו, לא נטל ברכותיו," ולא היה הנבחר להיות סגולה ולא היה נעשה אבינו השלישי.

GENESIS 29:1

Following God's revelation to him, Jacob lifts himself up and continues on his journey. Rashbam explains that the text's use of the poetic expression—"and Jacob lifted up his feet"[3]—illuminates Jacob's state of mind at this moment.[4] Buoyed by God's promises, Jacob continues on his journey to find a wife, bearing a lighter heart and a contented mien.

GENESIS 29:2–3

And Jacob saw, and behold [there was] a well in the field, with three flocks of sheep crouched beside it, as this well watered the flocks; and there was a great well-stone covering its mouth. And all the flocks [used to] gather there, [and all the shepherds] rolled back the well-stone from atop the mouth of the well, before they watered the sheep . . . and [afterwards] they returned the stone to its place, covering the mouth of the well.[5]

From the Torah's narrative, we are able to view this scene as a road-weary Jacob viewed it, happening upon the well after his arduous journey. The *Netziv* explains that the stone covering the well was not massive in size, so much as it was very wide, thin and heavy, almost like a giant stone wheel, defying any one person's ability to dislodge it from its resting place atop the well.[6] Jacob saw the three flocks ranged about the well, the shepherds lounging in the desert sun, awaiting the arrival of their companion shepherds so that—together—they could lift the well-stone and water their parched flocks. Radak emphasizes that the well-stone's unwieldy size and weight was historically essential to the survival of the desert community, ensuring that no single stranger could come upon their well and deplete their precious water supply. The stone's size and girth made it virtually impossible for it to be gripped and dislodged by

---

[3] וישא יעקב רגליו.

[4] מתוך שהבטיחו הקב"ה, הלך בשמחה ובמרוצה.

[5] וירא והנה באר בשדה והנה שם שלשה עדרי צאן רבצים עליה כי מן הבאר ההוא ישקו העדרים, והאבן גדולה על פי הבאר.

[6] והבאר גדלה. שלא היתה גדולה, אלא על פי הבאר באשר היה דק ורחב.

a single set of hands. It required the joint effort of all the shepherds working *in concert* to uncover the well and water their flocks.[7]

The Torah's somewhat wordy introduction to the portentous meeting scene at the well is deliberate and necessary according to the Ramban. The commentator points out that it is critical that the reader appreciate Jacob's strength and stature as it is immediately and graphically realized by the townspeople who are gathered at the well for the daily watering ritual. Ramban points out that Jacob, no doubt weary from his journeying and himself parched with thirst, was so powerful that he was able—alone—to lift the well-stone that required *all* the shepherds' strength to dislodge it from its place. The shepherds and townspeople were aware that none of them, acting alone, could so much as budge the well-stone. The Torah is preparing the reader for Jacob's act of dominance.[8]

Chizkuni concurs, stating simply that this entire introduction to the upcoming drama at the well was written for the single dramatic purpose of demonstrating, unequivocally, that Jacob's physical prowess is of heroic proportion.[9]

The reader here encounters a transformed Jacob. He was initially introduced to us as a sedentary tent dweller,[10] who by his dissembling behavior acquired the coveted birthright from his brother and the covenantal blessing from his father. We now view a physically vigorous man in his prime, his strength forged perhaps by months spent running for his life and surviving out-of-doors in harsh desert terrain. In addition, this new Jacob is confident in his knowledge that the God of his fathers, who appeared to him in Beit-El, has bestowed upon him the generational blessing securing the future for him and his progeny. Thus armed with physical as well as spiritual might, Jacob is poised to meet his destiny.

---

[7] שמו אבן גדולה על פי הבאר כדי שלא יוכלו להשקות אלא בהיותם **יחד**, וישקה זה אחר זה.

[8] יאריך הכתוב בספור הזה להודיענו . . . כי הנה יעקב אבינו בא מן הדרך עיף, והוא עיף, ויגל **לבדו** האבן אשר היו צורכים אליה **כל** הרועים, ושלשה עדרי צאן אשר להם רועים רבים ושומרים כלם רבצים עליה, אינם יכולים להניעה כלל.

Jacob greets the lounging shepherds and asks, "My brothers, where do you hail from?" They reply, "We all come from Haran." Mindful that he may well have arrived at his destination, Jacob asks, "Do you know of Lavan, son of Nahor?" The shepherds reply laconically, "We know him." Students of the text will recall that Lavan was the son of Betuel, and not of Nahor, who was in fact his grandfather. Jacob here uses Lavan's *grandfather's* name as an identifier rather than his father's name, for the clever purpose of revealing Lavan's character in a subtle fashion. *Kli Yakar* explains that by expressly relating Lavan to Abraham's brother Nahor—who was an honorable man—rather than to Betuel—who was widely known as a despoiler of virgins—Jacob was enabling the shepherds to inform him cryptically what he needed to know.[11]

Jacob wonders, Have I arrived at my destination? Are the daughters of Lavan the Aramean untouched and fit bridal prospects for the grandson of Abraham? And so Jacob inquired of [the shepherds], "Does it go well with [Lavan]?" And they replied, "Well enough. In fact, here comes Rachel his daughter with his flock of sheep."[12] According to the *Netziv*, when Jacob inquired whether all was well with Lavan, his choice of words allowed the shepherds to understand that Jacob was really interested in more than just a surface inquiry. He actually wished to know details concerning Lavan's character and that of his household. These details ordinarily are not divulged in an initial encounter with strangers.[13] Unwittingly, then, the shepherds tell Jacob what he needs to know: that his uncle Lavan is closer spiritual kin to Abraham's brother, Nahor, and that Lavan's daughters may be fit bridal prospects.

With his seemingly innocuous inquiry in verse six, Jacob acquires two critical pieces of data. According to Alshich, when Jacob asks the shepherds if Lavan is "at peace" (*shalom*) and the shepherds

---

9 כל הפרשה הזאת . . . לא נכתבה אלא להודיע כמה גדול כחו של יעקב.

10 יושב אהלים

11 כי על מעשיו שאל. אם הוא מתיחס אחר נחור, שהיה איש תם וישר, או אחר אביו בתואל הרמאי שהיה בועל כל הבתולות. ואמר הידעתם את לבן, אם הוא בן נחור, דומה **לו** בתולדה, ויאמרו ידענו, כי הוא בן נחור, מתיחס **אחריו** ודומה **לו** במעשיו.

12 ויאמר להם **השלום לו?** ויאמרו **שלום**, והנה רחל בתו באה עם הצאן.

13 הבינו שנדרש לו לדעת בפרטות משלום ביתו, מה שאין יודעים כל כך.

reply using the same word—*shalom*—Jacob has learned much. First, in addition to the data already gleaned, he also now knows that his uncle Lavan is a man to be wary of, because he is "at peace" with questionable neighbors, who countenance idolatry and paganism. But by the same token, Jacob can be secure that Lavan's daughters are untouched virgins, because the shepherds' response that Lavan is "at peace" with his neighbors also indicates to him that Lavan's daughter feels secure enough to appear at the public well alone, knowing she will not be molested by hostile men.[14]

Pirkei d'Rabi Eliezer (Chapter 36), quoting Rabbi Akiva, informs the reader that Jacob is explicitly under God's protection. The rabbis derive this from the phrase in verse six describing Rachel's imminent approach to the well. Rabbi Akiva taught that in our study of the Bible, whenever a man's entrance to a strange place is accompanied by the appearance of young maidens, we can infer that God has set his feet on the path to success.[15] Similar episodes occur with Eliezer, Abraham's servant, and later on with Moses, both of whom encounter maidens at a well upon their arrival in a strange setting. They, too—like Jacob—are subsequently proven to be under God's Divine protection.

---

[14] בזה ירצה כי אמרו אלה לו שלום והרעיה כי והנה רחל באה עם הצאן. כי אם לא היה שלום לו, לא היתה בוטחת בתו.

[15] רבי עקיבא אומר: כל מי שהוא נכנס לעיר ומוצא נערות לפניו, דרכו מצלחת לפניו.

FORTY

଼୦ଓଓ

Rachel
Appears at the Well

GENESIS 29:7

And the shepherds said to Jacob, "Here comes Rachel, Lavan's daughter, with his flock of sheep."[1] *So Jacob told the shepherds, "It is still early in the day, it is not yet the time to gather the flocks. Water the sheep, then, and take them out to pasture."*[2]

When the shepherds drew Jacob's attention to Rachel's approach, it is likely that his eyes remained riveted upon her. We can infer this from the abrupt switch in focus of Jacob's conversation with the shepherds. In verse six, *before* he sees Rachel, Jacob's only interest appears to be ascertaining Lavan's character. In verse seven, *after* watching Rachel's approach to the well, Jacob takes an almost officious tone with the shepherds, very nearly ordering them to be about their business and be on their way with haste. What is Jacob's purpose in interfering thus with the shepherds' routine?

According to Chizkuni, Jacob is instantly so attracted to Rachel that he is anxious to speak with her face-to-face. Yet, as she is driving her father's flock of sheep before her, intent upon her task, Jacob is fearful that the lounging shepherds were only waiting at the well for her to arrive, so that they all could take the flocks out to pasture

---

[1] והנה רחל בתו באה עם הצאן.

[2] ויאמר הן עוד היום גדול; לא עת האסף המקנה. השקו הצאן ולכו רעו.

together. In a flash of emotion, the commentator explains, Jacob practically orders them to begone in order that he will have his time with Rachel.[3] Jacob was well aware of the family lore of how his mother Rebecca was chosen to be his father's intended bride at the well. Perhaps he was filled with instantaneous attraction for this girl Rachel, and was moved to speak to her right away, lest the moment pass, and the opportunity be lost to him forever. Thus the *Netziv* adds that Jacob is smitten at his first glimpse of Rachel. The commentator explains that Jacob seizes the initiative and issues a perfunctory dismissal to the shepherds. His intention is to eliminate them completely from the vicinity, so that he can be alone with Rachel and speak to her in secret.[4]

GENESIS 29:8

The shepherds demur, replying that they are waiting at the well for the rest of the flocks to arrive, so that all the herdsmen, working together, can roll the well-stone from atop the well. "Only then can we water the sheep." According to Rashi, the shepherds respond to Jacob's directive to them in verse seven to water their flocks, saying, "We cannot!" because the stone covering the well is too large and too heavy for them. . . .[5]

GENESIS 29:9

While Jacob was thus speaking with [the shepherds], Rachel came with her father's sheep, because she was a shepherdess.[6]

The commentators uniformly stress that Rachel was at the well because it was her assigned task to tend the sheep. Her delegated family role, according to *Ohr Hachayim*, was to care for her father's

---

3   השקו הצאן ולכו רעו. למה היה ליעקב לומר להם כל כך? אלא מתיירא היה שמא תלך לה
רחל עם הרועים, והוא רוצה לדבר עמה.

4   בהיותו רוצה לדבר עם רחל בסוד; על כן השיאם שילכו מזה.

5   לא נוכל. להשקות, לפי שהאבן גדולה.

6   ורחל באה עם הצאן אשר לאביה כי רועה היא.

flocks. She had not gone out to the well for frivolous reasons.[7] Radak points out that it was the custom for females—as well as males—to tend the flocks.[†8] Sforno expands our appreciation of Rachel's skill level, explaining that she had a keen understanding of animal husbandry.[9] She was a valued shepherdess even at a young age.

Even though Rachel has an older sister—Leah—Ramban teaches us that Rachel alone was in charge of her father's flock on a daily basis. It was *she* who was the shepherdess *extraordinaire*.[10] One might wonder why *both* sisters did not assume the task of tending their family's flocks. It would have afforded them companionship and mutual protection, and was an accepted custom at the time for siblings to share in the responsibility of caring for the sheep. Ramban responds that perhaps Leah's eyes were particularly sensitive to the severe desert sun. Alternatively, that because Leah was the elder by a number of years and was suitable for marriage, Lavan, her father, was wary of sending her out into the uninhabited fields. Rachel was as yet not considered marriageable, as she was the younger of two maiden sisters. Lavan was not concerned that Rachel might attract suitors, because all the local men were aware of the custom that the elder unmarried sister is the first to wed.[11] Of course, Jacob—who was new to the town—did not know that Rachel had an older, unmarried sister at home. He was therefore able to give free rein to his attraction to her.

While Chizkuni agrees with Ramban that the desert sun and air were irritants to Leah's delicate eyes, he adds that another reason Rachel was the exclusive shepherdess was in order to afford respect

---

†The daughters of Jethro—a prominent figure in Midian whose daughter, Zipporah, ultimately became Moses' wife—were the shepherds for his flocks. וכן בנות יתרו, שהיה גדול מדין, היו בנות רועות.

---

[7] ורחל באה. ולא תאמר כי חס ושלום יצאנית היתה, אלא לטעם כי היא רועה אותם, ולזה יצתה ועם הצאן.

[8] כי רועה היא. כי מנהגם היה להיות גם הנשים רועות.

[9] כי רועה היא, יודעת חכמת מלאכת המרעה.

[10] להגיד כי אין לצאן לבן רועה אחר זולתה. כי **לה לבד** מסר אביה העדר והיא לבדה רועה אותם כל הימים, לא תלך בהם לאה אחותה כלל.

[11] ואולי בעבור כי עיני לאה רכות היה השמש מזיק לה, או בעבור שהיתה לאה גדולה ראויה לאיש, וחשש לה אביה . . . ורחל היתה קטנה ואין לחוש לה.

and honor to the elder sister.[12] The Zohar asks, Why did the Almighty not summon *Leah* to the well, as He was already summoning up a wife for Jacob? What was special about Rachel that *she* was summoned to this portentous assignation? The commentary responds (Zohar, 153b) that Rachel's beauty was so exquisite that she served God's purpose by riveting Jacob's eyes and heart so completely, that it acted as a magnetic force, causing Jacob to cease in his wandering, stake his claim and set down roots in Haran in order to possess her.[13]

GENESIS 29:10

And it happened that when Jacob saw Rachel, the daughter of Lavan, his mother's brother, and the [thirsty] sheep of Lavan, his mother's brother, Jacob approached [the well] and rolled the stone from atop the mouth of the well. And he watered the flock of Lavan, his mother's brother.

Rav Bachya draws the reader's attention to the thrice-repeated phrase "Lavan, his mother's brother." The first time it is used in this verse, the Torah is describing Rachel, the daughter of *Lavan, his mother's brother*. The second time, it is referring to the thirsty sheep belonging to *Lavan, his mother's brother*. And the third time is after Jacob has performed the improbable act of tremendous strength and thereafter watered the flock of *Lavan, his mother's brother*. The commentator teaches us that the repeated phrase highlights the underlying stimulus motivating Jacob in this verse.[14] Verbally linking Lavan's name with that of his beloved mother slows down the action and gives us insight into Jacob's state of mind. We can readily imagine his thoughts, as he first views the lovely Rachel. He is running the situation down his mental checklist: She fulfilled his mother's primary requirement, as she was the daughter of *Lavan, his mother's brother*. And he watered the parched and bleating sheep *because*

---

12 אבל לאה עיניה רכות והרוח והאויר קשים לה. לפיכך לא היתה רועה, ועוד כדי לחלוק כבוד לגדולה.

13 יעקב, שאשה נזדמנה בו על הבאר, למה לא נזדמנה לו לאה? . . . כדי להמשיך עינו ולבו של יעקב ביפיה של רחל, ויקבע דירתם שם.

14 הזכיר הכתוב הזה כמה פעמים "אחי אמו" להודיע כי כל מה שהשתדל יעקב בצאן להשקותם, ומה שהיה חומל על רחל בת לבן כי לא עשה לכבוד לבן, רק לכבוד אמו, בשביל ש[לבן] היה אחי אמו . . . וזכר בלבו את אמו אשר אהבתו, שנתנה לו העצה הזאת לבא עליו.

they belonged to *Lavan, his mother's brother*. Jacob demonstrated his strength and chivalry to Rachel, and in so doing he was heeding his parents' dictum not to take a wife from the daughters of Canaan, but rather from the family of *Lavan, his mother's brother*.

Without hesitation, Jacob moves from the passive act of "seeing" Rachel and the sheep in the first part of verse 10, to the heroic act of "rolling" the enormous well-stone later on in this same verse. Rabbi Abraham, son of the Rambam, resolves this improbable action sequence by explaining that Jacob's vision of Rachel arriving with her flock instantly aroused his strength so that he was miraculously able, single-handedly, to move the heavy obstacle and water his uncle's sheep.[15]

In fact, Rashi describes Jacob's strength as so impressive that he dislodged the well-stone with the practiced ease of one who removes the cork from a bottle.[16] The purpose of this scene, according to Rashi, is to instruct us as to Jacob's extraordinary strength. We can be sure that the import of his amazing feat was not lost on either Rachel or the gaping shepherds. The *Netziv* points out that the drama was unfolding on two levels: The ostensible consequence of Jacob's act of rolling the well-stone from the mouth of the well was to demonstrate to the onlookers that he was aiding his cousin and furthering his uncle's interests. The turbulent personal undercurrent that remained invisible to the shepherds was that Jacob was smitten with Rachel from his first glimpse of her. The simple script thus allowed Jacob to kiss his cousin Rachel in full view of the assembled shepherds even though he had only just met her.[17]

---

[15] מיד כשראה אותה ונתעוררו כוחותיו בעזר אלקי להסיר את האבן אף על פי שהייתה גדולה.

[16] ויגש יעקב ויגל. כמי שמעביר את הפקק מעל פי צלוחית. להודיעך שכחו גדול.

[17] הראה בזה לכל העומדים שם שהוא קרוב ללבן ורחל. ומשום הכי לא היה בזיון כשנשק את רחל.

FORTY-ONE

‱

The Kiss
and the Cry

GENESIS 29:11

And Jacob gave a kiss to Rachel; then he raised his voice and cried.[1]

The commentators raise the questions that must be on the readers' minds: How could Jacob kiss a young maiden, a virtual stranger? What was the precise nature of his kiss? What was it about Jacob that allowed Rachel to accept his kiss? Why did Jacob cry out after he kissed Rachel?

Ramban defuses the intensity of the kiss, explaining that it was platonic in nature. He derives this from the odd wording of the verse: *And Jacob gave a kiss to Rachel,*[2] The commentator cites Ibn Ezra as support for the notion that whenever a kiss is given "to" another, it is not a kiss on the mouth. Rather, says the Ramban, Jacob kissed Rachel on her forehead, or on her shoulder.[3] Similarly, *Midrash Rabbah* (70.12) includes Jacob's kiss to Rachel as one of the four types of non-passionate kisses that is permissible. The first is a kiss bestowed when a person is elevated to a high office; the second is a kiss at a reunion; the third is the kiss upon parting; and the fourth type

---

[1] וישק יעקב לרחל, וישא את קלו ויבך.

[2] וישק יעקב לרחל.

[3] נשיקה בלמ"ד איננה בפה, רק נשק אותה על ראשה או על כתיפה.

193

is a kiss between relatives.[4] According to *Midrash Rabbah*, Jacob's kiss to Rachel in this verse falls within the fourth permissible category.

Alshich differs from these *mephorshim*, confident that Jacob's kiss to Rachel reflected his ecstasy. Jacob is joyful, thinking that he has finally found his soul-mate and future wife in this beautiful young girl. The commentator believes this demonstrativeness to be a natural response to an initial infatuation.[5]

Rachel, the young shepherdess, has just led her father's flock to the well, as was her usual wont. She expected nothing out of the ordinary. In fact, as she approached, she could see that the well-stone was still in place, and thought that perhaps she was even a bit early for the daily watering ritual. We can envision Rachel, transfixed at the sight of one man, in a stranger's garb, moving purposefully toward the well, and rolling the giant stone off its mouth, single-handedly and with ease. Her eyes widen with awe and pleasure. And when the stranger takes time to water her father's flock, the *Netziv* comments that Rachel by now suspects that he is kin to her and her father.[6] When Jacob eventually looks at her and walks toward her to greet her, Radak explains that Rachel understands that his show of great strength and chivalry was born of his desire to impress her, and she accepts his kiss.[†7]

The commentaries, who up until now have given voice to the matriarchs even where the text remains silent, do not offer insight into Rachel's passive acceptance of Jacob's kiss. The silence itself may

---

[†]Students of the text will surely have noted the seemingly identical Hebrew words in verses 10 and 11: וישק, *VaYaSHK and VaYiSHaK*. In verse 10, it is used to mean "and Jacob **watered** the flock of Lavan." וישק את צאן לבן.

In verse 11, as we have just learned, the word is used to mean "and Jacob **gave a kiss** to Rachel," וישק יעקב לרחל. While it might be tempting to draw a parallel between the two words given their identical appearance in Hebrew, the fact is that the words emerge from separate root-words, and have different meanings. The word in verse 10 comes from the root שקה, *SHaKoh*, meaning "to give to drink," while the word in verse 11 derives from the root נשק, *NaSHoK*, meaning "to kiss."

---

4   כל נשיקה לתפלות בר מין תלת. נשיקה של גדולה, נשיקה של פרקים, נשיקה של פרישות . . . אף נשיקה של קריבות, שנאמר 'וישק יעקב לרחל',' שהיתה קרובו.

5   וישק לה מרוב שמחתו, כי בת זוגו היתה, ותנשא לו, והוא חבור הנפשות בנשיקה, כנודע.

6   שעד כה לא הבינה אלא שהוא קרוב, אבל לא ידעה מי הוא.

7   וישק. כיון שראתה שעשה כל בעבורה, זה שקבלה נשיקתו.

echo Rachel's reaction to Jacob. Perhaps she is not as passionate about him as he is about her. Her failure to respond to Jacob on any level here forebodes their future relationship.

And [Jacob] raised his voice and cried.[8] Jacob's cry in the second part of verse 11 follows immediately upon his kiss in the first part of this same verse. The proximity of the cry to the kiss should give us pause. Many questions may crowd our minds as we read verse 11. What prompted Jacob's cry? Was it happiness or was it a portend of future tragedy? At the very least, the commentaries teach us, the focus of the kiss in this verse is Jacob—the bestower of the kiss—and not Rachel, its recipient. It is Jacob's curious reaction that is recorded and dissected, almost as if the second part of his kiss is his cry. Jacob's cry was instinctual, according to Alshich. The commentator says that Jacob cried out as an expression of his ecstasy and relief, because Rachel was so very beautiful.[9] Also, his cry reflected his frustration, because he was prepared to declare his intention to marry her right then, and was hard-put to restrain himself.

Yet, According to Sforno, Jacob's first thought after kissing Rachel was regret, that his youth was spent in solitude. He was instantly sorry that he had not met her earlier, for he could have had children with her that were born while he was still a young man.[10] His cry, according to Sforno, is for those lost years.

The commentary of Rabbi Abraham, son of the Rambam, expands our understanding of Jacob's complex palette of emotions. This commentator states that Jacob's cry is a prayer of thanksgiving to God for directing him to the proper woman. Because his lovely cousin, Rachel, facially resembles his mother Rebecca—as she is, after all, his mother's niece—the correctness of his attraction for her is apparent to him.[11] Rashi explains that Jacob's cry was for the fact that he appeared at Rachel's feet as a penniless suitor, with nothing but the clothes on his back.[12] The commentator also adds that Jacob foresaw via Divine inspiration that Rachel would not be buried at his

---

[8] וישא את קלו ויבך

[9] בכה יעקב כי רחל היתה יפת יואר ויפת מראה.

[10] על שלא זכה לשאת אותה בנעוריו, והיו לו לעת כזאת בני נעורים.

[11] בכיתו בכית תנחונים לפי שנזכר על אמו, שהיא מגזעה וממשפחתה של רחל.

[12] לפי שבא בידים ריקניות. . . .

side, and his cry as he kissed her was filled with the anguish that they were destined to have only a short time together.[13]

Midrash Rabbah (70.12) tells us that Jacob saw the onlookers whispering with one another as he finished kissing Rachel. His cry reflected his concern that he should have caused her to be the object of their gossip.[14] The *Netziv* takes this one step further, saying that Jacob thought he already had sufficiently established himself as her cousin. Thus, he had hoped that his kiss would not have appeared lewd or promiscuous in anyone's eyes, since his intentions were honorable.[15] Jacob's cry expressed his distress that the kiss was misinterpreted.

Perhaps the most intuitive interpretation of Jacob's cry is that of *Ma'ayna shel Torah*. This commentator suggests that Jacob was agonized that to the world-at-large his kiss could be interpreted as common or vulgar, while in reality, to him, "the kiss" was something heavenly and sublime.[16]

---

[13] לפי שצפה ברוח הקודש שאינה נכנסת עמו לקבורה.

[14] למה בכה? שראה האנשים מלחשים אלו לאלו מפני שנשקה.

[15] בבכיה זו הראה לדעת שלא היתה בנשיקה זו פריצות ומחשבות אהבת אישות. . . .

[16] על שום מה בכה? על שום **שהעולם** יקבל זאת כדבר הדיוט, בו בזמן **שאצלו** היה "וישק" זה ענין שמימי נשגב.

FORTY-TWO

৪০৫৪০৫

Jacob Meets
Rachel's Father

GENESIS 29:12

And Jacob told Rachel that he was her father's brother, and that he was Rebecca's son; and she ran and told her father.[1]

The obvious difficulty with this verse is that Jacob is *not* Lavan's brother; rather, he is his nephew. Why, then, does Jacob describe himself thus to Rachel, since he then tells her his *actual* lineage, that he is her Aunt Rebecca's son? Rashi explains that Jacob merely sought to establish with Rachel their common family connection.[2] On a more subtle level, the commentator explains that Jacob used two means of identification with Rachel: He told her *both* that he was her father's "brother," *and* that he was her aunt's son. The *former* explanation was a hint to Rachel that just as her father was reputed to be a clever businessman, so, too, was he—Jacob— able to be Lavan's "brother" in cleverness. Jacob's *second* explanation reminded Rachel that he was also a biological and spiritual heir to a woman who was widely respected for her righteousness.[3]

---

1. ויגד יעקב לרחל כי אחי אביה הוא, וכי בן רבקה הוא. ותרץ ותגד לאביה.
2. קרוב לאביה.
3. אם לרמאות הוא בא, גם אני אחיו ברמאות. ואם אדם כשר הוא, גם אני בן רבקה, אחותו הכשרה.

197

The text uses the term *VaYaGeD* [4] to narrate that Jacob "told" Rachel about his lineage, instead of the more expected word *VaYoMeR*,[5] which translates as "he said." The term *VaYaGeD* [6] hints at a protracted conversation rather than a cursory greeting. The Talmud (*Megilla* 13b), seizes upon this verbal nuance to detail the first important conversation "between" Rachel and Jacob. The Talmud is exquisitely sensitive to the fact that *in the text*, however, this conversation is one-sided; Rachel has not spoken a word, nor has she reacted to Jacob's kiss.

The Talmud therefore fills this void with Rachel's spoken words, and allows us to overhear an extensive discussion between Rachel and Jacob at the well. The Talmud teaches that this was far from an insolent first kiss. Rather, that when Jacob saw his cousin Rachel and subsequently kissed her, he immediately asked her for her hand in marriage, and she consented. But with trepidation she also informed Jacob that her father was a sly man, whom Jacob would not be able to best in a bridal negotiation for her hand. It was in order to assuage Rachel's fear that Jacob responded, "I am your father's brother," comforting Rachel with the thought that he—Jacob—was equal in maneuvering ability to her father. "How will he try to trick me?" Jacob asked. Rachel told him, "I have a maiden sister who is older than I, and my father will not betroth me before her. He will surely try to give her to you in marriage in my stead." So Jacob gave Rachel secret codes—signs that only they would be privy to—and that only Rachel could reveal to him at their marriage.[7] In this way Jacob would be certain on the day of their marriage which sister he was taking to be his wife, and Lavan's trickery would be foiled.

Thus reassured, Rachel ran to tell her father that his nephew had arrived, had performed great feats of strength at the well, and had also watered his flock. Rashi informs us that the reason Rachel ran to her *father* with the news of her cousin's arrival, and not to her mother, is that her mother had died sometime before.[8]

---

4 ויגד

5 ויאמר

6 ויגד

7 וכי אחי אביה הוא? והלא בן אחות אביה הוא! אלא אמר לה: מינסבא לי? אמרה ליה: אין. מהו, אבא רמאה הוא, ולא יכלת ליה. אמר לה: אחיו אנא ברמאות . . . אמרה ליה: אית לי אחתא דקשישא מינאי, ולא מנסיב לי מקמה. מסר לה סימנים.

8 ותגד לאביה. לפי שאמה מתה, ולא היה לה להגיד אלא לו.

GENESIS 29:13

When Lavan heard from his daughter that his nephew Jacob had arrived, Lavan *ran* to the well to greet Jacob, and Lavan *hugged* him, *kissed* him, and *brought* him back to his house, where Jacob told him all that had transpired with him. Rashi explains that verse 13 is filled with action verbs in order to highlight Lavan's avid welcome of Jacob. Lavan surely remembers the servant Eliezer, the prior visitor from the house of Abraham, who came to the well years before, with ten camels laden with dower gifts for Rebecca, Lavan's sister. Lavan first *runs* toward Jacob, but perceives no caravan; he next *embraces* him, but feels no hidden pouches; he even *kisses* him, suspecting that Jacob may have hidden precious jewels in his mouth. But Lavan finally understands that Jacob has arrived empty-handed.[9]

Jacob, perceiving the mercenary objective of Lavan's effusive welcome, details for his uncle his precipitous flight from his own home. According to Sforno, Jacob tells his uncle that he is not destitute, rather he is on the run from his brother's murderous wrath, and seeks temporary refuge in his uncle's house, at his mother's instruction.[10] *Ohr Hachayim* credits Jacob with the ability to instantly perceive the character of his adversary. Jacob appears to be relating to Lavan the tale of his weeks on the run, while in reality he is conveying to his uncle that he—Jacob—is no innocent dupe intent on living off his uncle's largesse. By relating to Lavan that he outwitted his brother and obtained the birthright, and that he also impersonated his brother and acquired Abraham's special blessing, he is "telling" Lavan that he is at the very least his equal in matters of cunning. When Jacob went on to narrate the incident of his handling of the well-stone, this subtly added a layer of physical intimidation, which he immediately softened by mentioning that he watered his uncle's flock of sheep without being asked, and would be content to deal with his uncle in a straightforward manner.[11]

---

[9] כסבור ממון הוא טעון, שהרי עבד הבית בא לכאן בעשרה גמלים טעונים. ויחבק, שלא ראה עמו כלום..וינשק לו . . . שמא מרגליות הביא והם בפיו.

[10] להודיע שלא בא עליו לצורך פרנסה, אלא להמלט מאחיו ושבמצות אמו ישב עמו.

[11] נתחכם לספר לו כל הדברים שעברוהו כדי שבזה יחדל מהרשיע כשידע מה שנתחכם עד שלקח הבכורה והברכה ידע כי ערום יערים למה שיצטרך. וגם הודיעו אשר עברו ממעשה האבן, וזה יגיד כי הוא גבור חיל, גם מעשה השקאת צאנו. וזה יגיד חבתו בו והנהגתו הישרה עמו.

GENESIS 29:14–15

So Lavan offered Jacob, his sister Rebecca's son—his flesh and blood—a safe haven. After one month's time, during which Jacob competently tended to Lavan's flocks, Lavan asked Jacob to name the price of his hire. Lavan, pleased with Jacob's shepherding ability, sought to keep his nephew in his household by offering him paid employment. Although the text does not mention that Jacob actually labored throughout his first month in Lavan's house, Ramban tells us that from that first day when Jacob spared Rachel the task of watering her father's flock, out of his love for her he took over her work as shepherdess.[12]

---

[12] לא ספר הכתוב שהיה יעקב עובד אותו. ויתכן כי מעת שאמר וישק את צאן לבן אחי אמו, לא יצא מידו, כי בראותו את רחל כי רועה היא, חמל עליה שלא תשוב לרעות צאן עוד, והיה **הוא** רועה אותן באהבתו אותה.

FORTY–THREE

଼୦ଓ଼୦ଓ

Leah and Rachel:
Lavan's Daughters

GENESIS 29:16–17

Before Jacob has an opportunity to respond to Lavan's proposal, the Bible interposes a formal introduction to Lavan's two daughters.

> *And Lavan has two daughters: the elder is named Leah, the younger is named Rachel. And Leah has gentle eyes, but Rachel possessed beauty of face and form.*[1]

According to Rashbam, the Torah introduces Leah and Rachel at this point in the story because Rachel will be Jacob's negotiating price-point. Her hand in marriage will be Jacob's salary request.[2]

According to the *p'shat*, verse 17 is subtly derogatory of Leah's beauty because it is so starkly contrasted with Rachel's. The verse mentions only Leah's eyes, while it goes on to praise the totality of Rachel's beauty. The Hebrew adjective describing Leah's eyes is *RaKHoT*,[3] which has several positive definitions: soft, tender, or

---

[1] וללבן שתי בנות; שם הגדלה לאה, ושם הקטנה רחל. ועיני לאה רכות; ורחל היתה יפת תאר ויפת מראה.

[2] והפסיק תשובת דבריו של יעקב, כי לפי שהיה לו שתי בנות, והקטנה מצאה חן בעיניו, לפיכך בקש את הקטנה.

[3] רכות

201

gentle. The word also can be negatively defined as "weak." The commentaries predictably interpret this verse in several different ways. The *Netziv* calls Leah's eyes "lovely," but as was suggested above, the commentator explains that her eyes were sensitive to the strong rays of the sun, which exempted her from tending the flocks.[4]

The Talmud (*Bava Batra* 123a) contends that the text does not mention Leah's eyes in order to highlight a negative characteristic. On the contrary, the Talmud teaches us that we learn of Leah's sensitive and righteous qualities from the word *RaKHoT*. Leah overheard the townspeople matching up her aunt Rebecca's two sons with her father Lavan's two daughters, saying: the older daughter, Leah, is a match for the older son, and the younger daughter, Rachel, is a match for the younger son. So horrified was Leah at the prospect of being pressured to wed Esav, a known outlaw, that she sat and "cried her eyes out," and thus her lovely eyes became weakened.[5] Even if Leah's lovely eyes became weak, it resulted from her moral integrity: she refused to marry a hunter with a reprehensible reputation.

Rashbam, quoting the Talmud (*Ta'anit* 24a), agrees that Leah's eyes were lovely, and states further that when a young bride's eyes are lovely, one need not examine further in order to pronounce her to be "fine."[6] *Ohel Yaakov* elaborates on the Talmudic reference, saying that Leah's copious tears were shed in the course of her prayers to God that he avert the decree that she must marry Esav. God heeded Leah's prayers.[7] Radak states unequivocally that both sisters were equally lovely, though Leah's eyes were dimmed by her tears.[8]

From the scant clues provided in the text describing Leah only as the elder sister with delicate eyes, the commentators have created a composite portrait of her. Although she has yet actually to appear on the scene, we can now envision her: a doe-eyed woman, pretty

---

4   היו נאות, אבל מפני רכותן לא היתה יכולה לרעות בצאן משום שאור השמש היה מזיק להן.

5   מאי רכות? בגנות צדיקים דבר הכתוב?! . . . לא גנאי הוא לה, אלא שבח הוא לה. שהיתה שומעת על פרשת דרכים בני אדם שהיו אומרים שני בנים יש לה לרבקה, שתי בנות יש לו ללבן. גדולה לגדול, וקטנה לקטן . . . והיתה בוכה עד שנשרו ריסי עיניה.

6   רכות, נעות. וכלה שעיניה נעות אין כל גופה צריך בדיקה.

7   . . . לאה, להיות הגדולה שבבנות, היתה שמורה ומיועדת אל הבכור . . . ולכן היתה בוכה . . . תפילתה הועילה לה.

8   ועיני לאה רכות. יפת תאר היתה, אלא שעיניה היו רכות ודומעות. אבל רחל יפת תאר ויפת מראה בלא שום מום בעולם.

—though not as beautiful as her sister—a sensitive and spiritual young woman who prays to God in her unhappiness.

By way of contrast, in this same verse, the Torah belatedly describes Rachel's beauty, though she first appeared on the scene in verse six. Ibn Ezra tells us that each of her individual facial features was beautiful, and that her form was exquisite.[9] Rashbam adds that Rachel's complexion was delicately colored, like peaches and cream.[10] Rashi tells us that not only was Rachel's face beautiful, but her coloring was also extraordinary.[11] *Ohr Hachayim* rhapsodizes Rachel's appearance. He explains that there are two categories of *physical* beauty. The one describes individual features that are perfect in and of themselves, and the second occurs when the totality of a person's facial and physical appearance is considered beautiful. On another plane entirely is that special quality of beauty which transcends the physical, which emanates from a unique woman, and makes all men desire her. This latter quality of beauty also was embodied by Rachel.[12]

---

[9] כל אבר. כעין והאף והפה יפה, ומראה הכל יפה.

[10] יפת מראה. לבן ואדמדם.

[11] מראה. הוא זיו קלסתר.

[12] יש ב' בחינות ביופי. הא' בכל פרט ופרט . . . וב' הוא כללות הפנים וכללות הגוף . . . שהיו פרטי כל א' יפה בפני עצמו, וגם בדרך התקבצותם יחד. עוד ירצה יפת תאר כמשמע, ויפת מראה, שהיה לה חן שיתאוה לה כל רואה.

FORTY–FOUR

৪০০৪৪০০৪

Jacob Loves Rachel
and Offers a Proposal

GENESIS 29:18

*And because Jacob **loved** Rachel, he said [to Lavan], I will work for you for seven years for Rachel, your younger daughter.*[1]

What is the nature of Jacob's "love" for Rachel? It would seem—given that his love is mentioned immediately after the text's description of Rachel's extraordinary beauty—that Jacob's feelings are perhaps shallow, based only upon Rachel's external appearance. The reader should bear in mind, however, that according to the *p'shat*, Rachel was not simply an object of his physical attraction. On an objective level, Rachel was precisely the girl Jacob's parents commanded him to marry. But he may not have pursued her had he not been so attracted to her. We can envision that Jacob's initial infatuation with Rachel has intensified over the month of living under her father's roof. He must have observed her at her daily tasks, and most likely engaged her in extensive conversations during the long days that he tended her father's sheep under Lavan's watchful eye.

Radak asks rhetorically why the text belabors the fact of Rachel's external beauty. Should her beauty have been an irrelevant consideration for Jacob, the future patriarch? The fact that it was

---

[1] **ויאהב** יעקב את רחל, ויאמר אעבדך שבע שנים ברחל בתך הקטנה.

204

important enough for the text to highlight leads Radak to explore the implications of a woman's physical beauty and its effect upon her potential mate. The commentator explains that a beautiful woman arouses a man's desire, and that in a mate, this is an important quality, as an awakened desire will lead ultimately to more offspring, beautiful children, and a contented husband.[2] Chizkuni agrees that Jacob was drawn to Rachel from the moment he first set his eyes upon her.[3]

Ohr Hachayim delves more deeply into the human psyche. The commentator explains that the issue is not simply a woman's objective beauty, but whether she is perceived as beautiful by her mate. Rachel's loveliness ignited a "chemical reaction" within Jacob. This intrinsic "attraction," according to the commentator, is the ineluctable essence of a lasting relationship. Without it, a man may be tempted to look at other women.[4] The commentator stresses that the Torah's focus on Rachel's beauty, and on her magnetic effect upon Jacob, expresses a vital understanding of human sexual attraction.

It is odd that Jacob, so drawn to Rachel, suggests that he work for seven years before he weds her. Chizkuni endearingly explains that Jacob thought her beauty was so great that her father would surely not consent to part with her in exchange for only one or two years' labor.[5] Jacob thought she was well worth the wait.

According to the *p'shat*, Jacob's description of Rachel to Lavan was ordinary parlance: "My price for seven years' labor is your younger daughter, Rachel." But according to *Midrash Rabbah* (70.17), Jacob identifies her with strict particularity. The commentator asks us to read between the lines. Jacob is really saying to Lavan, "I will work for seven years, but *only* for Rachel (not for Leah), your *younger* daughter (in case you were thinking of substituting some

---

[2] יש לשאול אחר שכוונת הצדיקים לאשה לזרע, למה היו מחזירים אחר אשה יפה? . . . ויעקב אבינו בחר ברחל **לפי** שהיתה יפת תאר . . . ויש לומר כי כוונתם לטובה. לפי האשה היפה מעוררת התאווה, וכדי להרבות בנים היתה כוונתם לעורר תאותם, ועוד כדי שיהיו הבנים והבנות יפה מראה, . . . ועוד כי הצורה הנאה משמחת לב האדם.

[3] כבר נתן עיניו בה.

[4] לא לצד יופי אלא לצד מה שרחל בת זוגו . . . צריך שתהיה לו אשה נאה כנגד יצר הרע . . . על כל זה התורה תלמד אדם דעת.

[5] היה לו לומר שנה או שנתים, אלא לא היה בדעתו של יעקב שיתנו לו אשה יפה כרחל בשביל מועטת. לכן אמר שבע שנים.

impostor from the marketplace with the same name, or even your older daughter, by pretending that her name is Rachel)."[6]

GENESIS 29:19-20

Lavan [consented to Jacob's offer, and] said, "It is better that I should give Rachel to you [my own flesh and blood], than I should give her to a stranger. So stay and dwell with us." And Jacob worked for seven years in order to win Rachel, but the years flew by, seeming as but a few days, so great was his love of her.

Chizkuni explains that only in retrospect, *after* he completed his seven years of work, did Jacob think that the time seemed trifling. While he was laboring for her, each day of those seven years felt interminable.[7] Sforno says that Jacob would willingly have worked even longer than seven years for Rachel, since his labor was the only dower gift he could offer for her, and in his mind she was worth so much more. Responding to the reader's certain incredulity that Rachel was worth *more* than seven years' labor, the commentator quotes *Midrash Rabbah*, that "love warped Jacob's good judgment." For while Rachel was doubtless beautiful and desirable, how could seven years' labor ever seem but a trifle![8] The answer is that love—and its price—was truly in the *eye* of the beholder, Jacob.

Ma'ayna Shel Torah, reverting to the *p'shat*, is surprised that the text states that because of Jacob's great love, the seven years "flew by." According to the commentator, the opposite should have been the case, and each day he labored should have seemed like a year, because of his love for her. From verse 20, the commentator taps Jacob's longing and heroic restraint, and explains that only if a person is experiencing a self-centered drive for instant physical gratification will he be too impatient to wait for the right moment. For such a man, time will of necessity drag, and each day will truly seem like a year.

---

[6] ברחל ולא בלאה, בתך, שלא תביא אחרת מן השוק ושמה רחל. קטנה, שלא תחליף שמותן זו בזו.

[7] דבר מועט היה בעיניו לעבוד בשבילה ז' שנים, מרוב חיבתו בה . . . ד"א, **לאחר** שעבד, היו בעיניו כימים אחדים, אבל בשעת העבודה היו בעיניו כימים מרובים מתוך אהבתו אותה.

[8] שחשב שהיה ראוי לתת מוהר רב מזה באהבתו אותה, "שהאהבה מקלקלת השורה."

But here, Jacob's love also encompassed the spiritual, and was founded in more than base self-interest, and in the face of such a love as this, time had no real meaning, and the seven years seemed truly to fly.[9]

---

[9] בעצם הלא צריך להיות ההיפך, שכל יום יהיה בעיניו כשנה מחמת אהבה? ברם, רק באהבה שאדם מתכווין בה לעצמו, לשם הנאה חומרית, משתוקק הוא שהזמן יחלוף מהר, וכל יום כשנה בעיניו. אבל כאן, האהבה רוחנית, ללא כל פניה עצמית, ולגבי אהבה כזאת אין מקום למוקדם או למאוחר, ושבע שנים הן כימים אחדים.

FORTY-FIVE

Jacob Demands His Bride

GENESIS 29:21

[Having served his seven years,] Jacob went to Lavan and said, "Now give me my wife! For I have fulfilled my days [of our bargain], and now it is past time to take her to my bed."

The commentaries are a bit taken aback by the tone of Jacob's address to Lavan. Why was Jacob so brusque in demanding "his wife," and why was he so crude as to say "Give her to me so I may bed her?" Rashi, surprised by Jacob's demand, agrees that not even a common person would speak in such a manner.[1] What could Jacob have been thinking? The Talmud (*Megilla* 13b, quoting II Samuel 22, verse 27) rounds out our understanding of Jacob's difficult predicament. It cryptically states: A man must sometimes behave to his neighbor in a manner that befits him. With a pure one, you show yourself pure; but with a perverse one, you deal accordingly.[2] We are expected to understand that the validity of Rachel's early fears about her father's wiliness has slowly become apparent to Jacob over the course of the past seven years, and that Jacob has learned to distrust him. Moreover, as Jacob's time winds down, he realizes that Lavan is

1 והלא קל שבקלים אינו אומר כן!

2 כלומר, שעם כל אדם יש לנהוג כראוי לו. עם נבר תתבר; ועם עקש תתפל.

making no plans for the long-anticipated wedding. The Talmud is suggesting that Jacob spoke harshly to Lavan because Jacob knew that was the only language Lavan would understand.

Ohr Hachayim explains in more detail why Jacob is impatient with Lavan. The commentator offers two possible scenarios. If Rachel had become Jacob's *betrothed* on the day he and Lavan agreed that he would work for her for seven years, then at the instant of Jacob's *completion* of his last day of work, Rachel *became his wife*, and he was within his rights to claim her then.[3] Lavan should have had Rachel waiting for Jacob at Lavan's doorstep, poised to be given to him so they could begin their life together. Jacob's brusquely worded demand on Lavan came only *after* he saw that Lavan made no move to surrender Rachel to him.

Alternatively, it is possible that Rachel legally became Jacob's "wife" on the day—seven years previously—that he sealed the bargain with Lavan, but that the ultimate act of marital possession was not to occur until Jacob had fulfilled his condition. In this situation, we can well imagine that Rachel and Jacob's anticipation has built and crescendoed as the seven-year period comes to an end.[4] When Lavan fails to present Jacob's wife to him as agreed, Jacob demands that he live up to their bargain.

Ramban justifies Jacob's anger by explaining that Jacob had already presented himself to Lavan at the true time of completion of his seven years of labor, but that Lavan put Jacob off several times, dissembling that the time was not yet up. Jacob tolerated Lavan's perfidy only until his impatience for his bride overrode his attempts to appease his father-in-law's greed.[5]

Chizkuni adds that Jacob is finally aware that he is getting older, and that it is past time for him to wed Rachel.[6] Sforno tells us that Jacob has waited for Rachel for seven years, but that he has reached

---

3. טעם אמרו ואבוה אליה, והוא לשון בלתי נכון לצדיקו של עולם. יתבאר על דעת מה שאמר רמב"ם . . . הרי את מקודשת לי במלאכה זו שאעשה עמך, ועשה, **אינה** מקודשת . . . וצריך אני לקנותה בביאה.

4. אומרו, הבה לי אשתי, פרושו **כבר** היא אשתי . . . **וכבר** זכיתי בה, והגם שאין הדמים בעין ומה שאני אומר לך הבה לא לגמור הקנאה, שכבר קנויה היא. אלא לבוא עליה כדרך כל הארץ.

5. היה זה מחליף משכורתו עשרת מונים כי יעקב אמר לו מתחלה כי מלאו הימים, ולבן שתק . . . לכן, לא אמר הכתוב בתחילה ויהי במלאת הימים.

6. כי מלאו ימי. ימי הזקנה.

the point where a promise of marriage is not sufficient. He is ready now to father his own children, and to bring them into the covenant of his father, and of his grandfather before him.[7]

Unfortunately for Jacob, while Lavan takes pains to appear compliant in order to placate his nephew, and makes the wedding plans, in reality Lavan is secretly scheming to substitute Leah for Rachel.

---

[7] נעשה הנשואין, לא האירוסין בלבד, כי חפץ להסיג נחלת ד': בנים.

FORTY-SIX

଼ଡ଼ଓଡ଼ଓ

The Wedding Night

GENESIS 29:22

So Lavan gathered all the local menfolk and he made a [wedding] feast.

Lavan appears to have acquiesced to Jacob's demand. The *Netziv* points out that it is customary for a person to first prepare the feast, *and then* to gather the guests. Lavan's gathering of his fellow sheep herders *in advance* of the festivities was a calculated move on his part to make them all his accomplices in his scheme to trick Jacob.[1] *Midrash Rabbah* (70.19) sets the scene. When Lavan realizes that he can no longer keep Jacob working for him on the ruse that his seven years are not yet complete, he gathers his cronies about him and tells them that unless they collude with him to keep this man among them for seven *more* years, the extra water that their flocks have enjoyed during his tenure will disappear along with their newfound prosperity. The men reluctantly acquiesce to Lavan's veiled threat, and they agree not to disclose to Jacob Lavan's plan to substitute Leah for his intended, Rachel. Lavan has assured them that Jacob will surely stay among them and work an *additional* seven years in order to possess

---

1 להפך מיבעי . . . ללמד שמתחילה אסף אותם והתישב בדבר והמתיק סוד, ועשו מה שעשו.

his true love, so they can look forward to seven additional years of plentiful water for their flocks.

The sheep herders are slightly remorseful of their part in Lavan's cruel deception, however, so while all the wedding guests are occupied singing the groom's praises, the men chant, "Hee leah, hee leah!"[2]—"She is Leah!"—which had a double meaning as a wedding song refrain, and as a subtle attempt to hint to Jacob that Lavan had switched the sisters.[3] But of course, Jacob does not comprehend the warning.

Da'at Zekeinim explains that Lavan covertly plied Jacob with intoxicating drink throughout the feast as added insurance that Jacob would be unaware of the substitution.[4]

GENESIS 29:23

And it came to pass when evening fell, he took his daughter Leah, and brought her to [Jacob], and he came to her.[5]

Lavan craftily waits until the onset of the desert darkness to implement his subterfuge. *Ohr Hachayim* suggests that Lavan dragged Leah by force to the wedding tent, where Jacob awaited Rachel. The commentator derives this from the Hebrew word *VaYiKaCH,*[6] "and he took," which implies the use of physical force or coercion.[†] Ramban agrees, saying that Lavan actually grabbed Leah and thrust her into Jacob's tent.[7] Or, *Ohr Hachayim* continues, Lavan

---

[†]Students of the text will recall that this same root-word was used when Sarah was forcibly taken to Pharoah's palace. See above, footnote on page 10.

---

[2] "היא לאה"

[3] ויעש משתה. כינס כל אנשי מקומו. אמר להם: יודעים אתם שהיינו דחוקים למים, וכיון שבא הצדיק הזה לכאן נתברכו המים . . . אמר להון: אין בעיין אותן אנא מרמי ביה, ויהב ליה לאה, דהוא רחים להדא רחל סגי. והוא עבד הכא גבכון שבעה שנים אחורין. אמרין ליה עביד מה דהגי לך . . . וכולי יומא הוו מכללין ביה . . . ואומרין: הא ליא, הא ליא!

[4] לשכר את יעקב ביין כדי לרמותו, ולא יבחין בין רחל ללאה.

[5] ויהי בערב ויקח את לאה בתו ויבא אתה אליו, ויבא אליה.

[6] ויקח

[7] אחז בה והכניסה איליו.

could have pressured Leah via psychological manipulation to carry this substitution to its ultimate conjugal conclusion.[8]

Ohr Hachayim allows us to imagine the dense blackness of the nuptial tent, where Jacob hurried to greet his bride. After the torch-lit brightness of the wedding feast, it was customary for a modest bride to join her groom without benefit of candle light.[9] Jacob has longed for this night for years, and the moment is fraught with the immediacy of consummation. Overwhelmed by his desire *for Rachel*, Jacob fails to realize, until the break of dawn, that it is not she who shares his marital bed.[10]

The *Netziv* offers profound psychological insight into the integrity of marital passion. *This* was not a "marriage of true minds." A woman is not truly considered a man's "wife" unless both partners are mentally and physically synchronous. The commentator explains that this verse expresses none of this mutuality, for Jacob is unaware of the true identity of the woman in his marital bed. He proves this by pointing out that the Hebrew word for wife, *iSHa,*[11] is absent from this verse when Jacob unknowingly weds Leah. The *Netziv* asks us to read ahead and compare verse 28, where Jacob finally weds his beloved Rachel. There, the text states explicitly that Jacob takes Rachel *L'iSHa,* "as a wife."[12] Only when he weds *Rachel* does Jacob finally achieve the *Netziv*'s marital ideal.[13]

---

8 אולי שלא רצתה לרמות יעקב, ולקחה בעל כרכה או בריצוי דברים. וזולת זה לא היה צריך
לומר אלא "ויבא לאה בתו אליו."

9 לא הכיר בה כי כיבה הנרות כמשפט לאוהבי שמו, עד אור הבקר.

10 תקף ומיד בא אליה לשמור חומו.

11 אשה

12 לאשה

13 ולא כתיב "לאשה." כלשון דכתיב ברחל במקרא כ"ח. דבאותה שעה ודעי לא היתה לאשה כל
זמן שלא ידע ולא נתרצה יעקב בלאה.

FORTY-SEVEN

ଔଔଔ

Zilpah
the "Handmaiden"

GENESIS 29:24

The Bible interrupts this highly dramatic scene of wedding night deception with a parenthetical statement describing Zilpah, the woman whom Leah brings to the marriage. *And Lavan gave to [Leah] Zilpah, his handmaiden, to be handmaiden [to] his daughter Leah.*[1] The reader may wonder at the identity of the woman Zilpah. *Pirkei d'Rabi Eliezer* and Chizkuni both cite *Midrash Rabbah* for the proposition that Zilpah was another of Lavan's daughters. *Pirkei d'Rabi Eliezer* tells us that the word "handmaiden" (*SHiFCHa*[2]) is an understood reference to a man's daughter from his concubine.[3]

The story continues, and we read that Jacob discovers in the morning that he has been duped; that the elder sister, Leah, was substituted for his beloved intended, Rachel.

---

1 ויתן לבן לה את זלפה שפחתו ללאה בתו שפחה.

2 שפחה

3 לקח לבן את שתי שפחותיו ונתן לשתי בנותיו. וכי שפחותיו היו, והלא **בנותיו** היו. אלא ללמדך שבנותיו של אדם מפילגשו, נקראו שפחות.

214

FORTY-EIGHT

ಬಿಐಆಬಿಐಆ

The Morning After

GENESIS 29:25

And it came to pass in the morning that behold! she is Leah! . . .[1]

Jacob awakens with the sun, and turns his head to gaze upon his sleeping bride. According to Rashbam, he is utterly shocked to see *Leah* asleep by his side.[2] *Ohr Hachayim* explains that this sudden realization engendered in Jacob a penetrating depression because the woman he loves had been withheld from him.[3]

At first, the *p'shat* appears to be clear: Under cover of darkness Jacob thought it was Rachel, while the next morning he saw it was Leah. But the commentaries question why the text here emphasizes that *in the morning* it was Leah; was she not also Leah *the night before*? Rashi explains that during the night, Leah behaved *as if she were Rachel*; so in effect she "was not" Leah. Jacob had entrusted Rachel with secret passwords to foil any possible substitution of brides by Lavan. But at the last moment, when Rachel saw her father taking Leah toward Jacob's tent, her heart went out to her older sister, whom she knew would be profoundly shamed if she were to be

---

[1] ויהי בבקר והנה הוא לאה.

[2] והנה היא לאה. כדבר שלא נודע תחילה, אומר "והנה."

[3] ויהי בבוקר: לשון צער. יגיד על אשר נצטער אותו צדיק על מניעת רחל ממנו.

215

rejected by Jacob in the marriage tent. So Rachel stood by her sister and quickly disclosed to her the necessary secret signs that would allow her entrance to Jacob's bed.[4]

Midrash Rabbah (at *Eichah Rabbah* 24) embellishes this story, graphically demonstrating Rachel's devotion to her sister at the expense of herself. In the context of demonstrating the laudable qualities of selflessness and mercy, the *midrash* adds that after Rachel had passed the signs to Leah, she secreted herself inside Jacob's tent, underneath the marriage bed. Throughout that night, whenever Jacob whispered to Leah she remained silent, allowing *Rachel* to respond, so that Jacob would not recognize Leah by her voice. The *midrash* is highlighting Rachel's formidable determination to suppress her own natural passion for motherhood and rivalry with her sister, in order to spare Leah public mortification or spinsterhood.[5]

It was not only Rachel's compassion for her sister that led her to reveal Jacob's secret passwords. The Talmud (*Megilla* 13b) adds that Rachel also possessed the quality of modesty, evidenced by her having kept to herself—until the moment of the marriage—the code that contained explicit, intimate details of relations between a wife and her husband.[6] Rashi comments on this portion of the Talmud, and explains that Rachel's modesty is exhibited because she disclosed these intimate signs only to Leah, and only then in a private whisper.[7] The commentary on *Torah Temima* adds the necessary detail that the two sisters' voices were similar enough to fool a bridegroom in the dark.[8]

Da'at Zekeinim finally reveals to us the exact content of Jacob's secret passwords, and explains that Jacob never suspected that the woman in his tent that night was *not* Rachel, because Leah repeated for his ears only the words that Rachel had just disclosed to her: The

---

[4] אבל בלילה **לא** היתה לאה, לפי שמסר יעקב סימנים לרחל, וכשראתה רחל שמכניסין לו לאה, אמרה: עכשיו תכלם אחותי. עמדה ומסרה לה אותן סימנים.

[5] ולאחר כן נחמתי בעצמי וסבלתי את תאותי, ורחמתי על אחותי שלא תצא לחרפה, ולערב חלפו אחותי לבעלי בשבילי, ומסרתי לאחותי כל הסימנים שמסרתי לבעלי כדי שיהיא סבור שהיא רחל, ולא עוד אלא שנכנסתי תחת המטה שהיה שוכב עם אחותי. הוא היה מדבר עמה, היא שותקת, ואני משיבתו על כל דבר ודבר כדי שלא יכיר לקול אחותי. וגמלתי חסד עמה, ולא קנאתי בה.

[6] צניעות שהיתה בה ברחל . . . . מסר לה הסימנים . . . . מתוך סימנין שמסרה רחל ללאה, לא הוה ידע עד השתא.

[7] מסרתן ללאה והוא צניעות שלא יתפרסם הדבר שמסר לה הסימנין.

[8] בקול נשתוו.

intimate laws of *nidah*, detailing permitted and prohibited sexual relations; the tradition of *challah*, whereby a wife invites the spirit of God to enter the home during her weekly routine of baking bread; and the duty of kindling the Sabbath candles, which elevates the mundane atmosphere of the home to a higher spiritual plane.

The *midrash* allows us to "hear" the unrecorded conversation between Jacob and his bride at daybreak. The reader is led to envision Jacob's emotional devastation the next morning when he realizes that the passwords he entrusted only to Rachel had been repeated to him through Leah's lips. Is it any wonder, then, that in his anger Jacob calls Leah "a liar, and the daughter of a deceiver! All last night, when I called you 'Rachel,' you answered me! This morning when I call you 'Leah' you *also* answer me!" A rejected Leah cries out, "There is no teacher who does not have his disciple. Your father called you 'Esav' and you answered to *that* name. Yet when your father called you 'Jacob' you *also* answered him."[†] The commentator teaches us that this wedding night incident sowed seeds of distrust and hatred toward Leah in Jacob's heart.[9]

Although the *mephorshim* illuminate this morning scene for us by narrating the heated dialogue between Jacob and Leah, we should bear in mind that nowhere does the Bible text have Jacob expressing his anger and betrayal to Leah. According to the *p'shat*, Jacob accosts only Lavan.

GENESIS 29:25

*. . . And he said to Lavan, "What is this you have done to me? After all, did I not work for you **for Rachel**? Why then did you trick me?"* [10]

Ohr Hachayim describes Jacob's confrontation with Lavan on two levels. Jacob's first complaint is the obvious one, that Lavan

---

[†]Readers should refer to Chapter 34, "The Deception."

---

[9] כל הלילה היתה עושה עצמה כרחל מתוך השלושה סימנין שמסרה לה: נידה, וחלה, והדלקת נר, כמו שמסרן יעקב לרחל . . . אמר לה רמיתא! בת רמאי! בלילה קראתי לך רחל, וענית לי! השתא קרינא לך לאה, וענית לי. אמרה ליה: גבר דלית ליה תלמידי. אבוך קריא לך עשו וענית ליה. קרא לך יעקב וענית ליה . . . ומתוך הדברים התחיל יעקב לשנאתה.

[10] ויאמר אל לבן, מה זאת עשית לי! הלא **ברחל** עבדתי עמך, ולמה רמיתני?

substituted one daughter for the other. His second grievance is that
Lavan achieved his end by means of trickery. The commentator
explains that Jacob told Lavan that had he but confronted Jacob and
told him that he could only wed Rachel if he also married her older
sister Leah, Jacob would have done so in an above-board
manner—albeit reluctantly—in order to marry his beloved Rachel.
The commentator adds that Jacob places blame squarely upon
Lavan's head for inflicting certain humiliation upon Leah. For how
must Leah have felt, lying beside him in the marriage bed, knowing
that her marriage was achieved only by means of a deception? How
could this inauspicious beginning engender anything other than
anger, distrust and distance between them, especially considering that
Jacob took Leah as his wife *intending* that she was another? Our
sages understand that Lavan's treacherous substitution deprived both
Jacob and Leah of an intangible—but essential—element of a marital
relationship: a spiritual awareness of the "Other."[11]

The *Netziv* elaborates on *Ohr Hachayim*'s "intangible but
essential element." The commentator states that this indispensable
element is Jacob's knowledge and awareness that the woman on his
mind is the woman in his arms. If this physical and emotional unity is
absent, then the woman is being treated as a wanton.[12]

GENESIS 29:26–29

Lavan defended himself to Jacob in a calculated fashion, saying,
"Here in Padan-Aram it is not customary to give the younger
daughter in marriage before the elder. Wait only until this week is
ended, and then the other sister will be given to you, on condition
that you work for me yet another seven years." Faced with no
alternative, Jacob consented, and waited out the week, at which point
Lavan gave him his daughter, Rachel, as his wife. Rashbam fills in
some details of this bargain. He explains that the week that Jacob is
asked to wait is the seven days of Leah's wedding feasting. At the

---

11 אכן, יעקב יקבול על ב' דברים. הא' על מעשה שנתן לו לאה במקום רחל, והב' שעשה הדבר
בדרך רמאות . . . וטעם הקפדתו לצד מה? . . . **שנתכוון** אל רחל, **והיתה** לאה . . .
והצדיקים יקפידו למה שנוגע אל הרוחניות ביותר. ועוד, כי יש בזה גנאי ליושבת בחיקו,
שתהיה נשואה בדרך רמאות, וזה ירחיק חיבוב הזיווג.
12 למה רימיתני? לבעול אשה שלא בידעתי, והרי זה בעילת זנות.

very least, Lavan has allowed her to retain this one week alone with Jacob. Also, we are told that Lavan was crafty enough to know that he could not push Jacob so far as to induce him to work for Rachel for seven more years *before* he would wed her. The prospect of Jacob's achieving his heart's desire only one week after this bitter disappointment essentially assured Lavan that his plan would succeed completely, and that Jacob would consent to remain his sheep herder for another seven years.[13]

Jacob accepted Lavan's conditions, and after the week of wedding feasting, *Lavan gave Rachel his daughter **to him** to be a wife **to him**.*[14] *Ohr Hachayim* explains that the double use of the phrase "to him" emphasizes that *to him, Rachel* is his true mate. Jacob perceives that Rachel—and not Leah—will be the mainstay of his home.[15]

---

[13] מלא שבוע זאת: שבעת ימי המשתה של לאה. ותנתן לך גם את זאת, מיד.

[14] ויתן **לו** את רחל בתו **לו** לאשה.

[15] לו לאשה. מגיד הכתוב . . . כי עקרת הבית היא רחל, כי היא בת זוגו.

FORTY–NINE

Bilhah
the "Handmaiden"

After recounting that Lavan has at last given Rachel to Jacob, the text makes a detour, and informs us that once again Lavan gives a handmaid to his daughter; this time he gives Bilhah to his daughter, Rachel. The reader will note that the biblical text continually refers to Rachel and Leah as "Lavan's daughters," long after the filial relationship was first pointed out to Jacob in verse six of this chapter. We would suggest that this frequent repetition serves as a reminder to us that though Jacob is separated by time and distance from his parents, he has not forgotten their last exhortation to him to marry of Lavan's daughters. As was mentioned above, several of the *mephorshim* posit that Lavan's "handmaids," Zilpah and Bilhah, are also Lavan's daughters, albeit not from his main wife.

FIFTY

❧ೞ❧ೞ

Jacob Weds Rachel

GENESIS 29:30

*And Jacob came **also** to Rachel, and he **also** loved Rachel above Leah; and he worked with [Lavan] yet another seven years.*[1]

The text first mentions *both* that Jacob took Rachel conjugally as his wife, *and also* that he loved her. This phrasing is in stark contrast to verse 23, which says that Jacob "came to" Leah as his wife, with no mention of love. Rashbam points out that here, with Rachel, Jacob's love is sufficiently evident for the text to restate; in verse 18 we learned that he loved Rachel enough to offer to labor for seven years for her hand in marriage. Here, therefore, we are told that he *still* loved her, even *more* than before.[2] In contrast, according to Radak, this verse teaches us that Jacob did indeed love Leah, even though he did not choose her for his wife. He loved her the way most men love their wives, but he loved Rachel *more*.[3]

Ramban teaches us that it is human nature for a man to obsess over his *first* love. But here, Jacob loves Rachel—his *second* wife—more than Leah, his first. Ramban derives this from the second

---

[1] ויבא **גם** אל רחל, **ויאהב גם** את רחל מלאה; ויעבד עמו עוד שבע שנים אחרות.

[2] ויאהב גם את רחל. וגם: אהבה יותר מלאה. כלומר: בא אליה **וגם** אהבה.

[3] כי גם לאה אהב. להודיע כי גם לאה אהב, אע"פ שלא בחר בה מתחילה לאשה . . . אהבה כמו שאדם אוהב אשתו. אבל **יותר**, אהב רחל.

221

use of the word *GaM*,[4] meaning "more," or "more than what is natural."[5] Chizkuni expands upon Ramban, saying that the double use of the word *GaM*[6] indicates some degree of excess of emotion in Jacob for Rachel. The commentator says that this is counterintuitive to the way of the world, in which a man's *first* sexual experience leaves an indelible mark upon his heart. By such reckoning, *Leah* should have been the one who imprinted Jacob's emotions. Yet here, Jacob loves Rachel more than Leah, who was his first.[7]

We would suggest that Jacob's abiding love for Rachel as it is emphasized in this verse operates *according* to the commentaries' view of human nature. This is because throughout his wedding night Jacob *thought it was Rachel* who was in his arms. Therefore, *in Jacob's perception,* "Rachel"—and not Leah—was really his first, so his excessive love for her is understood.

Sforno understands the word *GaM*[8] in this verse to mean that Jacob's love for Rachel extended *beyond* just the physical; that he loved everything about her that made her Rachel.[9] *Ohr Hachayim* agrees that the Hebrew word *GaM*[10] implies Jacob's excessive love for Rachel. He adds that Jacob actually moved his bed into Rachel's tent because he loved her more than Leah. One would think, says the commentator, that Jacob's constant proximity to Rachel would have cooled his ardor, and that Leah's concomitant *in*accessibility would have increased his desire for *her*. But no! The unconscious motivating force at work here is that "stolen waters are sweeter." Because Jacob waited and worked for seven years before he could possess Rachel, *and because* she was "stolen" from him on his first wedding night, Rachel remained extremely desirable to him notwithstanding his nightly proximity to her.[11]

---

[4] גם

[5] הטבע לאהוב יותר האשה אשר ידע האדם בראשונה, והנה . . . יעקב אהב רחל מלאה, שלא כדרך הארץ; וזה טעם "גם."

[6] גם

[7] מהו גם? אלא נהוג שבעולם אשה ראשונה שאדם בועל, אהבתו תקועה בלבו עולמית. וכאן, יעקב אהב את רחל כשבא אליה, יותר מלאה, אע"פ שבא אל לאה תחלה. וזהו "גם."

[8] גם

[9] ויאהב גם את רחל: לא בשביל האישות בלבד, אבל גם **באשר היא רחל**, בשביל מעשיה הנמשכים לצורתה האישית.

[10] גם

[11] ויבא גם: שהיתה מטתו בקביעות אצל רחל . . . שאהבתה יותר מלאה . . . כי כפי הטבע ההתמדה תמעיט האהבה, וההרחקה תוליד התאוה. והוא סוד: מים גנובים ימתיקו. ולזה רמז

Kli Yakar continues analyzing the nature of Jacob's love for Rachel. He says that initially, Jacob loved Rachel on her own merit; this love grew as he compared Rachel to Leah, for in his mind's eye Rachel's worth became more and more apparent to him when he saw her *in contrast* to her sister.[12] While until now the commentaries have explained Jacob's love for Rachel as *he* experienced it, the *Netziv* alters the focus of this verse, allowing us to glimpse Jacob's love for Rachel from Leah's point of view. We are told that when Leah was Jacob's only wife, she did not feel that Jacob did not love her. This is because she thought, "after all, perhaps he is lukewarm to me, but at least he is taking me to his bed. His coolness does not mean that he hates me." But from the time that he *also* married Rachel, Leah's eyes were opened, and she was aware that Jacob was closer to Rachel than he was to her.[13]

הכתוב באומרו "ויבוא גם אל רחל" בתוספת קביעות, ואעפ"כ גם אהב אותה, ולא נתמעטה האהבה.

[12] ויאהב גם את רחל מלאה: כי אין ניכר איזו מעלה עד אשר רואין ההעדר, ורואין זה כנגד זה . . . יעקב היה אוהב את רחל מצד עצמה, ונוסף על האהבה זו עוד; הוסיף בה אהבה מצד לאה, כי ראה את זו כנגד זו, ונגלה בתותר יתרונה של רחל.

[13] וגם את רחל מלאה: שבמשך שלא נשא את רחל לא הרגישה לאה שאינו אוהב אותה. שהרי מ"מ התנהג עמה כדרך אישות. ויש אנשים שאין בטבעתם להיות מקורבים כל כך לנשותיהם, ולא מחמת שנאה הוא. אבל משעה שנשא **גם** את רחל, הרגישה לאה שמתקרב אל רחל יותר.

FIFTY-ONE

Unwanted Leah
is Redeemed

GENESIS 29:31

And God saw that Leah was hated, so God opened her womb; but Rachel was barren.[1]

Ramban answers a question that is implicit from this verse: Did Jacob "hate" Leah? The commentator explains that Jacob could not forgive Leah for two transgressions: First, that Leah tricked *him* when she went along with her father's duplicity—however reluctantly—and presented herself at his tent pretending to be his intended bride, Rachel. Second, that Leah betrayed not only Jacob, but also her sister when, once she had achieved her father's objective and tricked Jacob into marriage, she failed to divulge to him by word or sign anytime during that first night, but before consummation of their marriage, that she was not Rachel.[2]

Perhaps Rachel intended that the secret passwords she told Leah would be used by her sister *only* for the purpose of deflecting her acute embarrassment in full view of the assembled wedding guests if she were exposed as an impostor at the flap of Jacob's tent. Thus,

---

[1] וירא ד' כי שנואה לאה, ויפתח את רחמה; ורחל עקרה.

[2] "כי שנואה לאה" כי מאשר רמתה את אחותה, גם ביעקב, כי אם נאמר שנהגה כבוד באביה שאחז בה והכניסה אליו, ואל תמר בו, היתה לה להגיד או לרמוז כי היא לאה, אף כי היתה מתנכרת כל הלילה . . . ולכן שנאה יעקב.

224

Leah deceived *both* Jacob and Rachel when she used his secret passwords to secure for herself that first night in Jacob's bed, when the sisters had agreed that the ruse was not intended to go that far.

Abarbanel confirms Jacob's hatred of Leah. The commentator states that a person's thoughts can manifest themselves only in his speech or in his deeds. Jacob demonstrated his hatred for Leah not only in his thoughts, but also in his words *and* his actions. His hatred was always in evidence because he spoke to her in anger or rebuke. And Jacob's actions spoke for themselves, as he only rarely joined her in her tent, and his interactions with her at other times evidenced his dislike.[3]

Leah's betrayals continued to prey upon Jacob's mind until hatred for her took root in his heart. *Midrash Rabbah* (71.2) explains that Jacob's feelings of "hatred" toward Leah were so strong that he was on the verge of divorcing her! Only when she became pregnant did he relent, thinking, "How can I send away the mother of my child?"[4]

Some of the *mephorshim* interpret verse 31 to mean *not* that *Jacob* hated Leah, but that once Leah viewed herself through Jacob's eyes, over time *she* became filled with remorse and self-loathing. *Yefei To'ar* tells us that she wept copious tears, and lamented her bitter fate.[5] *Midrash Rabbah* (71.2) adds that Leah's self-esteem was at its lowest ebb not only because Jacob had begun to despise her, but also because she sensed the tide of public opinion had turned against her. All her life she had striven to be righteous and hence to be perceived as righteous by others. She was now aware that her participation in the deception of Jacob and of her sister altered her neighbors' view of her from righteous to tainted.[6] Therefore, Leah—who had so far been unable to conceive—in her deep despair confined herself to her house. God saw this, had pity upon her

---

[3] והנה השנאה ידוע שתראה לאדם מחבירו אם במעשים, אם בדבור. אם בשתי הדרכים האלה תצא השנאה מהמחשבה למציאות, ויעקב היה שונא את לאה בשתי הדרכים. רוצה לומר במעשים כי לא בא אליה רק בדרך מקרה. וכן בשאר הענינים, היה מתנהג עמה בדרך שנאה, וכן היה מורה תמיד שנאתו בדבריו, שתמיד היו בכעס ובגערה.

[4] כיון שראה אבינו יעקב מעשים שרימה לאה באחותה, נתן דעתו לגרשה. וכיון שפקדה הקב"ה בבנים, אמר: "לאמן של אלו, אני מגרש?!"

[5] וירא ד' כי שנואה לאה: שהיתה מרת נפש ושנאה את נפשה . . . שבכתה ויללה על מר גורלה.

[6] מהלכי דרכים היו אומרים, לאה זו, אין סתרה כגלויה. נראה צדיקת, ואינה צדיקת. אם היתה צדיקת, לא היתה מרמה באחותה.

because her actions were pardonable, and He opened her womb. Thus a depressed Leah, rejected by her husband, her sister and her neighbors, was redeemed in everyone's eyes when she became pregnant first. Her status was restored.[7]

Radak takes a softer view of the words "Leah was hated." He is convinced that she only *seemed* hated because she was the unfortunate "other wife" in Jacob's life. Because there were two wives—one of whom was so truly beloved—the other, by comparison, seemed "hated."[8] The commentary continues, saying that because Leah was acutely aware of the qualitative difference in Jacob's love for her and for her sister, she despised herself. God saw her suffering and opened her womb to console her.[9] *Ohr Hachayim* also views Leah's pregnancy as giving meaning to their fraught relationship. He says that had she been childless, the gossips would have pointed to that fact as confirmation that she and Jacob were not proper mates. God preemptively silenced them when he opened Leah's womb.[10]

The commentator reverts to *p'shat*, and alters the reader's view of Leah's predicament by emphasizing the verse as follows: *And **God** saw that Leah was hated*. The commentator tells us that *only God* saw into Jacob's heart and knew that Jacob had begun to hate Leah. Leah herself was spared this certain knowledge, and because Jacob treated her in a kindly fashion she believed only that Jacob loved her less.[11] *Ohr Hachayim* suggests that Leah's pregnancy will mitigate Jacob's disdain, because he sees that she is fertile, while Rachel remains barren.[12]

Radak emphasizes that *both* Leah and Rachel are barren, as were Sarah and Rebecca before them. God favors Leah with fertility

---

7 אלו העקרות שהן אסורות בתוך בתיהן, ועלוות. וכיון שהקב"ה פקדן בבנים, הן נזקפות. תדע לך שכן לאה, שנואת הבית היתה, וכיון שפקדה הקב"ה, נזקפה.

8 כי שנואה לאה: לא היה יעקב שונא אותה אבל היה אוהב אותה, אלא לפי שהיה אוהב את רחל יותר, קרא ללאה שנואה.

9 ולפי שהיתה עלווה בעיניה שלא היתה אהובה כאחותה, ראה ד' בעניה, ויפתח את רחמה.

10 אם לא היו לה בנים, היו מצדיקים הדברים כי לא בת זוגו של יעקב. לזה "ויפתח רחמה."

11 וירא ד' כי שנואה לאה: יכוין לומר כי ד' **לבדו** הוא שידע, והכיר כי היא שנואה. לא כן היא; שלא הרגישה בשנאתו, אלא שהיתה חושבת שאינה אהובה.

12 ואומרו "ורחל עקרה" . . . אולי יסורו שנאתה שזו אינה יולדת, וזו יולדת.

at this specific juncture, however—leaving Rachel still infertile—
perhaps in order to right the imbalance between them in Jacob's
eyes.[†][13]

[†]Our discussion of the matriarch's infertility appears in Chapter 3, "Infertile
Sarai Chooses a Surrogate."

---

[13] ורחל עקרה, נשארה עקרה כמו שהיתה. וכבר כתבנו הטעם למעלה למה היו האמהות עקרות.
ויפתח את רחמה, ובאומרו "ויפתח," מלמד שהיתה עקרה, וד' פתח את רחמה.

FIFTY-TWO

֍

Leah Bears Jacob's
First Four Sons

GENESIS 29:32-35

And Leah became pregnant, and she bore a son, and she named him Reuven; and she said, "because God saw my suffering, and now my husband will love me."[1]

With these verses, we hear Leah speaking for the very first time in the biblical text. The reader must recognize that until now, Rachel and Leah's words have been *absent* from the recorded text. It was the commentaries who provided Rachel and Leah's words as they understood them, and we have translated and presented these thoughts to the reader. How exciting it is, finally to hear the range of Leah's heartfelt emotions emerge here in her own words! Leah's first spoken words illuminate for us the essence of her deepest complementary emotions: suffering and desire. For Leah, the child himself—however beloved—is not her ultimate purpose. Her desire is focused entirely upon her husband. She says, *"Because God saw how I was suffering"* without Jacob's love, *"perhaps now,"* with the birth of this son I have given him, *"my husband will love me."*

Radak laconically explains that Leah's triumph in conceiving and bearing Jacob's first son is directed toward her husband. She names

---

[1] ותהר לאה ותלד בן, ותקרא שמו ראובן; כי אמרה כי ראה ד' בעניי, כי עתה יאהבני אישי.

228

him Reuven, which in Hebrew means *Re'u BeN*,[2] "look, I have borne you a son." Leah continues, "*now* my husband will love me . . ." Radak adds, ". . . as much as he loves my sister."[3] According to the *Netziv*, Leah's newborn son was the instrumentality for achieving marital closeness with Jacob.[4]

Pirkei d'Rabi Eliezer (chapter 36) echoes Leah's own anguished words from verse 32. The commentator says that Leah understood that her pregnancy was God's way of granting solace to her very soul.[5] Leah explicitly credits God with understanding her deepest inner torment: that she was unloved, and that this first fruit of her womb might obtain for her a measure of the love she so coveted.

Soon thereafter,

Leah again becomes pregnant, and gives birth to a son, and she says, "because God heard that I am hated, He also gave me this one." And she names him Shimon.[6]

The Hebrew word for "hear" or "listen and understand" is *SH'Ma*,[7] which forms the basis for Leah's second son's name. Leah knows that by granting her this second pregnancy God understood that her first was not sufficient to engender love for her in Jacob's heart. She is hopeful that Shimon's birth will dispel Jacob's continued hatred.

Alshich explains that once Leah saw that the birth of Reuven did not succeed in bringing Jacob's love to her, she understood that what she had hoped was Jacob's mere indifference toward her was actually a more potent lingering dislike. "With the birth of Shimon," she reasons, "if Jacob were merely indifferent towards me, then the birth of my first son would have been sufficient to 'purchase' his love." When Leah still senses his hostility even after Shimon's birth, however, she sees that Jacob's feelings against her are not so easily

---

[2] ראו בן

[3] ויאהבני. כאחותי.

[4] כי עתה יאהבני אישי . . . חשבה שעל ידי הבן ישוב להראות לה התקרבות ביותר.

[5] ראה הקב"ה בצרתה של לאה, ונתן לה הריון בטן ונחומים לנפשה.

[6] ותהר עוד ותלד בן ותאמר כי שמע ד' כי שנואה אנכי ויתן לי גם זה; ותקרא שמו שמעון.

[7] שמע

set aside. God heard and understood all this, and therefore gave her a *second* son.[8]

The *Netziv* agrees, saying that Leah saw that giving Jacob his first son was ineffective in earning Jacob's love.[9] Thus, her naming her second son "Shimon" reflected her hope that this birth might do so. Sforno explains that Leah saw Shimon as God's way to offset Jacob's hatred of her, which originated with the tangled events of his wedding night.[10] *Kli Yakar* offers two further possible interpretations of Leah's phrase "because I am hated." First, that she is surprised that Jacob did not have a change of heart from hostility to tenderness once she gave birth. Leah truly thought that with the birth of Reuven, Jacob would not be able to sustain his enmity toward her, for "how could he disdain the well, and enjoy its waters?" How could Jacob *not* be filled with love for the wife who bore his son? Sadly for Leah, she realized she was mistaken, "because I am [*still*] hated." Jacob's love was reserved for Reuven only.[11] Alternatively, the commentator suggests that Leah's statement is "because I am [*again*] hated." Perhaps Jacob's heart *did* soften towards Leah, and he did love her after the birth of Reuven. After all, it is only natural for a new father's joy to overflow onto his wife who labored to produce the fruit of his loins. But alas, Jacob's love toward Leah was only temporary, and it ebbed with each passing day until it was forgotten. We can infer this from Leah's repetition in the text of how "hated" she is in Jacob's eyes, and how distant his heart is from hers.[12]

---

8 מאי "שמע?" אך הנה יש שנאה, ויש העדר אהבה בלבד . . . בראות בן שני, אז אמרה אם לא
היה הענין רק העדר אהבה, היה מספיק בן א' להקנות אהבה . . . אך בהיות שנים אמרה אין
זה. כי אם . . . שנואה אנכי. ועל כן, ויתן לי גם את זה, ויהיה "שמע" לשון הבנה. על כן קרא
שמו שמעון.

9 בראותה שאין הבן מועיל

10 ותמורת השנאה המסובבת מן החשד נתן לי גם את זה.

11 היא סברה מאחר שאין אשה אלא לבנים, והבן אהוב בלי ספק, ואיך תהיה בור שנואה ומימיה
חביבין? אחר כך ראתה שהלכה בטעות.

12 ויכל להיות שבלידת בן ראשון אהב אותה . . . כי כן הוא המנהג, שבשעת הלידה ישמח האב
ביוצא חלציו, ואגבו ישמח גם באשתו אשר לכה. וברוב הימים הכל נשכח, וסרה אהבתו . . .
וידע זה מגודל רחוק לבבו.

*And Leah becomes pregnant once again, and she gives birth to a son and says, "now, this time, my husband will stay with **me**, because **I** have borne him three sons;" therefore **he** named him "Levy."*[13]

Leah's third son is named Levi, which means "to accompany" or "to stay with." Radak understands from this that Leah was hoping that Jacob would cling to *her* rather than to her sister now that she has given Jacob three sons, while her sister remains barren.[14] The reader will note that surprisingly, it is Jacob who names this son, while Leah named the first two. *Kli Yakar* concludes that while Jacob does in fact name his third son, he is actually echoing Leah's sentiment. The commentator concludes from this that Jacob must finally have been won over by Leah's fecundity, and that he has at long last come to terms with the fact that *she* is apparently his chosen wife for purposes of succession.[15]

Abarbanel suggests that Leah's first three sons' names may well reflect the three ways each birth mitigated Leah's suffering. Reuven's birth—his name is based upon the verb "to see"—caused Jacob to cease his *acts* of disdain; Shimon's birth—whose name means "to hear"—caused Jacob to refrain from his scolding *words*; and Levi's birth—whose name can also be a sound-play on the Hebrew word LeV,[16] meaning "heart"—removed from Jacob's heart and mind his hateful thoughts of Leah.[17]

Sforno seizes upon the fact that Levi is Leah's third son and tells us that she is finally optimistic that Jacob will cleave to her, rather than despairing over his love. This is not only because Jacob names this son Levi, meaning "to stay with," but primarily because as the mother of *three* sons Leah is *presumed* now to have an established claim on Jacob's affections. The significance of the number three is not lost on Jacob. This third son is the only son he names (until he names his final and twelfth son), and thus the name looms in

---

[13] ותהר עוד ותלד בן ותאמר עתה הפעם ילוה אישי אלי, כי ילדתי לו שלשה בנים; על כן **קרא** שמו לוי.

[14] יהיה נלוה אל אהבתי יותר מאהבת אחותי כי ילדתי *שלשה בנים*.

[15] ובן השלישי . . . **יעקב** קרא לו להראות שהוא מסכים לדבריה, וכי רצונו לידבק בה. אבל בבנים הקודמים **היא** קראה להם שמות, . . . אבל לא ראינו עדיין הסכמתו עד שילדה בן שלישי. אז גלה דעתו, כי סרה שנאתו מכל וכל.

[16] לב

[17] ואפשר לומר עודשראובן בא להסיר השנאה מהמעשים, ושמעון כדי להסיר השנאה מהדברים, ולוי בא כדי להסיר השנאה מהלב והמחשבה.

significance.[18] The Talmud (*Yevamot* 64b) teaches us that a "*chazakah*," or a presumption of an established claim, occurs when an event is repeated three times.[19] Clearly, Leah is somewhat endeared to Jacob after she has borne his third son.

Rashi points out that it is Leah who states—even *before* Jacob names the baby Levi—"this time my husband *will* cling to me." Leah speaks in the future tense, as if prophesying that Jacob will come to her yet again, allowing her to give birth to a total of six of his sons. Jacob's naming of this baby is a reflection of his agreement with Leah's prophetic statement. *Siftei Chachamim* states that all *four* of the matriarchs were prophetesses, but that Sarah is the only matriarch who is specifically named as a prophetess in the Talmud (see Chapter 1), because only *her* prophetic ability is clearly attested to in the biblical text. Also, the prophetic ability of Rebecca, Rachel and Leah was limited to knowledge about themselves and their children. Future prophecy concerning others was foreclosed to them.[20] Rashi tells us that Leah knew that after bearing Jacob this third son, she will have borne at least her fair share of the twelve tribes that she foresaw were destined to issue from him and his four wives.[21]

And Leah became pregnant still again, and she bore a son, and she said, "This time I will glorify the Lord." Therefore she named him "Yehuda;" and she paused in her childbearing.[22]

Consistent with her prophecy, Leah conceives a fourth time, and bears Jacob another son. She names him "Yehuda," from the Hebrew word *HoDaH*,[23] meaning "to give thanks" or "to glorify." Rashi teaches us that Leah was thanking God for granting her more than her one-fourth allotment of Jacob's prophesied twelve sons.[24] *Ohr Hachayim* says that Leah is praising God for his excessive

---

18 הפעם ילוה שכבר אני **מוחזקת** להיות רבת בנים.

19 הוא **דאתחזק** בתלתא זימני.

20 ושרה, הקרא מעיד עליה, "כל אשר תאמר אליך שרה, שמע בקולה. . . ." והמרש"ל תרץ שהאמהות לא היו מתנבאות כי אם על עצמן. שהיו יודעות מה שיבוא **עליהן**. אבל מה שיבוא לעתיד **על אחרים** לא היו יודעות.

21 לפי **שהאמהות נביאות היו**, וידעו שי"ב שבטים יוצאים מיעקב, וד' נשים ישא. אמרה, מעתה אין לו פתחון פה עלי, שהרי נטלתי כל חלקי בבנים.

22 ותהר עוד, ותלד בן, ותאמר, הפעם אודה את ד'. על כן קראה שמו יהודה; ותעמד מלדת.

23 הודה

24 שנטלתי יותר מחלקי, מעתה יש לי להודות.

goodness in opening her womb this fourth time. Thus, this son's name reflects Leah's appreciation of God's beneficence.[25]

Abarbanel prefers the interpretation that Leah—a conscientious mother who had her hands full with her three older sons, and having gone through the travails of childbirth and child rearing—sought to thank the Almighty for increasing her blessing with yet a fourth son. She was now more than content, and did not pray for more children, as she sensed that by now she surely had earned Jacob's love.[26]

The Talmud (*Brachot* 7b) extols Leah's expression of gratitude, saying that from the time God created the world and until Leah named her fourth son, no one had ever praised the Almighty in such language of gratitude and contentment.[27]

---

[25] כשניתן לה בן ד', אמרה, הפעם אודה את ד' . . . אין זה אלא הפלגת טובתו יתברך, כברכה על רוב טובה.

[26] והיותר נכון לפרש שלאה בראותה צער העבור וצער גדול בנים, והיו לה כבר שלשה . . . ואין חפצה בבנים יותר, ולכן אמרה "הפעם אודה את ד'," כאומר זה יספיק לי . . . עתה שנשלם המכוון שאני אהובה.

[27] ואמר רבי יוחנן משום רבי שמעון בן יוחai: מיום שברא הקדוש ברוך הוא את עולמו, לא היה אדם שהודה להקב"ה עד שבאתה לאה והודתו, שנאמר "הפעם אודה את ד'."

FIFTY-THREE

ഐരുഐരു

Rachel's Anguish
and Jacob's Ire

GENESIS 30:1–2

We can envision the anguish of Rachel, Jacob's beloved wife, watching as her sister effortlessly produced four sons in rapid succession, while she remains unable to conceive.

> *And when Rachel saw that she bore no children for Jacob, Rachel was filled with envy toward her sister; so she said to Jacob, "Give* **me** *children! For if not, I am dead!"* [1]

The *mephorshim* speculate about the precise reason for Rachel's envy. Radak says that Rachel envied Leah more as *each* son was born to her. It seemed to Rachel that God's blessing Leah with four sons was excessive, considering that she herself had yet to bear even one.[2] Chizkuni explains that Rachel's feelings of envy only surfaced with the birth of her sister's *fourth* son. For with *this* son's birth Rachel knew that Leah (only one of Jacob's prophesied four wives) already

---

1 ותרא רחל כי לא ילדה ליעקב, ותקנא רחל באחותה; ותאמר אל יעקב הבה לי בנים, ואם אין,
מתה אנכי.
2 קנאה בטוב, שראתה לאחותה שילדה ארבעה בנים ליעקב, והיא לא ילדה אפילו אחד.

234

had borne *more than* her allotted share of Jacob's twelve prophesied sons, and Rachel envied Leah her fertility.[3]

Torat Hachida understands that Rachel's "envy" of her sister is in reality a much more complex emotion than simple jealousy. The commentator invites the reader to view Rachel's plight as *she* has experienced it. First of all, we must remember that while Rachel may have fallen in love with Jacob at the time of their first meeting, she also had a close lifelong relationship with her older sister, Leah. It is this latter bond that caused her to reveal the secret passwords to her sister so that Leah would not be publicly humiliated at the wedding feast. Added to this tension was Rachel's true fear that after she had allowed her sister to be wed to her intended, perhaps her father might decide *not* to allow her *also* to wed Jacob. And even if her father did not go back on his promise, she was tortured by the doubt that perhaps Jacob himself might change *his* mind and decide he did not want to marry her also.

The commentator, exquisitely sensitive to Rachel's emotional turmoil, dramatically points out that *even with all these conflicting, competing loyalties*—to her intended husband; to her older sister; to her father; and yes, to her own happiness—Rachel nonetheless acted heroically, and passed the secret signs to her sister. She walked through this minefield of emotions and found the clear and righteous path. *This* act of Rachel's was a great and meritorious act.

What, then, is the true nature of Rachel's "envy?" The commentator continues that Rachel, in her heart of hearts, cannot understand why Leah—who is the one who carried the trick *too* far and pretended *throughout the night* to be Rachel—is the one to bear Jacob sons, while Rachel (who had pitied her sister and allowed her to save face) is herself afflicted with childlessness. Rachel envies Leah her seeming absolution (that is, her ability to bear children), while she—Rachel—is still being punished for her part in the deception, and remains barren. Thus, in her anguish born of the powerful emotions of guilt and righteousness, Rachel now fears that somehow Jacob holds the key to free her from continued punishment. She has convinced herself that if Jacob would only forgive her for her part in

---

3 לא נתקנאה בה עד שילדה בן רביעי, שעכשיו נטלה יותר מחלקה הראוי לה מי"ב שבטים.

her father's trickery—as he has apparently absolved Leah—then she, too, will surely be blessed with children.[4]

The *Netziv* adds that Rachel secretly thought that perhaps the fault of her childlessness lay not in her, but in Jacob. If only he would open his heart to forgive her, he would be blessed with children from *her* womb, also. The *Netziv* continues that this secret suspicion is consistent with the notion that she—and no other—was Jacob's preferred wife, and thus was entitled to bear his sons. Following this logic, if Rachel is *not* becoming pregnant, the "fault" must be in Jacob, who may in some manner be as yet unworthy of fathering Rachel's children. The time has come, to Rachel's way of thinking, for Jacob to humble himself sufficiently that God will determine that *he* is worthy.[5]

On the other hand, Rashi implies that Rachel is searching her own soul, looking for the lack within her own character, that may have led God to grant Leah children, yet withhold them from her. She fears, says Rashi, that Leah's heart is purer than hers is, that on a daily basis—even though she is functionally the "second wife"—Leah exudes selfless generosity and kindness toward others, including Jacob, and thus she is more deserving than Rachel.[6]

At this point in the text, at the midpoint of verse one, begins the *only* recorded dialogue between Rachel and Jacob. . . .

And [Rachel] said to Jacob: "Give me children, for if not, I am dead!"[7]
And Jacob's fury was kindled against Rachel, and he said, "Am I
instead of God, who has withheld from you the fruit of the womb?"[8]

---

4 שמסרה הסימנים ללאה כדי שלא תתבייש, והיא בתוקף אהבה ליעקב, ולא ידעה אם יתרצה
אביה להשיא גם היא ליעקב, ואם יעקב יתרצה לקחתה גם היא. **ועם כל זה** מסרה הסימנים,
והיה פשוט אצלה שעשתה מצוה גדולה . . . ותקנא רחל באחותה, שהיא דהטעיתה ליעקב
ממש יש **לה** בנים, והיא שהיתה גרמה, לקתה. ומזה חשבה דהכל תלוי ביעקב, דמחל ללאה,
ולה לא מחל, ולכך נענשה.

5 שחשבה שמה שלא ילדה הוא בשביל שלא זכה **הוא** להבנות ממנה . . . הלא היא לבדה עיקר
אשה אליו, ואם כן **הוא** לא זכה. ויש לו למסור נפשו ולעשות פעולה שיזכה.

6 ותקנא רחל באחותה. קנאה במעשיה הטובים. אמרה, אלולי שצדקה ממני, לא זכתה לבנים.

7 ותאמר אל יעקב, הבה לי בנים! ואם אין, מתה אנכי!

8 ויחר אף יעקב ברחל; ויאמר התחת אלקים אנכי, אשר מנע ממך פרי בטן?

This scene, far from a loving encounter, is an anguished confrontation. Avivah Gottlieb Zornberg[†] illuminates this fateful conversation.

> The only recorded dialogue between Jacob and Rachel can perhaps be read in the light of such an understanding of the dynamics of desire and frustration. . . . [The] commentators understand Rachel not to be having a feminine tantrum—threatening her husband with dire consequences if he does not "give" her children. Rather, she is simply describing a dull meaninglessness, a loss of sap in her life. And Jacob's anger becomes comprehensible. It is painful for him to hear his wife—whom he loves for herself, not as a means of procreation—declare so plainly that her primary passion is not for him.

The reader will note that up until this point, it was the commentaries who supplied us with Rachel's unrecorded words. Here, the biblical text records Rachel's own words for the first time. It cannot withhold them. Rachel's passion for a child is so strong that her voice bursts forth from the text. "Give me children!" she cries out to Jacob, "for if not, I am dead."

Rashi tells us that initially Rachel is begging Jacob to pray to God for her to become fertile, just as his father, Isaac, beseeched God on behalf of *his* childless wife. The alternative, Rachel cries, would be that she would be considered as good as dead.[9] The Talmud (*Nedarim* 64b) explains the substance of Rachel's emotional outburst. One who is childless, we learn from the Talmud, equates herself with one who is dead.[10]

The supercommentary on *Torah Temima* expresses, in metaphor, the reason for Rachel's anguish. He says that the essence of Rachel's request is that she understands that one's children are the thread that connects one generation to another. And thus, for one who is childless, this life-line has been abruptly cut, and it is as if she is

---

[†]Zornberg, A. G. (1995). *Genesis: The Beginning of Desire* (Philadelphia: The Jewish Publication Society), p. 210.

---

[9] הבה לי. וכי כך עשה אביך לאמך, כהלא התפלל עליה. מנה אנכי. מכאן למי שאין בנים שחשוב כמת.

[10] כל אדם שאין לו בנים חשוב כמת, שנאמר "הבה לי בנים, ואם אין, מתה אנכי."

dead.[11] The *Netziv* concurs, explaining that in this light we can appreciate Rachel's dissatisfaction even with Jacob's excessive, passionate devotion to her. Without children to follow in her footsteps, the love between her and Jacob seems empty and vain. Rachel desires a generational continuity of her line, so that she will be remembered long after she is gone.[12] *Sha'arei Aharon* defines Rachel's plea "for if not, I am dead!"—as a reflection of Rachel's immediate existential agony. The commentator says that she is not referring to the inevitable fact that she will eventually reach the end of her life in due course. Rather, that if she must live out her life *as a childless wife*, she will die an untimely death from the primal heartache this state of being engenders. Either that, or, driven by her own despair, she will come to a premature end.[13] Rabbi Abraham, son of the Rambam, comprehends from verse one the depth of Rachel's overwhelming anguish with her barrenness. He agrees that Rachel's existential state by this time has devolved into meaninglessness and hopelessness. She is crying out to Jacob saying, "if a child is not given to me, I will drown in my own sorrow!"[14]

Obviously, the commentators are struggling to understand Rachel's state-of-mind, and to validate both her choice of words and the accusing and anguished tone of her expression to Jacob in verse one. *Sha'arei Aharon* suggests that in her desperation, Rachel thinks that Jacob is indifferent to the emotional consequences of her barrenness, because *he* already has achieved fatherhood through Leah. She begins to suspect that Jacob is deliberately withholding children from her "for her own good." He is still so passionately in love with her that he seeks to spare her the agony and physical travail of childbirth, and the drudgery of housewifery and motherhood. He desires Rachel always to retain the virginal youthfulness of the young woman she was at the well. Rachel, however, has matured to the extent that a pampered but vacuous existence holds no attraction for her. She issues this seemingly outrageous ultimatum to her husband ("give me children or I am a dead woman!") in order to bestir Jacob

---

11 יש לומר כוונת העניין. כי מרוצת החיים הוא כפתיל הנמשך מאבות לבנים, וזה שאין לו בנים הרי פתיל החיים שלו נפסק, והוי כמת.

12 וכן רחל אמרה דעיקר הרעש שאינה מתפייסת באהבתו היתרה לה, הוא בשביל שאם אין מתה אנכי . . . כך הבן הוא המסייע להזכיר שמו האבוד מן העולם.

13 ואם אין, עתידה אני למות מרוב צער על היותי חשוכת בנים, או אסגף עצמי עד שאמות.

14 כלומר, אם לא יותן לי בן, אהיה אובדת בצערי.

to fathom, once and for all, how deadly serious she is in her desiring children of her own. She is provoking Jacob and in effect shouting at him, "Stop trying to protect me! I *want* the rigors of pregnancy! I *welcome* the changes that will overtake my body: the thickened waist, the engorged breasts, the breathless waddle of a beautiful woman heavy with child. *This* is why I was born, and without it I will wither and die!"[15]

The commentators turn now to Jacob's angry response to his wife's piteously desperate plea for children. Radak says that Jacob is irate at Rachel's implication that *he* has somehow withheld children from her. He responds to her provocation saying, "It is *God* who has withheld children from you, and not I! It is from God alone you should request children, because I am doing everything in my power to give them to you. After all, don't I come to your bed night after night! What more can you expect from me if it is God who has made you barren? Pray to *God* to open your womb as he did your sister's!" Therefore, says Radak, Jacob was incensed with Rachel's ultimatum, because he felt she unjustly attributed to *him*—and not to the Almighty—the power to induce fertility.[16]

Ramban is greatly troubled by Jacob's wrathful words and tone. The commentator asks rhetorically, what reason could Jacob have had for becoming so incensed with the woman he purportedly adored? If, as Rashi suggests, Rachel was begging Jacob to pray to God on her behalf—as his father had done for Rebecca—then Jacob's anger is surely uncalled for. If she were asking her husband to pray on her behalf because God listens closely to the prayers of the righteous, then still his angry response was inappropriate at best, or cruel at worst. Ramban is so distressed by Jacob's insensitivity to Rachel that he argues that historically, righteous men have been known to pray not only for their own wives, but even for nonbelievers! Surely Jacob's behavior in this episode is remiss. It is precisely because of Jacob's disproportionate anger and callousness here that the rabbis hold Jacob up to reproach.

---

15 ותאמר אל יעקב הבה לי בנים. יתכן שרחל חשבה כי אחר שהשיג מלאה בנים רבים, לא חשש
אם לא תלד, והיתה מניעת הבנים ממנה טובה בעיניו. לאהבתו אותה, להצילה מצער גדול
בנים, ושלא תכחיש, כי חפץ בבריאותה. ולכן העירה את רוחו שתזיק לה עד מות אם לא תהר.

16 **הוא** מנע ממך ולא אני, **וממנו** תבקשי שיתן לך בנים, כי אני נותן לך מה שעלי לתת, כי אני
שוכב עמך. מה אוכל אני לעשות אם את עקרה? **מהקל** תבקשי, שיפתח את רחמך כאשר עשה
לאחותך. בבקשה ממנו . . . לפיכך חרה אף יעקב, לפי שתלתה הכח **בו**, ולא בקל.

In fact, Ramban[†] quotes *Midrash Rabbah* stating that it is none other than the Almighty Himself who censures Jacob, saying, "Is *this* the proper way to answer one who is sorely oppressed?! You will live to see her sons born, and *your* sons will be subservient to *hers*!" Ramban explains that Jacob should have understood that in her tortured state, Rachel sought some measure of empathy from Jacob, and would have been comforted somewhat if he had donned sackcloth and ashes and prostrated himself before God, praying for her fertility. Unfortunately, says Ramban, Jacob allowed his temper—and not his sympathy—to be aroused by Rachel's overwrought ultimatum. He humiliated his wife by pointing out that God had seen fit to prevent *her* from conceiving, and not *him*. Thus debased, explains Ramban, a righteous Rachel—unable to rely upon her husband to pray on her behalf—appeals to God on her own merit.[17]

Siftei Chachamim succinctly captures the essence of Ramban's criticism of Jacob's anger. He says simply that Jacob should have spoken gently to his wife and comforted her, rather than allowing his anger to be kindled against her.[18]

It is possible that Jacob's anger at Rachel is rooted, perhaps subconsciously, in his having felt betrayed by Rachel when, years before, she gave the secret signs to her sister and enabled Lavan to trick Jacob into marrying Leah instead of Rachel. Jacob has suppressed his feeling of betrayal all these years because of his great love for Rachel, but now, when she very nearly blames him for her childlessness, his pent-up anger erupts. He never blamed Rachel for the marriage deception; he will not countenance her blaming him for her childless state. Rachel's desperation reminds Jacob that her

---

[†]Readers will recall that this is the second time that Ramban takes a patriarch to task over insensitivity to his wife. The first time was described in Chapter 2 above.

---

[17] וכי צדיקים אינם . . . ד' צדיקים אל ושומע . . . ? אפו חרה למה כן אם תמה, ואני
זה שבשביל ונראה נכריות! נשים בעד התפללו ואלישע אליהו והנה אחרים? בעד מתפללים
שבניך חייך המעיקות?!" את עונין "כך הקב"ה, לו אמר רבה, בבראשית אמרו רבותינו. תפסוהו
יתענה אותה באהבתו כי וחשבה בקנאתה, כהוגן שלא דברה . . . בנה." לפני לעמוד עתידין
הנשים געגועי דרך שדברה ובעבור . . . בנים לה שיהיו עד ויתפלל ואפר שק וילבש יעקב
ליסר וזה ממנו, ולא הבטן פרי נמנע **ממנה** כי . . . אפו חרה במיתתה להפחידו האהובות
עצמה. על להתפלל שבה יעקב, תפילת על להסמך תוכל שלא הצדקת והנה ולהחלימה, אותה
[18] בנחת. לו להשיב לו היה ליעקב? ויחר למה

"primary passion" has never been *for him*. Years before, her loyalty to Leah took precedence over her own marriage, and now her desire for a child of her own overshadows their entire relationship.

Ohr Hachayim offers a possible justification for Jacob's ire. The commentator suggests that he may have been subjected to Rachel's depression for some time, and no amount of his sympathy or coddling had sufficed to gentle her out of her misery. Perhaps for this reason, says *Ohr Hachayim*, when faced with her exclamation ("give me children or else I am dead!"), Jacob is genuinely fearful that Rachel's own words will become a self-fulfilling prophecy, and he reacts angrily. He knows that the words of the righteous, even though they erupt out of deep misery, may have irreparable consequences.[19] Thus, Jacob's disproportionate anger served to silence Rachel in her agitated state of depression.

Nehama Leibowitz[†] helps us to understand Jacob's explosive anger at his beloved wife, Rachel. Nehama cites the reader to the commentator *Akeidat Yitzchak*, who wrote about a woman's "two purposes" for living. The first is the same as man's, which is to "understand and advance in the intellectual and moral field just as did the matriarchs and many righteous women." A woman's second purpose is to exercise "the power of childbearing and [child] rearing." Nehama explains that

> Jacob's anger is here explained as being directed at Rachel's forgetting the true and chief purpose of her existence which, according to the *Akedat Yizhak* [sic] is no different from that of her partner, the man's. . . . She in her yearnings for a child saw her whole world circumscribed by the second purpose of woman's existence . . . to become a mother. Without it her life was not worth living. "Or else I die." This [cry] was a treasonable repudiation of her function, a flight from her destiny and purpose, shirking the duties imposed on her, not in virtue of her being a woman, but in virtue of her being a human being.[20]

[†]Leibowitz, N. (1973). *Studies in Bereshit*, p. 335.

---

[19] ויחר אף. הטעם לפי שהוציאה מפיה דבר קללה שאמרה "מתה אנכי," ודברי הצדיקים, אפילו בסדר זה, עושה רושם.

[20] נתבאר שיש לאשה שתי תכליות: האחד . . . תוכל להבין ולהשכיל בדברי שכל וחסידות . . . והשני עניין ההולדה . . . וגידול הבנים . . . על כן חרה אף יעקב ברחל . . . שהיא אינה מתה לפי התכלית המשותף, באשר מנע ממנה פרי בטן, כמו שיהיה בו העניין גם כן אם

It is not that Jacob is insensitive to Rachel's emotional turmoil; he understands it, but rejects it, in favor of the first role that Rachel can pursue, that of fulfilling her destiny as a moral and spiritual being, even though she is childless.

לא יוליד . . . . "ואם אין מתה אנכי"—והרי זו בגידה בתפקיד,, . . . השתממטות מן החובות
המוטלות עליה, לא בהיותה אשה, אלא בהיותה אדם.

FIFTY–FOUR

৪০ (৪৪০ (৪

Rachel Offers Bilhah
as a Surrogate

GENESIS 30:3–4

Rachel then presents Jacob with an alternative solution to her barrenness.

> *And she says, "here is my maidservant, Bilhah. Come to her, that she may bear a child upon my knees, and I will also be built up through her." So she gave him Bilhah her handmaiden as a wife, and Jacob came to her.*[1]

In verse three, Rachel tells Jacob "and I will *also* be built up through her." The *mephorshim* interpret the word "also" in different ways. Radak tells us that Rachel's intention is to breed children through Bilhah's union with Jacob, so she—Rachel—will *also* be a mother just like her sister Leah is.[2] Ibn Ezra writes that Rachel was referring to the well-known family lore that a barren Sarah offered Hagar to Abraham in order that she "be built up through her" (Genesis 16:2). Perhaps here the childless Rachel is following Sarah's instructive words, offering Bilhah to Jacob, so that she will *also*

---

[1] ותאמר הנה אמתי בלהה, בא אליה; ותלד על ברכי, ואבנה גם אנכי ממנה. ותתן לו את בלהה שפחתה לאשה; ויבא אליה יעקב.

[2] ואבנה **גם** אנכי. ר"ל כמו אחותי.

243

nurture a surrogate child.[3] Radak says as much. He describes Rachel's attitude here as expansive, telling Jacob to bed Bilhah, and she—Rachel—will treat the resulting child as her own, because it would be of her husband's seed.[4] *Sha'arei Aharon* explains that Rachel hoped to allow Bilhah to carry and deliver Jacob's child, while she—Rachel—was prepared to bear the child to her breast, and raise it as her own.[5]

Sforno's interpretation injects Rachel's strategy with the same psychological impetus that Sarah employed when she offered Hagar to Abraham. By offering yet another woman to her husband, Rachel seeks now to stimulate within her infertile body sufficient hormonal response so that she herself might conceive.[6] The Talmud (*Megilla* 13a) confirms the potential potency of envy as a psycho-biological stimulant to a woman's hormonal make-up. The Talmud states that a woman's jealousy can be most aroused by her husband's attraction for another woman.[7]

Thus, we can see that Rachel wisely is confronting her barrenness on two fronts. On the one hand, she is finally willing to consider raising a surrogate child as her very own. On the other, she also is still harboring a hope that a child will issue from her own womb.

Kli Yakar agrees, understanding the strength of Rachel's jealousy. This commentator credits Rachel with realizing, upon introspection, that she must somehow have erected an internal barrier between herself and the Almighty, for why else would her prayers for a child have gone unanswered. One whose fervent prayer to God *is* answered is considered as if she is in direct contact with the Almighty. Therefore, Rachel sought to dismantle this barrier within herself that blocked a spiritual relationship with God, and prevented her prayers for a child from being granted. To this end, Rachel closely examined her own heart and deeds, inquiring what she had done to cause this partition between herself and God. Rachel discerned that her overwhelming envy of her sister's ability to bear children was sufficiently great itself to constitute the psychological impediment to

---

3 ואבנה. מפורש בדברי שרה.

4 אחשוב שיהיה בני, כיון שיהיה משפחתי.

5 ותלד על ברכי. פירוש שתהא יולדת, ואני מגדלת, וטוענת בחיקי.

6 ממנה. ירך חברתי יתעורר טבע כלי הזרע לפעולותם.

7 אין אשה מתקנאה אלא בירך חבירתה.

her prayers. She therefore determined to truly repent of her envy, to conquer once and for all this destructive emotion. Once she did so, by dint of her enormous efforts, she not only ceased to envy her sister, but she also bore no envy even toward her handmaiden Bilhah.[8]

The commentaries next deal with the issue of Bilhah's status, because Bilhah will in fact conceive and bear two children. The status of these children becomes significant, as they are Jacob's sons, though born to neither Leah nor Rachel. In verse three Rachel offers Jacob her "maid" Bilhah.[9] Later on in the text, in verses four and seven, Bilhah is referred to by a different Hebrew word, SHiFCHa,[10] meaning "handmaid," which is also the same term used by Sarah (see our discussion in Chapter 3) when she referred to Hagar, her handmaid. The Netziv teaches us from Rachel's reference to Bilhah as aMaTi,[11] that Rachel had emancipated Bilhah, and that she presented her to Jacob as a free woman. The Netziv points to the similarity of the sound of the words aMaH and iMaH (meaning "mother"), as a sign that Bilhah also will be a mother to Jacob's sons.[12] Ohr Hachayim goes on to state specifically that even though Bilhah is later referred to in the text as a "handmaid,"[13] the text also clearly states in verse four that Bilhah was given to Jacob as a wife.[14] Bilhah's status as a wife was thus secured, and her sons from Jacob were free men.[15] Ba'al Haturim reminds us, in addition, that Bilhah was also Lavan's daughter, though not from the same mother as Leah and Rachel.[16] Although Bilhah was Lavan's daughter from a concubine, Chizkuni points out that Jacob took Bilhah as a wife according to Jewish law,

---

8 כל מי שנתקבלה תפילתו דומה כאילו עומד תחת אלקים ממש, ואין שום דבר חוצץ בינו לבין אלקים. אבל בזמן שאין תפילתו נשמעת, דומה כאילו יש מסך מבדיל וחוצץ בינו לבין אלקים . . . נתנה רחל אל לבה לפשפש במעשיה, איזה עוון גרם לה, ולא מצאה כי אם מידת הקנאה . . . על כן נתנה אל לבה לשוב בתשובה להטות אל קצה האחרון בדבר שחטאה בו, והוא שמתחלה נתקנאה אפילו באחותה, ואחר כך לא נתקנאה אפילו בשפחתה.

9 אמתי בלהה

10 שפחה

11 אמתי

12 אמתי . . . רחל שחררה אותה, ולא נקראה אלא "אמה," כמו אמה העברים.

13 שפחה

14 לאשה

15 שפחתה לאשה. אישיות יש לה בה, ובניה בני חורין.

16 הנה אמתי בלהה. לפי שהיתה בת לבן מפלגש.

and that therefore the sons that she bore him had the full status as tribes of Israel, and were categorically *not* the sons of a concubine.[17]

---

[17] בלהה שפחתה לאשה. שאף הם היו נשיו בכתובה וקדושין, ולא היו השבטים בני פלגשים.

FIFTY-FIVE

౭౦౪౦౪

Bilhah Bears Jacob
Two Sons

GENESIS 30:5–8

*So Bilhah became pregnant, and bore a son **for Jacob**.*[1]

R adak continues this line of reasoning, explaining that this verse stresses that Bilhah bore a son *for Jacob*, in order to acknowledge that Jacob considered her to be his wife, and thus her sons by him were legitimate heirs to his patriarchal blessing and material legacy.[2] Ramban points out that the text appears to emphasize that Bilhah and Zilpah's sons are born *to Jacob*. Surely the text could have noted that they each bore sons, omitting the words "to Jacob" as seemingly redundant. The commentator states that the text includes "to Jacob" in order to emphasize that Jacob *wanted* these sons, that he legitimized and acknowledged them as his full-fledged heirs.[3]

And Rachel says, "God has judged me, and He has also heard my voice, and has given me a son." Therefore she named him Dan.[4] The Hebrew word *DaN* is translated as "He judged." According to the *p'shat*, God judged Rachel's request for maternity to be worthy, and

---

[1]   ותהר בלהה ותלד **ליעקב** בן.

[2]   ותהר. זכר בארבעת בני השפחות **ליעקב** להודיע שהם נחשבים ליעקב כבני הנשים, וכן היו בברכה ובירושה.

[3]   ותלד **ליעקב** בן . . . הזכיר בכל השפחות "**ליעקב**" להגיד כי הוא חפץ ומודה בהם.

[4]   ותאמר רחל, דנני אלקים וגם שמע בקלי, ויתן לי בן; על כן קראה שמו דן.

247

He heeded her plea, allowing her to realize motherhood through Bilhah. Rashi explains that Rachel named her first "surrogate son" Dan, as a declaration that "God *has judged* me, found me guilty, and has now acquitted me" of any sin.[5]

To what "sin" was Rachel referring? The commentators explicate Rashi and outline Rachel's perceived offenses. Abarbanel says that Rachel's "sin" was that her first reaction to her obvious failure to conceive was to rail at her husband, Jacob. She should first have importuned God, in the manner of Sarah and Rebecca. This was her failing.[6] The *Netziv* tells us that Rachel's angry words toward Jacob ("give me children or else I am dead!") were the offense that required Divine forgiveness. The wonder of God's beneficence permeates the *Netziv*'s commentary here, because immediately after describing her "sin," the *Netziv* tells us that God excuses it, saying that it was Rachel's existential anguish at her childlessness that caused her to speak thus to her husband. God saw into Rachel's heart, and understanding her deep sadness, had mercy upon her, and granted her request that she be "built up" through Bilhah.[7] According to Abarbanel, God granted Rachel what she had recently requested, namely a surrogate son from Bilhah. Still, her consuming passion—to conceive and bear *her own* genetic child—remains unfulfilled.[8]

Immediately thereafter,

Bilhah, Rachel's handmaid, bears Jacob a second son. And Rachel says, "like bonds with the Almighty, so I am bound to my sister, but I have also prevailed." So she named [the son] Naphtali.[9]

According to the *p'shat*, once Rachel's handmaid, Bilhah, delivers yet a second son, Rachel names him "Naphtali," from either the Hebrew word *P'TiL*,[10] meaning "connecting cord" or "bond," or the Hebrew word *NaPHTuLaY*,[11] meaning "struggles." Clearly Rachel is referring here to her complex and intimate relationship with her

---

5 דנני וחיבני, וזכני.

6 חטאה היתה שלא קדמה פניו יתברך בתפילה, כמשפט העקרות.

7 שלא בצדק דברה ליעקב אבל מרוב צערה דברה, ורחמנא לבה בעי ויודע צערה.

8 שמע בקלי ותפלתי למלאות **קצת** משאלתי, ונתן לי את הבן הזה.

9 ותהר עוד ותלד בלהה שפחת רחל, בן שני ליעקב. ותאמר רחל, נפתולי אלקים נפתלתי עם אחתי וגם יכלתי, ותקרא שמו נפתלי.

10 פתיל

11 נפתולי

sister Leah. They share the same husband, but Leah is blessed with numerous children while Rachel is childless. Their present relationship is tainted by the formative drama of years ago, when Rachel allowed her sister Leah to be given in trickery to Jacob as a wife, and all the while Jacob thought he was marrying Rachel. Thus, the sisterly bonds have become entangled. Radak says that the text shows us that Rachel compares the complexity of her relationship with her sister to the multi-layered spiritual struggle one has with his Creator.[12]

The commentaries expound on Rachel's excessive absorption with her sister's role in her own barrenness. *Midrash Rabbah* (71.8) describes Rachel's internal struggle. She tortures herself by second-guessing every single action and feeling she has experienced since her father substituted Leah on the fateful wedding night years before. "If only I had sent Jacob a message saying, 'beware! They are tricking you!' Jacob would surely have withdrawn," and not married Leah.[13]

Alshich reveals for us Rachel's further self-recrimination. "Perhaps I am being punished with childlessness because I assisted in my father's trick, and allowed Jacob to marry my sister. I thus kept myself from Jacob for the full week when we should have been man and wife."[14] Alshich alternatively suggests that Rachel agonizes over her part in the deception, and thinks that God is punishing her with barrenness because she enabled the switch with Leah. "It is my collusion in my father's trickery that forever altered my natural, loving relationship with my sister."[15]

Ultimately, according to Alshich, with the birth of her two surrogate sons, Rachel grows to understand that her own childlessness is in no way connected with her sister. Rachel considers herself blessed with Bilhah's sons, and finally is coming to appreciate that her devotion to God and her bonds with the Almighty were the model for her behavior toward her sister. Her part in Lavan's trickery of Jacob years ago was motivated by the unselfish love of one sister for another, and that bond was proper and Godly.[16]

---

[12] נפתולי אלקים. להגדיל הנפתולים. כי כל דבר שרוצה להגדיל, סומך אותו לשם יתברך.

[13] אלו שלחתי ואמרתי לו "תן דעתך שהם מרמים בך!" לא היה פירש?!

[14] על שמנעתי עצמי מבעלי שבוע אחד.

[15] לעון לחשב לי מה שעשיתי בערמת חלופי לאה, מה שנתפתלתי שנתעקשתי לרמות, שלא כטבעי עם אחותי.

[16] הלא חששתי שחטאתי בדבר. אך בתת ד' לי גם את זה . . . חבורי אלקים ודביקות עמו היה מה שנתחברתי עם אחותי.

FIFTY–SIX

৪০০৪৪০০৪

Leah Offers Zilpah
as a Surrogate

GENESIS 30:9

*And Leah saw that no [more] children were forthcoming from her, so
she took Zilpah, her handmaid, and gave her to Jacob as a wife.*[1]

Ramban asks and answers the two questions that must be on the
reader's mind. First, why is Leah giving *her* handmaid to her
husband? After all, she already has borne four sons for Jacob; surely
she does not need "to be built up" through a surrogacy like her sister.
And second, on a deeper level, it is unnatural for a wife to foist an
additional woman into her husband's bed. The nighttime logistics
were complex enough with Jacob having taken three wives; what
could have motivated Leah to introduce a fourth variable into the
nocturnal schedule? Surely she would thereby be distancing her
husband from her even more? [2]

Ramban answers that Leah, who had been redeemed somewhat
in Jacob's affections with each successive son that she bore him,
watched with consternation as Rachel's handmaid, Bilhah, rapidly
brought Rachel into the sorority of motherhood. The issue for Leah,

---

1 ותרא לאה כי עמדה מלדת; ותקח את זלפה שפחתה ותתן אתה ליעקב לאשה.

2 לא ידעתי מה המעשה הזה ללאה, ולמה נתנה שפחתה לבעלה. והיא לא היתה עקרה שתבנה
ממנה. ואין דרך הנשים להרבות נשים לבעליהן.

says Ramban, was one of preeminence over her sister. Leah desperately wished to bear for Jacob the majority of the sons who were destined to emerge from him. The Torah tells us here that Leah, whose fertility was previously immediate and abundant, was presently experiencing a "dry" spell that she feared would become her permanent state. She therefore thrust her young handmaid, Zilpah, upon her husband, hoping that Zilpah's presumed fertility would secure Leah's primacy as matriarch to the tribes of Israel. For any children born to her handmaid would be credited to *her*, as she herself would name and mother them. Leah hoped that each child she bore for Jacob—whether her own or via a surrogate—would be a tether to secure her place in Jacob's heart.[3]

The *Netziv* presents a more unselfish view of Leah's giving her handmaid to Jacob. According to the *Netziv*, Leah's motivation for giving Zilpah to Jacob was compassion for the girl's unmarried state in Jacob's household. Leah uniquely understood Zilpah's feeling of exclusion from the anticipation of connubial intimacy, having initially been passed over by Jacob in favor of her younger sister. A magnanimous Leah sought to alleviate Zilpah's envy of Bilhah, whom Rachel had elevated in status from handmaid to wife. Leah felt she could do as much for Zilpah.[4] *Torah Shlema* explains that Leah approached Zilpah, and convinced her to be a wife to Jacob.[5] *Da'at Zekeinim* reminds us that Zilpah was Lavan's daughter, also. She was called a "handmaid" because she was born to Lavan's concubine.[6] Notably, Leah emancipated Zilpah, as Rachel did for Bilhah, allowing Jacob to take her to be his *wife* and not merely his concubine.[7] *Ohr Hachayim* agrees, reiterating that, as was the case with Bilhah, the text is clear that the sons Zilpah bore were "to Jacob."[8] She became his wife and the sons she bore him enjoyed the same status and property rights as all his other sons.[9]

---

[3] וַתֵּרֶא לֵאָה . . . אבל נצטרך לומר כי היו נביאות, יודעות שעתיד יעקב להעמיד י"ב שבטים, ורצתה שיהיה רוב הבנים לה ממנה, או משפחתה, שהיה ברשותה ולא תתגבר אחותה עליה בבנים.

[4] הבינה כי היא חוטאת על זלפה, שמקנאת בירך בלהה.

[5] ותקח. לקחה בדברים.

[6] הלא בנות היו; אלא . . . בנותיו של אדם מפלגש קרויות "שפחות."

[7] ותתן. לאשה ולא לפלגש. אלא שחררה אותה ודרך אישות לקחה.

[8] ליעקב

[9] ובניה בני חורין. וכמו כך עשתה לאה.

FIFTY–SEVEN

༄༅༄༅

Zilpah Bears Jacob
Two Sons

GENESIS 30:10–13

So, Zilpah, Leah's handmaid, bore a son to Jacob.[1]

M idrash Rabbah (71.9) points out that in every past instance where a son has been born to Jacob, the text prefaced the statement of his birth with the word *VaTaHaR*,[2] "and she conceived. . . ." Only here, regarding Zilpah, does the Torah omit mention of her pregnancy, and chronicle solely the birth.[3] The reason, according to *Yefei To'ar*, is to subtly inform us that Zilpah's pregnancy went undetected until late in her term because she was young, and her menses were not yet regular.[4] This is relevant, says Rashi, because it was the custom at that time to proffer the younger handmaid to one's younger daughter, and the older handmaid to the older daughter. Yet Zilpah, the youngest, was the handmaid to Leah, the eldest! Rashi states that it was Lavan, in his trickery years back, who switched not only Leah for Rachel, but also Bilhah for Zilpah. That is the reason

---

[1] ותלד זלפה שפחת לאה ליעקב בן.

[2] ותהר. . .

[3] בכולם כתיב "ותהר," וכאן "ותלד." אלא בחורה היתה, ולא היתה ניכרת בעיבורה.

[4] בחורה היתה . . . אולי בשביל בחורתה אין לה וסת עתה.

252

that there is no mention in the text of Zilpah's pregnancy; it was unnoticed the first few months.[5]

And Leah said, "my good fortune has arrived!" and she named him Gad.[6] Leah names Zilpah's son Gad, from the Hebrew term *BaGaD.*[7] This word has been interpreted in two diametrically opposed ways. The Torah's ancient tradition takes the single *written* word *BaGaD,*[8] and splits it into two, so that it is *pronounced* as *BaH GaD.*[9] In this rendition, according to Ibn Ezra, the term means "good fortune has come." On the other hand, the written version of the word, as it appears in the Torah text, is the single word *BaGaD,*[10] which Chizkuni interprets as "betrayal." He explains that Leah's unspoken wish when she offered Zilpah to Jacob was that he would *refuse* to sleep with her! She thought, "Why would Jacob need to take her to his bed? After all, haven't I already borne him four sons? The only reason he *had* to bed *Bilhah*, Rachel's handmaid, was that Rachel was barren!"[11]

Sforno delves more deeply into the source of Leah's anguish here. She names the baby Gad from the Hebrew word *BaGaD,*[12] meaning "betrayed," because she felt that in a way the baby's birth itself was a "betrayal," a symbol of her present lack of fertility.[13] However unjust this may seem, from her naming of Zilpah's son it is clear that Leah was ambivalent about giving Jacob her handmaid as a wife. On the one hand, she selfishly desired to mother the majority of the twelve tribes; on the other, she sought generously to allow Zilpah to be a wife like her other sisters. Yet still, Leah's quite human feeling of disappointment that Zilpah conceived when she—Leah—could not, was reflected in her naming of the boy.

---

[5] כדי לרמות ליעקב, נתנה לבן ללאה . . . שכך מנהג לתן שפחה הגדולה לגדולה, וקטנה לקטנה.

[6] ותאמר לאה בגד; ותקרא את שמו גד.

[7] בגד

[8] בגד

[9] בא גד

[10] בגד

[11] לשון בגידה. אף על פי שנתתי לו שפחתי, לא היה לו לשכב עמה, מאחר שילדתי לו ארבעה בנים. ואע"פ שבא אל שפחת רחל, לרחל לא היו לה בנים.

[12] בגד

[13] ונכתב בגד מלה אחת. כי היה ההריון לה בוגד כמו אכזב.

*So Zilpah, Leah's handmaid, bore a second son to Jacob. And Leah
said, "I am fortunate! For the women will consider me praiseworthy."
So she called him Asher.*[14]

The name Asher is translated from the Hebrew word *aSHeR*,[15]
meaning "fortunate" or "praiseworthy." Radak tells us that the name
that Leah gave Zilpah's second son demonstrates that she is basking
in the reflected happiness of the townspeople. Her neighbor-women
are all calling her fortunate indeed, for she now has *six* sons to her
credit, not withstanding that two of the six are from her handmaid.[16]
Sa'adia Gaon teaches that Zilpah's second son brings Leah much
praise.[17] *Sha'arei Aharon* adds that the praise is for Leah's strength of
character in giving her handmaid to Jacob when her chief desire was
not to share him, but to keep him to herself. The fact that she
suppressed this natural inclination and encouraged Zilpah to become
a wife and mother is greatly to her credit, and for this they praise
her.[18]

[14] ותאמר לאה, באשרי כי אשרוני בנות; ותקרא את שמו אשר.

[15] אשר

[16] כי הנשים אומרות עלי, אשרי שהיו לי כמה בנים; בן ממני, בן משפחתי.

[17] משבחי שתשבחנה אותי הנשים.

[18] אע"פ שיש לו בנים ממני, כבשתי את יצרי ונכנסתי את שפחתי, צרתי, בביתי.

FIFTY-EIGHT

৪০০ଔ৪০০ଔ

Rachel Barters for *Dudaim*;
Leah Barters for Jacob

GENESIS 30:14–15

These next verses carry momentous importance for our understanding of the passions motivating Rachel and Leah. For the first and only time in the Torah we are witness to a direct conversation between these two sisters, and the commentaries will reveal that this conversation is fraught with the discontented essence of their lives. The reader will see that their words reveal each woman's intrinsic desire. For Leah, it is her longing for Jacob's love; for Rachel, it is her hunger for her own child. Each woman faces the other, Leah bartering for an extra night with Jacob, Rachel negotiating desperately for what she perceives is a fertility amulet. The sense of human drama is palpable. There is much passion at play here.

> *And during the wheat harvest Reuven went and found "dudaim" in the field, and he brought them to Leah his mother; and Rachel said to Leah, "Please give me some of your son's dudaim." So Leah said to her, "Was taking my husband such a trivial matter to you that you now also seek to take my sons's dudaim?!" And Rachel said, "In that case, sleep with him tonight in exchange for your son's dudaim."*[1]

---

[1] וילך ראובן בימי קציר חיטים וימצא דודאים בשדה, ויבא אתם אל לאה אמו; ותאמר רחל אל לאה, תני נא לי מדודאי בנך. ותאמר לה, המעט קחתך את אישי, ולקחת גם את דודאי בני?!

Radak sets the scene, portraying a seven-year-old Reuven frolicking among the fields of wheat during the days of the harvest.[2] It is during his playful sojourns that Reuven comes by chance upon a sweet-smelling herb growing wild at the side of the field. Rashi tells us that the plant was a weed, growing in the public domain.[3] Sforno describes that the young Reuven was sensitive to his mother's constant saddened expression. Leah was depressed that she had stopped having children, and she was despairing that Jacob still did not love her as much as he loved Rachel. Seeing his mother's sadness, Reuven plucks the interesting plant for her to smell. Sforno informs us that the boy was doubtless attracted by the herb's pungent fragrance, and was anxious to cheer his mother.[4] The young Reuven, once he pulled up the plant to bring to his mother, was likely intrigued by the shape of its roots. Ibn Ezra tells us that the roots of the "dudaim" looked like a human form, with a discernible head and hands.[5] Despite the various descriptions, it is unclear precisely what the herb was that Reuven plucked for his mother. The Talmud (*Sanhedrin* 99b), asks the rhetorical question, "What are *dudaim*?" and offers three definitions. *Dudaim* could be "mandrakes," or "violets," or "the mandrake flower."[6]

The composite picture of *dudaim*, then, is a wild-growing, fragrant herb with an attractive flower, whose gnarled roots appear humanoid. Sforno adds that the herb was also thought to possess properties that induce fertility.[7] *Sha'arei Aharon* agrees, explaining that the *dudaim* enhance love and passion between a husband and wife. Their fragrance heightens desire, which then heats the blood, and in turn leads to stimulation of the reproductive faculties.[8] Ramban disagrees, saying that Rachel desired Reuven's *dudaim* only for their delightful fragrance and for her general pleasure. He states that

---

ותאמר רחל, לכן ישכב עמך הלילה תחת דודאי בנך.

[2] וראובן היה אז כבן שבע שנים.

[3] דבר הפקר שאין אדם מפקיד בו.

[4] כשראה שאמו מצטערת על שעמדה מלדת, וימצא דודאים, מין עשב טוב הריח.

[5] והם על צורת בני אדם, כי יש להם דמות ראש וידים.

[6] מאי דודאים? אמר רב, יברוחי; לוי אמר, סגלי; רב יונתן אמר, סביקי.

[7] ומכין כלי הזרע אל התולדה.

[8] הדודאים מוסיפים אהבה וחשק בין איש לאשתו, שריחן מביא את התאוה, ומחממת את המוח, ומוריד את הזרע.

Rachel relied upon her fervent prayer that moved God to ultimately open her womb, not upon a suspected aphrodisiac.[9]

The Zohar (*Vayetze*, 199) offers a compromise. According to the Zohar, Rachel's womb was not opened by the aid of the *dudaim*, because it is written in the Torah that it was God who eventually opened her womb, and not an external aid. But the commentary goes on to concede that the *dudaim* do possess some medicinal properties that *facilitate* pregnancy. Yet the *dudaim* do not of themselves *cause* a pregnancy; only Divine fate can do this.[10]

Leah's angry rejoinder to Rachel's request that they share the *dudaim* gives the commentaries pause. How is it that Leah chastises Rachel for "taking away *her* husband," when Leah knows that Jacob had never intended to wed Leah in the first place, and *Rachel* was the object of his desire? Chizkuni explains Leah's words to mean that whatever was initially intended, "the fact is that I did marry Jacob *first*, and you married him next, making you my tormenter, Jacob's *second* wife!"[11] According to Radak, Leah's angry words reflect her feeling of rejection by Jacob. Because he spent more nights in Rachel's tent than he did in hers trying to cause Rachel to conceive, Leah held Rachel responsible for Jacob's abandonment of her.[12] *Ohr Hachayim* explains that Leah is angry because Jacob had permanently installed his bed next to Rachel's, and any available time he had beyond the nights he was obligated to allocate to Leah, he voluntarily spent with Rachel. For this reason, Leah was bitter toward Rachel, because her existence in effect diminished Leah's conjugal time with Jacob.[13] Radak agrees, saying that Leah felt proprietary towards Jacob because once he took another wife they were expected to share the conjugal rights in equal measure.[14] But Jacob consistently spent excessive time with Rachel.

---

[9] הנכון כי רצתה בהן להשתעשע ולהתענג, כי בתפלה נפקדה רחל, לא בדרך הרפאות.

[10] ואי תימא דאלין דודאים פתחו מעהא דרחל. לאו, דהא כתיב וישמע אליה אלקים ויפתח את רחמה, קודשא בריך הוא. ולא מלא אחרא, בגין דאינון דודאים, אע"ג דחילא דלהון לעילא, בההוא חילא דלהון, לא אתמני פקידא דבנין.

[11] שהרי אנכי נשאתי לו תחילה, ואת נשאת צרתי.

[12] כי בעבור שלא היו לה בנים לרחל, היה יעקב שוכב עם רחל **יותר** משהיה שוכב עם לאה, כדי להפיס דעתה.

[13] כוונת לאה היא . . . כי קביעות מטתו של יעקב היה אצל רחל . . . חלק האודף אצלך היא נגרע מחלק לאה.

[14] כי אישי הוא כמו אישך.

Rashi teaches us that Rachel's response to Leah's angry rejoinder is a proposition to barter her allotted night with Jacob in exchange for the precious *dudaim*.[15] *Siftei Chachamim* expounds on Rashi, saying that Rachel and Leah each gave up to the other what was hers by right, in order to obtain something she valued more.[16] Sforno explains Rachel's bargain as well thought-out. She told Leah, "If you give me some of the *dudaim* now, you will get to sleep with Jacob this night. Therefore, even though I will have some *dudaim* in my possession, you will have no need of *them* tonight, because you will have *him* in your bed, and the remainder of the *dudaim, also*! I will not have the opportunity to try out the efficacy of the *dudaim* until one night later! And you are really ceding nothing by giving some *dudaim* to me, since I can go and pluck them for myself tomorrow, or send someone to obtain them for me, as they grow wild as weeds. So why not give me some of them *now*, and derive a benefit from your generosity; spend an extra night with Jacob?"[17]

Rashi explains that Rachel will be held accountable for spurning her night with Jacob. According to Rashi, because she disparaged this one night with her husband, she forfeited *all* her nights with him in the world to come, and it was Leah—and not she—who was buried beside Jacob for eternity in the Cave of Machpela, alongside Sarah and Abraham, Rebecca and Isaac.[18]

---

[15] **שלי** היתה שכיבת לילה זו, ואני נותנה לך תחת דודאי בנך.

[16] חליפין גמורים. שזה נותן שלו, וזה נותן שלו.

[17] שתקדם פעולת הדודאים וסגולתם בך לפעולתם בי, ולא יגיעך נזק במה שתתני לי מהם עתה, כי לא יחדל מי שימצא מהם בעדי אחרי כן, כל שכן בהיותם הפקר.

[18] ולפי שזלזלה במשכב הצדיק, לא זכתה להקבר עמו.

FIFTY-NINE

୨୦୦୫୨୦୦୫

Leah
Achieves Her Desire

GENESIS 30:16

*And Jacob returned from the field in the evening, and Leah **went out** to greet him, and she said, "Come to my [tent], because I have surely hired you with my son's 'dudaim.'" So he lay with her that night.*[1]

The commentaries are concerned with the propriety of Leah's *going out* to greet Jacob, thereby ostensibly soliciting her own husband. According to Sforno, the issue of the pursuit of intimate relations for the sake of childbearing—as regards the patriarchs—is reminiscent of the relationship of Adam and Eve before they were banished from the Garden. Their mating was not for their own pleasure, but was in order to perpetuate mankind's presence on God's earth. So, too, says Sforno, the intention of the matriarchs here was to fulfill their mission in God's eyes. Their preoccupation with the addition of concubines, and with the bartering of the *dudaim*, for example, all combined with their prayers to achieve their primary purpose. The righteous are justified to use all natural means to reach their desired goal of producing offspring, as long as they combine

---

[1] ויבא יעקב מן השדה בערב, **ותצא לאה** לקראתו ותאמר, אלי תבא כי שכר שכרתיך בדודאי
בני. וישכב עמה בלילה הוא.

259

these other means with religious faith. As our sages teach us, "God desires the prayers of the righteous."[2]

Thus, Sforno holds that Leah's "going out" to greet her husband was proper, as her goal was to have another child. Radak agrees, declaring that the Torah's *dudaim* episode proves to us that the matriarchs' overriding purpose was to bear Jacob's children.[3]

The *Netziv* ascribes to Leah a second worthy motive. For while her rushing out to greet Jacob may not have been the soul of modesty, it was preferable that she did so, thus sparing Rachel the embarrassment of having to turn Jacob away when he presented himself at *her* tent at the end of the day.[4] Alternatively, *Ohr Hachayim* suggests that Leah was fearful that Rachel would go back on her word, and for *this* reason Leah watched for Jacob's arrival and went out to greet him. Leah worried that Rachel was not specific when she told her sister "he will sleep with you the night." Perhaps Rachel did *not* intend that Leah could have Jacob *this* night, just that she could accumulate credit toward *a* night with Jacob sometime in the future. To preclude her own profound disappointment in the event that Rachel would seek to postpone the bartered night, Leah eagerly went out to greet Jacob, and for this she was rewarded.[5]

The Talmud (*Nedarim* 20b) mentions that a man whose wife solicits him will be blessed with sons who are wise. This stunning statement appears in the Talmud following a listing of im proper attitudes and actions concerning intimate relations with one's wife, where a brazen wife is specifically listed as un desirable. How does the Talmud reconcile the *merit* of a "forward" wife on the one hand, and her *censure* on the other? It answers that the meritorious wife makes her desires known to her husband in a subtle and fitting fashion, not

---

2 הודיענו אמנם שהיה ענין התולדה אצל האבות כמו שהיה ענינו אצל אדם ואשתו קודם חטאם,
כי לא היתה כוונתם בו להנאת עצמם כלל, אבל היה להקים זרע בלבד לכבוד קונם ולעבודתו,
והודיע שבהיות כונת האמהות רצויה לפני הקל יתברך. בהשתדלותן בהכנסת הצרות, ועניין
הדודאים, נשמע תפלתן על זה. כי ראוי לצדיק שיעשה ההשתדלות הטבעי האפשר אצלו
להשיג חפצו. ועם זה יתפלל שישיג התכלית, כאמרם ז"ל, שהקב"ה מתאווה לתפלתם של
צדיקים.

3 כל הספור הזה להודיע כי כל האמהות כוונתם להוליד בנים מיעקב.

4 אע"ג שלא היה מדת צניעות, מ"מ נוח היה לה להקל בכבודה משתבייש את רחל בבוא יעקב
לאהלה, ואח"כ יצא.

5 טעם עשותה ככה ולא מן המוסר, לפי . . . חששה לאה שתחזור בה רחל, ולזה קדמה ויצתה
. . . שלא דקדקה רחל לומר "הלילה הזאת." חששה שתתדחה אותה ללילה אחרת, והרי זו
זריזה ונשכרת.

in a crude or vulgar manner.[6] The *Ran*, a commentary on the Talmud, supports the aphorism that wise sons will result from the union of a husband whose wife entices him, by citing Leah's behavior in the incident before us (she went out to meet Jacob, and invited him to come into her tent) as positive proof of her meritorious behavior.[7] The Talmud affirms this, saying that the son that resulted from this union of Leah and Jacob had wise progeny.[8]

Rashi's commentary on the Talmud gives the reader a clearer understanding of Leah's actions. Rashi teaches us that Leah's modest words, "come into my tent," were the discreet enticement that the Talmud sought to praise, for her words allowed Jacob to *intuit* that she desired him and that he was hers for the night.[9] Delicacy such as Leah exhibited was a necessity in a polygamous relationship, and Jacob proved himself to be worthy of Leah's subtlety; he understood from her words and manner that it was *her* tent that he would enter that night.

So he lay with her at night; he . . .[10] This translation of the second half of verse 16 follows the *syntax* of the verse, rather than its plain meaning. The Hebrew text leaves the word *Hu*,[11] meaning the pronoun "he," dangling at the end of the sentence. This peculiarity leads the commentaries to ponder who "he" is. It would seem, according to the *p'shat*, that the last word should read *HaHu*,[12] "*that night.*" The extra Hebrew letter *hay*[13] is absent from this Torah text, producing the syntactical oddity that we translated above.

According to Rashi, the "he" referred to at the end of this verse is God. Rashi teaches us that this dangling "he" is a hint to the reader that He—God Himself—oversaw events so that Jacob and Leah conceived a child that very night.[14] *Siftei Chachamim* sets the scene. If, as Rashi says, *God* is the "he" at the end of verse 16, we are then led to ask, in what manner did God aid Jacob and Leah that

---

6 כל אדם שאשתו תובעתו, הוין לו בנים . . . נבונים . . . ההיא דמרציא ארצויי.

7 לאה, שיצאה לפני יעקב.

8 מבני יששכר יודעי בינה.

9 מראה לו **מתוך** דבריה, כגון לאה.

10 וישכב עמה בלילה **הוא**

11 הוא

12 **ההוא**

13 **"ה"**

14 בלילה הוא. הקב"ה סיעו שיצא משם יששכר.

evening? The commentator describes Jacob's arrival at his family camp that dusk. He was sitting astride his donkey, wending his way toward Rachel's tent, as was his wont. God miraculously gave sentience to the donkey, allowing it to appreciate the portentousness of the moment, and it brayed loudly, thereby alerting Leah, who then hurried to greet Jacob and invite him into her tent.[15] The commentary bases this vignette on a fragment of Jacob's blessings to his twelve sons, which he utters on his deathbed many years in the future. There (Genesis 49:14), Jacob singles out Issachar—the son who results from the night he spent with Leah—as "Issachar, [whom] the donkey caused."[16] Thus, we learn that a person's prayers can be answered by God in unpredictable ways. As subtle an occurrence as the simple bray of a donkey can alter a person's world.

In contrast, and more in line with the *p'shat*, Sforno and *Ohr Hachayim* both state that the "he" that ends verse 16 refers to *Jacob*. Sforno extracts from this word that he—Jacob—of his own mind, lay with his wife Leah that night. When he saw how eagerly she ran to greet him, and how well-intentioned her motives, he went to *her* tent knowing that his choice was the correct one.[17] *Ohr Hachayim* goes a bit further, saying that Jacob not only *knew* that Leah's tent was his proper destination, he also *desired* her that night, and deliberately accompanied her there.[18]

---

15 הוא, היינו הקב"ה, דאם לא כן **ההוא**, מיבאי לי, והיאך סייעו? יש לומר שיעקב בא מן השדה, ורוכב על החמור, והיה רוצה לרכוב באהל רחל. והקב"ה נתן דעה בחמור, והיה נוער כדי שתשמע לאה, ותצא לקראתו.

16 יששכר חמר גרם.

17 הוא. מדעתו, בראותו זריזות לאה וטוב כונתה בזה.

18 הוא. ברצונו ודעתו. שהשכים על הדבר.

SIXTY

୫୦୯୬୫୦୯୬

Leah Bears Jacob
Two More Sons
and a Daughter

GENESIS 30:17–21

*And God listened to Leah, and she conceived and bore a fifth son to
Jacob. And Leah said, "God has given me my reward because I gave
my handmaid to my husband." And she named him Issachar. And
Leah conceived again, and bore a sixth son to Jacob. And Leah said,
"God has bestowed a good bounty upon me. This time my husband
will honor me because I bore him six sons." So she named him
Zevulun. And thereafter she bore a daughter, and she named her
Dinah.*[1]

The text states in verse 17 that "God listened to Leah . . . ," but
nowhere does it tell us that Leah had beseeched God for anything.
Sforno explains that Leah had prayed to God for continued fecundity
after her fourth son was born, when she had paused in her
childbearing. Her prayers actually *preceded* her efforts to stimulate
her fertility with her handmaiden and with the *dudaim*.[2] Rashi reveals
that what God "listened to" were Leah's obsessive internal yearnings

---

1 וישמע אלקים אל לאה, ותהר ותלד ליעקב בן חמישי. ותאמר לאה, נתן אלקים שכרי, אשר
נתתי שפחתי לאישי; ותקרא שמו יששכר. ותהר עוד לאה, ותלד בן ששי ליעקב. ותאמר לאה,
זבדני אלקים אתי זבד טוב. הפעם יזבלני אישי, כי ילדתי לו ששה בנים. ותקרא את שמו
זבולון. ואחר ילדה בת, ותקרא את שמה דינה.

2 הקדימה השתדלותה הזה עם תפלתה.

to give birth to as many of the tribes as possible.[3] *Siftei Chachamim* states that even though the text never mentions that Leah prayed for children, her dearest wish was known to God, and so God treated it *as if* she had prayed, and granted her more children.[4]

In verse 18, Leah names the child who resulted from that night Issachar, from the Hebrew word *SaCHaR*,[5] meaning "hiring-price" or "reward." Leah states that she is naming her fifth son Issachar because the child is a *reward* from God for giving—albeit reluctantly—her handmaid, Zilpah, to Jacob. The commentaries query why Leah explained the baby's name thusly, when she could easily have relied upon her own words in verse 16: "because I surely hired you with my son's *dudaim*."[6]

Torah Temima acknowledges that *both* verses 16 and 18 presented good bases for naming the boy Issachar. The commentary credits Leah with incorporating *both* these reasons into the baby's name. First, that she "hired" Jacob that night by giving away some of the *dudaim*, and second, that God was "rewarding" her for her magnanimous gesture with Zilpah. He derives this from the fact that the Hebrew name Issachar is spelled with *two shin* letters. He explains that the Torah mentions only the second reason out of courtesy to Leah. We suppress any mention of the *dudaim* incident in the baby's naming because it is more honorable to Leah to name the boy after God's reward to her than after her bartering for her husband.[7]

With the naming of her sixth son, Zevulun, Leah's motives for desiring successive children by Jacob are starkly illuminated. It is imminently clear from the text that Leah's truest desire is to be cherished by Jacob, and that bearing his children is a means to that end. In vain Leah seeks to bind Jacob to her with each additional child she bears for him. According to Rashi, the name Zevulun is derived from the Hebrew word *ZeVuL*,[8] meaning "to dwell with," or "to honor." Leah's passion, her fervent fantasy, is that *her* tent will

---

[3] שהייתה מתאווה ומחזרת להרבות שבטים.

[4] נחשב לה **כאלו** התפללה, ונתן לה הקב"ה כרצונה.

[5] שכר

[6] כי **שכר שכרתיך** בדודאי בני

[7] תלתה בקריאת שם זה שני הטעמים, שכר הדודאים ושכר השפחה. ולרמז את זה קראתהו "יששכר" בשני שיני"ן, לרמז על שני עניני שכר. אך מפני כי הטעם משכר הדודאים אינו מכובד . . . משמיטין אנו את זה מפני כבודה של אמנו לאה.

[8] זבול

henceforth become Jacob's principal dwelling place. She thinks, "he will *dwell* with *me*, for I have *honored* him by giving him more sons than all his other wives."[9] The *Netziv* agrees with Rashi, emphasizing that Leah's nearly hopeless aim is to unseat Rachel from her position as "Jacob's wife." For even up until this sixth son's birth, except when Jacob was *required* to visit his other wives' tents, he dwelled principally with Rachel. *She* was his helpmate in all facets of his life, aiding in his daily affairs, as well as affording him physical and psychological succor. Leah is eternally hopeful that *this* time Jacob will tarry in *her* tent, that being among his own sons will give him sufficient satisfaction that he will linger with her.[10]

"*Afterwards, Leah gave birth to a daughter, and she named her Dinah.*" The first question is why, regarding Leah's six other births, the Torah first states, "and she conceived . . . ,"[11] before it mentions "and she gave birth,"[12] while here there is no mention at all of Leah's pregnancy. Chizkuni, joined by Ibn Ezra and Radak, believes that Leah's daughter Dinah was actually Zevulun's twin sister, and for this reason the Torah does not need to mention an additional pregnancy, because Dinah emerged from Leah's womb immediately after Zevulun was born.[13]

The other question implicit in this verse is why the text is silent as to Leah's *reason* for naming her daughter Dinah, when it has expressly stated Leah's explanations of her six sons' names. The commentaries offer their interpretations. *Midrash Tanchuma* allows us to glimpse Leah's inherent goodness here, because even though her only leverage for Jacob's affection was her ability to bear him sons, the *midrash* states that in this instance Leah prayed to God to *withold* a seventh son from her. The *midrash* portrays Leah's dilemma as follows: Leah knew prophetically that Jacob was destined to father twelve tribes. She reckoned that she already had given birth to six of those sons, and that each handmaid had borne two, totaling ten. When Leah discovered she was pregnant for the seventh time, she

---

[9] לשון "בית זבול". . . . מעתה לא תהה עיקר דירתו אלא **עמי, שיש לי** בנים כנגד כל נשיו.

[10] שעד כה היה ביום שלא בשעת עונה, עיקר דירתו בבית רחל, ומש"ה נקראת ביחוד "אשת יעקב." ש**היא** היתה לו לעזר בהליכות עולמו, בישוב הדעת. ואמרה, אשר **מעתה** תהיה דירתו באהל **לאה**. . . . שהיה נוח לפניו לשבת באהלה.

[11] ותהר

[12] ותלד

[13] ואחר ילדה בת. אין כתיב הריון ללמדך שהיא היתה תאומים לזבולון.

feared that her barren sister Rachel would be doomed to mother fewer tribes than even the handmaids, if Leah were to bear yet a seventh son to Jacob. Leah therefore beseeched God saying, "Here I am, pregnant for the seventh time, yet my sister Rachel still pines for a child. Have mercy on Rachel, and open her womb so that she, too, can bear a son to Jacob." *Midrash Tanchuma* says that Leah's supplication to God was for mercy for her sister Rachel, so that Rachel would not be shamed by comparison to the handmaids.

Alternatively, suggests the commentary, Leah could theoretically have had a boy fetus already growing in her womb, while she prayed to God for her sister to conceive. This latter possibility supplies the origin of the given name Dinah, from the Hebrew word *DiN*,[14] meaning "judgment." God answered Leah's prayer, and *judged* that the son that *would have* been born to her would be born instead to her sister Rachel.[15]

According to the *midrash*, then, Leah's request to God was: "Have mercy on my sister Rachel. Let *me not* give birth to a boy, then, in order to save the final two tribes for *her*." The Talmud (*Brachot* 60a) tells us that Leah was pregnant with a *male* child at the time of her prayer for Rachel. And that miraculously, because of her selfless request, God heeded her prayer, and changed the sex of the embryo from male to female. This segment of the Talmud teaches us that while in *this* instance God performed such a miracle, we should not *rely* on God to alter the course of natural laws as we lead our own daily lives.[16]

The Jerusalem Talmud (*Brachot*, chapter 9) states unequivocally that Leah's seventh pregnancy was originally with a *male* child. It diverges from the Babylonian Talmud quoted above, however, because it credits *Rachel's* supplications to God—and not *Leah's*—

---

14 דין

15 כיון שראתה לאה שילדה ששה בנים, אמרה, כך התנה הקב"ה עם יעקב שהוא מעמיד שנים-
עשר שבטים, והרי ילדתי ששה בנים, ושתי השפחות ד', הרי עשר . . . אמרה לאה, "הריני
מעוברת, ואחותי רחל לא ילדה." מה עשתה לאה? התחילה מבקשת רחמים על רחל אחותה
. . . "אל תמנע אחותי רחל מלהוליד בן." אמרה לה הקב"ה, חייך! את ריחמת על אחותך,
הריני עושה מה שבתוך מעיך נקבה . . . מהו דינה? ש**דיינה** מלהוליד בן על מנת שתלד רחל
בן.

16 היתה אשתו מעוברת ואמר, "יהי רצון שתלד וכו'," הרי זו תפלת שוא . . . לאחר שדנה לאה
דין בעצמה . . . "אם זה זכר, לא תהא אחותי רחל כאחת השפחות," מיד נהפכה לבת . . .
אין מזכירין מעשה ניסים.

with altering the gender of the fetus.[17] Whether it was Leah's merit or Rachel's merit that allowed Rachel to finally bear a son, we see that God heeds the prayers of righteous women.

---

[17] עיבור של דינה זכר היה. מאחר שנתפללה **רחל** נעשת נקבה.

SIXTY-ONE

৪০০৪৪০০৪

Rachel Finally Bears a Son, and Names Him Joseph

GENESIS 30:22–24

*And God remembered Rachel. And God harkened to her [prayer], and He opened her womb. So she conceived and bore a son. And she said, "God **has gathered** away my shame." So she named him Joseph, saying, "May God grant me an **additional** son besides." [1]*

The simple and familiar words of verse 23 ("and she conceived and she gave birth to a son. . . .") belie the momentous occasion of Rachel's long-awaited pregnancy. We must remember how difficult it must have been for Rachel, year after year, to watch Jacob fathering child after child—ten thus far—to her sister, Leah, and even to the handmaidens, while she herself remained childless. She watched as her sister Leah and her half-sisters Bilhah and Zilpah each successively swelled with child, while she remained empty. At long last, her prayers granted and her own belly heavy with child, Rachel now truly joins the ranks of the matriarchs.

Rashi enumerates reasons for the Torah's statement in verse 22, "And God remembered Rachel." According to Rashi, God "remembered" Rachel's selfless act, recorded in the *midrash*, of divulging the secret passwords to her sister, Leah, so that Leah would

---

1 ‏וַיִּזְכֹּר אֱלֹקִים אֶת רָחֵל; וַיִּשְׁמַע אֵלֶיהָ אֱלֹקִים וַיִּפְתַּח אֶת רַחְמָהּ. וַתַּהַר וַתֵּלֶד בֵּן; וַתֹּאמֶר, **אָסַף**‏ ‏אֱלֹקִים אֶת חֶרְפָּתִי. וַתִּקְרָא אֶת שְׁמוֹ יוֹסֵף, לֵאמֹר, **יֹסֵף** ד' לִי בֵּן אַחֵר.‏

not be shamed or rejected at the door to the marriage tent. Rashi
further suggests that God "remembered" Rachel's anxiety over her
fear that Jacob would divorce her—because she had failed to bear
him sons—and her compounded dread that she would then be fair
game for Esav, who had long desired her.[2] *Yalkut Shimoni* tells us
that God credits Rachel with remaining silent on that fateful wedding
night. God "remembered" that Rachel watched her intended groom
mistakenly welcome her sister into the marriage tent, but she stood
by, mute, allowing her elder sister Leah to be married in her stead.[3]
While Rashi and *Yalkut Shimoni* both credit Rachel's actions enabling
her sister to marry, Rashi's interpretation is based upon the *midrashic*
passwords, whereas *Yalkut Shimoni*'s understanding is based upon
the fact that Rachel is significantly silent throughout the entire nuptial
episode.

Sforno adds that God "remembered" that Rachel was so
desperate to mother a child that she offered Jacob her handmaid, so
that she could at least be surrogate mother to his issue, and also that
she bargained with Leah for the *dudaim*. Thus, according to Sforno,
God was "remembering" the psychological trials to which Rachel
subjected herself in order to mother Jacob's child.[4]

According to Alshich, God never ceased to "remember" Rachel
and her barren condition. Rather, God forbore granting her a
pregnancy for several years until it was deemed time to answer her
prolonged prayers. God did not wish it to appear that it was the
dudaim that caused Rachel's fertility, rather than Divine intervention.[5]
Rabbi Abraham, son of the Rambam, focuses on the words "and God
listened to [Rachel]" in this verse. The text teaches us that Rachel
never abandoned belief that a merciful God would remember her.
Rachel was steadfast in her trust, and when she prayed she never
failed to petition God for a son. It was Rachel's prayer that God
"heard."[6]

---

2   זכר לה שמסרה סימניה לאחותה, ושהיתה מצרה שמא תעלה בגורלו של עשו, שמא יגרשנה
יעקב לפי שאין לה בנים, ואף עשו הרשע כך עלה בלבו, כששמע שאין לה בנים.

3   מה זכירה? נזכר ששתקה לאחותה בשעה שהיו נותנין לו את לאה. היתה יודעת ושותקת.

4   שהשתדלה להוליד בהכניסה צרתה לביתה, ובענין הדודאים.

5   ויזכר אלקים את רחל. עד כה. אלא, שהמתין עד ש"וישמע, וכו'," לבל יראה שהדודאים פתחו
רחמה.

6   וישמע אליה אלקים. מורה שלא נתיאשה מן הרחמים, אלא היתה דבוקה בבתחון, מתפללת בלי
הפסק, ומבקשת בן.

Ohr Hachayim explains why the Torah first tells us that "God remembered" Rachel, *and then* informs us that "God listened" to her. Ordinarily, says the commentator, the "listening" should precede, or even prod, the "memory." Yet here the text presents the sequence in reverse. The commentator explains that God did not require Rachel's prayers as an impetus to remembering her desire for a child. The Almighty remembers the faithful and understands even their unexpressed desires. Therefore, the words "and God remembered" Rachel precede the words "and God listened" to her. God never forgot Rachel; the Almighty waited for her to give utterance to her deepest need before blessing her with its fulfillment.[7]

Ramban (at 30.1) refers to Rachel as a "righteous woman," who, when faced with the stark reality of infertility, first entreated Jacob to pray to God to give her a child. When she realized the futility of her reliance upon her husband's intercession, she then resorted to her own personal prayers to God, whom she was confident would hear her. That is the meaning of the words "and God listened" to Rachel in this verse. Ramban improves upon the notion of some sages who infer that Jacob failed to pray on Rachel's behalf. He says that it strains his belief that Jacob would fail to pray to God to bless his beloved wife with fertility. Rather, says Ramban, *Jacob's* prayer went unheeded. God "listened" to *Rachel's* supplications.[8]

These commentaries paint a heroic picture of Rachel. She never despaired of her belief that God would eventually remember her and heed her prayers for a child. When Jacob demurred, Rachel took the initiative, and prayed directly to God on her own behalf. This characteristic, the ability to confront God in an I-Thou relationship, informs the vital nature of the matriarchs.

So she conceived and bore a son, and she said, "God has gathered away my shame." The focus of Rachel's statement in this verse is her expression of gratitude and relief that God has lifted her shame from her. Rachel's simple phrase, "my shame,"[9] in this verse,

---

[7] מגיד הכתוב כי הגם שעלה זכרונה לפניו עוד הוצרכה לתפלה . . . ד' זוכר את חסידיו **מבלי** שיזעקו עליו. לזה אמר "ויזכור וגו'," **ואחר כך** "וישמע וגו'." לומר **שקודם** שהתפללה, עלה זכרונה לפניו יתברך.

[8] והנה הצדקת, בראותה שלא תוכל להסמך על תפלת יעקב, שבה להתפלל על עצמה אל שומע צעקה, וזהו "וישמע אליה אלקים." ואולי נתקן על דעת רבותינו. כי יעקב, אי אפשר שלא התפלל על אשתו האהובה כי עקרה היא. אלא, שלא נתקבלה תפילתו.

[9] חרפתי

elicits an outpouring of explanations by the *mephorshim*. Their sensitivity to Rachel's range of emotions exhibited by that single Hebrew word is evident in their commentaries.

Rashi says that God hid Rachel's shame so it would no longer be apparent. Her long-awaited pregnancy and childbirth reversed the humiliation of so many years of barrenness. Rashi allows Rachel to express in her own words the source of her dishonor. "I was shamed because I was childless," says Rachel, according to Rashi.[10] In granting her prayers, God not only blessed her with a son, but also eased her disgrace. Alshich adds that Rachel's shame had been compounded in her own mind by several factors. First, that Jacob had laid the blame for her childlessness squarely at *her* feet, telling her in his anger that "God has witheld fruit of the womb from *you*," and not from *me*. Also, Rachel felt shamed that despite her best intentions she failed to accept the sons of her handmaid as true substitute sons for her to raise. Her sister, Leah, was subsequently able to do so with the sons of her own handmaid, but perhaps this was because she already had borne four sons, while Rachel had borne none, and did not consider herself to be the true mother to Bilhah's sons. And finally, says Alshich, Rachel suffered the sharp pain of humiliation at the hand of her sister Leah, who accused her of "taking away my husband," when in fact the reverse was true: Jacob had always intended *Rachel* to be his first and only wife, and it was Rachel's act of immense charity that allowed Leah to marry first. Alshich sensitively points out to the reader, "behold, Rachel was subjected to shame and trials from all sides." He understood her existential loneliness.[11]

Ramban explains that all the humiliations that Rachel suffered both within her own family and among the community-at-large were mercifully "gathered away" by God when He granted her prayer for fertility. Once Rachel's pregnancy became obvious, and over the long months until she gave birth, the gossip concerning the negative

---

[10] הכניסה במקום שלא תראה . . . שהייתי לחרפה שאני עקרה.

[11] כי היו בעיניה חרפה מאמר יעקב, שאמר "אשר מנע **ממך** פרי בטן." וכמשז"ל, **ממני** לא מנע. וגם היה לה חרפה כי נתנה לאה שפחתה לאשה, וילדה לאה בזכות זה, והיא נתנה שפחתה תחילה לאשה וילדה, והיא לא נבנית ממנה. וגם מאמר לאה "המעט קחתך את אישי" כאלו **היא** העיקר, ונהפוך היה. הנה כי היה לה חרפה מבחינות רבות.

implications of her barrenness ebbed away until tales of her shame were no longer told in the marketplace.[12]

Sforno offers yet another reason for Rachel's feeling of shame. The commentator elevates Rachel's concern to a spiritual level, and she says, "I am shamed that I envied God's fulfillment of my sister's prayer for her fifth and sixth children (30:17), and I resented that God chose not to accept my prayer for even a single child."[13] Rabbi Abraham, son of the Rambam, explains that Rachel's shame was that her repeated nightly encounters with her husband failed to produce fruit of her womb. She began eventually to believe that a child of her own would give greater meaning to her sexual relationship.[14] In fact, according to the *Netziv*, since no child was forthcoming from Rachel's union with Jacob, she was shamed that people should perceive that her marriage was solely for Jacob's physical pleasure.[15]

The *Netziv* culminates this discussion with an existential interpretation of Rachel's "shame." He explains that a woman of Rachel's sensitivity must have felt shamed that she failed to fulfill her female biological destiny by remaining childless. Every creature on God's earth, says the commentator, must strive to reach its most essential reason for being. And a failure to reach this goal must yield him or her great shame. In particular, concludes the *Netziv*, a woman who is sterile experiences the most profound shame.[16]

So she named him Joseph, saying, "May God grant me an additional son besides." The name *YoSePH*[17] comes from the word *YaSaPH*,[18] meaning "to increase." In this verse, Rachel names her son with the hope that God *will increase* her fertility still again. Yet in the previous verse Rachel used a nearly identical Hebrew word, *ASaF*,[19] to mean God "has gathered" away her shame. The commentaries address this duality. Was Joseph named after Rachel's

---

12 ויאמרו אסיפה בחרפה שתתקבץ ולא תתפזר בין בני אדם להיות נדברים בה עוד בחוצות.

13 שקבל תפלת אחותי, ולא היה מקבל תפלתי.

14 שראתה כי הזיווג שאין בו פרי זרע חרפה היא, שהרי מה שמכסה על חרפת המשגל [היא] הסגת תכליתה הנכבדה בפרי הזרע.

15 . . . כל התשמיש עמה אינה לתכלית, רק להנאה ממנה, והיא חרפה.

16 לפי הפשט, כל בריאה שלא הגיע לתכליתו הרי חסר יביאנו וחרפה היא, וביחוד, אשה חסרון הולדה הוא חרפה.

17 יוסף

18 יסף

19 אסף

hope for a *future* son, or was his name an expression of gratitude to God for ending her shame by granting him this *present* son?

Rashbam says that if Rachel had named her son only out of gratitude to God, his name would have more precisely reflected that word, and he would have been named *ASaf* instead of *YoSePH*. However, Rashbam continues, Rachel named him using the Hebrew letter *yud*, **YoSePH**, which indicates a future tense, as she was also requesting that God that would add still another son to her credit in the future.[20] According to Rashbam, then, the name Joseph encompasses both meanings of the word. Rabbi Abraham, son of the Rambam, agrees, saying Joseph's name reflected not only Rachel's prayer of thanksgiving, but also her supplication for an additional child. The commentator adds, however, that perhaps the future *letter yud* in **YoSePH** hints at Rachel's Divine intuition that God *will grant* her one more son.[21] In fact, the Jerusalem Talmud (*Brachot*, chapter 9), refers specifically to the name *YoSePH*, with its future letter *yud*, to substantiate that the matriarch Rachel was one of the original biblical prophetesses. In her naming him "Joseph" Rachel specifically predicted that she would give birth only one more time. She says, "May God grant me an additional son besides."[22] Abarbanel explains that Rachel's prophetic ability allowed her to know that Jacob was destined to father twelve tribes, and that with Leah having already borne six sons, and two each to Bilhah and Zilpah, she herself was only allotted one more son after Joseph.[23]

Interestingly, the word *YoSePH* in this verse is spelled in two different ways. At first, it is spelled *with* the Hebrew vowel *vav*, as *YoSePH*,[24] which is referred to in Hebrew grammar as the "full"[25] spelling. At its second mention just two words later, the word *YSePH*

---

20 ותקרא את שמו יוסף. על שאמרה "אסף אלקים את חרפתי." ואם כן תקראהו "אסף." יו"ד של יוסף למה? על שם *שנתפללה* "יוסף ד' לי בן אחר." הרי שם זה משמש שני אמירות, אסף ויוסף.

21 יוסף ד' לי בן אחר. תפלה ובקשה . . . ואפשר שיש בו ידיעה שעתיד להיות כך.

22 ואמר רבי יהודה בן פזי בשם דבית רבי ינאי, אמנו רחל מנביאות הראשונות היתה. אמרה עוד **אחר** יהיה ממני. הדא הוא בכתיב "יסף לי **בן** אחר." בנים אחרים לא אמרה.

23 היו האמהות יודעות כמה בנים היה יעקב עתיד להוליד. כי בעבור שרחל ראתה שכבר ילדה לאה ששה בנים, ובלהה וזלפה ארבעה, לא היו נשארים לרחל לשתוליד אלא שנים . . . רצונו לומר לתשלום מנין הי"ב העתידין.

24 יוסף

25 מלא

is spelled *without* the *vav*, as *YSePH*,[26] which is referred to in Hebrew grammar as the "missing"[27] version. As expected, the *mephorshim* pick up on this contrast, and Alshich presents an interpretation that focuses precisely upon Rachel's state of mind after childbirth, when she is holding her long-awaited baby son and is preparing to name him. On the one hand, explains the commentator, the first spelling of *YoSePH* is "full" because Joseph ultimately will be considered *as two* of Jacob's twelve tribes. Joseph will eventually have two sons, Ephraim and Menashe, who will be counted in the same manner as *Jacob's* sons, Reuven and Shimon. This future honor is intensely gratifying to Rachel, who foresees its occurrence, and is thankful to the Almighty. On the other hand, with her second iteration of *YSePH* in the "missing" mode, Rachel also is indicating her fear that Joseph's two future sons—her grandsons—will be counted as *her* two allotted "children" out of the twelve tribes, which would mean that she will only bear *one* of Jacob's sons. Therefore, with the second spelling of *YSePH* Rachel is subtly requesting of God that He will grant her one more son *from her own womb*, namely Benjamin. Rachel does not wish to miss out *on bearing* her allotted complement of two of Jacob's sons.[28]

---

[26] יֹסֵף

[27] חסר

[28] וַתִּקְרָא שמו יוסף. מלא בוי"ו, ואח"כ אמרה "יֹסֵף ד' לי בן אחר," חסר וי"ו, לאמר כי יוסף יהיה
לו מילוי שיחשב לשנים, אפרים ומנשה כראובן ושמעון. . . . יֹסֵף ד' לי בן אחר, שיהיה לי
מבטני, והוא בנימין . . . ולא שיהיו שנים נכללים בזה.

SIXTY–TWO

෪෬෪෬

Jacob Begs Leave
of Lavan

GENESIS 30:25–26

And so it happened, at the time that Rachel gave birth to Joseph, that Jacob said to Lavan, "Let me go, and I will return to my home and my land. Give me my wives and my children, as I have served you well for them [for my wives], and then I will leave. Because you know the hard labor that I have performed for you.[1]

The commentaries ask, why, at this precise moment in time, does Jacob decide to leave Lavan's household? Why did he wait until after the birth of his eleventh son to make this move? Why not earlier? Rashbam states simply that only now, after fourteen years of marriage, with the birth of Joseph, were the agreed-upon, additional seven years' labor for Rachel fulfilled.[2] The *Netziv* presents the possibility that Lavan had been poised, even after all this time, to wed his daughter Rachel to another. In Lavan's mind, Jacob had not yet been deemed worthy to father a son by her. Jacob was aware of his father-in-law's predilection, and feared that Lavan would prevent him from taking his wives and family and returning to his home, or worse,

---

[1] ויהי כאשר ילדה רחל את יוסף, ויאמר יעקב אל לבן, שלחני ואלכה אל מקומי ולארצי . תנה את נשי ואת ילדי אשר עבדתי אתך בהן, ואלכה, כי אתה ידעת את עבדתי אשר עבדתיך.

[2] שלחני. כי עתה כשנולד יוסף, נשלמו שבע שנים אחרות של רחל.

275

that Lavan would take Rachel from him and marry her to another.[3] According to *Kli Yakar*, this was an opportune time for Jacob to return home. Up until the moment that Rachel gave birth to his son, Jacob feared the humiliation he would feel if he returned home to his father with such an exquisite—but barren—wife. He did not want his father to presume that he had selected a beautiful wife solely for the pleasure she would give him, perhaps even withholding his seed from her. But in light of Joseph's birth, Jacob felt he was at last free to return to his father's house.[4]

Kli Yakar also credits to Rachel alone—and not to her husband—the foreknowledge that Jacob was destined to sire twelve sons. Jacob only became privy to this fact when he overheard Rachel's prophetic reason for naming her newborn son *YoSePH*: "May God grant me an additional son besides." He discerned that she deliberately asked God for only one more son, and thus he inferred from her prophetic words that he would father twelve tribes. Amazingly, the commentators (Rashi, Abarbanel, *Kli Yakar* and Radak) are clearly saying that God granted Rachel and Leah the prophecy foretelling the twelve tribes, while this foreknowledge was not revealed to Jacob. As we explained in Chapter 52, these matriarchs were in fact "prophetesses" on matters concerning themselves and their families, and God did not funnel their prophecies through their husbands.

Kli Yakar adds that once Jacob overheard his wife's prophecy concerning the twelve tribes destined to issue from him, he lost his long-standing fear of his brother Esav's death threat. Jacob now felt secure that his brother would be unable to harm him because the prophecy had yet to be fulfilled, as his twelfth son, Benjamin, was not yet born. Moreover, Rachel had just given birth to Joseph, and so could not yet be pregnant with his final son. Jacob therefore considers himself to be protected from Esav's wrath during this window of time before his wife's prophecy of the twelve sons becomes realized.[5]

---

3 לפי הפשט משום שעד כה היה ירא לבן יעקב שלא את לבן באשר לא זכה להוליד ממנה, וירצה להשיאה לאחר.

4 קודם שילדה רחל, היה מתבייש לבא אל אביו, שלא יאמר שלקח אשת יפת תאר לשם תאווה.

5 היה מסופק אם יצאו ממנו י"ב שבטים. וכשאמרה רחל בנבואה "יוסף ד' לי בן אחר," ולא בקשה בנים הרבה, ש"מ שרוח ד' דבר בה שיצאו מיעקב י"ב שבטים ולא יותר . . . היה בטוח שלא יכל עשו להרגו שעדיין לא נולד בנימין, גם לא היתה מעוברת עדיין.

Abarbanel reveals that Jacob is still preoccupied, even after so many years have passed, with securing his grandfather Abraham's covenantal blessing. The commentary explains that until Rachel gave him a son, he had not felt that he had produced the spiritual heir worthy of inheriting his father Isaac's blessing. Since Rachel was his most favored wife, once he had a son with her, Jacob harbored the hope that surely their son would be the worthy recipient of Isaac's covenantal blessing. For this reason, Jacob only now grew impatient to leave Lavan's household and return to his father with his family while Isaac still lived.[6]

---

6 . . . ובעבור שיעקב עשה עקר נשיו רחל . . . חשב בלבו שהבן אשר יצא ממנה, הוא יהיה
יורש ברכות אביו . . . ולזה שנולד יוסף אמר ללבן "שלחני" וכו'.

SIXTY-THREE

୫୦୧୫୦୧

Lavan Detains Jacob

GENESIS 30:27–43

Once Jacob discloses to Lavan his intention to leave his household, Lavan appeals to him, saying, "If you have regard for me, please understand that I have seen, through means of sorcery, that it is because of you that the Lord has blessed me with good fortune." The *mephorshim* explain that Lavan's means of sorcery or divination was via his *teraphim*, which were household idols thought to have the ability to foretell the future. Ramban suggests as much.[1] Having first consulted his *teraphim*, Lavan begs Jacob, "Do not leave me, or my wealth will dissipate. Name your price, tell me what salary I can pay you to induce you to remain with me." So Jacob reiterates for Lavan how hard he has labored these past fourteen years.

"Bear in mind," Jacob tells Lavan, "how I have successfully shepherded your flocks, and how they have thrived and grown from virtually nothing to their present abundant number, all because God blessed you by prospering everything in my path. Now, however, is it not time for me to do the same for my own household?"

And Lavan asked Jacob what would induce him to stay. Jacob replied that he would remain to tend Lavan's flocks if he would

---

[1] ויש אומרים שהיה מנחש בתרפים.

receive as his salary all the speckled, spotted or brown animals; the prized solid-color black or white animals would belong to Lavan. Lavan agreed to Jacob's proposal, knowing that after Jacob culled all the mottled animals and put them in separate distant pens under Lavan's sons' watchful eyes, the remaining choice, all-black or all-white stock would continue to procreate, yielding Lavan abundant, choice herds, and presumably yielding Jacob only those few mottled animals that would result naturally by accident of birth or by mutation.

Jacob remained in Lavan's service and tended Lavan's pure-bred flocks. However, Jacob made a primitive attempt at genetically engineering the animals in order to alter the color of the hides of the next generation. He peeled the bark from fresh-cut trees, yielding brown-and-white striped rods. He then positioned these striped rods in the gutters of the watering-troughs, directly facing where Lavan's solid-colored flocks came to drink. Jacob hoped that this device would stimulate the flocks so that they would give birth to striped, speckled and mottled young. Of course, all the mottled animals that resulted would belong to Jacob under his bargain with Lavan, so following each mating season he separated out his own newborn mottled animals, leaving the solid-colored animals for his father-in-law as per their agreement. Jacob employed this technique whenever the strongest of Lavan's herd came to drink, hoping to induce these hardy stock to produce hardy, mottled young. Miraculously, over time, Lavan's solid-colored flocks produced hardy, variegated young *belonging to Jacob*, while the solid-color, pure-bred animals remained Lavan's sole property.

We must assume that Jacob's success in breeding hardy, mottled stock was due in no small part to his fourteen years of shepherding experience. Perhaps he observed some behavioral idiosyncrasy in the original mottled sheep, and he experimentally capitalized upon this. It is beyond speculation, however, that according to the Torah Jacob's breeding technique was tremendously successful.

While the *mephorshim* minutely analyze the details of Jacob's efforts at animal husbandry, Sforno and the *Netziv* present a broad understanding of the results of Jacob's actions. Sforno takes a behavioral approach, saying that Jacob's effort was aimed at visually

stimulating the animals in order to somehow affect their pregnancies.[2]
On the other hand, the *Netziv*'s approach is eminently theological.
He focuses on God's validation of Jacob's bold action, stating that
God's subsequent Divine intervention on Jacob's behalf informed
and effected Jacob's desired outcome: Lavan's solid-colored animals
gave birth to mottled young, who in turn multiplied many-fold. The
Netziv stresses that God's unseen intervention accompanied Jacob's
initiative, causing the miraculous consequences. This, then, is the
manner in which we are blessed by the Almighty: if a person but takes
the first step in his planned course of action, God will aid him in
reaching his goal.[3]

---

2   היה מציג המקלות לעיני הצאן כדי שיסתכלו בחדוש פעולת המציג, ומצייר בדמיונם בעת
ההריון, כי הציור בכח המדמה בעת הריון יפעל על הרוב בנולד דמות דבר המצוייר.

3   וראוי לדעת שאע"ג שעשה יעקב פעולה נמרצה, מ"מ בלי השגחה פרטית לא היה מקום שיוליד
כל כך כפי התנאי. אלא, העיקר היה השגחה בצירוף איזה פעולה כדרך נס נסתר. כך הוא
לברכה, פעולי האדם מעט גורם מעשה רבה מלמעלה.

SIXTY–FOUR

ဆၤလ္ၤဆၤလ္ၤ

Jacob Confers with
Rachel and Leah

GENESIS 31:1–13

A s Jacob's mottled flocks multiplied, Jacob heard that Lavan's sons were murmuring discontentedly, "Jacob has taken all that belonged to our father. He has become wealthy by dint of our father's property." And Jacob perceived that Lavan's attitude toward him was indeed no longer as favorable as it had been in the past. At this juncture, God said to Jacob, "Return to the land of your fathers, and to your birthplace, and I will be with you."

So Jacob sent for Rachel and Leah to come to him where he was tending his sheep in the field. And he said to them:

Your father is not as favorably disposed toward me these days as he was in the past. But the God of my father has remained with me. Both of you are well aware that with all my might have I served your father all these years. Yet your father has deceived me; he has changed my salary a hundred times. Still God did not allow him to prevail against me. Regardless of how your father altered the terms of our bargain—whether he promised me the speckled animals as my salary or the striped ones—God ensured that the result would be to my advantage. Thus, God effectively saved for me my due share of your father's herd. In fact, when one night I dreamt about my sheep, an angel of the Lord spoke to me in my dream, and called out to me. The angel said it was aware of all the tricks that Lavan was attempting in order to outsmart me. And in another dream, God told me, "I am the God of Beit-El, where you consecrated an altar and promised to dedicate it to me. Now rouse yourself! Leave this land and return to the land of your birth."

With God's exhortation echoing in his ears, Jacob takes pains to explain to Rachel and Leah the reason he and their extensive family must leave Lavan's household forthwith. According to Mizrachi, by explaining all of his motivations, Jacob sought to mollify any resistance his wives might present, so that they would willingly accompany him.[1] He appreciates that without their active cooperation and understanding of his reasons for immediately departing their lifelong home, he would be hard-pressed to go.

GENESIS 31:14–16

Rachel and Leah answered [Jacob] and said to him, "are we even considered inheritors in our father's house? He thinks of us only as strangers. He actually sold us [to you], and devoured our dowry. Certainly all the wealth that God delivered to you from our father [belongs] to us and to our children. Whatever God has told you [to do], obey." [2]

The commentaries assume that it is Rachel who apparently speaks up first, after Jacob presents his explanation for his desire to leave Padan-Aram at this time. They infer this from the Bible's striking use of the *singular form* of the Hebrew verb "to answer," *VaTa'aN*,[3] in the phrase "Rachel and Leah answered." If *both* Rachel *and* Leah had responded aloud to Jacob's words, the Hebrew text would have recorded that fact by the plural form of, *they answered, VaTa'aNu*.[4] In fact, *Sha'arei Aharon* questions why it is Rachel who answers Jacob's plea, considering that Leah was in fact the elder sister and Jacob's

---

1 הוא היה מפייסן ללכת עמו.

2 ותען רחל ולאה ותאמרנה לו, העוד לנו חלק ונחלה בבית אבינו? הלא נכריות נחשבנו לו כי מכרנו. ויאכל גם אכול מ את כספנו. כי כל העשר אשר הציל אלקים מאבינו לנו הוא ולבנינו. ועתה כל אשר אמר אלקים אליך עשה.

3 ותען

4 ותענו

first wife, and propriety would have dictated that *she* be the first to speak.[5] *Midrash Rabbah* (74.4) answers that in verse four the Torah states that Jacob "sent for *Rachel* and Leah," and so it was Rachel who more properly responded to him, since Jacob had sent for her first.[6]

The *Netziv* offers another explanation. In verse 13 Jacob tells his wives that he had sworn a solemn oath to God that he would return to his father's house and worship God there, and that God reminded him of his oath in a recent dream. The *Netziv* says that Rachel was first to answer Jacob because she was the more deeply affected by his confession of his sworn promise to return home. Most probably, Jacob had confided only to Rachel, his favored wife, his oath to return to his homeland, and she was first to speak up here because she was already privy to his anxieties.[7] According to Sforno, *Rachel* urges Jacob in the strongest terms to obey God's command immediately, and the commentator gives her voice. She says to Jacob, "Do as God commands, take control of what is yours and go! You have no need to seek my father's permission."[8]

Radak offers an interpretation that reveals a depth of emotion within Rachel for her husband, Jacob, that has hitherto been absent from both the text and the commentaries. Until now, we have read of Jacob's love-at-first-sight for Rachel; of Leah's unrequited yearning for Jacob's love; of Jacob's anger and subsequent indifference to Leah; and of Rachel's overwhelming desire for a child. There has been no mention in the text or the commentaries of any feelings of love flowing from Rachel to her husband, Jacob, in this turbulent marital triangle. Radak fills this void specifically at this verse. He explains that Rachel, at long last, has come to love Jacob as much as he loves her. She was quick to respond to his plea to return to his father's house because she was deeply pained by his anxiety, and empathized with his need to return home immediately. Perhaps Radak brings Rachel's "love" to the fore at this precise moment, because now that she has fulfilled her marital craving to bear Jacob's son, Rachel is open to respond to Jacob's needs. Rachel is experiencing a surfeit of emotions: adoration for her healthy, young

5 והקשה הטור איך לא נהגה רחל כבוד בלאה אחותה הגדולה ממנה והשיבה בפניה.

6 והלא **לרחל** קרא ורחל ענתה אותו.

7 הקדימה רחל ללאה . . . שהיא נרגשה ביותר מהזכרת הנדר באשר היא עיקר אשתו.

8 עשה, נהג ולך! ועל תטול רשות.

son; liberation from the suffocating stigma of childlessness; satisfaction that she shares the status of motherhood with her sisters. And, as Radak tells us, love for the man who has brought her to this moment.[9]

Both Rachel and Leah are obviously eager to leave their father's house. They were conspicuously silent in the text as regards Lavan's deceit at the wedding canopy years before, and also throughout subsequent periods of Lavan's perfidy concerning Jacob's employment and salary. Rashi gives them a strong voice in this verse, and we can appreciate from their "words" that the commentary understands that their silence for all those years did not signify acquiescence in their father's behavior. In fact, they remain hurt at their father's ready bartering of them for Jacob's strong back, intelligent mind, and shepherding skills. "Our father has treated us shabbily by not behaving in the manner of every father, and by not even gifting us with a dowry at the time of our marriage. Our father's behavior, from the time of your desire to marry Rachel years before, and until our father's present shifting of employment terms with you, has demonstrated that he treated us as little more than strangers."[10]

---

[9]   רחל היתה ראשונה למענה כי היתה אוהבת את יעקב מאד כמו שהוא היה אוהב אותה.

[10] הלא נכריות נחשבנו לו. אפילו בשעה שדרך בני אדם לתת נדוניא לבנותיו בשעת נישואין, נהג
עמנו כנכריות, כי מכרנו בשכר הפעולה.

SIXTY–FIVE

⚜️

Jacob and His Family Flee
Lavan's House

GENESIS 31:17–18

*So Jacob arose, and he placed his sons and his wives atop the camels.
And he led away all of his herds, and [carried away] all of his wealth
which he had accumulated, the herds that he had acquired while in
Padan-Aram, in order to go to his father, Isaac, in the land of Canaan.*[1]

Rashi notes that in verse 17 Jacob *first* placed his *sons* upon the
camels at the head of his caravan, and *then* he placed his *wives* upon
the camels, behind his sons.[2] The Maharal illuminates Jacob's
behavior, saying that the front of the traveling caravan was the secure
place to be, and that Jacob placed his sons in front, presumably right
behind himself, because he cherished them greatly.[3] After all, God
had desired their birth, and had designated Jacob to be the father of
the twelve tribes and the patriarch of Abraham's promised dynasty.
Poised to return now to his father's house, Jacob appreciates that his
most precious asset is his sons, perhaps even more cherished than his

---

[1] ויקם יעקב וישא את בניו ואת נשיו על הגמלים. וינהג את כל מקנהו ואת כל רכשו אשר רכש,
מקנה קנינו אשר רכש בפדן ארם, לבוא אל יצחק אביו ארצה כנען.

[2] הקדים זכרים לנקבות.

[3] יעקב לא נשא נשיו רק בשביל להעמיד תולדות שנים עשר שבטים, ובניו היו גורמים לישא
אשה. לקח בניו קודמים, שהם הסבה לנשיו. ועוד, כי תולדות יעקב הש"ית היה חפץ בהם קודם
שנבראו.

285

wives. Rabbi Abraham, son of the Rambam, explains that Jacob treated all his sons like precious cargo, as they were foremost in his mind, irrespective of who their mothers were.[4]

A careful reader will note that the text states only that Jacob is readying the caravan to return *to his father, Isaac,* with no mention of his mother, Rebecca. *Meshech Chachma* informs us that Rebecca was still alive when Jacob departed Lavan's house, but that Jacob was mindful of his mother's parting words to him. She had ordered him, twenty years before as he was about to flee for his life, to "stay with my brother Lavan until such time as your brother's fury has dissipated, and I will send for you to bring you back from there." (Genesis 27:45) The commentator reminds us that Jacob heeded his mother's warning, and took care not to return to her tent since she had not yet called him home. Jacob could correctly assume that his brother's fury against him had not yet abated.[5]

---

4   אמרו שהקדים בניו לנשיו לפי שבניו הם תכלית כוונתו עם נשיו, והם העיקר במחשבה אע"פ שהיו המסתעף במציאות . . . וזה דרש נעים.

5   ולא הזכיר רבקה שעדיין היתה בחיים, משום שהיא אמרה "ושלחתי ולקחתיך משם," וכל זמן שלא שלחה אליו, הרי מחלה לו כבודה.

SIXTY-SIX

৪০০৪৪০০৪

Rachel Steals
the *Teraphim*

GENESIS 31:19

Lavan had gone to shear his sheep; and Rachel stole the teraphim *that belonged to her father.*[1]

Unbeknownst to her husband, Rachel took advantage of Lavan's absence from home. He was away at the sheep-shearing, some three days' distant, according to Rashi.[2] Rachel stole into her father's tent, and took her father's *teraphim*. It is implied in the *p'shat* that Jacob had strategically loaded his caravan and made ready his departure deliberately to coincide with Lavan's week-long absence from his household in order to avoid a confrontational scene.

According to the *Netziv*, Rachel acted at the precise opportune moment.[3] She saw Lavan's tent standing empty, and moments before her departure, while her husband was otherwise occupied, she dashed inside and grabbed the *teraphim*. According to the commentator, the *teraphim* were Lavan's acknowledged means of divination, and Rachel feared her father would return home, see that

---

1 ולבן הלך לגזז את צאנו, ותגנב רחל את התרפים אשר לאביה.
2 דרך שלשת ימים בינו ובין יעקב.
3 ותגנב רחל. היה שעת הכושר לכך לעשות בביתו כך.

287

his daughters and grandchildren were gone, and consult his *teraphim* to discern their whereabouts.[4]

Because her place as mother of Jacob's sons was now firmly established, Rachel was willing to make an escape from her father's house, but she was equally determined that no harm should come to her husband or to her young son. She knew that her father's anger, upon discovering their escape, would be great indeed, and thus she sought to place as much time and distance between them as possible. The *Netziv* credits Rachel with the courage and foresight to act swiftly and decisively, preemptively taking her father's *teraphim*.

The commentaries are perplexed by the nature of these *teraphim*. What precisely were the *teraphim* that Rachel stole, and why did she take them? According to Rav Sa'adia Gaon, the *teraphim* were Lavan's house-idols.[5] Ibn Ezra tells us that the *teraphim* were copper implements in the nature of a sundial, used to foretell the future. Alternatively, they were idols shaped in the image of a human.[6] Radak continues that their fortune-telling utility was limited, however, as they were wrong as often as they were correct.[7]

Pirkei d'Rabi Eliezer, one of the earliest written commentaries on the Torah, graphically describes a macabre version of the nature of Lavan's *teraphim*. He explains that the *teraphim* were embalmed shrunken heads that were hung upon the wall. Names of demons were written on a golden thread that was laid under their tongues, and they were treated as talking gods.[8]

In light of the idolatrous nature of Lavan's *teraphim*, the *mephorshim* help us to understand why Rachel took them. The *Chatam Sofer* states that Rachel took her father's gods in order to preclude his consulting their "magical" powers to disclose not only the fact of Jacob's secret departure, but also the whereabouts of his fleeing caravan.[9]

---

4 והיא עשתה כדי שלא ינחש לבן בהודעו, ולא ידע מאומה מאופן הבריחה.

5 תרפים, פסלים.

6 יש אומרים שהוא כלי נחושת העשוי לדעת חלקי השעות . . . ושעות ידועות תדבר הצורה. והקרוב אלי, הם על צורות בני אדם, והיא עשויה לקבל כח עליונים, ולא אוכל לפרש.

7 ויראו בו העתידות, ופעמים רבות יכזב.

8 מה הן התרפים? שוחטין אדם בכור ומולקין את ראשו ומולחים אותו במלח ובשמן, וכותבין על ציץ זהב שם רוח טמאה, ומניחין אותו תחת לשונו ונותנין אותו בקיר ומדליקין נרות לפניו ומשתחוים לו, והוא מדבר עמהם.

9 דלקה התרפים כדי שלא יהיה נודע ללבן שברח ואנה ברח. שבתרפים עשו קסמים לידע עתידות.

When Rachel bartered with Leah for the *dudaim* (Genesis 30:14–15, and *see* our discussion in Chapter 58), the commentaries were rife with explanations of the plants' commonly-accepted power of inducing fertility. The reader might think, therefore, that Rachel's absconding with the *teraphim* might also have had some connection with her quest for another pregnancy. On the contrary, as regards the *teraphim*, we have been unable to find even one commentary who vests Lavan's *teraphim* with power to induce fertility. The text repeatedly refers to them as "Lavan's gods" (Genesis 31:19, 31:30 and 31:32), implying that Rachel had no use for them other than to prevent Lavan's consulting them. *Torat Hachida* explicitly says as much. The text refers to the *teraphim* here and elsewhere as belonging *to her father*. From the moment that Rachel took the *teraphim* she never had any intention of appropriating them for herself. The commentator understands Rachel's mind and heart, and deduces that although she took physical possession of her father's gods, they always remained exclusively *her father's* idols.[10] Rashi assigns to Rachel a spiritual reason for absconding with her father's idols. He explains that Rachel took her father's house-idols in order to remove the idolatrous influence from Lavan's proximity.[11] Rav Bachya suggests that it was Rachel's plan that Lavan would renounce his idols once he returned home to find they had been stolen. Surely he would think, says the commentator, "my stolen gods cannot possess any true powers if they allow themselves to be stolen away." He also suggests that it was Rachel's intention to uproot idolatry from her father's house.[12]

---

[10] את התרפים **אשר לאביה**. כלומר שבעת שלקחתם, פירשה שאינה רוצה לקנותם, ח"ו . . . והיא פרשה בפה ובלב שאינה ח"ו רוצה לזכות בהם, שהם עבודה זרה **והם לאביה**.

[11] להפריש את אביה מעבודה זרה נתכונה.

[12] שגנבה אותם כדי לעקר עבודת גלולים מבית אביה.

SIXTY–SEVEN

Lavan Pursues Jacob

GENESIS 31:20–30

Jacob stole "the heart" from Lavan the Aramean, and fled Lavan's house while Lavan was gone at the sheep-shearing. Jacob crossed the Euphrates River [Radak] on his way to the Mountain of Gilead. On the third day after Jacob's flight, Lavan was told of his [Jacob's] escape, and he took his men and pursued Jacob for seven days until he finally overtook him at the Mountain of Gilead. There Lavan also pitched his camp, and that night God appeared to Lavan in a dream, saying, "Take heed! Do not attempt to manipulate Jacob with your words by offering him incentives, or by threatening him."

So [the next morning] when Lavan encountered Jacob face-to-face, he said to Jacob, "What have you done? You have stolen away my heart by treating my daughters as if they were prisoners of war! Why did you feel the need to flee secretly and to mislead me? By not informing me of your departure you prevented me from sending you away with joy, song and music. You did not allow me to kiss my daughters and grandchildren farewell. But you have outsmarted yourself, because now I have caught up with you, so that you are now within my power. It is only because your God spoke to me last night and warned me not to influence you either positively or negatively that I am restraining myself from harming you. While I can understand your great desire to return forthwith to your father's house, why did you also steal my gods?"

Lavan's words are ripe with dramatic irony. The reader is of course aware that it is none other than Lavan's own daughter, Rachel, who has taken her father's gods. Lavan's broadside attack at Jacob is unjustified in light of this secret fact. But Lavan's diatribe enlightens us as to the complex array of emotions at play upon his discovering Jacob's clandestine escape. Primarily, we must appreciate the egotistical sting of Lavan's anger that he—a master of deception—has been doubly outwitted by his son-in-law.

First, he has "lost" Jacob, the journeyman shepherd whose presence, methods and expertise have brought unprecedented prosperity to Lavan and his neighbors. Lavan is angered because it is his accumulated wealth, after all, that is his "heart," and which he prizes above all else, and he fears will be lost with Jacob's absence.

Second, hastily summoned, Lavan returned to find an empty house. Not only is Jacob gone, but so, too, are his daughters and grandchildren. Lavan's anger at his family's absence is now seasoned with confusion. He reasons that surely his daughters would not have absconded from his home voluntarily. He therefore paints Jacob as his daughters' captor, and rants without concrete justification. Yet Lavan can see that Leah's and Rachel's eyes are not red from weeping at having been taken from their home against their will. Neither are they being restrained from even now returning home with their father should they but so desire. Lavan is forced to confront the reality that Jacob has not acted perfidiously, but had departed in secret out of justifiable necessity and for his very survival. Lavan knows he would never have parted with Jacob voluntarily.

Lavan's righteous anger becomes tinged with his characteristic cunning, and he attempts to tantalize Jacob with the sumptuous farewell banquet that he—Lavan—would have thrown had he but known of Jacob's imminent departure. The reader should hark back to the only other lavish banquet hosted by Lavan in the text, because we can be sure that Jacob is not blind to this irony: it was the fateful wedding of the stranger Jacob to Leah instead of to his beloved Rachel. There, Lavan's carefully orchestrated banquet festivities provided the backdrop to the calculated deception that informed his daughters' lives. Here, Lavan's promise of a catered banquet complete with musicians is followed by his veiled threat of physical harm to Jacob. We can imagine Jacob silently congratulating himself that after more than twenty years in Lavan's house he has learned his lesson, not to allow his father-in-law to host a banquet in his honor, for surely no good would have come of it.

Faced with Jacob's apparent resolve never to return to his house, and suddenly bereft of his source of wealth, his daughters and his grandchildren, Lavan posed the first question to Jacob: "Why did you steal away in secret?" Now, finally discerning that he may truly have lost Jacob and his daughters, Lavan seeks at least to salvage his *teraphim*. He thus poses his second query to Jacob: "Why did you steal my gods?"

SIXTY-EIGHT

࿓࿓࿓࿓

Jacob Utters
a Fateful Curse

GENESIS 31:31–32

So Jacob answered and said to Lavan: "[I left] because I was afraid. I said [to myself], perhaps you will take your daughters from me by force. With whomever you will find your gods, he will not live. Before our kinsmen, if you recognize anything of yours among my [belongings], take it back." And Jacob did not know that Rachel had stolen them.[1]

Rashi explains that Jacob has distilled Lavan's raving monologue into its two essential components, and Jacob answers him in the order the questions were asked.[2] To Lavan's first question, "Why did you steal away in secret?" Jacob answers, "because I was afraid you would wrest my wives from me by force." To his second question, "Why did you steal my gods?" Jacob answers by figuratively holding his arms wide, and inviting Lavan to search his caravan. Because Jacob himself has no interest in Lavan's idols, and he has instilled in his entire household a belief in the One God, he is confident that Lavan will not find his *teraphim* anywhere in his caravan. Jacob

---

[1] ויען יעקב ויאמר ללבן, כי יראתי כי אמרתי פן תגזל את בנותיך מעמי. עם אשר תמצא את אלהיך לא יחיה נגד אחינו הכר לך מה עמדי וקח לך. ולא ידע יעקב כי רחל גנבתם.

[2] השיבו על ראשון, ראשון. . . . .

293

therefore makes the emphatic and portentous statement consigning to death the person in whose possession Lavan finds his stolen gods.

Jacob's first response to Lavan's first question, "Why did you steal away in secret?" is understood in a straightforward manner by the commentaries. Sforno tells us that Jacob knew that Lavan considered his wealth, his daughters and his grandchildren to be solely *his* possessions, and thus he regarded Jacob as a thief, even of the wealth that Jacob had justly acquired as his salary while in Lavan's employ. Therefore, Jacob deliberately effected his escape in secret, in order to avoid being outnumbered and detained against his will by Lavan and his cohorts.[3]

In contrast, Jacob's response to Lavan's second question, "Why did you steal my gods?" is not readily understood. At the outset, Rashi states that Jacob's overconfident vow—"with whomever you find your gods he will not live"—is the curse that unwittingly seals Rachel's fate, as she in fact dies an untimely death.[4] Jacob's zealous response to Lavan reflected his aversion to the possibility of idolatry within his own household. He is adamant that if any member of his household such as a servant or a handmaid took Lavan's *teraphim* in order to engage in idol worship, that person would suffer an untimely death, the punishment for idolatry. The commentator notes that it is obvious from Jacob's response to Lavan that if one of his servants *by chance* purloined any common household item either deliberately or in error in their haste to pack and leave Lavan's home, such a possibility did not provoke such an extreme response in Jacob. He mildly told Lavan "if you find anything else of yours mixed in with my belongings, just take it back." It was only the thought of idol worship under his own roof that provoked him to make this rash vow.[5]

The commentators, troubled that Jacob's own impulsive words could have been the catalyst for Rachel's death, continue to address the implicit issue of why Jacob's conditional vow should have such a tragic effect. The commentators take for granted that surely Jacob

---

3 כי באמרך שלא נתת את בנותיך להרחיקם מעליך, תגזול אותן מעמי לעכב גם הבנים והממון, כענין אמרו אח"כ [פסוק מ"ג], הבנות בנותי, והבנים בני, והצאן צאני. וכל זה אולי היית עושה בעזרת אנשי ארצך בהיותי שם, ולא תשיג זה אחרי שיצאת מארצך.

4 ומאותה קללה מתה רחל.

5 היינו מאשר כלי הבית לא היה יעקב בטוח כ"כ. ואולי איזה עבד או שפחה לקח איזה כלי בלי ידיעתו . . . אבל על אלהיו הקפיד גם הוא דאם אחד מבני ביתו לקח, הרי בדעתו לעבוד ע"ז בבית יעקב, מש"ה לא יחיה.

would never have pronounced such a serious conditional curse had he even suspected that Rachel had taken the *teraphim*. Also, they grapple with the fact that Lavan *never* finds his idols even after he methodically searches through Jacob's caravan. And Jacob's curse specifies that *only* "with whomever *you will find* your gods, he will not live." Logically, then, Jacob's curse should not ever have taken effect.

Pirkei d'Rabi Eliezer's response is that such an impulsive vow, uttered aloud by Jacob the patriarch, had the impact of words uttered from the mouth of an angel. Jacob's impulsive words carried much weight, and as we will see, incurred dire consequences, even though the conditions of the curse were unfulfilled.[6]

Moreover, *Midrash Rabbah* (74.9) compares the effect of Jacob's curse to a monarch's edict. Even if such a royal pronouncement is mistakenly harsh, it is not easily retracted. So too here, Jacob's harsh words took effect even though he uttered them in error.[7] The Abarbanel agrees, stating that had Jacob but known that Rachel was the person who took the *teraphim*, he never would have issued such a curse, intuitively assuming that her motives must have been justifiable, and certainly not deserving of her death.[8]

Torah Shlema relates a touching allegory that illustrates the tragedy of Jacob's miscalculation. The commentary likens Jacob to a watchful shepherd who spied a wolf about to snatch a sheep from his flock. The shepherd took up a rock, launched it at the wolf, but hit his prized sheep instead. So it was with Jacob's curse. Jacob thought that Lavan's story of stolen idols was merely a fabrication intended to further detain him and his family. Therefore, had the idols still been in Lavan's possession as Jacob suspected, Jacob's curse would have befallen Lavan and not Rachel. Alas, Jacob's pronounced curse unintentionally sealed Rachel's fate.[9]

According to *Meshech Chachma*, the fact that the idols were never found in Rachel's possession did not vitiate the effect of Jacob's curse. The curse of a sage, even though it may be conditional, will still

---

[6] ויעקב לא ידע בכל אלה, ואמר, כל מי שגנב את התרפים, ימות בלא עתו. והיוצא מפי צדיק, כיוצא מפי המלאך.

[7] והוה כאן כשגגה היוצאה מלפני השליט.

[8] כי אלו ידע, לא היה מקלל, כי ידע כי לשם שמים נתכוונה.

[9] למה הוא דומה? לרועה שראה את הזאב שנכנס לחטוף כבש. נטל אבן לזרוק בזאב, והלך בכבשו. וכך יעקב קלל, והיה סבור שהוא מקלל לבן. ולא היה יודע שקללתו הולכת על כבשתו.

come to pass.[10] The Talmud and the commentaries help us to comprehend why it is that Jacob's harsh words took effect, bringing Rachel to an untimely death, even in light of two potentially mitigating facts: First, that Rachel may have had a noble reason for taking her father's idols, namely to prevent him from consulting or worshipping them; and second, that the condition Jacob attaches to his curse, namely that Lavan must first find them in the thief's possession, never comes to pass.

The commentaries derive from this difficult episode that ultimately—as Rachel did in fact take her father's *teraphim*—she was unknowingly caught up in Jacob's and Lavan's emotional maelstrom. The commentaries do not at any time suggest that Rachel deserved the punishment of death for her actions. But they do suggest that the words of a sage such as Jacob are imbued with great potency. Here, even though the precise *letter* of Jacob's curse is unmet, because the thief is never uncovered, the *spirit* of his curse condemning the perpetrator is tragically effected. The *mephorshim* are aware that their explanations of possible future fulfillment of Jacob's curse may not be completely satisfactory. Still, they remain unwilling to consign Rachel to death for the reason that the biblical text itself never connects Rachel's death in future verses to Jacob's curse here.

The modern commentator Yehuda Nachshoni gives voice to the reader's difficulty with this episode. He is careful to begin his commentary with an introduction explaining that this entire scenario of Rachel's theft of the *teraphim* and its tragic aftermath is beyond our comprehension. He therefore offers an alternative explanation of verse 32 that completely avoids interpreting Jacob's words as a conditional curse. Consider Nachshoni's reading of Jacob's words in that verse:

> So Jacob answered and said to Lavan: Even if you find your gods among one of us, what good will they do you? Your gods are lifeless corpses! With our kinsmen as witnesses, recognize instead what *I* have: a true and living God. Take *my* God to be your religion instead.[11]

---

[10] לפי המדרש, מתה רחל מאותה הקללה. **אף על גב שלא מצא**, בכל זאת קללת חכם, אפילו על תנאי, אינו חוזר, כדאמרו ז"ל במכות יא, א.

[11] בכל אופן מהווה גנבת התרפים על ידי רחל **דבר סתום וטעמה אינו מבורר** . . . "עם אשר תמצא את אלוהיך לא יחיה," אפילו תמצא את האלהים שלך בידי מישהו מאתנו, תוכח לדעת, כי מצאת רק פגר מובס, שאין בו חיים. לכן, "הכר לך מה עמדי," "התבונן והתעמק באמונתי אני

Nachshoni interprets Jacob's impassioned monologue to Lavan as a last-ditch attempt to sway his errant father-in-law from his reliance upon idols. Nachshoni concedes that this exegesis may be farfetched, but he stresses that it is compatible with the rabbis' unwillingness to use Jacob's own words to condemn Rachel.

בקל חי וקיים. "וקח לך," אמונה באלוקים בחוזרך הביתה. זה כמובן דרוש, אך משתלב ברעיון
הנאמר למעלה של חז"ל.

SIXTY-NINE

໖໒໖໒

Lavan's Futile Hunt
for the *Teraphim*

GENESIS 31:33–35

*So Lavan came into Jacob's tent and into Leah's tent, and into the tent
of the two handmaids, but he found nothing. So he went out of Leah's
tent and came into Rachel's tent. Now Rachel had taken the* teraphim,
*put them in the camel-saddle, and she sat upon them. And Lavan
touched everything in the tent, but found nothing. And she said to her
father, Let not my lord view me with vexation, that I am unable to
stand in your presence, but the way of women is upon me. So he
searched but did not find the teraphim.*[1]

Ramban teaches us that Jacob righteously assigned each wife *her
own* tent, in order to preserve the privacy of his nocturnal comings
and goings. In fact, Jacob's modest behavior here, highlights for us
the importance of privacy in intimate marital relations. It was Jacob's
own tent that served as the family's central gathering place. It was
there that Jacob's entire household—wives, children and
servants—gathered for meals and discussions.[2] *Sha'arei Aharon* adds

---

1 ויבא לבן באהל יעקב ובאהל לאה ובאהל שתי האמהת ולא מצא; ויצא מאהל לאה ויבא באהל
רחל. ורחל לקחה את התרפים ותשמם בכר הגמל, ותשב עליהם; וימשש לבן את כל האהל ולא
מצא. ותאמר אל אביה, אל יחר בעיני אדני כי לוא אוכל לקום מפניך כי דרך נשים לי; ויחפש
ולא מצא את התרפים.

2 אהלים היו לכלם כי היה זה מצניעות הצדיק, כי לכל אחת מארבעה הנשים היה אהל מיוחד

298

that Jacob's tent was the designated site for prayer en route to Canaan.[3] The reader will note that the precise order of Lavan's search of Jacob's caravan is unclear from the *p'shat*. According to the *p'shat*, Lavan began his search in Jacob's tent, went through Jacob's belongings, and proceeded to Leah's tent. From there he went on to search Bilhah and Zilpah's tent. The text then states that Lavan "left *Leah's* tent and went into Rachel's tent." According to Rav Bachya, the path of Lavan's search would have been easy to follow had the text said, "Lavan left the tent *of the two handmaids*" *and then* said "he went into Rachel's tent." Did Lavan first *return* to Leah's tent after searching the handmaids'? Why is Leah's tent mentioned *twice*?

Rav Bachya's explanation of the plain text resolves the apparent confusion of verse 33 by telling us that Leah's tent was the largest of all, because Bilhah and Zilpah's chambers were located *within* it. So when Lavan exited the tent of the two handmaids, he was still standing inside Leah's tent, and thus had to walk through Leah's tent once again, on his way to search Rachel's. Now the plain text is clear. According to Rav Bachya, verse 33 can be read as follows: Now Lavan came into Jacob's tent, and into Leah's tent *(and into the tent of the two handmaids)*, and he found nothing; so he exited Leah's tent, and entered Rachel's tent.[4]

The commentator's interpretation that Rachel's tent was apart from the other wives', harks back to the text's original thesis (stated in Genesis chapter 29, verse 18), "Now Jacob loved Rachel. . . ." It is consistent with Jacob's strong desire for Rachel that he gave her separate living quarters. Even after Jacob's anger at Rachel many years before, and even after Rachel's pregnancy and childbirth, Jacob's special love for Rachel endured.

Midrash Rabbah states (74.9) that not only did Rachel have her own, separate tent, but "Rachel's tent" became *synonymous* with "Jacob's tent."[5] Rashi adds that Rachel's tent *became* Jacob's tent because he was habitually with her.[6] Rashi would therefore explain

---

[3] בעבור שלא תדע האחרת בבואו אל רעותה, גם אסור הוא בדין תורה . . . וליעקב אהל מיוחד, ושם תאכלנה על שלחנו עם בניו ועם בני ביתו.

באהל יעקב. שהיה מיוחד לו לתפלה.

[4] יתכן לומר כי אהל לאה היה גדול מכלן עד שהיה אהל שתי האמהות **בתוכו**, ומשיצא מאהל שתי האמהות עדיין היה עומד באהל לאה, ולכך הצרך לומר ויצא מאהל לאה.

[5] באהל יעקב. שהוא אהלה של רחל.

[6] באהל יעקב. הוא אהל רחל, שהיה יעקב תדיר אצלה.

verse 33 as follows: Lavan first searched "Jacob's" tent, which the commentary states was in reality Rachel's tent, because it was in Rachel's tent that he spent most of his time. Lavan then searched Leah's tent, and finally the handmaids', but found nothing. When Lavan emerged from Leah's tent—still suspecting Rachel—he *returned* to search Rachel's tent before he searched the chambers of the handmaids. Rashi sees the first part of the verse as the outline of Lavan's search. The text then continues to tell us that Lavan returned to search through Rachel's belongings *a second time*, because he suspected her, as she often handled household curios.[7]

According to Ramban, Rashi's interpretation (that when the text refers to "Jacob's" tent it really indicates Rachel's tent), is not consistent with the *p'shat*. It is unlikely, according to Ramban, that the text would refer to Rachel's tent by two different names in one verse.[8] Therefore, the precise sequence of Lavan's search remains unresolved.

Ibn Ezra offers yet another alternative reading of the search. According to Ibn Ezra, with a concurrence by Ramban, the text in verse 33 is chronicling the locations that Lavan searched *unsuccessfully* : *He went to Jacob's tent, to Leah's tent, and to the tent of the two handmaids, but found nothing*. The commentary adds, Lavan found nothing *because there was nothing there to be found*. The text reserves discussion about the search of *Rachel's* tent until *last*, until it has first disposed of the other suspects. According to the text, the order of Lavan's search is that he entered Rachel's tent to search it after he searched Leah's. The second half of the verse would thus read: when Lavan *had emerged* from searching Leah's tent, he *had gone* into Rachel's tent next. It is telling us *last* what had occurred *earlier* in Lavan's hunt. Ibn Ezra concludes that by the time Lavan emerged from searching Leah's tent—his third searching place—Rachel already had removed the *teraphim* from her tent and hidden them in the camel-saddle.[9]

---

7 ויבא באהל רחל. כשיצא מאהל לאה חזר לו לאהל רחל קודם שיחפש באהל האמהות. וכל כך
   למה? שהיה מכיר בה שהיא משמשנית.

8 ועל דרך הפשט, איננו נכון שיקראנו בפסוק אחד בשני שמות.

9 וכך היה. בא באהל יעקב ואחר כך באהל לאה, ואחר כך באהל רחל, ואחר כך באהל שתי
   האמהות. והטעם, שבקש באהל יעקב, ובאהל לאה, ובאהל שתי האמהות, **ולא מצא, כי לא
   היו שם כלום.** ובעת צאתו מאהל לאה, ובא באהל רחל, שהיו התרפים **שם, כבר לקחתם רחל
   ושמה בכר הגמל.**

According to Rashi, Rachel hid the *teraphim* inside the cushion of her camel-saddle.[10] *Sha'arei Aharon* reasons that Lavan returned to search Rachel's tent because he saw her sitting on the camel-saddle, and this odd behavior fueled his suspicions.[11] Ibn Ezra explains that Rachel had taken the *teraphim* and hidden them amidst the caravan's numerous, arrayed camel-saddles, and there she sat, *outside* her tent, while Lavan conducted his search.[12] *Torat Chayim*, commenting on Ibn Ezra, agrees that Rachel was seated just outside her tent, and he also places her upon her *unmounted* camel-saddle.[13] According to nomadic practice, one's saddle was placed close by each camel's rider at day's end, because the saddle contained that person's individual possessions. *Sha'arei Aharon*'s explanation of the *p'shat* attempts to put to rest any discussion of where Rachel was during the latter part of Lavan's search. He, however, places Rachel *inside* her own tent, possibly seated upon her camel-saddle, not unlike a traveling couch. *Sha'arei Aharon* agrees with Ibn Ezra and *Torat Chayim*. He states emphatically that it is clearly incorrect to assume that Rachel is seated outside, atop the camel during Lavan's search. The commentator reiterates that Rachel secreted the *teraphim* inside her camel-saddle, and then sat upon it inside her tent, awaiting her fate.[14]

In light of Lavan's meticulous search of Jacob's caravan, the reader may well wonder how Rachel was able successfully to avoid detection. To arrive at our answer, perhaps it would be helpful to envision the biblical scene. Jacob has camped at the foot of Mount Gilead with his extensive entourage on his way home to Canaan, after having extricated himself from Lavan's household in Padan-Aram. An angry Lavan has caught up with him there, and Lavan is publicly hurling denunciations at his son-in-law, accusing him of taking everything of value from him. Jacob responds by throwing open his caravan to Lavan's searching hands, so sure is Jacob that Lavan's missing gods are not in his—Jacob's—possession. Each of

10 בכר הגמל. לשון כרים וכסתות.

11 ראה רחל יושבת על הכר . . . וחשדה עליה.

12 והנה רחל לקחה התרפים ושמה אותם במקום ששם כר הגמל, ותשב עליהם. ולא היתה באהל.

13 לא היתה באהל, אלא במקום ששם עמד כר הגמל.

14 ורחל לקחה את התרפים ותשימם בכר הגמל, ותשב עליהם כלומר שלקחה את התרפים ותשם אותם בכר הגמל, ותשב עליהם **באהל**. ולא כמו ששמעתי שטועים, שישבה על הגמל וזהו פשוט.

Jacob's wives has surely emerged from her tent to watch the confrontation between her husband and her father. Perhaps the women are thinking, Will we have to return to our father's house? Will Jacob stand strong against our father?

Only the reader is aware of the one person in Jacob's retinue who is preoccupied with other thoughts as well. Rachel, who unbeknownst to all has taken her father's *teraphim*, is surely thinking, Will I have the opportunity to hide them from my father's questing hands? Will they be discovered? If they are found, will I be incriminated? Will I be denounced? Will I be banished?

We can envision Jacob's household servants, huddled together and wringing their hands, perhaps thinking that if one of them has taken Lavan's gods, their master Jacob would be as furious as Lavan, and the entire caravan would be in an uproar. As Lavan's search proceeds, we can further imagine Rachel standing back from the small crowd that follows Lavan from one tent to another, their mutterings increasing as Lavan emerges empty-handed from each successive tent. Rachel can perhaps take advantage of the confusion engendered by the hunt, and secure a hiding-place for the *teraphim*. While we can never know Rachel's true motivation for taking the *teraphim*, because the text omits any rationale for the act, we must deduce that Rachel had her own, solid reasons for doing so. She employed all her clever faculties to successfully carry out her mission undetected.

The *Netziv* summarizes our understanding of these dramatic events by explaining that the import for the reader is that between one thing and another, amid the confusion and disturbance caused by the search, Rachel had ample opportunity to hide the *teraphim* in her camel-saddle, undetected, demonstrating that it was surely Divine Providence that prevented Lavan from uncovering their hiding-place. *Midrash Rabbah* (74.9) explains that in order to protect Rachel, God miraculously altered the shapes of the hidden *teraphim*, turning them into goblets.[15] This miracle on Rachel's behalf prevented the *teraphim* from being discovered. When Lavan felt in Rachel's saddle bags he felt only these innocent objects. God was guarding Rachel's honor, and did not wish her to be humiliated by Lavan's discovery of the *teraphim* in her possession. Rabbi Abraham, son of the Rambam, concurs, teaching us that Lavan's search involved not only searching

---

with his *eyes*, but with his *hands* as well.[16] Thus, God's miracle on Rachel's behalf was necessary to protect her from Lavan's questing hands.

According to the *Netziv*, God guarded Rachel from certain humiliation and the possible dire consequences of discovery.[17]

> *And she said to her father, Let not my lord view me with vexation, that I am unable to stand in your presence, but the way of women is upon me. So he searched but did not find the* teraphim.[18]

Rachel is evidently uncomfortable under Lavan's piercing regard. According to the *Netziv*, Rachel is ever-perceptive, and she sees that her father is eyeing her, seated up on her camel-cushion, while the rest of Jacob's household stands anxiously behind him as he searches each tent. She senses that Lavan is growing progressively aggravated, his wariness of her behavior very nearly boiling over into overt suspicion. To preempt his searching in her camel-saddle, Rachel addresses her father saying, "Do not stare at me so, my lord! I am sitting here because it is impossible for me to rise in your presence because the way of all women is upon me." Upon hearing her words, Lavan averted his eyes.[19]

A reading of verse 35 reveals an oddity of spelling. The Hebrew word *Lo*,[20] usually spelled *either* with the *vav*[21] (meaning "to him"), *or* with an *aleph*[22] (meaning "no" or "not"), is here spelled with *both* letters. The Maharam explains that *both* meanings of the homophones are implied in the text's spelling. The text is hinting to the reader that Rachel is telling Lavan that she can*not* get up off her camel-saddle in *his* presence, (because she is sitting on his *teraphim*). If she were required to arise in order to show respect for someone else

---

16 ומישוש, לשון חיפוש. והמחפש ימשש בידו מה שהוא מחפש.

17 ובין כה וכה, היתה יכולה רחל להשים את התרפים בכר הגמל, ומשום הכי, ספר הכתוב כל זה. השגחה פרטית שהיתה בזה, שאלו נמצא התרפים, מלבד שנתבייישה, מי יודע מה שהיה עושה.

18 ותאמר אל אביה, אל יחר בעיני אדני כי **לוא** אוכל לקום מפניך, כי דרך נשים לי; ויחפש ולא מצא את התרפים.

19 אין משמעות "יחר" כעס אלא . . . לשון כדחת ורתיחה . . . ולבן הביט הרבה על ישיבת רחל באשר היה קשה לו הדבר, וחששה שלא יחפש מושבה. על כן אמרה "אל יחר בעיני אדני" כלומר "אל יביט כמתפלא הרבה על זה, כי לא אוכל וגו'." ולא הביט יותר.

20 לוא

21 "ו"

22 "א"

who was not suspicious of her, however, she would get up off her camel-saddle.[23]

According to the *p'shat*, Rachel excused herself from the duty of rising in the presence of her father because "the way of women" was upon her. Ramban observes that of course, women do not typically become immobilized with the onset of their menses. In this instance, explains the commentator, Rachel may have meant that her limbs were heavy, and that her head ached, and that she was actually ill. These are well-known symptoms that accompany menstruation. Rachel's symptoms may even have been more severe than those faced by other women, suggests Ramban, because she suffered from irregular periods and infertility, and thus when she experienced a menses it was unusually painful. Also, continues Ramban, because a menstruating woman in those days kept herself removed from the society of men, Rachel was unable to do her duty and rise to kiss her father's hand. Her brief statement that "the way of women" was upon her strategically insured that Lavan would not dislodge her as she sat upon her camel-saddle, and the *teraphim* remained undiscovered.[24]

Rabbi Abraham, son of the Rambam, implies that even in a society where a menstruating woman would avoid contact with men, Rachel still could have gotten up in her father's presence as a show of respect notwithstanding her menses. That she remained seated would therefore have seemed suspicious to Lavan *unless* her claim "the way of women is upon me" was meant—and understood by Lavan—as "the way of women *has just at this moment* come upon me." This commentator suggests precisely that. He continues to describe in detail that had Rachel been forced to stand up in Lavan's presence, she would have been mortified to display to him her soiled garments and saddle-pillow. The commentator derives all this from the phrase "the way of women,"[25] meaning "I am menstruating." He harks back to Genesis 18:11, when Sarah, a very old woman, had ceased to

---

23 כי **לוא** אוכל לקום. מפניך. **לא** אוכל לקום מפניך מפני התרפים. אבל מפני אדם אחר אקום. כלומר, **לו**, לא אוכל לקום.

24 לא הבנתי מה התנצלות זה. וכי הנשים אשר להם האורח לא יקומו ולא יעמדו? אולי אמרה כי ראשה ואיבריה כבדים עליה והיא חולה בבא הארח, כי כן דרכן. וכל שכן, במעיטות הלידה כרחל שדמיהן מועטין והארח יכבד עליהן מאד. והנכון בעיני כי היו הנדות בימי הקדמונים מרוחקות מאד . . . כי לא יתקרבו אל אדם . . . ולכך אמרה רחל ראויה הייתי לקום מפני אדוני לנשק ידיו, אבל דרך נשים לי, ולא אוכל להתקרב עליך . . . והוא החריש ממנה.

25 דרך נשים

have her regular menses. The Hebrew term used by the Bible there is a similar phrase to the one spoken by Rachel here, and also translated as "the way of women"[26] (see Chapter 5). Here, Rachel's menses came upon her unexpectedly according to the commentator. Perhaps this onset of bleeding was her first menses since before her pregnancy.[27]

The onset of Rachel's menses was propitious indeed. Rav Bachya adds that Lavan was silenced by Rachel's revelation to him. So accustomed were men at that time to avoiding contact with women who were menstruating that they even refrained from speaking to them.[28] Thus, these two *mephorshim* echo the opinion of the *Netziv*, that evidently God has come to Rachel's rescue with this timely recurrence of her natural bodily function.

Breishit Rabbati adds that Rachel's statement to Lavan (that she was unable to rise in his presence) would not have saved her without God's miraculous intervention on her behalf—altering the *teraphim* into goblets—for Lavan entered her tent nevertheless, and felt about in her saddle-pillow as she sat there. Lavan felt only the shape of goblets, and looked no further for his *teraphim*.[29]

---

26 ארח כנשים

27 דרך נשים. כנוי לוסת הנדה. דוגמת מאמרו במעשה שרה "ארח כנשים". והיא)רחל(נתכוונה כאן, "הגיע לי **עכשיו** וסת הנדה, ואיני יכולה לעמוד כדי שלא יתגלה בזיוני בלכלוך דם הנדה, ולא נשמרתי עכשיו מלידת הנשים.

28 זה יורה כי קדם מתן תורה היו הקדמונים נוהגים טמאה בענין הנדה, ומחזיקין אותה בטמאה כמעט המת . . . ועל כן החריש לבן ולא דבר עמה כלל.

29 כי דרך נשים לי. אף על פי חן לא הועילה כלום. נכנס וחפש את הכר . . . שרחל יושבת עליו, שנאמר, ויחפש ולא מצא את התרפים.

SEVENTY

ಬಂ⊙ಲ⊙ಲ

The Aftermath
of the Search

GENESIS 31:36–32:1

N ow Jacob, who had suppressed his resentment of Lavan's ill-use and distrust of him for the twenty years he served his father-in-law, releases his pent-up emotions in the aftermath of Lavan's fruitless search. Jacob has suffered Lavan's humiliating public ransacking of his caravan, and takes long-overdue satisfaction in his exoneration. He finally confronts Lavan and catalogues aloud that he endured the scorching sun by day and freezing, sleepless nights keeping watch over Lavan's flocks these past twenty years. Jacob describes his own scrupulous honesty, and relates within earshot of the entire caravan how Lavan has taken advantage of him, repeatedly altering his wages.

Jacob continues admonishing Lavan, saying that had the God of his fathers not protected him, Lavan would even now rob him of his due and leave him empty-handed. But God has appreciated his suffering and the labor of his hands, and has warned Lavan not to hinder Jacob's successful departure.

Lavan's response is a stubborn adherence to his possessive belief that the women whom Jacob married nevertheless remain first and foremost *his daughters*; the sons they bore Jacob are *Lavan's sons*; and the flocks that Jacob cultivated as his own under agreement with Lavan nevertheless remain *Lavan's flocks*. Lavan points to Jacob's wealth and tells him that all of it belongs *to him*. Nonetheless, Lavan gestures toward his daughters and grandchildren, ranged nearby and doubtless terrified, and he relents. He concedes that he cannot separate his daughters and their children from Jacob. So he offers to pledge a covenant of peace between himself and Jacob, and Jacob accepts his offer, and builds a cairn of stones to seal the bargain.

Lavan designates the cairn as witness to Jacob's agreement *never to torment his daughters*, nor to take additional wives over them.[1]

To what "torment" is Lavan referring in verse 50? From a *p'shat* reading of the text, Lavan is warning Jacob on two counts: not to afflict his daughters "in any way," *and* not to take any additional wives. According to the Talmud (*Yoma* 77b), the "torment" that Lavan is cautioning Jacob against refers to sexual activity; the second half of the verse warns Jacob not to take any additional wives.[2] Rashi and Ibn Ezra, with exquisite sensitivity, clarify verse 50. According to Rashi's commentary on the Talmud, the "torment" that Lavan fears is that Jacob might at some future time *cease* having sexual relations with his wives.[3]

Ibn Ezra takes the issue one step further, adding that the Hebrew word for "torment" in the biblical text when used with regard to women usually refers to the woman being forced to engage in intimate relations *against her will*. Here, says the commentator, the word "torment" not only encompasses the withholding of sex, as Rashi indicated,[†] but cautions against Jacob putting his own physical pleasure above that of his wives. According to Ibn Ezra, Lavan is

---

[†]The reader will recall from our discussion of Sarai and Hagar (Chapter 3) that the *mephorshim* were also similarly compassionate of the "torment" that Hagar suffered in Genesis 16:6. There, *Midrash Rabbah* interpreted the identical Hebrew root, ותענה שרי, *VaTe'aNe*, "Sarai tormented Hagar," to mean that Sarai removed Hagar from Abram's bedroom once Hagar became pregnant. They do not flinch from terming denial of conjugal pleasures to be a "torment," *even* if this implicitly chastises Sarai.

---

[1] . . . **אם תענה את בנתי** ואם תקח נשים על בנתי.

[2] "אם תענה," מתשמיש. ו"אם תקח," מצרות.

[3] אם תענה מתשמיש. **להשבית** ענותן.

warning Jacob not to cause his daughters *any* ill, either by withholding pleasure from them, or by imposing his desires upon them. According to the commentators, it is the *woman's* desires that take priority in the intimacy of marital relations.[4]

Therefore, in verse 50, according to the commentators, Lavan wishes Jacob to be finely attuned to his wives' desires, even if Jacob must suppress his own desires in deference to theirs. It is the *mephorshim* who imbue Lavan's warning to Jacob with the sensitive nuances they wish us to appreciate between husbands and wives.

The two men then swear never to harm one another, and they offer a sacrifice, and share a covenantal meal to seal their pledge. Early the next morning Lavan arises, kisses his daughters and their children, and blesses them, thereafter returning to his home in Padan-Aram.

---

4 אם תענה את בנותי. אמר הגאון, פירושו אם **לא** תשכב עם נשיך. וזאת לשון נכרייה. לא נשמע כמוה בכל המקרא. ואם כמשמעו, מה יזיק? והטעם שלא יעשה להם רע, ויכריכם על דבר שאינם חפיצות בו.

SEVENTY-ONE

ଏଠ&ଠଏଠ&ଠଏ

A Nocturnal Encounter
and Jacob's Name
Is Changed to Israel

GENESIS 32:4–33

After Lavan's departure, Jacob continues his journey homeward to his father's house. On his way, intending to make peace with his estranged brother Esav, Jacob sends messengers to Esav offering him words of supplication and conciliation, and a peace offering of abundant valuable gifts and livestock. Jacob is informed that Esav has received his message, and is now coming toward him with four hundred men. Jacob, mortally terrified, divides his own camp into two, strategizing that even if his flocks and possessions are decimated by Esav's men, perhaps the remainder will be salvaged. Thereafter, Jacob prays fervently to the God of his fathers to save him, his children and their mothers.

Late that night, Jacob directs his wives and children across the Jabok River. He is the last person remaining on shore and, left alone, he endures a mysterious and inexplicable encounter with an unknown being. During the nightlong struggle, Jacob is wounded in his thigh. As dawn breaks, Jacob releases his adversary only after extracting a blessing from him. The stranger complies and says (Genesis 32:29):

309

No longer will your name [only] be called "Jacob;" your [new name] is now "Israel," because you strove with God and with men and you have prevailed.[1]

While the text is unclear about the precise nature of Jacob's struggle, it is undisputed that he emerges from this nocturnal episode physically wounded, but spiritually fortified.

---

1   ויאמר, לא יעקב יאמר עוד שמך, כי אם ישראל, כי שרית עם אלקים ועם אנשים ותוכל.

SEVENTY-TWO

৪০ে৪৩৪০ে৪৩

Esav and Jacob:
A Dreaded Reunion

GENESIS 33:1–17

A s the sun rises, Jacob crosses over the river and sees, in the distance, the daunting sight of Esav and his four hundred men coming toward him. He rapidly separates out his wives and children so that the handmaids and their children are first, Leah and her children thereafter, and Rachel and Joseph safely in the far back. Jacob places himself in front of them all, and prostrates himself again and again as he draws near to his brother. Esav runs to Jacob, embraces him and falls on his neck and kisses him, and they weep together and are reconciled. At Esav's inquiry, Jacob introduces him to his family members one-by-one, again keeping Rachel from Esav's regard until last. Despite Esav's expressed reluctance, Jacob presses gifts upon him as restitution for their past enmity. Jacob refuses Esav's offer to escort him home, under pretext that his young children and nursling livestock would be unable to withstand Esav's grueling pace, and the brothers part amicably.

SEVENTY-THREE

৪০৫৪০৫

Jacob's Tragedies Begin

GENESIS 33:18–34:31

E ventually, Jacob journeys to Shechem where, tragically, Dinah—his daughter with Leah—is raped. In a violent act of revenge, Dinah's brothers massacre the city, and Jacob is devastated.

GENESIS 35:8

Nearing home at long last, Jacob receives word that his mother Rebecca's beloved nursemaid, Deborah, has died. As we have described above in Chapter 36, the commentaries equate nurse Deborah's death with the death of Jacob's mother, Rebecca.

GENESIS 35:9–15

God reiterates to Jacob that his name is now Israel. God further comforts him in the wake of these recent tragic events by explicitly restating the promised blessing that a great nation consisting of kings would yet emerge from him, and that the land which God gave to Abraham and Isaac he will give to Jacob and his progeny. Jacob erects a stone monument in the place where God spoke to him, naming the place Beit-El, the same location that he had named Beit-El during his escape journey to Padan-Aram some twenty years earlier.

Now, Jacob is making the return journey, this time not as a fugitive, but as a man of means with four wives, eleven sons and one daughter. In fact, we learn from the following verses of biblical text that his beloved Rachel is far along in her second pregnancy.

SEVENTY–FOUR

೮೦ಉ೪೦ಉ

Rachel Suffers
a Perilous Labor

GENESIS 35:16–17

Having resumed their journey from Beit-El, and still some distance from Ephrat, Rachel went into labor, and suffered severe complications. During her hard labor the midwife said to [Rachel], "Fear not, for this [one] is also a son for you."[1]

The *Netziv* explains that in verse 16 Rachel has not yet given birth; she is suffering in the throes of a long and difficult labor. The commentator adds that even though the *p'shat* in this verse could be interpreted as stating "Rachel gave birth," *VaTeLeD*,[2] this is not quite so.[3] For if such were the interpretation of the verse, its events would be out of chronological order, reading first, "Rachel gave birth," followed by "she suffered a difficult labor." The logical order is of course for the labor to be followed by the childbirth. The *Netziv* infers from the Talmud (*Shabbos* 129a) that "childbirth" begins either when a woman first sits upon the birthing stool, or from her first show of blood, or from the time her women friends must carry her to the

---

1 ויסעו מבית-אל ויהי עוד כברת הארץ לבוא אפרתה; ותלד רחל ותקש בלדתה. ויהי בהקשתה בלדתה ותאמר לה המילדת, אל תיראי כי גם זה לך בן.

2 **ותלד** רחל

3 ותלד רחל. עוד לא ילדה ממש. אלא אחזוה חבלי לידה.

314

birthing bed. According to the *Netziv*, the term *VaTeLeD* [4] can be used from even the very first signs of labor, and not only at the time a woman actually gives birth. There exists an awareness among the rabbis in the Talmud that childbirth begins from the moment a woman first begins to experience labor. From that moment on, a woman is in an extremely vulnerable and precarious state, and consideration must be given to her needs, even including desecrating the Sabbath.[5]

In fact, according to *Midrash Lekach Tov*, we learn from verse 16 that although all women are *especially vulnerable* at the time they are giving birth (see our discussion at Chapter 26), Rachel's *critical* state here is due not to any transgression of her own. Rather, according to the commentary, Rachel's state of extremis is attributed directly to the rash curse of her husband, Jacob. In Genesis 31 verse 32, the reader will recall that Jacob told Lavan in a heated exchange, "with whomever you find your gods, he will not live!" It was his words that tragically condemned Rachel. She was to meet her fate not on the day of Lavan's demeaning tent-by-tent search, however, but in the future, when in the perilous throes of a difficult childbirth.[6]

The commentaries are troubled that Rachel has been fated to meet an untimely end due to the impulsive words of her husband. *Yalkut Shimoni* confirms that Rachel's death was a tragic consequence of Jacob's curse, which had the effect of a monarch's mistaken edict that could not be recalled.[7] And *Pirkei d'Rabi Eliezer* (chapter 36) explains that the effect of Jacob's curse (he condemned the person who took the *teraphim* to die before his prescribed time), was deferred until her vulnerable moment of childbirth.[8]

The Zohar not only holds Jacob responsible for his impulsive words regarding the *teraphim*, but further states that unfortunately,

---

[4] ותלד

[5] מאימתי? . . . אמר אביי, משעה שתשב על המשבר; רב הונא בריה דרב יהושוע אמר, משעה שהדם שותת ויורד; ואמרי לה משעה שחבירותיה נוסעות אותה באגפיה. . . . בין אמרה "צריכה אני" . . . ובין אמרה "אין צריכה אני" מחללין עליה את השבת.

[6] מלמד שאין האשה נבדקת אלא בשעת לידה. והיינו דתנן על שלשה דברים נשים מתות בשעת לידתן: על שאינן זהירות בחלה, בנדה, ובהדלקת הנר. ואף על פי שבכל אלו הג' **לא נתחייבה רחל אמנו,** מכל מקום לפי שנאמר)בר' לא:לב("עם אשר תמצא את אלהיך לא יחיה," נענשה רחל ולא נגבה דינה אלא בשעת לידתה.

[7] לא מתה אלא מקלליו של זקן . . . והוה כשגגה שיוצאה מלפני השליט.

[8] ויעקב לא ידע בכל אלה ואמר "כל מי שגנב את התרפים ימות בלא עתו."

Rachel's tragic fate serves as a punishment *to Jacob* for his own delayed fulfillment of his vow to God to return to his father's house (Genesis 28:20). Justice was therefore meted out to Jacob in the person of Rachel, when she herself was experiencing her most hazardous hours. At that precise time, says the Zohar, judgment was effected.[9]

The *Netziv* evidently also believes that Rachel suffers for Jacob's failure. The commentator takes pains to demonstrate that Divine justice assails Jacob because he delayed his vow to return to his parents' house, and he suffers the punishment of losing Rachel, the person he cherishes as dearly as himself.[10]

Ramban even goes so far as to suggest that Rachel died just as Jacob's caravan set foot in the land of Israel so as to prevent Jacob from transgressing the future biblical prohibition against a man's being married to two sisters simultaneously (Leviticus 18:18). According to Ramban, because Jacob wedded Leah first, Rachel was unfortunately the "forbidden" sister. The holy land of Israel could not abide Jacob's dual marriage to both sisters at one time. According to Ramban (at Leviticus 18:25), it was Rachel's own merit that prolonged her life, allowing her to enter the land of Israel, even if she did so only at the moment of her death.[11]

Midrash Rabbah (74.4) presents and then rejects out-of-hand the argument of Rav Yuden, which suggests that perhaps Rachel herself is culpable for her untimely death. Rav Yuden's reason is Rachel's failure to defer to her elder sister by speaking first (Genesis 31:14) when Jacob summoned them both to the field to discuss his plan to escape Lavan's household. Rav Yosi destroys this hypothesis with the irrefutable argument that in the *p'shat* (Genesis 31:13) Jacob summoned Rachel first, *and then* he summoned Leah. Therefore, it was entirely proper for Rachel to speak first.[12] For this reason, according to *Yefei To'ar*, Rachel justifiably was the first to respond,

---

9 ותא חזי . . . בגין דיעקב אחר נדריה דנדיר קמי קודשא ב"ה אתתקף דינא . . . ובעא דינא
בשעתא דסכנה דהות רחל בה.

10 פגע ביעקב מדת הדין. ונענש באשתו האהובה לו כגופו בשעת הסכנה.

11 שמתה רחל בדרך בתחלת בואם בארץ, כי בזכותה לא מתה בחוצה לארץ, ובזכותו לא ישב
בארץ עם שתי אחיות, והיא היתה הנשאת באיסור האחוה.

12 למה מתה רחל תחלה? . . . רב יודן אמר שדברה בפני אחותה. אמר לו רב יוסי . . . והלא
לרחל קרא, ורחל ענתה אותו.

and therefore her response could not have been the reason for her untimely death.[13]

During her hard labor the midwife said to her, "Fear not, for this [one] is also a son for you." [14] From the use of the emphatic Hebrew word *BeHaKSHoTa*,[15] describing Rachel's unbearably difficult labor, Ibn Ezra deduces that her travail was excessively heavy, to the point that Rachel herself realized that this was not merely a difficult labor, but that her very life-blood was flowing from her.[16] *Karnei Ohr*, a supercommentary on Ibn Ezra, adds an existential dimension to Rachel's labor. He explains that the Hebrew word *BeHaKSHoTa*[17] signifies more than *physical* labor pains. It refers specifically to Rachel's awareness that her life, and perhaps the life of her unborn child, were hanging by a thread. She probably also was conscious that she might not even live to raise Joseph, the son for whom she had yearned her entire life.[18]

Rashi continues that the text's use of the midwife's words to Rachel, "Fear not, this is *also* a son,"[19] indicates simply that the midwife is reassuring Rachel that she is bearing forth a second son, in addition to Joseph. Sforno adds that the midwife's solace to Rachel is that the child she is bearing is in fact a boy and not a girl.[20] Rashbam explains that the importance to Rachel of the midwife's merciful consolation was her disclosure that the infant that Rachel was laboring to deliver was in fact a boy, and thus would be Jacob's twelfth son. This assurance is vital to Rachel because she had long feared that if she were to be blessed only with *one* son, her status vis-a-vis the handmaids would be diminished (see our discussion at Chapter 61 above). According to Rashbam, the midwife is comforting the dying Rachel that God has heard her prayer to grant her yet another son[21]

---

13 וכן הכא מן הדין ענתה רחל תחלה אחרי שאליה קרא תחלה.

14 ויהי **בהקשתה** בלדתה ותאמר לה המילדת, אל תיראי, כי גם זה לך בן.

15 בהקשתה

16 בהקשתה. מהבנין הכבד הנוסף. והטעם, שהקשתה הלידה על נפשה.

17 בהקשתה

18 כי היה לה **קושי וצער גדול** מהלידה, עד שמתה ממנה.

19 אל תיראי, כי **גם** זה לך בן

20 אל תיראי שיהיה הולד נקבה . . . כי גם זה לך בן.

21 יוסף לי בן אחר

(Genesis 30:24). God has granted Rachel a second son who will live to carry on the patriarchal blessing.[22]

Radak conveys the imminent crisis at Rachel's birthing-bed by explaining that the midwife's cry to Rachel, "Fear not, for this [one] is also a son for you!" was intended as a rallying cry to her beloved mistress. "Now be strong!" the midwife was urging Rachel. "Now that you know God has answered your prayer for another son, hang onto life, and live to be mother to him also!"[23]

The *Netziv* appreciates that the time for words of consolation and rallying is past, and that the text is informing us that Rachel's extreme pain will end only with her imminent death. Simultaneously, her healthy son will be born. Rachel's penultimate emotion, the fear that her labors will not even bring forth a living son, is relieved by the midwife's final words to her, "Fear not, for this [one] is also a son for you!" Rachel is sent from this world with the echo of the midwife's words in her ears. According to the *Netziv*, the midwife's words meant, "You have given birth to a son who will be a staff for you to lean on, and a mainstay after your death." We can imagine, from the *Netziv*'s explanation, that Rachel's ultimate emotion was gratitude.[24]

---

22 אל תיראי וגו'. כאשר התפללת "יוסף לי בן אחר" (ל:כד), ולא חפץ להמתיך, אלא קיבל
תפילתך, ולדבר על לבה נתכוונה.
23 כי גם זה לך בן. ועתה התחזקי!
24 בהקשתה בלדתה. שגמר הקישוי היה בלידה ממש, ובזה הרגע יצאת נשמתה והיתה יראה שמא
מת הולד . . . כי גם זה לך בן. גם זה יהיה לך חוטרא לידך ומרא לקבוריך.

SEVENTY–FIVE

ფიცჯფიცჯ

A Dying Rachel
Names Her Newborn Son

GENESIS 35:18

As her soul departed when she was dying, she named him Ben-oni,
but his father called him Ben-yamin.[1]

Jacob's last son is born to Rachel with her final burst of strength,
and she names him with her dying breath. Radak explains that Rachel
is hovering on the brink of imminent, certain death with no hope that
she will survive the ordeal of childbirth.[2] Chizkuni characterizes
Rachel's last moment as an instant of transition, when she is still
sufficiently conscious to bestow a name on her newborn son, yet
coincident with her naming him, she expires.[3]

Rachel's birthing-bed has become her deathbed. But her life-
blood has yielded a healthy son, securing for Rachel her place as
matriarch of her rightful share of Jacob's children. She names the
infant Ben-oni,[4] which Rashi translates as "son of my *sorrow*."[5]
Initially, agrees Ibn Ezra, Rachel names her son "son of my lament."[6]

---

1 ויהי בצאת נפשה, כי מתה, ותקרא שמו בן-אוני; ואביו קרא לו בנימין.

2 ויהי בצאת נפשה, בעוד שהיתה יוצאת נפשה. כי מתה, קרובה למות ואין בה תקוה. קראה לו
קודם שתמות.

3 בצאת נפשה, כי מתה. מתה, ולא מתה.

4 בן אוני

5 בן אוני, בן **צערי.**

6 בן אוני, בן **אבלי.**

319

The *mephorshim*, however, are sensitive that there exists a duality in the interpretation of this son's name. For the text tells us, "*she* named him Ben-*oni*, but his *father* called him Ben-*yamin*." Ultimately, the name he is known by is Ben-yamin, translated by Ramban as "son of my right hand," or "son of my strength." Since the word *oNi* [7] has two interpretations, meaning, ironically, *both* "my sorrow" *and* "my strength," the commentator explains that Jacob chose to interpret his dying wife's name, Ben-*oni*, in its positive sense, namely as Ben-*yamin*, denoting goodness and valor instead of sorrow and lament.[8] Avivah Gottlieb Zornberg[†] agrees with Ramban: "On the face of it, the child is named twice, to record the anguish of his dying mother, and the virile triumph of his father. . . . The word *oni* in Hebrew means both pain and strength."

These commentators concentrate on the double meaning of the Hebrew word *oni*,[9] Rachel's name for her son. The Rashbam, however, focuses on Jacob's name for the child, Ben-yamin. He teaches us that the Hebrew word *YaMiN*,[10] is really intended as *YaMiM*,[11] meaning "days." Benjamin, like Joseph, is a son of Jacob's old age.[12] Rabbi Abraham, son of the Rambam, teaches us that Jacob's name for his son reflected his own awareness of his mortality, and that his future years no longer spread out before him in uncounted abundance. Alternatively, that in the absence of a nurturing mother to guide the growth of this last son, the boy would be raised with the passage of time as his nursemaid.[13]

[†]Zornberg, A. G. (1995). *Genesis: The Beginning of Desire* (Philadelphia: The Jewish Publication Society), p. 215.

---

[7] אוני

[8] בן אוני, בן צערי . . . . והנכון בעיני כי אמו קראתו בן אוני, ורצתה לאמר בן אבלי. ואביו עשה מן "אוני" "כחי" . . . . ולכן קרא אותו בנימין, בן הכח או בן החוזק כי הימין בו הגבורה וההצלחה. . . . רצה להיות קורא אותו בשם שקראתו אמו כי כן כל בניו . . . . והנה תרגם אותו לטובה ולגבורה.

[9] אוני

[10] ימין

[11] ימים

[12] בנימין, בן זקונים, בן ימים.

[13] בנימין, דוגמת "בן ימים," ואמר אבי אבא, ז"ל, כי יעקב, ע"ה, כיון בזה כי קרב זמנו, ע"ה, ולא נשאר לו ממנו אלא ימים מועטים. ומה שאני רואה בזה כי כיון שהימים יגדלו אותו אע"פ שחסרה לו האם המגדלת אותו.

SEVENTY–SIX

⸮⸜⸝⸝

Rachel's Death

GENESIS 35:19–20

So Rachel died, and she was buried on the way to Ephrat, which is Beit Lechem. Then Jacob set up a monument on her grave, which is the monument on Rachel's grave to this day.[1]

This verse states, once again, that Rachel died. The *Netziv* explains that when a parturient woman is in dire straits during delivery, it is possible for her to appear to be dead, when in reality she may be slipping in and out of consciousness, due to the confluence of her pain and weakness. Her attendants may endeavor to resuscitate her, as was the case with Rachel. The commentator tells us that Rachel's midwives strove mightily to revive her after her soul departed, but to no avail. Therefore the text restates, "So Rachel died."[2]

The reader may be wondering at the seeming haste of Rachel's burial on the road to Beit Lechem so soon after her death. Why did Jacob bury his beloved wife so quickly? Surely he could have transported her the short distance from Beit Lechem to Hebron, to be

---

[1] ותמת רחל; ותקבר בדרך אפרתה היא בית לחם. ויצב יעקב מצבה על קברתה; הוא מצבת קברת רחל עד היום.

[2] ותמת רחל. באשר יולדת המתקשה בלדתה, נראית כ"פ מתה. ומ"מ אין זה אלא התעלפות שבא מחמת כאב וחלישות, ומשתדלים להשיב רוחה. כן עשו כאן ועסקו עמה הרבה, אולי תשוב לחיות, אבל **ותמת רחל**.

buried in the ancestral burial place, the Cave of Machpela. The commentaries, too, are struck by the fact that Jacob does not bury Rachel in the cave where he will eventually be laid to rest. Chizkuni presents the most practical reason for Jacob's behavior. He explains that because Rachel hemorrhaged to death following a difficult childbirth, Jacob feared that transporting her body even a short distance under the hot desert sun would be exceedingly unseemly and unsanitary. Jacob made the expedient decision to bury her where she died.[3] *Meshech Chachma* reasons that the text mentions Rachel's death and burial in one breath, so-to-speak, in order to emphasize the correctness of immediately burying a woman who dies in childbirth. Speedy interment accords her the necessary reverence.[4] The *Meshech Chachma* bases his commentary on the Talmud (*Moed Katan* 27b), which states that the bier of a woman who has died in childbirth must never be carried on the roadway; she must be buried forthwith, out of a sense of respect for her dignity and sacrifice.[5]

Alshich posits that even though Jacob was constrained by strict custom to bury Rachel where she died, he must have resisted leaving her on the road. The commentary derives this from the text's use of the word *VaTiKaVeR*,[6] meaning Rachel "was buried." Surely the text could have better used the word *VaYiKBeRa*,[7] meaning "and he buried her." The choice of the indirect expression "she *was buried*" teaches us that *against Jacob's will* Rachel was buried where she died. God therefore took pity on Jacob's desolation, and consoled him with the foreknowledge that Rachel's roadside grave would serve to hearten future generations of exiles of Israel who would pass it by on their path to dispersion in hostile lands, and would thereby be inspired to return.[8]

And Jacob set up a monument. . . .[9] Jacob did not continue on his journey until he had put a substantial monument upon Rachel's

---

[3] ותקבר בדרך אפרתה. בשביל שבקישוי לידה מתה, וירא היה יעקב פן תתלכלך בדמיה כשאר נשים יולדות. לפיכך לא הוליכה עד המערה.

[4] ותמת רחל ותקבר . . . סמך מיתה לקבורה, שאין משהין מטה של חיה מפני הכבוד.

[5] אין מניחין את המטה ברחוב . . . ולא של נשים לעולם מפני הכבוד.

[6] ותקבר

[7] ויקברה

[8] הנה מאומרו "ותקבר," ולא אמר "ויקברה," מורה מאמרם ז"ל שעל פי הדבור קבר אותה שם ולא בבחירתו, למען תבקש רחמים על ישראל בעברם בגלות, שישובו מארץ אויב.

[9] ויצב יעקב מצבה על קברתה.

roadside grave. The monument was not solely a means of marking a memorial to his adored wife before he moved on. According to Sforno, the monument also served the utilitarian purpose of keeping Rachel's grave secure against scavenging animals and plundering grave robbers.[10]

Abarbanel adds that the very existence of Jacob's monument over Rachel's grave proclaimed to one and all that a great woman was buried there. The commentator implicitly understands that Jacob could not convey Rachel's body the distance to the Cave of Machpela in Hebron, but still presents the question why, if Rachel died on the road but a mile from Beit Lechem, did Jacob not simply carry Rachel's body the short distance to *that* town, so as not to bury her on the desolate roadway? He responds that Jacob did not transport Rachel's body there because he foresaw that the town of Beit Lechem would, in future years, fall within the territorial province of the tribe of Judah, while the roadside sliver of land where Rachel died was destined to fall within the territory of the tribe of Benjamin. Therefore, Jacob buried Rachel on the very spot where she died giving birth to Benjamin.[11]

. . . *Which is the monument on Rachel's grave* **to this day**.[12] The Zohar (175b) expounds on the text's use of the words *aD HaYoM*,[13] meaning "to this day." To which "day" is the text referring? The commentary responds that Jacob's monument prevented Rachel's burial place from falling into obscurity. To the contrary, says the Zohar, her burial-place will be remembered until the "end of days."[14]

In fact, even after hundreds of years after her death, the matriarch Rachel is mentioned in the book of Jeremiah (31:14) in the course of his optimistic vision of the ingathering of people at the "end of days." There, the prophet reveals God's promise that Rachel's

---

[10] מצבה על קברתה. מפני שהקבר על אם הדרך, ויש לחוש לחטוטי קברי.

[11] כלכבודה הציב מצבה גדולה על קבורתה . . . כדי שיודע לכל שנקברה שמה אשה גדולה.
והנה קבר אותה יעקב בדרך ולא בבית לחם, שהיה קרוב לשם פחות ממיל . . . לפי שצפה
יעקב שעתיד בית לחם אפרת להיות בחלק יהודה, ולכן לא רצה לקברה שמה, רק בדרך בגבול
שהוא בבנימין . . . וכן אמרו בספרי "רחל בחלקו של בנימין מתה."

[12] הוא מצבת קברת רחל **עד היום**.

[13] עד היום

[14] אמר רבי יוסי, מאי טעמא בגין דלא אתכסיא אתרה עד יומא? דזמין קידשא ב"ה לאחייא
מתייה.

exiled children will ultimately return to their homeland, and that Rachel herself will eventually be consoled.[15]

Rachel's death marks the end of the most positive and productive years of Jacob's life. When he fled his home so many years before at his mother's urging, he had been a "dweller of tents," who was forced by circumstances to survive alone in the wilderness. Thus, a physically honed and strengthened Jacob presented himself at the desert oasis that day, able to single-handedly remove the well-stone and confidently establish himself as Rachel's suitor. Now, twenty-one years later, having witnessed his beloved Rachel's death in childbirth, we will see that Jacob is once again a changed man, his present existence and that of his wives and children ever shadowed by Rachel's death.

---

[15] כה אמר ד', קול ברמה נשמע. נהי בכי תמרורים. רחל מבכה על בניה, מאנה להנחם על בניה
כי איננו. כה אמר ד', מנעי קולך מבכי ועיניך מדמעה . . . ויש תקוה לאחריתך, נאום ד',
ושבו בנים לגבולם.

SEVENTY–SEVEN

୪୦୯୫୫୦୯୫

The Bilhah Affair

GENESIS 35:21–22

A fter Rachel's burial, Jacob (Israel) continued on his homeward journey and pitched his tent in Migdal-Eder.

> And it happened that while Israel was encamped there, Reuven went and lay with Bilhah, his father's concubine; Israel heard of this; now Jacob's sons numbered twelve.[1]

According to Rashi, the incident that befalls the patriarch Jacob in verse 22 is the latest in a series of tragic events that have taken place as a direct consequence of Jacob's delay in returning to his father's house in Hebron in the land of Israel. The first was the rape of his daughter Dinah (Genesis 34:2), the second was the death in childbirth of his wife Rachel (Genesis 35:19), and the third tragic event occurs here in verse 22, when Jacob's eldest son, Reuven, subverts his father's authority with Bilhah.[2]

The *p'shat* of verse 22 appears to leave little room for discussion about precisely what Reuven's act was. Radak points out that the text

---

1   ויסע ישראל; ויט אהלה מהלאה למגדל-עדר. ויהי בשכן ישראל בארץ ההוא וילך ראובן וישכב
את בלהה פילגש אביו; וישמע ישראל; ויהיו בני יעקב שנים-עשר.

2   בארץ ההוא. עד שלא בא לחברון אצל יצחק ארעוהו כל אלה.

325

uses the term *VaYeLeCH*,[3] meaning "and Reuven went" purposefully to Bilhah's tent and slept with her there. Radak suggests that even if Reuven mistakenly thought that Bilhah was not forbidden to him because of her status as a handmaid and then as a concubine, this was incorrect. Bilhah is referred to in the text as a full wife to Jacob (Genesis 30:4), and thus was absolutely taboo to Reuven. In fact, continues Radak, because of his illicit act with Bilhah, Reuven forfeited his firstborn's right to inherit a double portion at his father's death.[4]

The *mephorshim* differ about what actually took place in Bilhah's tent as they camped at Migdal Eder. According to the Zohar (176a), Reuven resented what he perceived as the injustice that Bilhah, Rachel's handmaid, should "inherit" his own mother's "rightful place" as the next in line for Jacob's conjugal attentions. Therefore, says the Zohar, Reuven moved Jacob's bed from Bilhah's tent to Leah's, and for this act Reuven is later punished.[5]

Rashi explains that apparently, after the death of his beloved Rachel, Jacob moved his own bed into Bilhah's tent, as Bilhah was Rachel's lifelong handmaid whom the barren Rachel had given over to her husband as a wife. According to Rashi, Reuven did not sleep with Bilhah. Reuven's improper act was that he went into Bilhah's private tent and lifted his father's bed out of there, thus audaciously defiling his father's sleeping place.[6]

The Talmud (*Shabbat* 55b) explains that Reuven, Leah's firstborn, ever-protective of his mother, wishes to spare her the brunt of the insult that her husband prefers even her dead sister's *maid* to Leah herself. The reader will recall that years before it was Reuven who, as a young child, brought Leah the *dudaim*. The Talmud explains that Reuven, now an adult, was acutely aware of his mother's humiliation caused by her husband's habitually making his bed in Rachel's tent. The additional indignity concerning Bilhah following Rachel's death cut Reuven to the heart, and he hastily

<hr />

3 וילך

4 וילך ראובן. הלך לאהל בלהה ושכב עמה. פלגש אביו היתה, וקראה "פלגש" לפי שראובן חשב כי לא היתה אסורה עליו לפי שהיתה תחלה שפחה. וא"כ לקחה אביו לפלגש. והכתוב מעיד עליה שהיתה לו **לאשה**, והיתה אסורה עליו . . . לפיכך נטל ממנו בכורתו.

5 ואתא ראובן ובגין דחמא דבלהה ירתה אתרא דאמיה, אזל ובלבל ערסה.

6 כשמתה רחל. נטל יעקב מטתו שהיתה נתונה תדיר באהל רחל . . . ונתנה באהל בלהה.

removed his father's bed from Bilhah's tent, and placed it in Leah's, before his mother could suffer from the affront.[7]

The reader can well appreciate Reuven's protective outrage on Leah's behalf. For if we follow Rav Bachya's configuration of the matriarchs' sleeping arrangements (as we described in Chapter 69), Bilhah's smaller tent was situated *within* Leah's larger one. Jacob could not enter Bilhah's tent time after time without passing through Leah's domain. *This* was perhaps the affront to his mother's honor that Reuven could not bear.

Ramban attributes a less altruistic motive to Reuven here. According to Ramban, Reuven removed his father's bed from Bilhah's tent solely in order to prevent her from conceiving and giving birth to more children. Reuven, the eldest, was mindful of his destiny to inherit a double portion at his father's death. He, therefore, stood potentially to lose more than his brothers by the possibility of Jacob's siring more offspring. He did not fear this eventuality from his own mother, Leah, however, because she was already past her childbearing prime. As for Zilpah, Leah's handmaiden, Ramban posits from the text's silence regarding her, that perhaps Zilpah has already died. Alternatively, suggests Ramban, perhaps Reuven avoided Zilpah entirely, out of his respect for his mother. It is for this reason—that he sought to prevent the birth of additional siblings—that Reuven forfeited his birthright, according to the commentator.[8]

The *Netziv* agrees that Reuven did not actually sleep with Bilhah. According to this commentary, however, Reuven, in a misguided action, stood guard at Bilhah's door and prevented his father from exercising his marital rights with her. It is because of this disrespectful and intrusive act that the text states, "[*it is as though*] Reuven lay with Bilhah, his father's concubine."[9]

The next two *mephorshim* consider this episode from *Jacob's* vantage point, rather than from Reuven's. *Siftei Chachamim* explains

---

[7] אמר רבי שמואל בר נחמני אמר רבי יונתן, כל האומר ראובן חטא אינו אלא טועה . . . מלמד שבלבל מצעו של אביו ומעלה עליו הכתוב **כאלו** שכב עמה . . . עלבון אמו תבע. אמר, אם **אחות** אמי היתה צרה לאמי, **שפחת** אחות אמי מהא צרה לאמי?! לכך בלבל.

[8] יתכן שבלבל ראובן יצועי בלהה מפחדו שלא תלד ליעקב עוד, כי הוא הבכור, וחשב לקחת שני חלקים, ויפסיד יותר מכל האחים. ולא פחד מאמו, כי זקנה היתה. ואולי מתה זלפה, או חשש לכבוד אמו בעבור שהיתה שפחתה. **ולכן** נטלה ממנו הבכורה.

[9] וישכב את בלהה. שלא היה מעשה, ח"ו, אלא **שמר** שלא יבוא אביו לחדרה.

that Jacob had his bed brought into *Bilhah's* tent instead of into *Leah's* because Jacob believed that Leah would have rejected such an overdue overture on his part if he had sought a place inside her tent. Jacob reasoned that because he had maintained his bed in Rachel's tent during her lifetime, Leah would reject being cast, once again, as Rachel's stand-in. However, the commentary continues, Reuven, who understood his mother's abiding yearning for Jacob, knew that Leah would have welcomed Jacob even though she knew that the memory of Rachel remained foremost in Jacob's thoughts.[10]

Breishit Rabbati reminds the reader of the tragic practicality of Jacob's predicament. His wife Rachel had just died in childbirth, leaving him with a suckling infant. Jacob of necessity installed Bilhah in Rachel's tent as his wife's surrogate, and she served as wet-nurse to the infant Benjamin. For even though Bilhah had not given birth in recent years, she was still able to nurse the infant with her own milk, and Jacob was satisfied with the arrangement, as it kept Rachel's newborn by his side.[11]

Israel heard [what Reuven did]; now Jacob's sons numbered twelve.[12]

The text's iteration that "Israel heard" invites the reader to expect a reaction to Reuven's behavior. Surprisingly, the text simply states that "Jacob's sons numbered twelve." The *mephorshim* grapple with this seeming *non sequitur*. Ramban, for instance, explains that these two phrases, "Israel heard" and "Jacob's sons numbered twelve," must be read together, just as the text presents them. Even though "Israel heard" that Reuven had defiled his (Jacob's) bed, Jacob refrained from ousting his firstborn son, choosing for the moment to retain his family's unity. This is the reason that even after "Israel heard" what Reuven did, *nevertheless,* "Jacob's sons [*still*] numbered twelve." Although Reuven ultimately will lose his firstborn's

---

[10] וישכב את בלהה. ואם תאמר מ"ט דיעקב, ולמה לא נתן מטתו באהל לאה, י"ל לפי שיעקב היה סבור שלאה לא תרצה ליקח משום שלא נתן מטתו בחיי רחל באהלה, גם כן עכשיו לא תרצה ליקח. אבל ראובן, שהיה רגיל אצל אמו ויודע שתקף, משום הכי הלך ובלבל.

[11] כיון שמתה רחל, הכניס את בלהה באהל רחל ועמדה במקומה והיתה מינקת בנימין. אף על פי שעמדה מלדת כמה שנים, בא לה חלב והניקתו.

[12] וישמע ישראל; ויהיו בני יעקב שנים-עשר.

right of inheritance, he is forever considered the first of the twelve numbered tribes.[13]

According to Chizkuni, these phrases form a transition between Reuven's behavior—whatever form it took—and the forthcoming verses of the text which enumerate the genealogy of Jacob's sons. The commentary construes the sequence of these phrases as teaching us that from that day forward, after "Israel heard" what Reuven did, Jacob had twelve sons *but no others*. After Rachel's death, Jacob initially tried to resume some semblance of married life with Bilhah, Rachel's handmaid. He ultimately lost all desire to cohabit with his wives, however, following the incident with Reuven. The commentator goes on to say that the phrase "now Jacob's sons numbered twelve" heralds the next segment of the text, and informs us that Jacob *and his twelve sons* returned home to Isaac's house in Hebron. The text's forthcoming recap of Jacob's sons' matrilineal descent highlights for the reader the names and provenances of Jacob's successors.[14] Radak infers from this phrase that not only did Jacob withdraw himself from the physical aspect of marriage so that he sired no more children, but he also disengaged himself from his worldly endeavors and confined himself solely to theological matters until the end of his days.[15]

GENESIS 35:23–29

The text now lists Jacob's sons by each of his four wives.

Leah's sons are Reuven, Jacob's firstborn, and Shimon, Levi, Yehuda, Issachar and Zevulun. The sons of Rachel are Joseph and Benjamin. The sons of Bilhah, Rachel's handmaid, are Dan and Naphtali. And the sons of Zilpah, Leah's handmaid, are Gad and Asher.

---

13 וישמע ישראל. שמע בחלל בנו יצועיו, ולא צוה שיוציאוהו מביתו מכלל בניו, ולא ינחל עמהם. אבל ימנה עמהם, "ויהיו שנים-עשר." והוא ימנה ראשון. ולכך עשה משתי הפרשיות פסוק אחד.

14 ויהיו בני יעקב. משם והלאה שנים-עשר ולא יותר, שלא הוסיף עוד יעקב להזקק עם נשיו . . . חזר ושנה מספר "בני יעקב" ללמדך שבא הוא ושנים-עשר בניו אל אביו.

15 ויהיו בני יעקב שנים-עשר. כי לא היה עוד בן, והיה פרוש עוד כל ימיו מאשה וממדרכי העולם, והתעשק בעבודת הקל.

The text next restates that these are "the sons of Jacob that were born to him in Padan-Aram." Ibn Ezra points out that the text makes this blanket statement even though admittedly it is the first eleven of Jacob's sons who were in fact born in Padan-Aram, while Benjamin, the twelfth son, was born within the boundary of the land of Israel. Ibn Ezra goes on to say that the text here is summarizing this chapter of Jacob's life by stating, in effect, "all of Jacob's twelve sons that were born to him *before* he returned to his father's house."[16]

---

[16] עשתי-עשר נולדו לו שם. כי בנימין נולד בארץ כנען, והכתוב כתב על הרוב.

SEVENTY-EIGHT

ഓൽഭ൧ഭ

Finally,
Jacob Returns Home

GENESIS 35:27

Jacob returned to his father, Isaac . . .[1]

Although Jacob is returning to his birthplace, the text states only that he is returning specifically *to his father*. The pointed absence of Rebecca's name in this verse reminds us that Jacob has arrived home too late to see his mother before her death (please see Chapter 36 for a fuller description of Rebecca's death). Jacob arrives home with his numerous children, his surviving wives and his large household, and is made painfully aware of his mother Rebecca's empty tent. It was from this very tent, more than twenty years ago, that Rebecca had sent her beloved son Jacob into exile, promising him she would summon him to return when it was safe. Surely Jacob now recalls his mother Rebecca's final embrace, as he slowly approaches her desolate tent. Rebecca's name is not mentioned here in verse 27 because she has died during Jacob's journey, and Jacob is only now confronting the physical reality of his mother's absence.

Jacob's life, henceforth, is filled with even more tragedy. He is deceived by his older sons—who themselves sold their seventeen-year-old brother Joseph to a passing caravan—and believes that

---

[1] ויבא יעקב אל יצחק אביו. . . .

331

Joseph, Rachel's firstborn, is "killed" by wild beasts. Jacob mourns him for years. Thereafter, a severe famine forces Jacob to allow all his surviving sons, with the exception of Benjamin, to travel down to Egypt to purchase food for their families. Unbeknownst to Jacob, his son Joseph is not only still alive, but he has risen to a position of great prominence in Egypt over the course of the past twenty-odd years. While Joseph, the viceroy of Egypt in charge of distributing food during the famine, recognizes his ten older brothers when they come to Egypt to purchase food, they do not identify him as their long-lost kin. Joseph-as-viceroy is anxious to behold Benjamin, his sole sibling from his mother Rachel, and so he sets a condition upon the brothers' further purchase of food: they must bring their youngest brother with them the next time they come to Egypt. Under great duress and only after seeing that his family is starved for food does Jacob eventually cede Benjamin into Judah's care and allow him to go down to Egypt to meet the viceroy.

The Bible text tells us (Genesis 44:27) that Jacob referred to his precious son Benjamin as one of the "*two sons* that *my wife* bore to me."[2] The Ramban asks rhetorically, how can Jacob say the words "*my wife*," when in fact we know that he had *four*? More poignantly, how can Jacob claim to have only *two* sons, when we know that in fact he had *twelve*? The Ramban's answer is quietly explosive. He explains that when Jacob uses the term "one wife," he is referring of course to Rachel, the wife he married *knowingly*. And only two sons were born to this wife, the only wife he also married *willingly*. It is upon Rachel's two sons that Jacob lavished the great love he felt for Rachel, and he showered them with this love as if he had no other sons. The other ten sons, says the commentator, even those born to Leah, were considered, in Jacob's affections, as if they were the sons of concubines.[3]

The *Netziv*'s understanding of this verse softens the Ramban's interpretation. According to the *Netziv*, Jacob, recounting his life experiences, was only explaining to his sons how harshly fate had treated him, because his *most treasured wife* only bore him two sons.[4]

---

2 אתם ידעתם כי שנים ילדה לי **אשתי**.

3 אשתי. כי יעקב לא לקח אשה מדעתו, רק רחל. וזה טעם "ילדה לי אשתי," כי לא נולדו לי מאשה אשר היא אשתי ברצוני, רק שנים. ושמתי אהבתי **בהם,** כאלו הם יחידים לי. והשאר כבני פילגשים הם אלי.

4 הסביר לנו כמה קשה המזל הוא, כי מראש לא ילדה לו **אשתו העיקרית** כי אם שנים.

Eventually, Jacob is reunited with Joseph in Egypt, and Jacob is treated honorably there, as the venerable father of the viceroy. Jacob has moved with all his fortune, with his daughter Dinah, with his sons and their wives, and with his grandchildren and their wives and daughters down to Egypt, until all seventy of Jacob's family are united there. No family members remained in Canaan, and Jacob lived in Egypt, close to his son Joseph and with his entire extended family, for seventeen more years. When Jacob was very old and on his deathbed, he summoned Joseph to him, and extracted a solemn promise that Joseph would not allow his father Jacob to be buried in Egypt, but that he would carry his body back to Canaan, to be buried with his ancestors. As Jacob's health worsened, he again summoned Joseph to him. Joseph brought his two sons, Ephraim and Menashe, to his father's side, where Jacob bestowed upon them the covenantal blessing of land and progeny. Most importantly, he formally adopted his grandsons, Ephraim and Menashe, as his own sons, gifting each with a portion of his future legacy equivalent to that of his sons, Reuven and Shimon, *et al*. In effect, then, Jacob has granted Joseph with a double inheritance, the traditional legacy of a firstborn son.

SEVENTY-NINE

୧୦୧୫୧୦୧୫

On His Deathbed, Jacob Reflects Upon Rachel

GENESIS 48:7

When I arrived from Padan [Aram], Rachel died upon me [suddenly] in the land of Canaan on the road still some distance from Ephrat; so I buried her there on the way to Ephrat, which is Beit Lechem.[1]

In the midst of blessing his two grandsons, Jacob, on his deathbed, veers from the covenantal benediction and in an ostensibly rambling manner harks back in time to the death of his beloved wife, Rachel. *Ohr Hachayim* explains that Jacob's purpose in interrupting his blessing is to hint to Joseph that had his mother not died in childbirth, it is likely that she would have given birth to more sons. Therefore, reasons the commentator, Jacob here considers Joseph's two sons as if they are his own.[2]

The reader may recall that Jacob already extracted a promise from Joseph to bury him in Canaan. The *mephorshim* feel, however, that Jacob's request of Joseph in Genesis 47, verses 29 to 31, and Joseph's oath of acquiescence, obviously have not yet given Jacob

---

[1] ואני בבאי מפדן, מתה עלי רחל בארץ כנען בדרך בעוד כברת-ארץ לבא אפרתה; ואקברה שם בדרך אפרת, היא בית לחם.

[2] ואני בבאי מפדן. כתוב זה אין לו קשר עם מה שלמעלה ממנו. וגם אין ידוע כוונת הודעה זו . . . ואלו היתה קיימת רחל, היו יוצאים ממנו. ועכשיו יבאו מיוסף, שהוא בחינת יעקב, גם בחינת רחל.

the peace-of-mind he seeks. Jacob still fears that notwithstanding his vow, Joseph will be reluctant to make the significant effort to carry his father's bones to Canaan to be buried in the Cave of his ancestors, when Jacob himself shunned the much shorter trip to bury Rachel there many years before. Therefore, because Jacob is desperate for Joseph to fulfill the oath to bury him with his ancestors, Jacob here reminds his son of the dire consequences of taking an oath lightly. Here, according to the commentaries, Jacob openly alludes to the untimely death of Rachel, his beloved wife, because he still bears the guilt of having caused Rachel's death, either because he failed to timely fulfill his oath to God that he would return home to Canaan (see Chapter 39), or because of his precipitous vow concerning Lavan's missing teraphim (see Chapter 68).

Meshech Chachma explains that verse 48:7 is Jacob's intimation to Joseph that untimely death can result from a person's delayed fulfillment of his vows.[3] Alshich interprets Jacob's hint to Joseph to mean that Jacob blamed himself for Rachel's death because of his heedless utterance to Lavan before he searched for his missing teraphim ("With whomever you find your gods, he will not live!"). According to Alshich, Jacob has for years borne the guilty certainty that from the instant of his utterance Rachel's untimely death was irrevocably fated.[4] Thus, in 48:7 Jacob is issuing a *veiled warning* to his son to be scrupulous about keeping his vow to bury him in the Cave of Machpela, to avoid similar dire consequences.

Other commentaries see 48:7 not as a warning to Joseph, but as an attempt by Jacob to convince Joseph that he could not have acted otherwise but to bury Rachel by the roadside. This verse, then, presents Jacob's *justification* of his actions many years before. The following commentaries offer their varying interpretations of Jacob's cryptic words, "Rachel died upon me [suddenly] in the land of Canaan."

Ramban views Jacob's words as an obvious *apology* to Joseph in order to forestall any anger his son might be harboring against him for failing to bury his mother in the Cave of Machpela. Jacob's objective is to be laid to rest in the Cave of his ancestors, and he is

---

3 מתה עלי רחל. שחשש שמא יאחר שבועתו להליכו לארץ ישראל. רמז לו כי רחל מתה **עליי,** היינו **בשבילו,** שאיחר את נדרו.

4 מתה עלי רחל. כלומר, **בשבילי.** על קללות "אם אשר תמצא את אלהיך לא יחיה, וכו'," כי מאז נגזרה מיתתה.

troubled at his deathbed by the fear that Joseph will resent that *Leah* was buried in the Cave, while his own mother was not. For this reason, says Ramban, Jacob elaborates that Rachel died unexpectedly during the journey from Padan-Aram. There were no physicians available, nor were there medicaments with which to properly embalm her. Even though the measured distance from the road where Rachel died to the Cave was not far—perhaps only half-a-day's journey—Jacob explained to his son that he had been heavily laden with all his worldly possessions. Thus, a half-day's journey for a single, unencumbered traveler would have taken him many days to complete, traveling as he was with his great flocks and the numerous members of his family and household. For this reason Jacob was constrained to bury Rachel where she died.[5]

Chizkuni presents a different view of Jacob's long-ago predicament on his way from Padan-Aram to Canaan. This commentator tells us that at the time of Rachel's death, Jacob did not yet feel secure in his claim to the Cave of Machpela, as Esav had begun to undermine Jacob's title to the plot. Also at that time, Esav was nearby with four hundred armed men at his disposal, while Jacob was traveling with his family in an exposed caravan. In this vulnerable state, Jacob chose not to instigate trouble with his brother over title to the Cave, as the two had just become reconciled. It is for this reason, according to Chizkuni, that Jacob buried Rachel by the roadside. However, by the time of *Leah's* death years later, Esav had long since departed for his home in the land of Se'ir, abandoning the entire Cave to Jacob.[6]

According to Rashi, Jacob here admits to Joseph that he is asking of his son the specific kindness that he himself failed to accord Joseph's mother, *i.e.*, to be buried alongside Sarah and Abraham, Rebecca and Isaac in the family crypt in the Cave of Machpela. Jacob offers Rachel's son, Joseph, a combination explanation-cum-apology, expressly recognizing that Joseph must surely bear bitterness in his heart against his father for burying his mother on the road. Rashi states that Jacob was explaining to Joseph that he had been obeying

---

[5] ועל דרך הפשט גם כן אמר לו כן כמתנצל שלא יחר ליוסף בראות חפצו בקבורת המערה על
שלא קבר אמו שם, וכאשר קבר שם את לאה . . . ולכך אמר לו כי מתה . . . בדרך בפתע
פתאום, ולא יכול לקברה שם . . . ואיה הרופאים והרפואות לחנט אותה. וזה טעם "עלי."

[6] עדיין לא הייתי מוחזק במערה, שהרי עשו מערער עליה. לפיכך, קברתיה בדרך. אבל
כשקברתי את לאה, כבר הלך לו עשו אל ארצו, והניח לי הכל.

a Divine order to bury Rachel where she died. "My reason for doing this was to comply with *God's command* to me, to bury Rachel on the exact road that her exiled children were fated to pass on their way to Babylonia in years to come." She would serve as an aid and a comfort to them in the future, as they are led past her burial place.[7]

Breishit Rabbati expands on Rashi, and offers us a glimpse of the emotionally charged, unwritten dialogue between Jacob and Joseph on the subject of Rachel's roadside burial. After Jacob broached the subject with Joseph that he bury him in the Cave of Machpela, Joseph proceeded to question his father as to why he failed to accord Rachel the same honor. Clearly, says the commentator, this question has burned within Joseph for many years. Thus, it is this verse—a seeming *non sequitur* amidst Jacob's blessing of his grandsons—that offers Jacob's response to Joseph's *unrecorded* interrogation of his father. We know this, says the commentator, because the verse begins with the words ". . . *And as for me* . . . ,"[8] implying that this unrecorded conversation already is in progress.

The commentary continues that Jacob responds as follows to Joseph's question, justifying Rachel's burial by the roadside: "Just as *you* wish for Rachel to enter the Cave of Machpela, my son, so did *I* desire this."

Joseph retorts, "If that is to be believed, tell me, then, why did you not carry her there to be laid to rest? Was it perhaps the rainy season, making such transportation impossible?"

To wit, Jacob is compelled to admit, "No, it was not the rainy season. She died on the way to Ephrat, during the dry season between Pesach and Shavuot."

Says Joseph, sensing that his father failed to advance a compelling reason for burying Rachel by the road, "Well, then, I will issue a command forthwith, to disinter my mother and to bury her in the Cave!"

"Alas, my son," replies Jacob, "you must not do this. For I buried her in the road according to the word of God, as it is His

---

7 ואעפ"י שאני מטריח עליך להוליכני להקבר בארץ כנען, ולא כך עשיתי לאמך, שהרי מתה סמוך לבית לחם . . . ולא הולכתיה אפילו לבית לחם . . . וידעתי שיש בלבך עלי, אבל דע לך, **שעל פי הדיבור** קברתיה שם, שתהא לעזרה לבניה כשיגלה אותן נבוזראדן, והיו עוברים דרך שם.

8 **ואני**

intention that she will lay forever by the roadside for a purpose, so that future generations of her descendants will pass your mother's burial place and derive solace from her."[9]

Now that the *mephorshim* have advanced Jacob's justification for having buried Rachel by the roadside, they next explain the use of the enigmatic phrase "Rachel died *upon me*."[10] Although these words can be read colloquially, meaning simply that "Rachel died," the commentaries derive a deeper meaning. *Torat Hachida* takes Jacob's words literally, teaching us that because of Jacob's abundant love for Rachel, once he learned that she was truly *in extremis*, Jacob burst into the birthing tent and gathered Rachel into his arms as she lay dying. So his words to Joseph in this verse, "Rachel died upon me," come vividly to life.[11]

Sforno takes a psychological approach, and attributes Jacob's failure to bury Rachel in the Cave of Machpela to the drastic change that befell him when she died. The commentary portrays Jacob's deathbed argument as an attempt to explain to Joseph that his life force quite simply deserted him nearly as finally as it departed Rachel on that awful day on the road from Padan-Aram. His extreme misery and mourning so overwhelmed him that he could not muster the strength to carry Rachel's body to the burial place in Beit Lechem. Sforno has Jacob uttering these ardent words to his son: "It is beyond question that for me, from the moment of Rachel's death my heart became a hollow shell. I never again experienced feelings of desire, and I could not rouse myself to attempt to sire more sons."[12] Sforno wishes the reader to see that it was only Jacob's imminent death that compelled him to thus confess his deep-seated anguish to Joseph.

---

9 ואני בבאי מפדן. התחיל יוסף שואלו על עסק רחל, למה לא נכנסה לקבורת מערת המכפלה, שהיה יוסף מצר על הדבר מאד. והוא משיב עליה "ואני . . . " אינו אומר "אני," אלא "ואני."

א"ל, חייך! כשם שהיית מבקש שאמך תכנס במערת המכפלה, כך [אני] הייתי מבקש . . .

א"ל יוסף, למה [לא] הכנסת אותה לקבורה? שמה עונת גשמים היתה? א"ל, לאו, בדרך מתה, בעוד כברת ארץ לבא אפרתה בין פסח לעצרת היה . . . א"ל יוסף, גוזר אני עכשו ומעלה אותה למערה! [א"ל], אין אתה יכול לעשות בני, שלא קברתיה בדרך אלא על פי הדיבור . . . ובני עתידים לצאת לגולה לבבל, והם הולכין . . . בדרך. הם באים ומחבבין קבורת אמך, והיא מבקשת עליהם רחמים.

10 מתה **עלי** רחל.

11 מתה עלי רחל בדרך. כתב רבינו אפרים, "מרוב חיבתי מתה **על ברכי**." וזה "עלי."

12 וכל כך גברה עלי תרדתי ואבלי שלא עצרתי כח להוליכה לבית קברות בית לחם. ואין ספק כי מאז היה לבי חלל חלל בקרבי, ולא שלט עוד בי יצר הרע להתלכלך בחטא, ולא נשאר בי כח להוליד בנים.

Although Jacob did not actually apologize for his action in the text, this verse is, in effect, an apology. Perhaps he never could bear to relive the day of Rachel's death, or even to speak of it before now, and only the dire prospect of being buried in Egypt impels him to explain himself so passionately to Joseph.

The Talmud (*Sanhedrin* 22b) confirms Jacob's deep love for Rachel, and his concomitant sense of abiding profound loss at her untimely death. His laconic statement, "Rachel died upon me," belies the intensity of his feelings as he is left alive without her by his side. "The death of a woman is most keenly felt by none but her husband," teaches the Talmud. And it brings our verse 48:7 as the proof-text for this statement.[13] It is noteworthy that of all the married couples in the Bible who suffer death of a spouse, the Talmud singles out the depth of Jacob's bereavement after Rachel's death as the paradigm.

Rabbi Adin Steinsaltz,[†] in his commentary on this talmudic passage, adds to our understanding of why the Talmud selected Jacob as the prime example of a husband who so profoundly suffered the death of his wife. Rabbi Steinsaltz explains that death irrevocably severs the husband/wife bond. *Halachically* (legally), when a wife dies, the husband is permitted—even encouraged—to remarry and seek solace with another. Jacob could not even bring himself to do this, so existentially wounded was he by Rachel's death.[14]

[†]Steinsaltz, A. (1989). *Babylonian Talmud*, Vol. 1, *Sanhedrin* 22b.

---

[13] אין אשה מתה, אלא לבעלה, שנאמר, "ואני בבאי מפדן, מתה עלי רחל."

[14] במדרשים מוגדש אותו ענין מכמה צדדים . . . והיה שהוסיף שדבר זה יש לו גם משמעות **הלכית.** שכן קשר הקרבה שבין אשה ובעלה קיים רק בעוד האשה קיימת. ואלו לאחר מותה פוקעת קרבה זו. ומכאן שמבחינת ההלכה, האשה מתה ומתרחקת במתה רק מבעלה בלבד.

EIGHTY

༺ఔ༻

But Jacob is
Buried with Leah

GENESIS 49:29–33

At the moment before his death, after he blessed each of his twelve sons, Jacob then commands them all to bury him with his ancestors in the Cave of Machpela, which Abraham purchased from Ephron the Hittite, which is located on the Plain of Mamre in the Land of Canaan (*see* Chapter 12).

> *[Bury me] there, [where] they buried Abraham and Sarah his wife; there, [where] they buried Isaac and Rebecca his wife; there, [where] I buried Leah.*[1]

Following this directive to his sons, Jacob gathers his feet upon his bed, and he dies.

Although Jacob speaks here of Leah's burial, her death is never mentioned in the text. It is here that we learn of her death obliquely, via Jacob's mention of Leah's burial in the Cave of Machpela. It is ironic that Leah, Jacob's unfavored wife, obtains in death the position of honor: to be laid to rest beside her beloved Jacob. Yet it is noteworthy that Jacob, even with his dying breath, avoids referring to

---

[1] שמה קברו את אברהם ואת שרה אשתו; שמה קברו את יצחק ואת רבקה אשתו; ושמה קברתי את לאה.

340

Leah as his wife. Despite his own reference in the text to the burials of Abraham *with Sarah, his wife;* and of Isaac, *with Rebecca, his wife*, Jacob breaks the textual rhythm and leaves out any mention of Leah as "my wife." Avivah Gottlieb Zornberg[†] points out the related irony that the Cave of Machpela, which in Hebrew means "Cave of *Couples*," became the eternal resting place of Jacob *and Leah*, while Rachel, Jacob's soul-mate, is buried alone. How can this be reconciled?

The Zohar (222b) poses this precise question. Why is it that Rachel, who is referred to as the "essence" of Jacob's household, is not buried in the Cave alongside him? This ancient commentary offers two reasons. First, in all fairness, *Leah* merited this honor because of the irrefutable fact that it was she who gave birth to six of the twelve tribes. The Zohar then goes on to offer an additional reason, built upon the *midrash* that Leah had long ago cried a sea of tears, praying that it would be Jacob who would wed her, and not his wicked brother Esav. The Zohar explains that because Leah spent time in her youth crying for Jacob, she would merit being buried alongside him for eternity. Rachel, however, who had never spent time pining for Jacob, would spend eternity in her roadside grave, "crying" for her children.[2]

Alshich offers a different perspective of the same scene. While the Zohar asserts that the Cave of Machpela is the burial place of honor, Alshich suggests that perhaps the *true* burial place of honor is Rachel's roadside grave, which was dictated by God so that she could perform the essential task of "pleading" successfully with the Almighty for the redemption of future generations of her exiled children.[3]

Tanna de'be Eliyyahu (30/28) would agree. According to this commentary, the prophecy (Jeremiah 31:14) that the matriarch

---

[†]Zornberg, A. G. (1995). *Genesis: The Beginning of Desire* (Philadelphia: The Jewish Publication Society), p. 212

---

[2] ות"ח אבהתא זכו לאתקברא תמן, אינון וזווגייהו. יעקב, הוא ולאה, מ"ט רחל לא? והא כתיב ורחל עקרה, דאיהי עקרא דביתא. אלא, לאה זכתה ביה, לאפקא שית שבטין . . . א"ר יהודה, לאה כל יומהא הות בפרשת אורחין קיימא, ובכת בגיניה דיעקב . . . והיינו דכתיב . . . רחל דלא בעאת למיפק ולמשאל בהדיה, בג"כ קבורתה בפרשת אורחין.

[3] כי הלא "ואקברה שם בדרך אפרת" שהוא על פי הדיבור. למען תהיה מבכה על בניה בעת החורבן. מידי עברם לשם.

"Rachel weeps for her [exiled] children"[4] can perhaps be read slightly differently. The Hebrew name *RaH-CHeL* can be parsed into two words: *Ru'aCH eL*, meaning "the spirit of God." According to this reading, then, Rachel's roadside burial place is deliberate, eminently correct and even prophetic. This commentary suggests that Rachel's "presence" on the road to her "children's" exile caused the spirit of God to weep *with* her, and ultimately to console her descendants.

Midrash Rabbah (in *Eichah Rabbah* 24) indirectly confirms the primacy of Rachel's burial place when it depicts a scene in the Heavenly court. Venerable character witnesses appear before God in this commentary, pleading that the Almighty should redeem the children of Israel from exile and return them to their land. In vain do Abraham, Isaac, Jacob and Moses importune God. Only Rachel's plea succeeds in moving God to bestow mercy upon them, and to return "Rachel's children" from captivity (see Chapter 76).[5]

Alshich counters rhetorically that as *Leah* was the mother of six of Jacob's sons, surely it would have been more fitting for *her* to be buried by the roadside to comfort *her children* in exile? No, concludes Alshich. The Torah text is clearly offering *Rachel* the "place of honor." Though she gave birth to only two of Jacob's twelve sons, Jacob at all times considered *her* to be his essential wife, and thus it is fitting for her to be chosen to weep for *all* of Jacob's children.[6]

Students of the text will appreciate that it is clear from the *p'shat* that the Cave of Machpela was the burial place of honor for the patriarchs and matriarchs. Otherwise, it would have been unnecessary for Jacob to justify his failure to bury Rachel there, and also Jacob would not have insisted so adamantly that his sons bury him there, as well. Yet, it emerges from the commentaries that the Cave may not be the only burial place of honor for the matriarchs. Perhaps their alternative readings of the text reflect their own discomfort with Rachel's burial place.

We suggest that the text's burial of Leah in the Cave of Machpela, and Rachel by the roadside, may actually be most fitting.

---

4 רחל מבכה על בניה

5 קפצה רחל אמנו לפני הקב"ה ואמרה: . . . וגמלתי חסד עמה ולא קנאתי בה . . . ואתה מלך חי וקיים, מפני מה קנאתה לעבודת אלילים . . . והגלית לבני? . . . מיד נתגלגלו רחמיו של הקב"ה ואמר, **בשביל רחל** אני מחזיר את ישראל למקומם.

6 שהלא יקשה, למה יקרא כל ישראל "בניה?" והלא אדרבה. טוב, טוב תקבר שם **לאה**, שכמעט כל ישראל ממנה. אלא ודאי שהיא [**רחל**] עיקר הבית.

Leah's primary passion, as we have discussed, was, quite simply, Jacob. Her desire for his love informed her entire life. Rachel's primary passion, on the other hand, was her desire for children. She yearned for them above all else, and ultimately gave up her life bearing a son. Their burial places properly reflect their life-passions: Leah is buried beside Jacob for eternity, and Rachel is buried where future generations of the children of Israel will receive her solace.

EIGHT–ONE

80CX80CX

Epilogue
to Rachel and Leah

*God should establish you as He did Sarah, Rebecca, **Rachel and Leah**.*[1]

T his portion of the story began with love at first sight. From the moment Jacob saw Rachel at the well, all his energies were directed toward winning her. But this idyllic beginning is mitigated by the absence of reciprocity. While the text clearly records Jacob's love for Rachel, in contrast, the text is silent about Rachel's feelings for him. In fact, Rachel's first words in the Bible express not her love for Jacob, but her existential pain at her childless state. The story is complicated by the fact that Rachel's older sister, Leah, who had been given to Jacob in marriage by means of subterfuge, easily bore him children. Yet the fact that Leah bore Jacob the children that he desired still did not earn her his affection; Leah's love for Jacob was unrequited. Jacob remained constant in his love for Rachel.

This triangle of passions—Jacob for Rachel, Leah for Jacob, and Rachel for children of her own—becomes even more intricate when injected with the rivalry between the two sisters as well as their handmaids. In addition, their lives are punctuated by tragedy. Leah's daughter, Dinah, is raped; Leah's sons extract murderous revenge on an entire city; her sons later sell their brother into servitude, and

---

[1] .ישמך אלקים כשרה, רבקה, **רחל ולאה**

344

perpetuate a lifelong deception on their father. Rachel, unable to conceive, is fated to watch her sister and the two handmaidens, Bilhah and Zilpah, effortlessly deliver one child after another. Years later, Rachel, finally able to bear one son, dies giving birth to her second.

As was the case with Sarah and Rebecca, these matriarchs' lives are fraught with misfortune. We must therefore ask once again, why do we bless our daughters to be like Rachel and Leah? We are assisted in this inquiry by the *mephorshim*, who illuminate the qualities of Leah and Rachel that immortalize them in our tradition.

The commentaries derive that Leah was devout, and that she prayed for a husband who kept Abraham's covenant with God. She was steadfast in her love for Jacob, and was singular among the matriarchs in that she was blessed with fertility. Importantly, she was mother to six sons and one daughter, and she nurtured her handmaid, Zilpah's, two sons as well.

We are taught that Rachel was exceedingly beautiful. Further, she possessed a tender heart, having sacrificed her wedding night in order to spare her older sister the grave humiliation of spinsterhood or an unwanted marriage. The commentaries refer to Rachel as *iKeReT HaBaYiT*,[2] the essence of Jacob's household. She initiated the surrogacy of her handmaid, Bilhah, and though barren herself, vicariously mothered *her* two sons. She was also, at long last, a mother herself, who nurtured one son and died giving birth to a second. Rachel remained desirable to Jacob until the end of her life, and even beyond, as her husband was forever unable and unwilling to shed her image from his consciousness.

Although the Talmud enumerates only the matriarch Sarah as one of the seven biblical prophetesses, Rashi and other commentaries also vest the other three matriarchs with prophetic intuition, albeit of a more limited nature. Both Rachel and Leah possessed a degree of prophecy sufficient to allow them to perceive their role as mothers to the twelve yet-unborn tribes of Israel.

Interestingly, an earlier form of this blessing was bestowed upon Ruth, the great-grandmother of King David, at her marriage to Boaz close to three thousand years ago. In the Book of Ruth (4:11), the righteous Ruth is blessed in the name of the matriarchs Rachel and Leah.

---

[2] עיקרת הבית

*So the assembled people said [to Boaz], with the elders as witness: "May God grant that this woman who is [hereby] entering your household should be **like Rachel and like Leah**, who, together, both built the house of Israel."*[3]

This ancient version of our blessing mentions only Rachel and Leah, and states explicitly that *they both* built the nation of Israel. At this point in our study, after having so closely followed the lives of the matriarchs, the reader can readily appreciate that while it may have sufficed for Abraham and Isaac each to have produced only one covenantal son, it was necessary for Jacob, the third patriarch, to produce numerous progeny in order for his family to physically become a nation. In addition to their other attributes, Rachel and Leah, along with their handmaids, Bilhah and Zilpah, were mothers to the progenitors of the twelve tribes of Israel. It was their passionate desire for bearing and raising children that formed the dominant theme of Rachel and Leah's lives, and this driving force is the basis for the millennia-old blessing of Ruth. The elders, *invoking the names of Rachel and Leah*, were intoning the benediction of family, generational continuity, and covenantal inheritance upon Ruth.

According to the modern Bible commentator Rabbi Aaron David Goldberg, in his work *Shirat David*, Rachel and Leah's legacy to us is highlighted in the closing phrase of Ruth's benediction: . . . *Rachel and Leah, who **both** built the house of Israel. Shirat David* focuses on the grammatical oddity of the Hebrew word for "both," which appears in the text in the *masculine* form[4] even as it describes the two women, Rachel and Leah. One would have expected the Scripture to have used the *feminine* form when referring to the two matriarchs, unless it intended for us to derive a deeper meaning from the masculine usage. The commentator reasons that the Bible uses the masculine form with reference to these biblical women when they take equivalent action to that of their male counterparts. The elders blessed Ruth to be like Rachel and Leah because *both* these matriarchs built the "house of Israel" as partners with the patriarchs.[5]

---

3 ויאמרו כל העם אשר בשער והזקנים עדים; יתן ד' את האשה הבאה אל ביתך **כרחל וכלאה** אשר בנו שתיהם את בית ישראל. . . . .

4 שתיהם

5 ועוד יש לעיין למה כתיב "אשר בנו **שתיהם**" בלשון זכר, והיה צריך לכתוב "שתיהן" בלשון נקבה . . . הרי שכשהנקבות עושות מעשים כזכרים יתכן להכתב בלשון זכר, וה"נ **בנין בית ישראל על ידי רחל ולאה היה כבנין האבות הקדושים.**

Acting in this inspired manner, the matriarchs propelled the covenantal vision to successive generations, and created the Jewish nation. Therefore, when we bless our daughters, we invoke the benediction that they will walk in the footsteps of the matriarchs, meeting life's challenges by choosing the correct path, guided by God's teachings.

GLOSSARY

ഓൽ൙ഓൽ൙

Abarbanel   Rabbi (Don) Isaac Ben Yehuda (1437–1508) was a Spanish Bible commentator, philosopher and statesman. He suffered various misfortunes culminating in the expulsion of Spanish Jewry in 1492. Abarbanel's extensive commentaries to the Bible are arranged by chapters introduced by numerous questions that he then proceeds to resolve.

Abraham, Rabbi, Son of the Rambam   (1186–1237) The *nagid*, or rabbinic leader, of the Egyptian Jewish community, and the only son of the Maimonides. He studied Torah, philosophy and medicine with his father, and was well known for his mystical religious views. He completed a biblical commentary of Genesis and portions of Exodus.

Akeidat Yitzchak   Isaac ben Moses Arama (1420–1494) was a Spanish rabbi, teacher, and philosopher. After the expulsion of the Jews from Spain in 1492 he settled in Naples, Italy. He delivered hundreds of sermons dealing with the weekly Torah readings, which were compiled under the title of "Akeidat Yitzchak," which was published in Salonika in 1522.

Alshich   Rabbi Moshe Alshich (1508–c.1593) was a Torah scholar who spent most of his life in Safed, in Israel, and who was a disciple of Rabbi Yosef Karo, the author of the *Shulchan Aruch*, the Code of Jewish Law. His primary interest was *halacha*, Jewish law, but Alshich also studied Kabbalah, Jewish mysticism, and biblical exegesis. His Shabbat sermons formed the basis of his popular commentaries on most of the Bible.

Bachya, **Rav** Rabbi (Rabbeinu) Bachya ben Asher (d. 1340) was a Spanish Bible commentator and kabbalist. He wrote his popular commentary on the Torah in 1291.

Ba'al Haturim Rabbi Yaakov ben Asher (c.1270-1340), was born in Germany, but fled with his father to Spain, and there he served as the *dayan*, or Judge of Jewish law, in the City of Toledo. His father was "The Rosh," Reb Asher ben Yechiel, who wrote an authoritative commentary on the Mishna. He is called the Ba'al Haturim because of his major work, entitled the *Arba'ah Turim*, which for 200 years, until the appearance of the *Shulchan Aruch*, was considered the standard code of Jewish law.

Breishit Rabbati A commentary on Genesis attributed to Rabbi Moshe Hadarshan of Narbonne, France, written in the first half of the eleventh century. His commentary reflects a wide range of sources, namely Breishit Rabbah, the Babylonian and Jerusalem Talmuds, and the Apocrypha, and both Rashi and Ramban refer to it in their writings.

Chatam Sofer Rabbi Moses Sofer (1762–1839), was born in Frankfurt, but moved to Hungary at a young age, where he remained until the end of his life. He served as rabbi of Pressburg, Hungary for 33 years, during which time he established the largest yeshiva, or house of Jewish study, since the Babylonian *yeshivot*. His many writings include commentaries on the Bible and Talmud, numerous responsa, sermons, letters, poems and a diary.

Chizkuni Hezekiah ben Manoah was a Bible scholar who lived in France in the mid-thirteenth century. He is known for his *midrashic* commentaries on the Torah and on Rashi's vast exegesis. His work was published in Venice in 1524.

Da'at Zekeinim Miba'alei Hatosfot Thirteenth-century compilation of commentaries on the Torah originating with the French Tosafists, the Talmudic commentators who were the disciples of Rashi.

Gr'ah, The   Hagaon Rabbi Eliyahu ben Shlomo Zalman, also known as the Gaon of Vilna (1720–1797), was one of the greatest Talmudic authorities in Eastern Europe and the leader of non-Chassidic Jewry at that time. His teachings and leadership did much to shape the "Litvak" *Mitnagdim* culture, which centered on the supreme importance of *halacha*, or Jewish law. He authored more than seventy works, of which *Aderes Eliyahu* is his commentary on the Torah.

Hirsch, Rabbi Samson Raphael   (1808–1888) The rabbi of Frankfurt-on-Main and the defender of Orthodox Judaism against the upsurge of the Reform movement. Among his many works is his monumental German translation of and commentary on the Torah.

Ibn Ezra (of Tudela), Rabbi Abraham   (1089–1164) A Spanish poet, grammarian, philosopher, and physician whose commentary on the Bible dwells on the meaning, grammar and etymology of the words in their different contexts.

Karnei Ohr   A late-nineteenth-century supercommentary on Ibn Ezra compiled by Rabbi Yehuda Leib ben Reb Yitzchak Krinsky of Minsk, Russia.

Kli Yakar   A homiletic commentary on the Bible written by Rabbi Ephraim Solomon ben Haim of Luntshitz (1550–1619), the Rabbi of Prague and head of the yeshiva in Lemberg.

Leibowitz, Nehama   Born in Riga, Latvia, in 1905, "Nehama" was a twentieth-century Israeli teacher and Bible scholar. For a half-century her renowned "Pages" on the study of the weekly Torah portion reached Bible students the world over. She was a Professor of Bible at Tel Aviv University whose unique method of critical analysis of the Bible and its commentaries challenged generations of students to understand the nuances of meaning in the Torah text. She died in Israel in 1997.

Lekach Tov   Also known as *Pesikta* or *Pesikta Dutarta*, *Lekach Tov* is a late-eleventh century collection of *midrash* on the Torah written by Rabbi Tobias (Tuvia) ben Eliezer, from Castro, Bulgaria. His work includes material from the Babylonian Talmud, *halachic midrashim*, early *aggadic midrashim*, and early mystical literature.

Levush Haorah   A supercommentary to Rashi written by Rabbi Mordechai ben Avraham Jaffe (c.1535–1612), who succeeded the Maharal as the *Av Beit Din*, head of the Jewish High Court, in Prague. He is known as the *Ba'al Halevushim* because he authored the "Ten Attires" (*Levushim*), commentaries on a range of Hebrew texts. It is the sixth *Levush* that is the supercommentary on Rashi.

Maharal   Rabbi Judah Loew ben Bezalel (c.1525–1609), born to a noble Worms family, was a scholar of Bible, mathematics and astronomy, and served as Chief Rabbi of Moravia, Posen and Prague. His many writings on ethics, law, philosophy and homiletics had *kabbalistic* leanings. He is the author of the *Gur Aryeh*, a supercommentary on Rashi.

Maharam   Rabbi Meir ben Rav Baruch of Rothenberg (c.1215–1294) was a Tosafist, scholar, teacher and *dayyan*, or judge, in Germany. Considered the greatest scholar of his generation, he served for almost fifty years as the highest court of appeal for Jews of Germany and surrounding countries, and as such he shaped the laws and customs for Ashkenazik Jewry.

Malbim   The acronym of Rav Meir Leibush ben Yechiel Michel (1809–1879), known as the "illui [prodigy] of Volhynia" in the Ukraine. He was a staunch supporter of Orthodox exegesis, and wrote an esteemed commentary on the Torah.

Matnot Kehuna   A commentary on the *Midrash Rabbah* written by Rabbi Yissacher Ber Hakohen (c.1520–1590).

Ma'ayna Shel Torah   A twentieth-century anthology and commentary written by Rabbi Alexander Zushia Friedman. It combines ethical and moral teachings with the weekly biblical portions. Written originally in Yiddish in Warsaw, Poland, it was translated into Hebrew and published in Palestine in 1938.

Mephorshim A generic term that refers to traditional Jewish biblical commentators whose words were recorded from the third century before the Common Era to the present day.

Meshech Chachma A commentary on the Torah written by Rabbi Meir Simcha Hakohen of Dvinsk (1843–1926), where he served as rabbi for forty years. His commentary on the Torah combines Talmudic and *midrashic* material with philosophical insights. He also wrote commentaries on Maimonides' *Mishna Torah* and on the Talmud.

Midrash From the Hebrew root-word *DaRoSH*, meaning to search, seek, examine or investigate. Commentaries that discuss the *legal* texts of the Torah comprise *midrash halacha*. *Midrash aggadah,* on the other hand, which is the essence of our book, is rabbinic interpretation whose focus is the biblical narrative combined with historical events, and ethical and philosophical matters. According to Daniel Boyarin in his book, *Intertextuality and the Reading of Midrash* (Indiana University Press, 1994), pages 10–20, *midrash* represents the "intertext" of the Bible, or the rabbis' attempts to fill in the gaps that may appear to exist in the Bible's spare narratives and dialogues. In Boyarin's words, the authors of the *midrash* are "lonely geniuses in communion with the biblical heroes," reproducing the "essences" of these biblical heroes. *Midrash* represents the timeless "double-voicedness" of the Torah, by setting up a dialectic between rabbinic interpretations. Certain biblical ambiguities naturally invite the *midrashic* intertexts, thereby generating more than one legitimate *midrashic* reading. Biblical *midrash* thus preserves intimate contact with and context for the Bible, and provides a rabbinic model of the relationship between the present and the past.

Midrash Lekach Tov A twelfth-century anthology of Torah commentaries ascribed to Rabbi Tuvia ben Reb Eliezer of Mainz (Mayence).

Midrash Rabbah The general title of a compilation of numerous interpretive sources. Each collection of these commentaries is named after the biblical text it expounds. It is based on Palestinian sources dating from the time of the *Tanaim* and *Amoraim*, and was compiled between the years of 400 to 500 C.E.

Midrash Tanchuma A collection of interpretations of the Torah originally written in Aramaic by the fourth-century Talmudic scholar Rabbi Tanchuma bar Abba. The work, first published in Venice in 1545, was comprised mainly of Tanchuma's sermons on the biblical text.

Mishna d'Rabi Eliezer An important commentary on *Midrash Rabbah* attributed to Rav Eliezer ben Yehuda. This work is also known as *Midrash Agur*, and is thought to have been compiled sometime between the seventh and ninth centuries.

Mizrachi Rabbi Eliyahu Mizrachi (1450–1526) of Constantinople. Known as the Re'im, he is the premier supercommentary on Rashi. He served as the rabbinical authority throughout the Ottoman Empire, and was considered the greatest *posek*, or authority on Jewish law, of his time. Mizrachi's supercommentary itself became a subject for study of succeeding generations of rabbinic commentators.

Nachshoni, Yehuda Twentieth-century Israeli rabbi, scholar, and Torah commentator whose Hebrew-language work on the weekly Torah portions combines traditional commentaries with original exegesis.

Netziv The acronym of Rabbi Naphtali Zvi Yehuda Berlin (1817–1893), the prodigy Talmudist who served as the head of the Yeshiva of Volozhin for forty years, until the yeshiva was closed by the Russian authorities in 1892. Berlin's commentary, *Ha'amek Davar*, incorporated his daily lessons on the weekly Torah portion.

Ohel Yaakov The eighteenth-century Torah commentary of Rabbi Jacob Kranz, a pupil of the Gaon of Vilna. Rabbi Franz was known as "the *Maggid* of Dubno."

Ohr Hachayim Rabbi Chayim Ibn Attar (1696–1743), a Moroccan Torah scholar and kabbalist who encouraged resettlement of Palestine and established a yeshiva there. His commentaries on the Talmud, *halacha* and the Torah were widely circulated in Germany and Poland.

Onkelos   The Torah commentary written *circa* first century C.E. by Onkelos the Proselyte, referred to in the Talmud (*Megilla* 3a) as a student of Rabbi Eliezer and Rabbi Yehoshua after the destruction of the Second Temple in Jerusalem in 70 C.E. Known as "the Targum," Onkelos' work aimed for literal translation of the Hebrew biblical text into Aramaic, but in fact it liberally employed paraphrase for clarity or in order to avoid anthropomorphism. It was highly valued by the Babylonian Talmudists, who referred to Onkleos as "our targum."

Otzar Ishei Hatanach   A one-volume encyclopedia of biblical personalities anthologized from the Talmud, *midrash*, and rabbinic writings. First published in Jerusalem in 1964 by Rabbi Yisrael Yitzchak (Yishai) Chasidah.

Perush Yonatan   An ancient biblical commentary on Targum Yonatan Ben Uziel/Yerushalmi, an Aramaic translation on the Torah of uncertain authorship.

Pirkei d'Rabi Eliezer   A commentary of *midrash aggadah* compiled in the eighth century, attributed to Rabbi Eliezer, son of Hyrkanos, who lived in the latter half of the first century C.E. He was renowned for his erudition, but was ultimately excommunicated for revealing kabbalistic mysteries in his commentary. He is cited in the Tosfot commentary to the Talmud (*Ketubot* 99a), as well as by Rashi and Maimonides, and it is believed that much of his commentary has been incorporated into the Zohar.

P'shat   The plain-sense meaning of the Bible text, or its strict textual reading.

Radak   Acronym of Rabbi David Kimchi (1160–1235), Bible commentator and grammarian of Provence, France. Known for his plain-sense commentary on the Bible, he was interested in science and philosophy, as well as the rationalism of Ibn Ezra and Maimonides.

Ralbag   Acronym for Rabbi Levi ben Gershom [Gershonides] (1288–1344), of Provence, France. He was a biblical commentator, philosopher, mathematician and astronomer, whose scholarship favored philosophical inquiry over strict literal meaning of the text.

Rambam Acronym for Rabbi Moses ben Maimon [Maimonides] (1135–1204) of Fostat, the Old City of Cairo, Egypt. He was a brilliant Rabbinic authority, codifier, philosopher, and royal physician. Among his great works are his commentary to the Mishna, the *Mishnah Torah,* and *Guide to the Perplexed.* Rambam is considered a towering figure of Judaism in the post-Talmudic era.

Ramban Acronym for Rabbi Moshe ben Nachman [Nachmanides] (1194–1270) of Gerona, Spain. He was a physician as well as a Talmudic authority who authored biblical commentaries distinguished by an in-depth analysis of the larger significance of the Torah's stories and themes. His work on the Torah often quoted the writings of Rashi and Ibn Ezra as his point of departure, explaining or challenging their comments.

Ran Acronym of Rabbeinu Nissim ben Reuven Gerondi (c.1310-c.1375), a Spanish Talmud and Bible commentator, physician and philosopher. He is best known for his *halachic* works, notably his commentary on the "Rif," Rabbi Isaac Alfasi. He authored numerous responsa, a book of sermons and a commentary on the Torah.

Rashbam Acronym of Rabbi Shlomo ben Meir (1085–1174) of Troyes, France. The grandson of Rashi, Rashbam's Bible commentary favors the literal or plain-sense meaning of the Torah text. Rashbam was one of the earliest Tosafists.

Rashi The acronym of Rabbi Shlomo Yitzchaki (1040–1105) of Troyes, France. Rashi's exhaustive biblical exegesis, the first known Hebrew commentary to be printed in 1475, spawned more than 200 supercommentaries. He employed literal as well as *midrashic* interpretations, and said of his own commentaries (at Genesis 3:8): "As for me, I am only concerned with the literal meaning of the Scriptures and with such [*midrash*] *aggadot* as explain the biblical passages in a fitting manner." Rashi also wrote a commentary to virtually all of the Babylonian Talmud.

Rokach The acronym of Rabbi Eleazar ben Judah of Worms (c.1165-c.1230), a Torah scholar in medieval Germany. He lived during the horror of the Crusades, and so feared for the future of German Jewry that he committed his learning to writing in case the oral transmission should falter in the uncertain and dangerous future. He authored the *halachic* work, *Sefer Harokeach*, as well as numerous books of biblical commentary.

Sa'adia (ben Joseph) Gaon   Born in Egypt (882–942), he translated the entire Torah into Arabic, incorporating into the translation his authoritative biblical commentary.

S'fat Hayeriya   A nineteenth-century supercommentary on Ohel Yaakov written in Warsaw by Rabbi Abraham Dov Barosh Flaum, a student of Rabbi Jacob ("the *Maggid*") of Duvna, author of *Ohel Yaakov*.

Sefer Tosfot Hashalem   A modern compilation of *tosafistic* commentaries on the Bible from the Middle Ages, published in Jerusalem by Yaakov Gelis beginning in 1982. The work presently covers Genesis and Exodus, and fills fifteen volumes, listing as its sources 172 manuscripts and 56 other published works.

Sforno   Rabbi Ovadia ben Jacob Sforno (1475–1550) was an Italian Bible commentator and physician. In Bologna, Sforno established a *beit medrash*, or house of learning, over which he presided until his death. He is best known for his Bible commentary which often highlighted the medical and biological aspects of the text.

Shirat David   A commentary to the Book of Ruth authored by Rabbi Aaron David Goldberg. Rabbi Goldberg, born in Chicago in 1951 and educated in Cleveland's Telshe Yeshiva, also studied at the Brisker Kollel in Israel. He presently lives in Ohio with his wife, Rivka, and their children.

Siftei Chachamim   The Torah commentary written by Rabbi Shabbetai Bass (1641–1718) is the most popular and widespread supercommentary on Rashi. Bass was born in Poland but was forced by a pogrom to flee to Prague in 1655, where he became a publisher and bibliographer. In 1680 he published this commentary as well as the first Jewish bibliography written in Hebrew.

Sha'arei Aharon   The Torah commentary of Rabbi Aharon Yeshaya Rotter, a survivor of the holocaust of Eastern European Jewry. Rabbi Rotter fled the Nazis in Hungary and ultimately emigrated to Israel via the Ukraine, and a displaced persons camp in Cyprus. He is currently living in B'nei Brak, Israel. His encyclopedic work explains the Torah text, Rashi, Onkelos, and numerous other rabbinic sources. He also incorporates his original interpretations in a verse-by-verse explication of the Bible.

Soloveitchik, Rabbi Joseph B.   (1903–1993) Known as "The Rav," Soloveitchik was born in Russia into a prominent rabbinic family. He earned a Doctorate of Philosophy from the University of Berlin in 1931, and emigrated to the United States the following year. From 1941 to 1985 the Rav served as *Rosh Yeshiva* at Yeshiva University. A talmudist and philosopher of vast erudition, he was one of the preeminent teachers and scholars of the twentieth-century.

Steinsaltz, Rabbi Adin   A modern author and Torah scholar whose towering translation of the Babylonian Talmud into Hebrew includes his original commentary. Rabbi Steinsaltz also has written a commentary on the *Tanya*, the classic treatise of Lubavitch Chassidic thought, as well as numerous philosophical works. He lives and teaches in Jerusalem, and lectures worldwide.

Torah Shlema A verse-by-verse, encyclopedic compilation of *midrashic* commentaries on the Torah, authored by Rabbi Menachem Mendel Kasher, and published in Jerusalem in 1992.

Torah Temima   The Bible commentary written by Rabbi Baruch Halevi Epstein (1860–1942), a Russian talmudic scholar whose father, Rabbi Yechiel Michel Epstein, authored the monumental work entitled the *Aruch Hashulchan*, and whose uncle was the *Netziv*. In his introduction to his Torah commentary he explained that his aim was "to show that this Torah, the written law, is a twin sister . . . to the oral law. They are inseparable, as body and soul." Epstein perished at the hands of the Nazis in the Pinsk Ghetto.

Torat Chayim   A verse-by-verse analysis of the Bible (*mikra'ot gedolot*) by classical biblical commentators (including Rav Saadia

Gaon, Rashi, Rashbam, Ibn Ezra, Radak, Ramban, Maharam, Chizkuni, and Sforno), published by the Mossad HaRav Kook in Jerusalem in 1986. This seven-volume work is enhanced by extensive footnotes by modern Torah scholars.

Torat Hachida   Rabbi Chayim Yosef David Azulai (1724–1806), author of *Torat Hachida*, was a native of Jerusalem. Azulai, a leading scholar of his generation, traveled extensively in Europe as an emissary of the houses of Torah study in the Land of Israel, and was esteemed by the Jews of the Ottoman Empire, Italy and Germany. He authored literary diaries, *halachic* works, and mystical interpretations of the Bible.

Talmud, Babylonian and Jerusalem   Foundational multi-volume works consisting of discussion and commentary on the Mishna, or Oral Law, as expounded in the Jewish academies of study in Babylon and Palestine between the years 200 and 500 C.E. by the *amoraim*, the rabbinic scholars of that period. The Babylonian Talmud was completed in c.500 C.E., about a century later than the Jerusalem Talmud, and is considered more *halachically* authoritative.

Tanna de'be Eliyyahu   A very early *midrashic* work whose precise authorship and date is uncertain, though it is thought to be the work of Rabbi Anan, a Babylonian jurist who lived in the third century B.C.E. It is known that the one-volume book predates the Zohar and the writings of the Safed mystics, and it presents coherent moral and ethical lessons based upon the lives of the patriarchs and matriarchs.

Yalkut Shimoni   Considered the most extensive *midrashic* anthology, spanning the entire Torah, including the Prophets and the Writings. Its authorship is attributed to Rabbi Shimon Hadarshan of Frankfurt, in thirteenth-century Germany. The Yalkut collected more than 10,000 *halachic* and *aggadic* opinions.

Yefei To'ar   A commentary on *Midrash Rabbah* authored by Rabbi Shmuel Yafeh Ashkenazi (1525–1595) of Constantinople.

Zohar   Meaning "Book of Splendor," the Zohar is the foundational work of medieval Jewish mysticism, the Kabbalah. It is a commentary on the Bible whose authorship is obscure, and is presented not as a homogeneous work, but as a compendium of material spanning numerous authors and several centuries. Some credit it to Shimon Bar Yochai, the fugitive from Roman persecution in the second century C.E., but it is more commonly attributed to the thirteenth-century kabbalistic writer Moses de Leon of Grenada, Spain, who was the first to make it known to the general public.

Zornberg, Dr. Avivah Gottlieb   A modern-day Torah scholar and author of two books of biblical commentary on Genesis and Exodus. Born in England to a rabbinic family, she grew up in Glasgow, Scotland, where her father was head of the rabbinical court. She holds a Ph.D. from Cambridge University, and emigrated to Israel twenty-five years ago, where she lives with her husband, Eric, and their family. She now lectures widely in Israel, Europe and the United States.

Z'ror Hamor   The biblical commentary of Rabbi Avraham ben Yaakov Saba (c.1440-c.1508). With the expulsion of Spanish Jewry, Saba relocated to Portugal, where he wrote commentaries on the Torah, the *Megillot* and *Pirkei Avot*. When Portugal decreed forced conversion of Jews in 1497, he buried his manuscripts under an olive tree and was never able to retrieve them. After he escaped imprisonment in Portugal, he settled in Fez, Morocco, where he attempted to rewrite his books from memory. He succeeded only in completing his commentaries on the Torah, Ruth and Esther before he died.